Java Programming:

An IS Perspective

Java Programming:

An IS Perspective

Jan L. Harrington

Marist College, Department of Computer Science and Information Systems

John Wiley & Sons, Inc.
New York   Chichester   Brisbane   Toronto   Singapore   Weinheim

Cover photo by Javier Romero/The Image Bank

Acquisitions Editor	Beth Lang Golub
Marketing Manager	Leslie Hines
Production Editor	Kelly Tavares
Senior Designer	Dawn Stanley

This book was set in Adobe Garamond by Black Gryphon Ltd. and printed and bound by Malloy Lithographers. The cover was printed by Lehigh Press.

This book is printed on acid-free paper. ∞

The paper in this book was manufactured by a mill whose forest management programs include sustained yield harvesting of its timberlands. Sustained yield harvesting principles ensure that the numbers of trees cut each year does not exceed the amount of new growth.

ISBN 0-471-19665-7

Printed in the United States of America

10 9 8 7 6 5 4 3 2 1

Preface

It's not uncommon these days for someone to hear the word "Java" and conjure up visions of startling animation dancing across World Wide Web pages. And let's not forget all those Java applications that will run on any platform, revolutionize computing, and make us instant web masters. If you were to believe all the hype, then you might think that Java a program could brew its own beverages, at the same time it was creating world peace.

Now that that's out of the way, let's get real, folks … Java is a full-featured, object-oriented programming language that, when used properly, can create platform-independent applications, some of which can be run through a World Wide Web browser. For people working in an IS environment, it can be an invaluable tool that eases the deployment of applications across networks of computers running different operating systems.

This book provides an introduction to Java programming for IS, CIS, and MIS majors. Although there are a lot of Java books on the market today, this one is well suited to your students because:

- It is the only Java book specifically written for students whose majors have a business focus. The majority of the examples in the book are business oriented. (Those that aren't are a few games included just to keep things light and fun.) The end-of-chapter exercises also focus on topics that will be meaningful to such students.
- It builds upon programming knowledge your students already have. It assumes that students know either COBOL, Pascal, Modula-2, C, or C++. Certainly, those who know C or C++ will have an easier time moving to Java because the languages share so much syntax, but any student with two semesters of programming experience can handle this book.
- It is a true text book—not a trade book—and it has therefore been written to help students learn. It has the pedagogical elements you have come to expect in a text, such as chapter objectives, summaries, and exercises.

Because Java is a complete language, learning to use it requires the same care and study as learning to use any other object-oriented language. As far as Java is concerned, the old aphorism "you've got to walk before you can run" really holds true. Students who want to work with Java must learn what it means for a program to be object oriented, how to structure classes, and how to write methods using Java's program structure such as selection and iteration.

Then they can turn to inheritance, which is essential for creating Java programs with a graphic user interface. Once they know how to write event-driven GUI programs, then they are ready to prepare applets for World Wide Web use. And animation? That requires multithreading and exception handling, two very advanced topics.

All of the preceding concerns have had a major impact on the organization of this book, which tries to make it possible for students to create Java applets as soon as possible. Nonetheless, there's a lot to learn before students are ready to work on the web:

- Chapter 1 presents an introduction to Java and the object-oriented paradigm. Because everything in a Java program is part of a class, there is no way to write a Java program without it being object-oriented. (In the mind of this author, that is a very good thing.)

- In Chapter 2, students learn about the Java programming environment and get their first look at a complete Java program.

- Chapter 3 focuses on Java data types and variable declarations. Because Java is a strongly typed language, students are also introduced to typecasting.

- Chapter 4 covers the structure of Java methods. Students learn to write simple methods such as constructors that perform initialization and accessor methods ("get" methods).

- Chapter 5 presents Java's basic programming elements. With the exception of string handling, the syntax presented in this chapter is identical to C and C++. This means that if your students happen to know either of those languages, they will be able to skim most of Chapter 5, with the exception of the material on strings at the end of the chapter.

- Chapter 6 focuses on inheritance. Inheritance is absolutely necessary for creating programs with a GUI, which in turn is required for an applet.

- Chapter 7 turns to GUI and event-driven programming. Because GUI programs are event-driven, students must learn an entirely new way of looking at the structure of a program.

- In Chapter 8, students learn how to turn stand-alone applications into applets.

Now that students can put their programs on the World Wide Web, the book returns to elements of the language that have been temporarily pushed to the side. Most of these chapters also introduce additional features of a graphic user interface.

- Chapter 9 covers one- and two-dimensional arrays and the Java vector.
- Chapter 10 extends the coverage arrays by looking at arrays of objects and introduces container classes to show students how object-oriented languages handle data structures. It also covers Java hash tables.
- Chapter 11 is devoted totally to the graphic user interface. It covers a variety of GUI functions that couldn't be logically worked into the preceding chapters.
- Chapter 12 presents stream I/O in the context of file I/O. Although it would be wonderful to present this material earlier, stream I/O requires exception handling, an advanced language topic that is rarely covered, even in C and C++ texts for CS majors.
- If you have time, and you feel your students can handle it, you may choose to use the images, animation, and multithreading coverage in Chapter 13.

Support Files

This book is supported by a collection of files that can be obtained by downloading them from my web site: http://members.aol.com/blgryph/home.html. The files are of two types: sample source code for all the examples in the book and files that students will need to use for the programming exercises.

The student files include source code for the exercises at the end of Chapters 2 through 4. In addition, they include a Java package (*text.zip*) that provides keyboard input support for use through the first six chapters of the book and number formatting for use throughout the book.

Java's support for console I/O is very primitive, and not all Java development environments support direct console input. Therefore, the *text.zip* package includes a system input window that can display a prompt and receive one value (simple data type or string) from a user. Documentation for the use of classes within the package appear in the book as students are ready to use them.

Acknowledgments

I'd like to thank all the following people who helped make this book possible:

- Beth Lang Golub, my editor at Wiley, who as always is a pleasure to work with.
- Kelly Tavares, production manager, who guided the production process so smoothly.
- Amy Haggarty, editorial assistant, who was always there when I needed something.
- Pam Landau, the copy editor, who has a great eye for all the weird things I type.
- The reviewers:
    - Dr. Douglas M. Kline, Sam Houston State University
    - Dr. Craig W. Slingman, University of Texas at Arlington
    - Dr. Billy Lim, Illinois State University

JLH

Contents

Chapter 5: Writing Methods (Part II) 97

Introducing Java and the Object-Oriented Paradigm

OBJECTIVES

In this chapter you will learn:

- Why Java is a good choice for a programming language.
- How objects provide a way of looking at the elements of a program's environment.
- About the characteristics of objects.
- About how objects with the same properties are represented as classes.
- How classes work together to structure the logic of a program.

If you look at recent articles in computer journals and magazines, you'll notice an emphasis on something known as *object-oriented programming* (often abbreviated *OOP*). Object-oriented programming is a method for developing and organizing the logic of application programs. Object-oriented concepts have also had an impact on systems analysis and design procedures, operating systems, and database systems. As a whole, object-oriented technology represents a *paradigm* (a theoretical model that can be used as a pattern for some activity).

There are a number of languages that allow a programmer to write object-oriented programs, including C++, Eifel, Smalltalk, and Java. This book will teach you to program in Java, a language that is gaining widespread popularity for a number of reasons. The first section of this chapter therefore provides you with an overview of Java so that you understand why it is a good choice for a programming language.

There are many reasons why application programmers are increasingly deciding to write object-oriented programs. To make these reasons easier to understand, we'll start by looking at an example of the object-oriented approach that has absolutely nothing to do with computers. We'll compare it to structured programming, the more traditional way of describing and organizing instructions with which you are familiar.

Then we'll turn to technology, beginning with a look at how the object-oriented paradigm originated, followed by an introduction to the basic elements of an object-oriented program. As we go along, we'll identify those features of object orientation that make it the paradigm of choice for many programmers today.

Why Java

The Java programming language was developed by a team at Sun Microsystems, led by James Gosling, in the early 1990s. Originally intended as a language for handheld and set-top consumer devices, Java became popular because of a Netscape Navigator 2.0 plug-in that made it possible to run small Java programs within a World Wide Web browser. These programs, known as *applets*, have made Java the fastest growing language in computing history and given many people the impression that all Java can do is create cute animations for the web. However, Java is a lot more. It is a full-featured programming language with capabilities similar to those found in other general-purposes such as C, C++, Pascal, and COBOL.

Gosling and Henry McGilton published their goals for the language and a description of the language's environment in a white paper (*The Java™ Language Environment: A White Paper*). They summarized their ideas with the following:

"The massive growth of the Internet and the World-Wide Web leads us to a completely new way of looking at development and distribution of software. To live in the world of electronic commerce and distribution, Java must enable the development of *secure, high performance,* and highly *robust* applications on *multiple platforms* in *heterogeneous, distributed networks.*

Operating on multiple platforms in heterogeneous networks invalidates the traditional schemes of binary distribution, release, upgrade, patch, and so on. To survive in this jungle, Java must be *architecture neutral, portable,* and *dynamically adaptable.*

The Java system that emerged to meet these needs is *simple,* so it can be easily programmed by most developers; *familiar,* so that current developers can easily learn Java; *object oriented,* to take advantage of modern software development methodologies and to fit into distributed client-server applications; *multithreaded,* for high performance in applications that need to perform multiple concurrent activities, such as multimedia; and *interpreted,* for maximum portability and dynamic capabilities."

Note

You can find the complete Java white paper along with other Java documents prepared by Sun Microsystems at http://java.sum.com/docs/white/index.htm.

As you read the preceding paragraphs, you probably noticed that there is one major characteristic that differentiates Java from other languages you have used: Java is designed to create programs that work on multiple computing platforms. In other words, a developer can create one version of a program that can then run on a variety of hardware and software platforms. Today, Java programs that adhere to Sun Microsystems's "pure Java" standards run under Windows 95, UNIX, and the Macintosh OS without modification.

Note
One of the problems with pure Java code is that it runs more slowly than programs compiled for a specific computing platform. Currently there is a great deal of controversy over whether portability is worth the trade-off in performance. Some developers would prefer to have platform-tailored versions of Java that produce programs that execute as fast as possible.

In addition to program portability, as a language Java has a number of characteristics that make it a good language for business software development, including the following:

- Java is simple in that it retains much familiar syntax. If you know C or C++, you'll feel right at home. If you don't, you'll find the basic syntax easy to learn.
- It is *strongly-typed*. This means that everything must have a data type. It also means that Java doesn't perform automatic data type conversions across an assignment operator; a programmer must request the conversion and therefore pay attention to what the conversion is actually doing to a value.
- Java performs its own memory management, avoiding the *memory leaks* that plague programs written in languages such as C and C++. (A memory leak is a block of main memory that becomes inaccessible to—and therefore unusable by—a program). Java, however, regularly performs *garbage collection,* during which it collects all unreferenced memory so that it can be reused.
- Java is completely object-oriented. With the exception of some basic data types (for example, numbers, characters, and booleans), everything in a Java program is an object. Java therefore forces you to write object-oriented code. The benefits of this will become clear throughout the rest of this chapter.
- Java handles arrays as objects rather than as a basic data type. Java can therefore provide significant control over arrays, including automatically checking for out-of-bounds errors.
- Java is multi-threaded, allowing a program to do more than one thing at a time. Multi-threading is fundamental to animation as well as programs that require periodic actions.

Now that you have an overview of Java as a programming language, it's time to turn to Java's fundamental programming paradigm: the object-oriented model.

Performing a Real-World Task

Object-orientation is a way of organizing what is occurring in an environment. It doesn't apply solely to computer programs. As a first example of what it means to be object-oriented, let's look at a real-world example that has nothing to with computing. This will make it easier to see the contrast between object-orientation and the way in which you organized logic in languages such as Pascal, C, and COBOL.

One of the things we do frequently is prepare a meal. Whether you're cooking a standing rib roast for an elegant dinner or making a peanut butter and jelly sandwich for a quick lunch, there is a general process that you follow.

- First, you must decide what to prepare to eat.
- Next, you must figure out what ingredients the food requires.
- Third, you must look to see if you have the ingredients on hand.
- If you're missing an ingredient, you must either go to the store, or change your mind about what you're going to fix.
- Once all the ingredients are in place, you can follow the recipes and prepare the meal.

The recipes for the items you are preparing can be very simple ("Put peanut butter on one piece of bread; put jelly on a second piece of bread; smash together.") or very complex. Nonetheless, there is a specific set of instructions that you follow whenever you are preparing food in any way.

The preceding bulleted list describes a general process for preparing a meal; it doesn't depend on what specific foods are going to be prepared. However, the ingredients used and the recipe for preparing any given dish are specific to that dish.

Now assume that you have been asked to write instructions for preparing a meal for two people consisting of an egg salad sandwich, carrot sticks, potato chips, and soda. A traditional way to assemble such a set of instructions might appear as in Listing 1.1.

Listing 1.1   Steps to prepare lunch

1. Decide to serve egg salad sandwich, carrot sticks, potato chips, and soda.
2. Put two eggs, mayonnaise, four pieces of bread, lettuce, two carrots, potato chips, and two cans of soda on the list of ingredients. Place small pot, mixing bowl, tablespoon, fork, paring knife, two lunch plates, and two glasses on the list of equipment needed.
3. Check the refrigerator for eggs, mayonnaise, lettuce, carrots, and soda; check the cupboard for bread and potato chips.
4. You have everything except eggs.
5. Do you want to change your mind about the egg salad sandwiches? No. Then go to the store and buy eggs. (If yes, go back to Step 1.)
6. Make the egg salad sandwich: Boil two eggs for 15 minutes. Peel the eggs. Put the eggs in a bowl and mash them with a fork. Put the mashed eggs in the freezer for 15 minutes to cool. Remove from the freezer. Add two tablespoons of mayonnaise and mix. Divide the mixture evenly between two pieces of bread. Cover with lettuce. Spread mayonnaise on two remaining pieces of bread. Place bread on top of lettuce. Place each sandwich on a separate lunch plate.
7. Prepare carrot sticks: Wash two carrots. Peel the carrots. Cut each carrot in half lengthwise; cut each half in half again. Place on a lunch plate next to the sandwiches.
8. Prepare potato chips: If necessary, rip open the bag of potato chips. Shake approximately one cup of chips onto each lunch plate.
9. Prepare the soda: Place one can of soda and a glass on the table next to each lunch plate.

As you read through these instructions, you're probably thinking that they seem fairly straightforward: They tell someone what to do in a step-by-step manner. In fact, until the advent of object-oriented programming, the instructions that made up computer programs were organized in a very similar way. This type of program organization is known as *structured programming*.

Listing 1.1 illustrates some of the basic principles of structured programming. First, and most important, instructions are executed in order, beginning at the first instruction, until something in the set of instructions indicates that you should do something different.

At several places in the instructions you are asked to make a decision. For example, you need to figure out whether you have the ingredients needed. If you don't, you have to decide whether to go to the store or to change your mind about what you are preparing. In our particular example, we decided to go to the store. However, if you were to change your mind about the dish, you would need to return to Step 1 and start again with a different decision about what to serve. Making decisions between two sets of alternative actions is something that computers also do frequently.

So, what's wrong with this picture? If the instructions and the way they have been prepared seem so straightforward, why would people try to find another way to describe them? To understand the problem, consider what would happen if you *did* decide to make something other than an egg salad sandwich. In other words, at Step 5, you decided to return to Step 1 and make tuna fish sandwiches instead. Notice the problem: the instructions that follow are no longer appropriate for what you're going to make. Instead of eggs, you need tuna fish. Rather than boiling, mashing, and cooling eggs, you need to open the can of tuna and drain the liquid.

The instructions, as written, are specific to one particular menu. If we want a different menu, we need to modify almost all the instructions. We could avoid needing to redo the instructions if we separated the instructions into pieces. One type of "piece" could be a dish that we know how to prepare. The ingredients and the instructions for preparing a given dish belong to the dish. When we want information from the dish, we ask for it. If we rewrite the meal preparation instructions under the assumption that the dishes will give us information when we ask for it, then the instructions might look like Listing 1.2.

Listing 1.2   Steps to prepare lunch when the dishes we prepare can give us information

```
1. Decide which dishes to prepare (Dish1, Dish2, Dish3, Dish4)
2. Ask each dish to list its ingredients.
3. Verify that we have all the ingredients.
4. If an ingredient is missing, either go to the store or go back to Step 1.
5. Ask a dish to tell us how to prepare it. Follow the instructions given to us
   by the dish.
6. If all dishes are prepared, stop. Otherwise, go back to Step 5.
```

There are two major differences between Listing 1.2 and Listing 1.1, aside from Listing 1.2 being much shorter:

- The specific ingredients and recipe needed to prepare any given dish are hidden from the list of instructions. We have to ask the dish to give us information when we need it.
- Because the ingredients and the recipe aren't included in the instructions, a change in the dishes that are being prepared doesn't require a change in the instructions.

The second set of instructions that we have been studying exhibits many of the characteristics of object orientation. In this particular example, there are actually five objects: the four dishes being prepared and the set of instructions itself. The dishes we prepare are typical objects: they have data that describe them (the ingredients and amounts of those ingredients needed) and they have things that they know how to do ((1) tell us the ingredients and (2) tell us how to prepare the dish). They hide the details of how they do their work from the object that is manipulating them (the set of instructions).

The beauty of working with the dishes as objects is that the set of instructions that uses the objects can be written generically. We can switch objects at any time (for example, swap egg salad with tuna fish) without making any other changes. Our set of instructions doesn't need to include the details about preparing a given dish; all it needs to do is ask the dish for the ingredients and recipe when appropriate. In addition, we can take one of the dish objects and reuse it in another procedure, without having to make any changes to it.

Object-oriented programming takes much the same approach, hiding the details of objects from objects of other types. When an object needs information from another object or needs another object to perform a task, it sends a message to the object requesting whatever it needs. As a result, object-oriented programs can be written more generically than structured programs. Usually, making changes to the programs is then easier than changing structured programs.

Objects that have the same data that describe them and know how to do the same things in the same way are said to belong to the same *class*. For example, the egg salad sandwich, the tuna fish sandwich, carrot sticks, potato chips, and soda objects all belong to one class, which we might name *LunchFood*.

If we want to add a new dish to our collection of things that we can have for lunch, we use *LunchFood* as a pattern for creating the new dish. The class definition tells us what data any object of the class will have (the ingredients and the amounts of those ingredients) and what objects of the class know how to do (tell us about the ingredients and tell us the recipe). A class therefore functions as a template for creating objects.

Classes are independent of where they are used. For example, we are currently using objects created from the *LunchFood* class in a set of instructions that tells us how to prepare lunch. However, we could also use objects created from the *LunchFood* class in a set of instructions that tell us how to prepare a printed cookbook. Because class is independent of the instructions that are using it, the class can be reused in many programs. The ability to reuse classes is another major benefit of object orientation. An organization might, for example, collect a group of classes fundamental to its operations into a library, from where they can be used repeatedly throughout the organization's programs. Using previously developed and tested components can save a lot of programming time.

Now that you have a general understanding of why many people believe the object-oriented approach is better than a sequential approach, let's take a more formal look at objects and computer programs.

A Bit of History

The object-oriented paradigm was developed in 1969 by Dr. Kristin Nygaard, a Norwegian who was trying to write a computer program that described the movement of ships through a fjord. He found that the combination of tides, the movements of the ships, and the shape of the coastline were difficult to deal with using existing programming methods. Instead, he looked at the items in the environment he was trying to model—ships, tides, and the fjord's coastline—and the actions each item was likely to take. Then he was able to handle the relationships between them.

The object-oriented technology we use today has evolved from Dr. Nygaard's original work on ships and fjords. The paradigm retains the concept of combining the description of the items in a data processing environment with the actions performed by those items.

Objects

At the heart of the object-oriented paradigm is the *object*, an entity in the data processing environment that has data that describe it and actions that it can perform. An object can be something that has a physical existence, such as a boat, product, or computer (or a lunch dish that we know how to prepare!). It can also be an event (for example, the sale of a product, a professional conference, or a business trip), a place, a part of a program's user interface (for example, a menu or a window), or even the program itself (an *application object*). You will read more about classifications of objects later in this chapter.

Any given object-oriented program can handle many objects. For example, a program that handles the inventory for a retail store uses one object for each product carried by the store. The program manipulates the same data for each object, including the product number, product description, retail price, number of items in stock, and the reorder point.

Each object also knows how to perform actions with its own data. The product object in the inventory program, for example, knows how to create itself and set initial values for all its data, how to modify its data, and how to evaluate whether enough items are in stock to satisfy a purchase request. The important thing to recognize is that an object consists of *both* the data that describe it and the actions it can perform.

An object in a computer program isn't something you can touch. When a program is running, most objects exist in main memory. Objects are created by a program for use while the program is executing. Unless a program explicitly saves an object's data to a disk, the object is lost when the program ends.

Messages

An object performs one of its actions when it receives a *message* instructing it to do so. A message includes an identifier for which action the object is to perform, along with the data the object needs to do its work. Messages therefore constitute an object's window to the outside world.

An object can also send messages back to the outside world. When an object finishes performing one of its actions, it may send a single message to whatever object requested the action. The returned message may be used by the external object to continue data processing or it may be used as input to another message the external object needs to send.

Data Encapsulation

An object hides its internals from other objects. In most cases, an object's data are accessible only within the object. Other objects cannot access the data directly; they must ask the object for it. In addition, the details of how an object performs its actions are hidden from other objects. When an external object requests an object to perform some action, the requesting object has no knowledge of the process used to complete that action.

This hiding of an object's details from other objects is known as *data encapsulation* or *information hiding*. It has one major benefit: It makes objects self-contained units whose details can be changed without affecting any external objects that use them. This means that modifying programs is much easier because modifications affect only limited, localized parts of a program. It also makes it easier for someone who didn't write a program to understand what the program does because actions are associated with the specific data they affect.

Classes

The template from which objects of the same type are created is known as a *class*. A class contains specifications for the data that describe an object along with descriptions of the actions an object knows how to perform. These actions are known as *services*, *methods*, or *member functions*. The term *method* is most commonly used with Java. Objects from other classes can send messages to a class's methods, but because of data encapsulation, the way in which the methods operate are hidden.

A class also includes all the data needed to describe objects created from the class. These are known as *attributes* or *variables*. The term *attribute* is used in object-oriented analysis and object-oriented databases; the term *variable* is used in object-oriented programs. In most cases, all of a class's variables are hidden from objects of other classes. However, a class can contain methods that provide data to external objects.

Types of Classes

Object-oriented theorists often place classes into one of three broad categories:

- Entity classes: An entity class represents data. For example, classes such as Employee, Appointment, Sale, Project, Order, and Order Line Item all represent data that a business may need to manipulate. A systems analyst identifies entity classes by conducting an analysis of the business environment that a program will serve.

  An entity class doesn't need to be something you can touch. Entity classes therefore can be further subdivided into three additional categories:

- Concrete classes: A concrete class is used to create objects that represent things that have a physical existence, such as a person, place, or thing.
- Conceptual classes: A conceptual class is a template for objects that don't have a physical existence, but that exist as concepts in the human mind, although often the concepts can be recorded on something physical (for example, a piece of paper or a disk file). Such classes include abstractions such as organizations, agreements (for example, contracts or leases), floor plans, business strategies, and maps.
- Event and state classes: Events are things that happen in the business environment (for example, sales, shipments, and deliveries). State classes classify other objects as to some condition, such as terminated employees or overdue rentals. Such classes therefore represent things without physical analogs.

Note

An entity class is much like a database entity that would be depicted on an entity-relationship (ER) diagram. In fact, one part of an object-oriented systems analysis is drawing an ER diagram.

- Interface classes: Interface classes are used to define an object-oriented program's user interface. They provide a way for a user to communicate with entity objects. An object-oriented program uses objects for windows, menus, dialog boxes, buttons, and so on.
- Control classes: Objects created from control classes act as coordinators for all the objects used in an object-oriented environment. They often work with data from many classes. In an object-oriented program, the most common control class is the application class, which represents the program itself.

This classification of classes is really an aspect of the idea of data encapsulation. There are two basic reasons why it brings significant benefits to an object-oriented program:

- The separation makes a program easier to modify. If you think about the categories of classes, you'll notice that the data we manipulate are separate from the user interface, which in turn is separate from the classes that control the action of a program. This means, for example, that you can change the user interface by redesigning a dialog box without having to make any changes in the data manipulated by the dialog box. By the same token, you can change the details of how an entity class performs calculations or stores data in a file without changing the user interface of a program.

- The separation makes it easier to create program elements that can be reused. When entity classes are distinct from the user interface and from the programs that control them, you can reuse the same classes in more than one program without changing the classes. This can significantly speed up the development of new software, especially when an organization can develop a library of thoroughly tested entity classes for use throughout all its programs. The same holds true for interface classes, which are typically provided to programmers as libraries that accompany program development software. (Control classes are usually too specific to their environment to be reusable.)

Note

For a more extensive discussion of entity, interface, and control classes, see page 135 of *Object-Oriented Software Engineering* by Ivar Jacobson, Magnus Christenson, Patrik Jonsson, and Gunnar Overgarrd (ACM Press/Addison-Wesley, 1992).

A Short Introduction to Object-Oriented Development

It seems relatively straightforward to state definitions that define classes, objects, methods, and variables. However, the task of identifying the classes that make up a program can be challenging. It means looking at the environment that a program is to serve and being able to view it in terms of objects and object relationships.

Determining which entity classes are needed by a business takes place during the analysis phase of the object-oriented development life cycle (OODLC). The OODLC is similar to the system development life cycle (SDLC) used in structured analysis—you need to perform many of the same tasks—but the focus is on identifying objects and their uses rather than on data handling processes. The steps in the OODLC are summarized in Table 7.1.

Table 7.1   Steps in the object-oriented development life cycle

Phase	Task	Deliverables
Analysis	Object-oriented analysis	Requirements document Object model
Design	Object-oriented design	Object-oriented design model
Construction	Object-oriented programming	Object-oriented programs
Testing	Object-oriented testing	Debugged object-oriented programs
Maintenance	Repetition of preceding steps	Modified object-oriented system that continues to meet an organization's changing needs.

Like the SDLC, the OODLC begins with the fundamental task of discovering and documenting what the users need the system to do. However, an SDLC analysis usually involves creating data flow diagrams that document data processes, how data move through an organization. In contrast, an object-oriented analysis looks at uses of data to develop *use case scenarios*, descriptions of the contexts in which users (known as *actors* because they act upon the system) can make use of some part of the system.

Along with system requirements, the analysis phase of the OODLC documents the entity classes that are needed for the new information system in the object model. Interface classes are added during the design phase, during which developers decide how the system should interact with its users. The construction phase uses object-oriented programming techniques like those you will be using in this book. Testing and maintenance follow guidelines similar to those used in the SDLC.

Note

For in-depth material on object-oriented analysis, see *An Introduction to Object-Oriented Analysis* by David Brown (Wiley, 1997).

Designing an Object-Oriented Program: A First Example

Unfortunately, there aren't any simple rules designing an object-oriented program. As with any business analysis task, the process is somewhat imprecise because there is often more than one way to view the data entities in a given environment. Choosing between alternative object models involves weighing the advantages and disadvantages of each; it's not unusual for there to be no clear-cut best model. To make the process a bit easier, let's start by looking at a simple example. At the end of the chapter, we'll generalize some guidelines you can use when you approach your own programs.

The Office Supply Inventory

Hard times have hit the major international management consulting firm of Rye Associates Inc. Top management has ordered financial cutbacks in every aspect of the organization, including the purchasing of office supplies. Instead of simply ordering whatever anyone needs, office managers have been instructed to keep detailed records of office supply levels. In other words, corporate management wants to know the state of the current office supply inventory at any given time. It also wants office managers to reorder only when levels drop below a predetermined reorder point.

Although the demand to keep track of office supplies is a major burden for many office managers, the head of Information Systems has come up with a relatively simple solution. She asks one of the programmers to create a program that will track current inventory levels of office supplies. At the end of each month, one of the department secretaries will take a physical inventory of all the office supplies. (The monthly physical inventory is a lot simpler than trying to capture data every time someone takes something out of the supply cabinet.) These data will be entered into the program, which will then print out a summary of the inventory. By comparing summaries from many months, the IS manager can get a good picture of how supplies are being used.

The program will also generate a monthly order list. All supplies for which the current stock level has dropped below the reorder point will be placed on that list, which can then be sent directly to Purchasing.

In this case, the needs of the user (the IS manager) have been well specified. The first task facing the Java programmer therefore is deciding what classes to use in the program, beginning with identifying the necessary entity classes. The office supply inventory program actually deals with only one thing: the office supplies that make up the inventory. However, just what is the business entity?

The entity is a type of office supply, in this particular situation called Inventory Item. From a class that describes this entity the program will create one object for each type of supply used by the IS department, such as floppy disks, black fine-line pens, or Post-It notes. The class might be diagrammed as in Figure 1.1. Each item is described by an item number, a text description of the item, the number on hand as of the most recent physical inventory, and the reorder point.

Figure 1.1   The Inventory Item class and the data that describe it

One of the most common mistakes made by people who are just starting to work with object-oriented concepts is to look at the entire inventory, rather than the inventory item, as the class. Keep in mind, however, that a class is a template from which you stamp out objects. Each object represents one real-world occurrence, or *instance*, of the business entity. If the inventory were the class, then each object would represent a separate inventory (the contents of a separate supply cabinet, if you will). This is clearly not what the Java programmer is trying to represent. In this example, the inventory is actually the collection of all the objects created from the Inventory Item class.

Because an object represents an instance of a class, the verb *instantiate* is often used to refer to the process of creating an object from a class.

The Java programmer must also define the actions that the Inventory Item class will perform. Given the requirements defined by the IS manager, the programmer comes up with the following list:

- Create a new inventory item.
- Modify the data describing an inventory item.
- Delete an item from the inventory.
- Check to see if the item needs to be reordered.
- Return information about the item's current stock level.
- Return information about the item's description.

This list illustrates one very important characteristic of methods. Each method acts on only one object at a time. Therefore, there is no method to print a report of items that need to be reordered. Instead, there is a method that checks a single object to see if it needs to be reordered.

A user interacts with the inventory program in the following ways, each of which is a separate use case scenario:

- The user enters, modifies, and deletes data about individual inventory items.
- The user prints a report showing inventory levels at the end of the month.
- The user prints a report that shows items needing to be reordered.

The program must therefore include interface elements to allow the user to enter data about a new inventory item, find an item for modification or deletion, and print a report. For example, the interface objects might include a menu bar, a dialog box for data entry and modification, a dialog box for finding an item, and a window for viewing the summary and reorder reports on the screen. Each of these interface objects will probably be made up of other objects. A dialog box used for data entry, for example, typically contains text fields and push buttons, each of which is an object.

To prepare the report of items that need to be reordered, the program also needs a class that can manipulate the many objects that have been created from the Inventory Item class (a control class). In a simple object-oriented program, this class will be the application class.

For this particular example, one object will be created from the application class, which will create objects from the Inventory Item class and organize them in some way. If we were to diagram the relationship between the entity and control objects used by the supply inventory program, we might draw something like Figure 1.2. The application object can be thought of as the manager of or container for the Inventory Item objects.

Note

There are many ways to organize multiple objects created from the same class. You will learn about some of those methods—in particular arrays, vectors, and hash tables—in this book.

Figure 1.2   The objects used by the inventory supply program

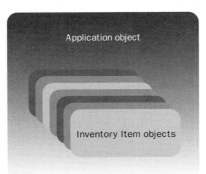

The application object will access the Inventory Item objects one at a time to determine which items need to be ordered, and will add only those that do need to be reordered to the report.

The last two methods in the Inventory Item class send data from an object back to whatever is manipulating the object. In this particular program, the application object uses these methods to create the monthly inventory summary report. They are necessary because, as you will remember, an object's data are hidden from any method using the object. The inventory program's application object, however, needs the item description and stock level for the monthly inventory summary report.

Inheritance

Classes are often related in a hierarchy that moves from general to specific. For example, assume that you are writing a program that computes an amortization table for three types of loans: fixed-payment, variable-payment, and mortgage. (You will see an implementation of this program in Chapter 11.)

All of the types of loans share some attributes (principal and interest rate). However, in addition to the common attributes, each type of loan has some attributes that are specific to it:

- Fixed-payment: payment amount
- Variable-payment: payment percent, minimum payment, and minimum interest
- Mortgage: number of payment periods, number of payment periods per year, and payment amount

One way to structure the loan program is to create three separate classes, each of which duplicates the principal and interest rate attributes. However, the objects can be related in a hierarchy that captures the idea that there is a generic class—a loan—from which other specialized classes branch. This type of relationship, which goes from a general class to specialized classes, is known as *inheritance*. For our particular example, it might be diagrammed as in Figure 1.3. The Loan class is known as a *base* class; the other three classes are *derived* classes.

Figure 1.3   Classes in the loan program

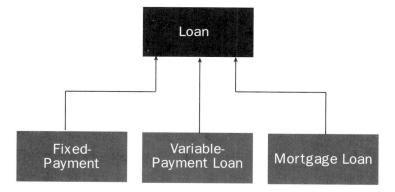

When the classes are declared in a program, the Loan class will include the principal and interest rate attributes. The derived classes include only their class-specific attributes. They "inherit" the common attributes from Loan.

Using inheritance has three major advantages:

* It avoids duplicating attributes in related classes.
* It imposes organization on the classes in a program, making the structure of a program easier to understand and maintain.
* It simplifies creating additional related classes because the new classes can use parts of base classes that have already been developed and tested.

Note

Methods can also be inherited, but the situation is a bit more involved than with data.

It isn't always easy to determine when inheritance is appropriate for a program. To explore the situation a bit further, we'll look at two examples involving entity classes.

The Office Supply Company

One of the companies from which Rye Associates purchases office supplies is Country-Wide Supplies. Country-Wide uses an object-oriented Java program to keep track of the supplies in its catalog. The program manages information about all available merchandise items, including their price, shipping weight, and other descriptive characteristics.

As you might expect, the basic entity class in Country-Wide's program is the office supply item. The data manipulated by the program could therefore be based on a single class like that in Figure 1.4. The problem with this design, however, is that the descriptive characteristics that are stored about the items vary, depending on the general type of the item; not every type of product has values for every data item. For example, paper products are described by their size and color, whereas writing products are described by type of tip, size of tip, and color.

Figure 1.4   A class to handle an office supply company's merchandise

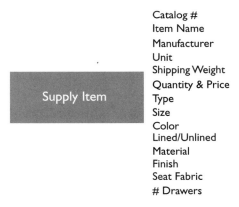

Your first thought may be that Country-Wide can simply leave data items that don't apply to any given type of merchandise without values. Although such a solution will certainly work, it isn't very efficient in terms of storage space. Whenever an object is created, space is allocated in main memory for the entire object. That means that even if no values are assigned to some data items, those data items still consume storage. The unnecessary storage may also consume extra disk space when the object is transferred to external storage.

The fact that there are many variations on one type of object suggests that Country-Wide is dealing with some generic properties of an item (the price and shipping weight, for example) along with other properties that apply to more specific types of items. Such a situation can be handled through inheritance.

A portion of a possible entity class hierarchy for Country-Wide appears in Figure 1.5. (Because an office supply company typically handles so many types of products, showing the entire class hierarchy in one drawing isn't particularly practical!) Notice that the hierarchy begins with the base class—`Supply Item`—and is then made more specific with derived classes. For this example, there are three derived classes on the second level of the hierarchy—`Writing Instrument` (pens and pencils), `Paper Product`, and `Furniture`. The `Furniture` class has two derived classes—`Chair` and `Desk`.

Only the four classes with black circles in their boxes in Figure 1.5 (`Writing Instrument`, `Paper Product`, `Chair`, and `Desk`) are actually used to create objects. When an object is created, it receives its own data along with the data of its base class. For example, a `Writing Instrument` object inherits all the data that are defined as part of the `Supply Item` class.

The `Furniture` class also inherits the data defined as part of the `Supply Item` class. The `Desk` class therefore inherits not only the data defined as part of the `Furniture` class, but also the data that the `Furniture` class inherited from the `Supply Item` class.

The major advantage to using the design in Figure 1.5 is that no storage space is wasted when objects are created: Every data item is used for every object. However, in this particular example, you might think that using the class hierarchy instead of a single class can make the objects harder to use. For example, if the program using this class hierarchy needs to display or print every product carried by Country-Wide, wouldn't the program need to use separate code for each class? The answer is "no."

Another of the benefits of inheritance is that we can work with objects created from derived classes as if they were objects of their base class. For example, objects created from `Writing Instrument` and `Desk` can be manipulated by the same program code, as if both were objects of the `Supply Item` class. This means that a program can gain the benefits of having specialized derived classes yet still be able to manipulate all objects derived from the same

Figure 1.5   A portion of the class hierarchy for an office supply company

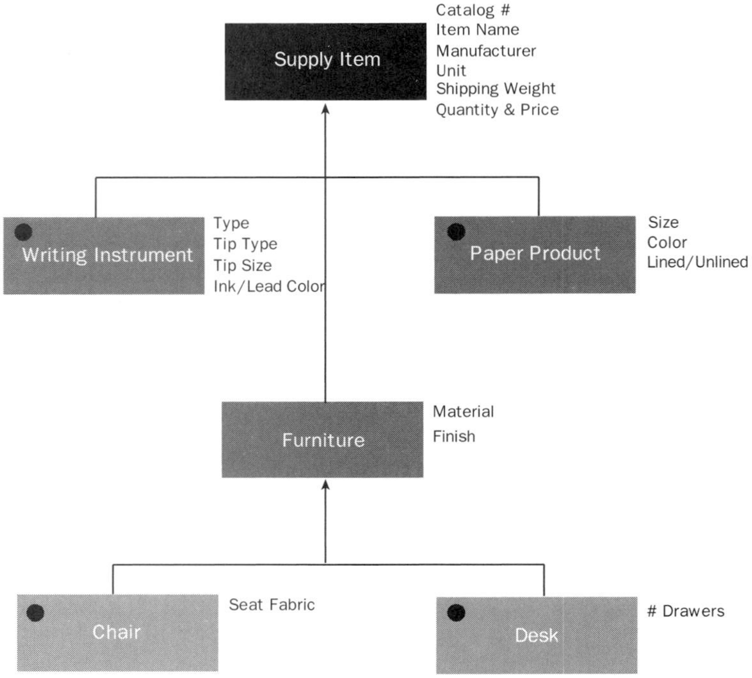

base class as a group. This means that it will be easy to search through all the supply item objects for a single item or to list them all in a catalog, even though the specific details of the objects are somewhat different.

The Corner Pharmacy

The Corner Pharmacy is a full-service drugstore owned and operated by George and Gladys Bellows. It has been in the Bellows family for three generations and currently isn't part of any national chain. In addition to containing a pharmacy, the store sells cosmetics, personal care items, and other merchandise typically found in a drugstore. Both Mr. and Mrs. Bellows are registered pharmacists; the store employs two other pharmacists as well as a 10-person sales staff.

The Bellows are concerned that their business may be suffering because they aren't managing their prescriptions on a computer like the drugstores that belong to national chains. Among other things, the national chains advertise that they can check for drug interactions. The Bellows are therefore going to have someone write a program that will handle prescriptions.

Note

The Bellows looked at existing pharmacy management software packages, but discovered that those packages were designed for much larger stores and provided functionality the Bellows didn't need. The cost of custom programming that would exactly match the Bellows's specifications was less than the purchase of a ready-made package with capabilities that would never be used.

As you know, the first step in the process is to analyze the needs of the users of the program. The Bellows sat down with the programmer and identified three major things about which they needed to store data: customers, drugs, and prescriptions. They stated that it is vital that data about drug interactions be part of the program. The Bellows also emphasized that there is a slight difference in the handling of prescriptions for controlled and noncontrolled substances.

After listening carefully to the Bellows's description of the data the program needs to store and how the users will interact with the program, the programmer produced the entity classes shown in Figure 1.6. There are three stand-alone entity classes (`Customer`, `Drug`, and `Prescription`). The `Prescription` class also has two derived classes, one for a controlled substance and the other for a noncontrolled substance.

There is certainly a relationship between the three stand-alone classes. Each prescription is for one customer and one drug; a customer can have multiple prescriptions, each for a different drug; multiple prescriptions will be written for the same drug, each for a different customer. Why, then, isn't `Prescription` a derived class of `Customer` and `Drug`? If the classes were designed in that way, the class hierarchy would look like Figure 1.7. (Deriving a class from more than one base class is known as *multiple inheritance.*)

This design may initially seem very intuitive, especially if you've taken a data management course and are familiar with the design of relational databases. Inheritance, however, isn't a logical relationship (for example, one-to-many) between classes; it's a migration of class data and methods down a hierarchy, a progressing from the general to the specific. To be strictly correct,

Figure 1.6   Classes to manage a pharmacy's prescriptions

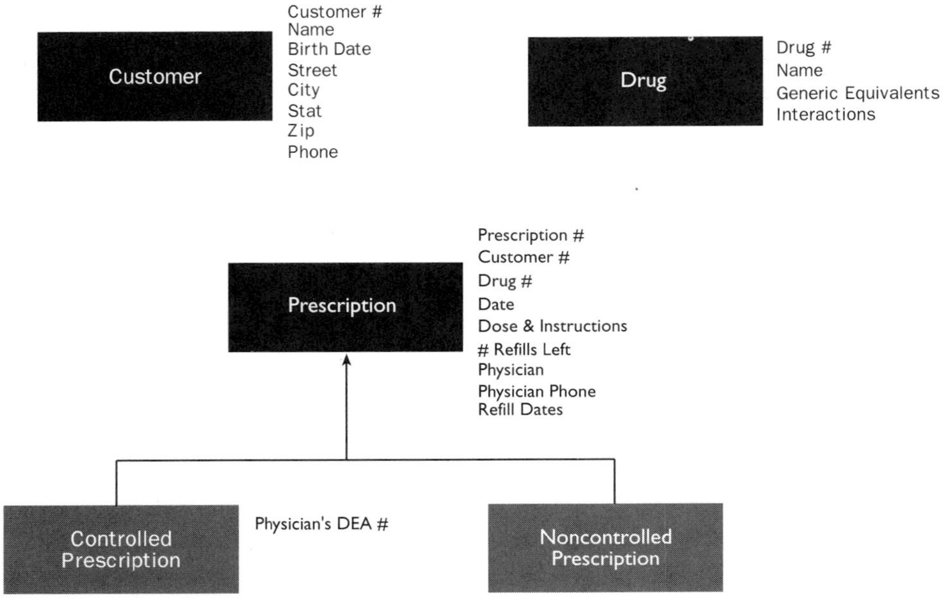

inheritance is an expression of the "is a" relationship. If inheritance is appropriate, then we can say that a derived class "is a" more specialized version of its base class.

The diagram in Figure 1.7 makes the following assertions:

- A Prescription is a Customer
- A Prescription is a Drug
- A Controlled Prescription is a Prescription
- A Noncontrolled Prescription is a Prescription

The first two assertions are not valid; the second two are. This makes it clear that inheritance is appropriate between the three prescription classes, but not between Customer, Drug, and Prescription.

Figure 1.7   Attempting to use inheritance in the prescription class hierarchy

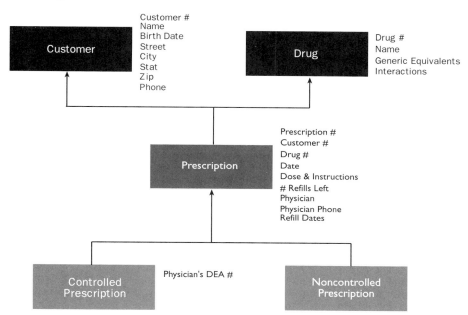

Instead, the `Customer`, `Drug`, `Controlled Prescription`, and `Noncontrolled Prescription` classes will be managed as stand-alone classes. The application program that manipulates objects created from these classes will use the Customer # and Drug # to search `Customer` and `Drug` objects to locate objects related to any given prescription.

Interface Classes and Inheritance

As you have been reading, one category of class is a user interface class. As an example, consider the four types of windows in Figure 1.8. Although all are rectangular and approximately the same size, they have different characteristics. The document window at the top left of Figure 1.8 has scroll bars, a title bar, a close box, a size box, and a zoom box. The shadowed window to its right and the alert window below have none of those characteristics but instead have distinctive borders. The round-cornered window at the lower right has a title bar and close box, but no scroll bars, grow box, or zoom box; its title bar is also rather different from the title bar of the document window.

Figure 1.8   Sample window types

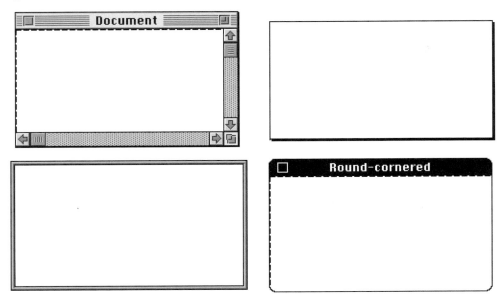

Because these windows are variations of a generic rectangular window, they lend themselves to a class hierarchy like that shown in Figure 1.9. The base class, `Window`, includes a unique ID number for a window along with the coordinates of the window's position on the screen. These coordinates also represent the window's size.

There is one derived class for each type of window in Figure 1.8. The `Document` class includes data that describe all the possible types of elements that a programmer might choose to include in a window; the same is true for the `Round-cornered` class. However, the `Shadow` and `Alert` classes don't have any data other than what they inherit from the base class.

Why, then, are the `Shadow` and `Alert` classes necessary? The answer lies in the methods. In particular, each class has a method that draws the window on the screen. The way in which that method acts varies among the four types of windows because each type of window looks different. Even though the `Alert` and `Shadow` classes don't add any data to that of the base class, the way in which they respond to a "draw yourself" message is different.

Figure 1.9   A window class hierarchy

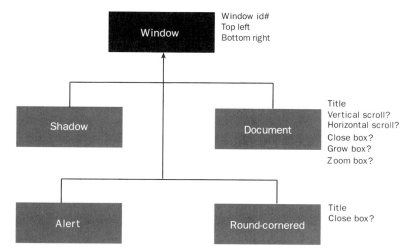

Some Guidelines for Defining Classes

Based on your reading of the preceding examples, several general principles should have emerged for identifying classes, class hierarchies, and methods. When identifying classes, you should pay attention to the following guidelines:

- Create entity classes to represent the most specific entities in the data processing environment. When representing an inventory of items, for example, choose classes for the items in the inventory, rather than the inventory itself.
- Consider inheritance when you have similar types of items that share some data, but have data specific to a given item type. Create a base class that contains the common data and use derived classes to represent the item-specific data. Apply the "is a" test to verify that inheritance is appropriate.
- Consider inheritance when you have similar types of items that react differently to the same message.
- After identifying the entity classes that will store program data, consider classes that will be used to manage the user interface.
- Create a control class that will represent the application itself. As you have read, you will create only one object from this class.

When deciding what methods to define for a class, consider the following:

- Each class needs at least one method that is run when the object is created (a *constructor*).
- A method acts on just one specific object rather than on all objects of the same class. Therefore, a method must represent an action appropriate for a single object. If all objects of the same class need to be processed, then it is the responsibility of a control class designed to handle multiple objects of another type to do so.
- Because the data that describe an object are hidden from the program manipulating the object, classes often need methods that return data values to whatever is manipulating the object.
- In addition to methods that return data values, classes also need methods to change the values in their attributes.

The object-oriented paradigm also makes provisions for a method that is executed automatically when an object is destroyed (a *destructor*). Traditionally, you would use a destructor to free any memory allocated by the object so that the memory could be reused by other parts of the program. Java, the language you are studying using this book, makes destructors largely unnecessary because it performs its own garbage collection, a process during which all unused memory is collected for reuse.

Summary

The object-oriented paradigm is a way of organizing the logic of a program. It has the following major characteristics:

- Entities in the programming environment—data, the user interface, and the program itself—are represented as objects.
- Objects have data that describe them (variables) and things they know how to do (methods).
- The general pattern from which an object is created is known as a class.
- A class's variables are usually private (hidden from methods outside the class).

- The way in which methods are called is public. The details of how methods operate are private (known as information hiding or encapsulation).
- General classes (base classes) share their variables and methods with more specific classes created from them (derived classes); this is known as inheritance.
- Objects communicate by sending messages to one another. A message indicates the object that is to receive the message, the method that is to be executed, and the data that are to be used as input to the method.

Exercises

These exercises will give you a chance to explore the current state of the Java language as well as to practice identifying the classes that might be required by an object-oriented program.

1. At the time this book was being written, the controversy between "pure Java" proponents, led by Sun Microsystems, and those who want to produce versions of Java tailored to specific platforms was unresolved. Using both print and World Wide Web resources, research and report on the current state of the Java standards controversy.

   a. Is there a "standard" version of Java?

   b. What has Sun done to try to promote a Java standard? To whom have they applied for recognition of the standard? What has been the result of those applications?

   c. According to "pure Java" proponents, what are the benefits of writing pure Java code?

   d. According to those who want Java tailored to specific platforms, what are the benefits of the specialized versions of Java?

   e. In your opinion, based on what you have read, in which direction should the development of Java as a language proceed?

2. Java has many uses beyond creating applets. Using both print and World Wide Web resources, research and report on answers to the following questions:

    a. Some developers see Java as the basis for an operating system. What is the state-of-the-art in the development of a Java OS? What products, if any, currently exist? In what environment are they intended to be used?

    b. What is the relationship between Java and database management systems? What capabilities does the Java Database Connectivity kit (JDBC) provide? What is the state-of-the-art in using Java as a development language for database applications?

    c. What other uses for Java can you find, beyond creating applets and stand-alone application programs?

3. Draw a diagram like those used in this chapter to describe the entity classes you would create for the programs described in the following. If your classes include inheritance, be sure to apply the "is a" test to determine whether inheritance is appropriate. On a separate page, list the methods you would need for each class.

    a. A program that would manage a student's calendar, including class schedule, reading assignments, assignments to hand in, and exam schedules. The program should also track school holidays.

    b. A program that keeps track of grades a student receives during the semester, identified by course, type of graded item, and the weight of that item in the overall course grade.

    c. A program that helps someone building a house pick the options for that house, including siding material and color, inside wall covering and color/pattern, and floor coverings for each room.

    d. A program that manages a video store, including the movies in inventory, the people who rent them (the customers), and the actual rentals of those items.

e. A program that a salesperson could use to manage his or her contacts with customers, including when each contact was made, the substance of the contact, and how the contact should be followed up.

f. A program that a student could use to manage a bibliography for a term paper, including sources of research material, quotations taken from the research, and data to be used in writing the paper.

g. A program to manage a Human Resources department (formerly called "Personnel"), including employees, their job history with the company, and their dependents.

h. A program that a hobby shop could use to control its inventory. The program should track items in inventory along with the sales of those items. (*Hint:* Don't forget about the people making purchases.)

i. A program to manage the service department of an automobile dealership. The program should handle cars and their owners, service appointments, and work done during those appointments.

j. A program to handle accounts payable (money a company owes). The program should track the vendors to whom money is owed, the statements that are received from those vendors, and payments made. When developing your classes, consider the effect of writing checks on a company's bank account.

4. You have been asked to complete the object-oriented design for the term paper bibliography program described in Exercise 3(f). This design needs to include entity, interface, and control classes. Since you've already identified the entity classes and your program will use only one control class (the application itself), all you need to do is draw a diagram for the interface classes:

The user interface needs to do the following:

- Provide a main menu
- Provide a dialog box for entering data collected from a single bibliographic source.

- Provide a dialog box for searching for bibliographic information.
- Provide a window for displaying information that is retrieved.

(*Hint:* When identifying interface classes, don't forget that each element you put on a dialog box, such as a field for text entry, a check box, or a button, is an object created from some class.)

5. You have been asked to complete the object-oriented design for the hobby shop inventory program described in Exercise 3(h). The design needs to include entity, interface, and control classes. Since you've already identified the entity classes and your program will use only one control class (the application itself), all you need to do is draw a diagram for the interface classes.

   The user interface needs to do the following:

   - Provide a main menu.
   - Provide dialog boxes for entering inventory items, customers, and sales. (The same dialog boxes can be used to modify and delete as well.)
   - Provide dialog boxes for finding inventory items and customers so their data can be modified or deleted.
   - Provide windows for displaying a sales slip for a single sale, an inventory report, and a weekly sales summary.

   (*Hint:* When identifying interface classes, don't forget that each element you put on a dialog box, such as a field for text entry, a check box, or a button, is an object created from some class.)

2

Running Java

OBJECTIVES

In this chapter you will learn about:
- The environments in which a Java program can execute.
- The difference between an application and an applet.
- How Java programs are prepared for execution.
- How Java programs are executed.
- The overall structure of a Java program.
- Creating objects and calling methods.
- Placing comment statements in a program.

Although Java shares a great deal of syntax with C++, Java has some unique characteristics that make it distinct from any other high-level language (structured or object-oriented) that you may have encountered. In this chapter you will read about where Java programs run, how they are prepared for execution, and how they are actually executed. In addition, you will see your first complete Java program and be introduced to its overall structure.

Java Execution Environments

A Java program can run as an application, or it can run inside a World Wide Web browser. Java programs that run inside browsers are known as *applets*. Although there are a few structural differences between applications and applets, basic programming techniques are the same for both. In addition, an applet must use a graphic user interface; an application can use either a graphic user interface or perform text-based console I/O.

Note

Much of the excitement that surrounded the release of Java centered on the ability to run applets. In the ensuing furor, it was forgotten for a time that Java is a complete programming language, and that it is the only programming language that has a graphics toolbox that supports applications with a graphic user interface on a variety of computing platforms without any source code changes

Although a Java application doesn't run inside a web browser, it still isn't a complete stand-alone application. Instead, like an applet, it runs with the help of an *interpreter*. An interpreter is a language processor that takes a program and translates it to machine language as the program is running. In contrast, a compiler—like those you may have used with COBOL, Pascal, C, or C++—performs the complete translation before the program is run. Compiled programs therefore can run on their own.

The original interpreted language was BASIC. A BASIC interpreter takes source code and performs the translation, line-by-line, as the program is running. Interpreted BASIC programs therefore execute rather slowly. Java, however, is only partly interpreted.

The Java interpreter isn't working with your Java source code. Instead, it is working with *bytecodes*. A bytecode is an intermediate form of a program, where source code has been translated to a generic, binary format that is unrelated to the instruction set of any specific computing platform. The interpreter takes the bytecode and translates it to the machine language required by a specific computer as the program is running.

There is one major advantage to this arrangement: As long as you have a Java interpreter for a computing platform, you can take Java bytecodes created on any platform and run them, without any modification. A Java program in bytecode format is therefore truly platform-independent. Given the speed of today's CPUs, the interpretation of the bytecodes and translation to machine language while the program is running doesn't seem to introduce any noticeable execution slowdowns. Nonetheless, a partially interpreted, partially compiled program will execute more slowly than a completely compiled program.

Note The first language to use bytecodes was UCSD Pascal. We often speak of UCSD Pascal as being "pseudocompiled" and call the bytecodes produced by the compiler "p-codes." A UCSD interpreter therefore translated the p-codes to machine language at runtime, just as a Java interpreter does.

The bottom line is that a Java program is both compiled and interpreted. When you are developing a Java program, you compile the program into bytecodes. Then, when you run the program, the interpreter translates the bytecodes to machine language.

The program that interprets a Java program is often called a *Java virtual machine*. Depending on your computing platform, it may be stand-alone application or integrated into your operating system.

Java Programming Environments

There are many Java programming environments available today, each with its own rules for how a program should be assembled. For example, Microsoft's J++ requires that each class be in a file of its own; the file must have the same name as the class, with a *.java* extension. In contrast, Metrowerks CodeWarrior couldn't care less how many classes are in a file or what the files are named (although *.java* extensions make life easier), but you do need to tell the development environment the name of the class containing the start of the program (the `main` method, which we'll discuss in the next major section of this chapter).

The result is that the details of creating and naming the files that make up a Java program are very dependent on the development software you are using and therefore beyond the scope of this book. However, there are some basic characteristics of the programming environment that are the same.

Java Class Library

Like most high-level languages, Java development software provides the developer with a toolbox of prewritten routines that can be used in a program. These libraries of classes provide support for I/O, the graphic user interface, string manipulation, math, and so on.

The basic Java library that accompanies your Java development software is stored in a file called *classes.zip*. (Exactly where this file is stored on your computer depends on both your operating system and the development software you are using.)

Note

You will also probably have the source code for all the classes in *classes.zip*. You can therefore look at how the classes you are using were written.

Inside *classes.zip* is a hierarchy of *packages*, each of which contains a group of related Java classes. There are four basic packages inside *classes.zip* that you will use in this book:

- `java.lang`: Contains support for arithmetic manipulations, numeric data types, and arrays.
- `java.io`: Contains support for I/O, although support for console (line-oriented) I/O is very primitive.
- `java.util`: Contains a variety of utility routines, including a random number generator and a date class.
- `java.awt` (Alternative Window Toolkit, or AWT): Contains classes for a graphic user interface as well as some simple drawing routines.

The *classes.zip* file also contains `java.net`, which provides support for interacting with a network.

Because Java's support for console I/O is so limited, you will need to use a special package that goes along with this book—*text.zip*—for the first few chapters, until you learn how to use AWT to create a graphic user interface.

The classes in *text.zip* make it easier to read values from the keyboard and to format numbers for console output than working directly with what Java provides.

Warning A Java compiler expects the classes in a *.zip* library file to be zipped. Don't attempt to unzip the file, although you can browse the file with a Windows 95, UNIX, or Macintosh utility. However, don't open the file with an MS-DOS or Windows 3.1 version of an unzipping program. Java requires long file names, but those programs will truncate file names to the MS-DOS 8.3 naming convention, making the library's contents inaccessible.

Preparing a Java Program

The details of how you will prepare a Java program will depend on the specific development software you are using. However, the general steps in assembling the program and getting it ready to run are as follows:

1. Enter and save source code files. Give each file a *.java* extension.
2. Create a *project* for the program. A project is a mechanism for letting the compiler know which source code files and libraries are part of a single program. Exactly what goes into the project depends on your development software. The project may require you to specify just source code files or it may require you to specify both source code files and libraries.

Note The easiest way to organize all the source code files for a single program is to place them all in one directory that is dedicated to just that program.

3. Compile the program with the Java compiler to produce bytecodes. The compiler will check your source code for syntax errors. If no errors are found, it will generate bytecodes for each source file. Then, your program development software will link the individual bytecode files, along with those from the libraries used in your program, into a single Java program file.

At this point, you can test the program. If the program is a stand-alone application, you will need to run your Java interpreter and execute the program. (Exactly how you do this depends on the software development environment.)

If the program is an applet, you have two choices:

- If you have an applet viewer, you can run the applet without using a web browser.
- Alternatively, you can create an HTML file that runs the applet. Then, you open the HTML file with a web browser that has a Java plug-in.

The advantage to the second strategy is that you can see how the applet actually will appear when it is downloaded by a World Wide Web user.

The Anatomy of a Java Program

In Listing 2.1 you can see a complete, albeit very small, Java program. Although the specific visual elements of Java development environments and virtual machines differ widely, if you were to run this program, you would see something like Figure 2.1.

Listing 2.1   hello.java

```java
import java.lang.*;
import java.io.*;
import java.awt.*;
import text.*;

public class HelloApp
{
    void Run()
    {
        SystemInput sysIn = new SystemInput();
        String theName = sysIn.readString ("Enter your name:");
        System.out.println ("\n\nJust saying 'hello,' " + theName + "!\n\n");
    }
    public static void main (String args[])
    {
        HelloApp theApp = new HelloApp();
        theApp.Run();
    }
}
```

Figure 2.1   Sample output of the Hello program

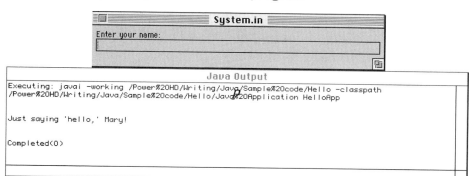

Some Java development environments do not support input directly into a console window. Therefore, until you learn to provide a graphic user interface for your programs, you will be using a system input window. This window, which is an object of the class `SystemInput`, is part of the `text` package supplied with this book. When you use a system input window, you specify a prompt to tell the user what data to enter (for example, "Enter your name:" in Figure 2.1). The user then types something into the input window's text edit box and presses Enter.

Text output appears in a console window (the window underneath the system input window in Figure 2.1). Although output formatting in this window is quite limited and not necessarily very attractive, it will be convenient to use while you are mastering basic Java syntax.

Every Java program must have at least one class. In most cases, that class will have the following characteristics:

- The class will be an application class. In this book, the names of such classes end with **App**.
- For programs that use console I/O like the Hello program, the class will contain a method called **Run**. This is where the program begins its real work.
- The class will contain a method called `main`. This is the first method executed by the program. Its task is to create an application object and, when we are using console I/O, to call the `run` method.

Class Structure

In Figure 2.2 you can see the basic, skeletal structure of a Java application class. (The major difference between this class and other Java classes is the presence of the main method.)

Figure 2.2   Basic class structure

```
public class someApp
{
    private variable declaration
    private variable declaration

    public someApp()
    {
        // constructor
    }

    public void Run()
    {
        // a method
    }

    public int someMethod(int value1, int value2)
    {
        // another method
    }

    public static void main (String args[])
    {
        someApp theApp = new someApp()
        theApp.Run();
    }
}
```

Every class begins with a header line that contains the keyword class followed by the name of the class (in this example, someApp). The body of the class is surrounded by braces ({ and }). Java uses braces not only to group a class, but to group methods and compound statements (for example, loops of more than one statement) as well.

There are many styles for organizing braces in source code. In this book, pairs of braces will always be on separate lines and indented so that the parts of the pair line up. This makes it easier to see the structure of a class or method.

Class names can include letters, numbers, and underscores (_). Like all words in Java, they are *case sensitive*. In other words, the Java compiler distinguishes between upper- and lowercase letters. Therefore, someClass and SomeClass are different names. By convention, Java names that include more than one word use either an underscore between the words—as in some_class—or use embedded uppercase letters to indicate where words begin—as in theClass.

The body of the class contains a collection of variable and method declarations. Each declaration begins with a keyword that describes the element's accessibility:

- public: The variable or method is accessible to objects of any other class. Variables are rarely public. (In fact, you won't see any public variables in this book.) Most methods are public so they can be called by objects of other classes.
- private: The variable or method is accessible only to objects created from the class. Variables are almost always private. You will also occasionally create private methods when you need a utility method that is used only within the class. Private methods are sometimes known as "helper methods."
- protected: The variable or method is accessible only to the class and objects derived from the class. Classes that aren't in the inheritance hierarchy cannot access the class element. Typically, we use protected access for base class variables. Methods remain public.

In Figure 2.2, the variable declarations appear at the beginning of the class, followed by the class's methods, and then the main method. There is no particular reason that the internals of a class need to be laid out in this way. However, by convention we keep variable declarations together and place the main method at the end.

Method Structure

With the exception of the `main` method, constructors, and destructors, all methods have the same general structure:

```
accessibility return_data_type methodName (parameter_list)
{
    // body of method
}
```

The body of the method is contained within a pair of braces. The method's first line—its header—contains the following elements:

- The accessibility of the method (`public` or `private`)
- The data type of the method's return value. Each method returns at most one value. The value returned can be a simple data type (for example, an integer or character) or a complex data type (for example, an array or an object).

Note   It is possible to modify data within a method in such a way that you end up with the *effect* of returning more than one value. However, the return mechanism handles only one value.

- The method's name. Like classes, method names are case sensitive. They can include letters, numbers, and underscores.
- The method's *parameter list*, where all input parameters are declared. An input parameter is a value that is passed into a method when the method is called. (You will read more about declaring input parameter when we discuss variable declarations in Chapter 3.) The entire parameter list is surrounded by parentheses

Optionally, a method may include the keyword `static` in its header immediately after its accessibility. Nonstatic methods perform their actions on an object created from their class. Static methods, however, don't operate on objects created from their class. As you will see throughout this book, the difference becomes important when you need to call the method.

Overloading

The complete identifier for a method includes both the method name and its parameter list (the method's *signature*). Method signatures must be unique within their class, although method names do not need to be. You can therefore have more than one method with this same name, as long as the parameter lists differ in some way.

Having more than one method in a class with the same name but different signatures is known as *overloading*. Overloading can simplify a programmer's task considerably by giving methods that perform the same task the same name. For example, assume that you write a program that can search a group of objects either by some identification number or by a key that is a string of characters. You would then include two methods:

```java
public String find (int ID_numb)
{
    // body of function goes here
}

public String find (String name)
{
    // body of function goes here
}
```

Both methods have the same name and the same return data type. However, their input parameter lists are different. All a programmer needs to remember is the name of the method. Regardless of the type of search key, the programmer knows that the method is named find.

Constructors

Most classes have one or more *constructors*, methods that are executed automatically whenever an object is created from a class. Constructors are similar to other functions with two exceptions:

- The name of a constructor is always the same as the name of its class.
- A constructor has no return data type.

Note

Many people use the word *instantiate* to describe creating an object from a class. This term comes from the idea that an object is an *instance* of a class.

Constructors are used to initialize parts of a program's environment. A constructor might, for example, read values for a data-handling object from a file. In a game program, a constructor might initialize a random number generator. Nonetheless, if there isn't any initialization that you need to do, you can theoretically omit writing a constructor.

The program in Listing 2.1, for example, has no constructor methods. However, it isn't good programming practice to omit a constructor. Doing so may make it harder for someone to modify your class at a later date. We should therefore add the following constructor to Listing 2.1:

```
public HelloApp ()
{
}
```

The presence of this empty constructor will help make it clear to a maintenance programmer that no actions take place when an object is created.

Note

To be strictly correct, if you don't include a constructor, the compiler creates a default constructor without any input parameters for you.

Classes often have more than one constructor. You can overload constructors just like you can overload other methods. A typical set of constructors might include:

- A constructor to initialize an object with data accepted from a user working at the keyboard.
- A constructor to initialize an object with data read from a disk file.
- A constructor to initialize an object with data copied from another object of the same class (a *copy constructor*).

The main Method

The `main` method is different from other methods in several ways:

- It appears only once in a program. Ordinarily, method names don't need to be unique. In fact, as you have just read, there are times when we consciously create more than one method by the same name.
- It is always `static`.
- It rarely returns a value and therefore usually has a return data type of `void`.
- Its input parameter list is always the same:

  ```
  (String args[])
  ```

- It is usually the only method in a program that creates an object of its own class.

The issue of input parameters and a return value for a `main` method has its roots in command-driven operating systems such as UNIX. Many UNIX programs return a single value to the operating system when they finish executing. For example, a 1 meant that the program ended successfully and a 0 meant that something unwanted occurred. The operating system could then take that return value, evaluate it, and if necessary, display an error message for the user.

By the same token, when a UNIX user would run a program, he or she could send arguments to the program by typing them on the command line along with the name of the program. For example,

```
Labels 12345,12346
```

might run a mailing list program that would print mailing labels for addresses in the two zip codes following the program name.

Although we typically run Java programs in a graphic user interface environment, the language is nonetheless equipped to both handle arguments input from a command line and to return a value to the operating system.

Note There is a subtle difference between the words "parameter" and "argument," although many people use the terms interchangeably. A parameter is a variable into which data are received by a called method. Parameters can then be used within the body of the method like any other local variable. Arguments are the values that the calling method sends to the method being called. In other words, arguments are passed into parameters.

Gaining Access to Class Libraries

If you look back at Listing 2.1, you'll notice that the first four lines of the program contain the keyword `import`. The import mechanism gives a program access to classes contained in the Java class libraries.

When you import a package, the Java compiler will look in that package to find a class or method references in a program file. Although the word "import" might suggest some sort of merging of the package into your program, that isn't what occurs. Importing simply alerts the Java compiler to additional locations it should consult to find classes and methods you've used.

You can import specific classes by giving the entire class name. For example, if you want the `SystemInput` class from the `text` package, you could write:

```
import text.SystemInput;
```

However, it is usually easier to import all the classes in a package with * wildcard:

```
import text.*;
```

This makes the entire package accessible, and because you aren't really merging anything with your program, but simply alerting the compiler to a source of additional classes, importing the entire package won't slow down compilation time.

Note   All Java statements end with a semicolon. As you will see in Chapter 3, this includes complex statements, such as the multiple statements that form the body of a loop, as well as simple statements such as assignment statements.

Creating Objects

One of the most fundamental things a Java program does is create objects from classes. The `main` method in the Hello program, for example, creates an object from its own class.

When you create an object, a Java program does the following:

- Allocates main memory for the object's variables.
- Connects (*binds*) the object to the code of its class's methods.
- If the class from which the object was created has a constructor, runs the constructor.
- Returns the main memory address of the beginning of the object's data storage (a *pointer*) to the program.

To use an object, a Java program needs to know the location in main memory where the object's data are stored. Therefore, when a program creates an object, it must store the pointer to an object's storage location in a variable. The variable is declared from the object's class. For example, the variable that holds the object declared from the `HelloApp` class could be declared with:

```
HelloApp theApp;
```

The first element in the statement is the data type (the class `HelloApp`); the second element is the variable that will hold the main memory address of the object. Because the variable holds the location of the object (a *reference* to the object's location), this type of variable is known as a *reference variable*.

To create the object, a program uses the `new` operator:

```
theApp = new HelloApp();
```

The `new` operator initiates the steps in the creation process and, when it finishes, assigns the main memory address of the object to the `theApp` variable.

The `new` operator is followed by the name of the class from which the object is to be created. The parentheses after the name of the class contain any arguments that are to be passed to the constructor. In this particular example, there aren't any arguments, so the parentheses are empty.

In Listing 2.1, the declaration of the variable and the creation of the object have been combined into one statement:

```
HelloApp theApp = new HelloApp();
```

What is actually occurring here is that the variable is being initialized at the same time it is being declared. The end result is exactly the same as using two statements, one to declare the variable and another to create the object. (You will learn more about initializing and declaring variables in Chapter 3.)

Calling Methods

A second task that a Java program performs frequently is to call methods. To execute a method, the program needs to know which object to use, which method to invoke, and what data to send to the message. For example, to read a string of text from the system input window, a program needs to know which window (the object), which method (the method to read a string), and what data (the prompt the user sees).

The syntax for calling a method is as follows:

```
Object_variable.Method_name (argument_list);
```

Because there is a period between the name of the variable that contains a pointer to the object and the name of the method, this syntax is often called *dot notation*. The complete syntax to read the string from the system input window is therefore:

```
sysIn.readString ("Enter your name:");
```

When there is more than one input argument, the arguments are separated by commas in the argument list.

Adding Comment Statements

Although you may find them a bother, comment statements are an important part of any program. (Try putting aside a program you're working on and coming back to it a couple of weeks later. How much of your logic will you understand?) Java supports two types of comments, one that is suited for short, single-line comments and another that works well for long comment blocks.

The block comment syntax brackets the comment with /* and */, as in:

```
/* This is a block comment */
```

The comment can be placed on a line by itself or at the end of another line, or it can span several lines.

In contrast, the single-line comment format begins each comment with //. Like block comments, single-line comments can be placed on a line by themselves or at the end of a line of executable code.

Which style should you use? It really doesn't matter. However, as you can see in the following example, it's often easier to use the block comment style for long comments:

```
// When you use the single-line comment style for multi-line
// comments, you must precede each line with the double
// slashes. This can be a bit of a bother for a long comment.

/* With the block style comment, you can run a comment onto
multiple lines without needing special characters to
indicate that a line belongs to a comment. However, you must
be very careful to close the comment. If you don't the rest
of your source code will be considered to be part of the
comment. */
```

Tracing the Hello Program

At this point, you know enough to understand everything the Hello program does. To begin, let's trace through the execution of the Hello program.

- The program begins with the `main` method. (If this seems somewhat odd, try to think up some other convenient way for a Java compiler to figure out where a program starts!)
- The `main` method creates an object of its own class, `HelloApp`, and stores a pointer to the main memory storage for the object in a variable named `theApp`.
- The `main` method calls the `HelloApp` class's `Run` method.
- Program control transfers to the `Run` method.
- The `Run` method creates an object of the `SystemInput` class and stores a pointer to the main memory storage for the object in a variable named `sysIn`.
- The `Run` method calls the `SystemInput` class's method `readString` to display a prompt in the system input window and store the text entered by the user in a variable called `name`.
- The `Run` method displays some text and the value the user entered in the console window by calling the `println` method of the `System.out` object.
- The program stops.

If you look again at the Hello program, you'll notice that the line that displays output to the user doesn't declare an object of the `System.out` object. The `System.out` object is declared for you by the compiler to provide support for simple, line-oriented console output.

Note

The Java specifications also include a `System.in` object. There are two drawbacks to basing the sample code in the first part of this book, however. First, not all Java development environments support `System.in`. Second, `System.in` reads only one character at a time, forcing the programmer to perform a significant amount of data conversion. That is why you have been given the `text` package, which does all that work for you.

Summary

Java programs are both compiled and interpreted. A program developer compiles Java source code into bytecodes, an intermediate, platform-independent form of a program. When the program is run, the bytecodes are interpreted and translated into machine language for the computer on which the program is running.

Java programs can be stand-alone programs or they can run inside a World Wide Web browser. In the latter case, they are known as applets.

A Java program is a collection of classes, which are made up of variables and methods. One class in a Java program must contain a method named `main`, which is always the first method executed when the program is run.

Java programs have at least one class: an application class from which an object is created to represent the program itself. In many cases, a program uses at least one other class to hold the data being manipulated by the application class.

An object is created with the `new` operator, which sets aside main memory storage for the object and returns a pointer (main memory address) of the object's storage to the method that created it. To call a method, a program uses the name of an object, followed by a period ("dot"), the name of the method, and the method's argument list.

Exercises

The first two exercises below will give you a chance to debug some simple Java programs as well as write your own `main` methods. The errors that are in these programs are typical of those that people make when learning to program in Java and involve the structural elements of a Java program that were presented in this chapter. You can enter the programs yourself or obtain the source code from your instructor. In either case, you will need to create a project file for each program.

The remaining exercises provide extra practice with some of the important concepts you've learned.

1. Shipping companies often ask you to compute the total dimensions of a package by adding the package's width, length, and height. The Package-Size program therefore asks the user for three integers (width, length, and height) and, when working correctly, displays the total dimensions in the console output window. For example, if the user entered 10, 15, and 20, the output would be:

    ```
    The size of the package is 45 inches.
    ```

    a. Enter (or obtain from your instructor) the source code in Listing 2.2 and Listing 2.3.
    b. Write a `main` method for the program. Place it in *Size.java*, replacing the comment statement "//Add the main method here." Your `main` method should declare an object of the `SizeApp` class and then call its `Run` function.
    c. Create a project and add the two source code files to the project. If required by your Java development environment, add the Java class libraries and the `text` package to the project.
    d. Run the program to see what errors the compiler detects. There are three errors you must find and correct before the program will run correctly. (*Hint:* One error in *Pkg.java*; the other two are in *SizeApp.java*.)

2. One of the facts of life in business today is the need to add sales tax to retail sales in most states. A simple program to compute the tax asks the user for the purchase price and for the tax rate. If the purchase price is 29.95 and the tax rate 0.0725 (7.25%), then the output of the program will be:

    ```
    The tax is $2.17
    ```

Listing 2.2   SizeApp.java

```java
import java.awt.*;
import java.io.*;
import java.lang.*;
import text.*;

public class SizeApp
{
    public void Run()
    {
        SystemInput sysIn = new SystemInput()
        int iwidth = sysIn.readInt ("Enter the width of the package:");
        int ilength = sysIn.readInt ("Enter the length of the package:");
        int iheight = sysIn.readInt ("Enter the height of the package:");

        pkg thePackage = new pkg (iwidth, ilength, iheight);

        int totalSize = thePackage.computeSize();

        System.out.println ("The size of the package is " + totalSize);
    }

    // Add the main method here
}
```

Listing 2.3   Pkg.java

```java
import java.io.*;
import java.lang.*;

public class pkg
{
    private int length;
    private int width;
    private int height;

    public pkg (int ilength, int iwidth, int iheight)
    {
        length = ilength;
        width = iwidth;
        height = iheight;
    }

    public int computeSize ()
        { return length + width + height;}
```

a. Enter (or obtain from your instructor) the source code in Listing 2.4 and Listing 2.5.

Listing 2.4   taxApp.java

```
import java.awt.*;
import java.io.*;
import java.lang.*;
import text.*;

public class taxApp
{
    public void Run
    {
        SystemInput sysIn = new SystemInput();
        float iPrice = sysIn.readFloat ("Enter the purchase price of the
item:");
        float iRate = sysIn.readFloat ("Enter the tax rate as a fractional
percentage (0.XX):");

        tax theTax = new tax (iPrice, iRate);
        float amount = theTax.computeTax();
        System.out.println ("The tax is $" +
NumberFormat.floatFormat(4,2,amount));
    }

    // Add the main method here
}
```

Listing 2.5   tax.java

```
public class tax
{
    private float Price;
    private float Rate;

    public tax (float iPrice, float iRate)
    {
        Price = iPrice;
        Rate = iRate;
    };

    public float computeTax()
        { return Price * Rate; }
};
```

    b. Write a `main` method for the program. Place it in *taxApp.java*, replacing the comment statements "//Add the main method here." Your `main` method should create an application object and call the object's `Run` method.

    c. Create a project for the program's two source code files. If necessary, add the Java class libraries and the `text` package to the project.

    d. Run the program to see what errors the compiler detects. There are three errors you must find and correct before the program will run correctly. (*Hint:* There is one error in *taxApp.java*; the other two errors, which are actually two instances of the same error, are in *tax.java*.)

3. Describe how a Java program is prepared for execution and how it is run. How is the way in which a Java program runs different from a program written in C, C++, Pascal, or COBOL?

4. Describe how the `import` statement makes it possible for a Java program to use classes and methods that aren't part of a program's source code.

5. Why must every Java program have a `main` method? How is the `main` method different from other methods?

6. What purpose do braces ({ and }) serve in a Java program?

7. Using resources available on the World Wide Web, research and report on what software is required to run a Java applet in a web browser.

8. Using both print and WorldWide Web resources, research and report on how operating system developers are integrating Java virtual machines into their software.

3 Variables and Data Types

OBJECTIVES

In this chapter you will learn:

- To understand Java's simple data types.
- How to declare variables using simple data types.
- About the scope of variables.
- How to use assignment to give variables values and how to use type-casting to change variable data types.
- About Java's String class.

The variables in an object-oriented program can belong to a class, in which case the values given to the variable describe an object created from the class, or they are used as temporary storage by methods (*local variables*). Nonetheless, both types of variables are declared and initialized in much the same way.

All Java variables must have a data type. For this reason, Java is what we call *strongly typed*.

In this chapter we will look at Java's simple data types and how to create variables from them. In addition, we will talk about the scope of variables (their accessibility, visibility, and length of life throughout a program) as well as look at techniques for initializing them. This chapter also introduces Java's String class, which provides support for manipulating strings of characters. Finally, we will discuss how variables are passed into methods as arguments.

Variables of Simple Data Types

Java's eight simple data types handle integer, floating point, character, and boolean data. Although many programming languages share the same simple data types, Java's simple data types are unique in that a variable of a given type always occupies the same amount of storage, regardless of the platform on which it is running.

All variables must be declared before they are used. To declare a variable, you specify the variable's data type followed by its name:

```
data_type variable_name;
int theInteger;
```

As with all Java statements, variable declarations are followed by a semicolon.

If you want to declare more than one variable of the same data type, you can do so by separating the variable names with commas:

```
data_type variable_name1, variable_name2, variable_name3;
int Integer1, Integer2, Integer3;
```

Local variables need only the data type and variable name. However, variables that belong to a class (in other words, those that will hold data describing an object) must also be preceded by `private`, `protected`, or `public` to indicate their accessibility.

```
private int theInteger;
```

As you read in Chapter 2, variables that are part of a class are usually `private` or, when inheritance is involved, `protected`. They are almost never `public`.

Integers

Java has four integer data types, which are summarized in Table 3.1. Notice that the typical integer type (`int`) is 32 bits. In other high-level programming languages, many PC implementations use only 16 bits for an `int` and use 32 bits for a `long`. As a result, a Java program can use `int` storage for most integer manipulations.

Table 3.1   Java's integer data types

Data Type	Range	Main Memory Requirements
int	-2,147,483,648 -> 2,147,463,648	4 bytes
short	-32,768 -> 32,767	2 bytes
long	-9,223,372,036,854,775,808 -> 9,223,372,036,854,775,807	8 bytes
byte	-128 -> 127	1 byte

Note When choosing a data type for a variable, keep in mind that one of your software development goals should be to minimize the size of your program. (If a Java program is an applet, someone will need to download it over the World Wide Web!) Therefore, you should pick the smallest size storage location that will hold each value you need. For example, don't use a `long` when an `int` will do.

The following are all legal integer variable declarations:

```
int theNumber, the_Number, THENUMBER;
short smallQuantity;
long bigNumber, big_number, bigNumber1, bigNumber2;
byte counter, how_many;
```

Floating Point Numbers

Java has two floating point data types, which are summarized in Table 3.2. The `float` data type provides about seven digits to the right of the decimal point; the `double` provides about 15. This means that even if you don't need the wide range provided by `double`, you may want to use it to obtain the extra *precision* (significant digits to the right of the decimal point) that it gives you. In particular, if you are doing financial calculations, `float` storage usually doesn't provide enough precision. We therefore often store currency values as `double`.

Table 3.2   Java's floating point data types

Data Type	Range	Main Memory Requirements
float	≈±3.40282347E±38	4 bytes
double	≈±1.7976931348231570E±308	8 bytes

The following are legal floating point variable declarations:

```
float theFloat, float_var;
double bigFloatingPointNumber, theDouble, Double2;
```

Character Data

The basic building block for handling character data is the `char` data type, which holds one ASCII character. A `char` variable therefore occupies one byte of storage. Character variables, for example, are often used to hold data such as single-letter codes (such as *s*, *m*, or *l* for sizes):

```
char T_ShirtSize;
```

In business programs, most character data are part of strings. Although Java does not have a String data type, it does have a `String` class that you will use extensively. You will be introduced to that class later in this chapter.

Booleans

Variables declared from the `boolean` data type can accept only one of two values: `true` or `false`. They are therefore most useful when testing the result of logical conditions. You therefore might, for example, use `boolean` variables to hold flags used by a program:

```
boolean More, finished, Done;
```

Variables for Objects

An object is an instance of a complex data type (a class), in that its main memory representation is a collection of values declared from other data types. Therefore, when you declare a variable to hold a pointer to an object's main memory storage, you use the class from which the object will be created as the variable's data type. For example, you would create a variable to point to an object from an `Employee` class with:

```
Employee theEmployee;
```

Note

Don't let anyone tell you that Java doesn't use pointers! It does. Every reference to an object is a pointer. Because you have just this one way to reference an object, you don't have to distinguish between using pointers or regular variables when you want to access an object.

Because an object variable contains the main memory address of the starting location of an object's storage, you can assign the contents of one object variable to another:

```
Employee theEmployee = new Employee();
Employee theManager = theEmployee;
```

Does the statement above mean that you are making a copy of the first object? No, not at all. After executing both statements, the variable named `theManager` holds a copy of the main memory location of `theEmployee`. In other words, both variables point to the same place in memory and are therefore two ways of referencing the same object.

Now consider the following two lines of code:

```
Employee theEmployee = new Employee();
theEmployee = new Employee();
```

The first statement creates an object from the `Employee` class and assigns it to the variable `theEmployee`. The second statement creates a *second* object from the same class and assigns it to the same variable. What happens to the space in main memory allocated to the first object? It's orphaned because the memory's address is no longer stored anywhere. Executing the second statement erased the pointer to the first object.

In many languages, the preceding would produce a *memory leak*, memory space that is allocated and then lost and never recovered. Memory leaks can cause enormous program problems because they consume and fragment the memory used by the program, making it difficult (and sometimes, impossible) for the program to allocate space for more data while it is running. Java, however, avoids memory leaks because it performs its own *garbage collection*, through which it periodically collects all unreferenced memory and frees it for use again.

Scope of Variables

Unlike other languages that you may have used, variables in a Java program can be declared just about anywhere. However, the accessibility, visibility, and length of life of a variable (its *scope*) depends on where the variable is declared. As an example, take a look at the code in Listing 3.1, a class that we'll be examining in more depth in Chapter 5.

The class has one variable that belongs to objects of the class (`theNumber`). Because this is a private variable, its contents are accessible to all of the class's methods. The variable stays in memory as long as the object it belongs to stays in memory. However, the variable's contents are *not* accessible to any methods belonging to objects outside the class.

Most of the methods in this class use local variables. For example, in the `binary` method, there are four local variables declared at the beginning of the method. These variables are accessible and visible only within the method. When the method finishes execution, the variables are removed from main memory, destroying their contents.

If you look at the `factorial` method, you will see a variable declaration buried in the `for` statement. The variable `i`, which is used as an index in the loop, is visible and accessible only within the body of the loop. When the loop terminates, the variable disappears.

Listing 3.1   A sample class containing object and local variables

```
public class NumberManip
{
    // variable that belongs to objects of the class
    private int theNumber;

    public NumberManip (int iNumber)
        { theNumber = iNumber; }

    public long factorial()
    {
        long result = theNumber;

        // local variable--i--exists only within the for loop
        for (int i = theNumber-1; i >= 1; i--)
            result *= i;
        return result;
    }

    public long binary()
    {
        // local variable declarations
        int bit, placeValue = 1, numberTemp;
        long binaryTemp = 0;

        numberTemp = theNumber;

        while (numberTemp != 0)
        {
            bit = numberTemp % 2;
            numberTemp /= 2;
            binaryTemp += bit * placeValue;
            placeValue *= 10;
        }
        return binaryTemp;
    }

    public double root()
        { return Math.sqrt(theNumber); }
}
```

There is actually one guiding rule behind all of these scopes: A variable is accessible, visible, and alive only inside the "statement" within which it is defined. When the statement finishes execution, the variable disappears. The trick here, of course, is how we define "statement." In this context, assume that a statement is anything that terminates with a semicolon (for example, the `for` statement in the `factorial` method) or anything that is bounded by a set of braces. Therefore, in this situation a method might be considered a "statement," as well as a class.

Literal Values

When you use a numeric literal value in a program, Java makes some assumptions about the data type of the data. For example, Java assumes that an integer literal such as 123 is an `int` and that a floating point value such as 3.456 is a `double`.

If you want the Java compiler to treat an integer as a `long`, follow the literal value with an L. For example, `123L` will be stored as a `long` rather than an `int`. To get a `float` rather than a `double`, follow a literal value with an F, as in `3.456F`.

Character literals should be surrounded by single quotes, as in `'a'` or `'X'`. String literals, which will be discussed in more depth later in this chapter, are surrounded by double quotes (for example, `"test"`).

Boolean literals have only two possible values, the keywords `true` and `false`.

Initializing Variables

All variables must be initialized before they are used. There are two ways you can do so:

- Assign the variable a value when it is declared. The value that is given to the variable can be a literal or the result of evaluating some Java expression.
- Assign the variable a value using an assignment statement at any point before the variable is used on the right side of an assignment operator.

In either case, initialization requires use of the Java assignment operator, an equals sign. To perform assignment, place the variable on the left of the assignment operator and the value to be assigned on the right.

The following statements initialize variables declared from simple data types:

```
private int employeeID = 0;
private float salary = 0.0F;
```

```
char Size = 's';
boolean Done = true;
```

As you saw in Chapter 2, to create an object and allocate storage space for its variables, you use the new operator. Although we typically create objects within methods, there is no reason that you can't create an object where the variable to holds its pointer is declared as part of a class. For example, all the following object declarations and initializations are acceptable:

```
private someClass theObject = new someClass(); // LEGAL
private someClass theObject; // LEGAL

public void someMethod ()
{
    someClass theObject = new someClass(); // LEGAL

    someClass theObject;
    theObject = new someClass(); // LEGAL
}
```

Typecasting

Java is very fussy about data types. Unless you explicitly request a change of data type, Java will not let you assign a value of one type to a variable of another. Explicitly requesting a change of data type is known as *typecasting*.

To perform a typecast, you precede a value with the data type to which you want to convert it, surrounded in parentheses. For example, to convert an int to a long, you would use:

```
int theInteger = 6;
long theLong;
theLong = (long) theInteger;
```

Java will allow you to typecast any numeric type to any other. However, sometimes the results may not be what you expect. For example, what do you think will be stored in anInteger after a program executes the following statements?

```
int anInteger;
float aFloat = 4.568F;
anInteger = (int) aFloat;
```

The variable `anInteger` will contain 4. Why? Because when you typecast a floating point value to an integer value, Java truncates the value, removing anything to the right of the decimal point.

You can also typecast a character to an integer, and vice versa. However, you cannot typecast a `boolean` to any other type.

String Objects

A string of characters is a complex value. To make it possible for you to handle strings as a unit, rather than requiring you to work with each individual character, Java provides a `String` class. However, when it comes to initializing and assigning strings, you can work with them as if they were simple values. For example, the following statements are all legal:

```
String name;
String firstName = "Jeff", lastName = "Stone";

private String name;
private String name = "";

String name1, name2;
name1 = "Jane";
name1 = name2;
```

charAt

To access individual characters in a string, you use the `String` class method `charAt`. The method requires the position of the character you want as its input parameter:

```
char theLetter;
String theString = "My dog has fleas.";
theLetter = theString.charAt (3);
```

The positions characters in a string are counted beginning with 0. In the string My dog has fleas, the letter d is at position 3.

Although you can retrieve the individual characters in a string, you cannot modify them while they are a part of a string. For this reason, we often say that Java strings are *immutable*.

Static Variables and Constants

Java does not support global constants (unchangeable values available to an entire program); all variables must be part of a class. Nonetheless, you can establish variables within a class whose values can't be changed. To do so, you use the keyword `static`, along with the keyword `final`. For example, the following statement establishes a value that is accessible to all methods in a class:

```
static final float TAX_RATE = .0725F;
```

The constant declaration is placed outside any methods, along with the variables that describe objects created from the class. However, static variables belong to the class as a whole, not to individual objects.

Static variables are often referred to as *class variables* because their values apply to the class as a whole, rather than to individual objects. (That is why we don't use that term to describe the variables that hold the data describing objects created from a class.) When you declare a variable that is part of a class as `static`, the computer maintains only one copy of the variable, regardless of how many objects you create from the class.

You could, for example, declare a variable that holds the number of objects created from a class:

```
static int objectCount = 0;
```

All objects created from the class would have access to the variable and could modify its contents. However, there would be only one, central copy of the variable stored in memory.

Static local variables are different from static class variables. When you declare a local variable as `static`, the variable won't be removed from memory when the statement in which the variable was created finished executing. The variable will remain intact, retaining its contents.

Data Type Classes

The Java class libraries contain a class that corresponds to each simple variable type. For example, there are classes named `Integer`, `Long`, `Float`, and `Double`. Most of the methods in these classes are *static methods*, which means that they don't operate on an instance of a class, but instead work with individual data values provided by a program. As a result, when you call a a method from one of these classes, you use the name of the class rather than the name of an object declared from the class.

For example, one of the methods you will use frequently from these classes is `toString`, which converts a number to a string of ASCII characters. `toString` To convert a `float` to an equivalent string, you could do the following:

```
float theValue = 1.256F;
String stringEquivalent = Float.toString (theValue);
```

Notice that the `toString` method takes a single parameter: the value being converted.

The `toString` method is available for the `Integer`, `Long`, and `Float` classes. Converting a `double` to a string is a bit more involved than simply calling a single method; the technique will be discussed later in this book.

Summary

Every Java variable must have a data type that indicates the type of data that will be stored. The amount of storage allocated to a variable depends on the data type, regardless of the platform on which the program is running.

All variables must be declared before they are used. They should also be initialized because the declaration process doesn't erase any previous value the main memory storage location may have had.

Java does not support global constants. However, static class variables can be used to provide constants within a single class.

Object variables hold the main memory location of where the data that describe the objects are stored. When you assign the contents of one object variable to another, you assign a main memory location rather than copying actual data values. Assigning a second object pointer to an object variable can orphan the data originally pointed to by the variable. However, Java's garbage collection mechanism collects inaccessible memory, preventing memory leaks.

Character strings are handled by the class `String`. Strings can be declared and assigned like simple variable types. However, access to characters within a string requires calling a class method.

Exercises

In this set of exercises, you will first work with some variable and constant declarations with pen and paper. Then you'll get a chance to declare variables and constants in a sample program, as well as to debug some errors involving constant and variable declarations. You may either type in the source code for the programs or obtain the text files from your instructor. In either case, you will need to create your own project.

1. Write the following declarations:

    a. A character variable that will hold a letter that represents the size of a piece of clothing.
    b. An integer variable that will count the number of people who visit a web site.
    c. A string variable that will hold a person's first name.
    d. A character variable that will hold a single-letter response to a question asked by the computer.
    e. Two integer variables, one for a student's test score at the beginning of a one-week training course and the other for the same student's test score at the end of the training course.
    f. A floating point variable that will hold the price of a gallon of home heating oil.
    g. A string variable that will hold the name of a company that sells home heating oil.
    h. Three floating point variables that will hold the winning times of the first three heats of a foot race.

2. Write the following constant declarations:

    a. An integer constant for the number of people who responded to a survey.
    b. Two integer constants, one for the number of salespeople employed by a company and another for the number of consultants employed by the same company.
    c. Three character constants to represent the three sizes that are available for a line of sweatshirts (medium, large, and extra large).
    d. A floating point constant for the commission rate that salespeople receive on their sales.
    e. Two floating point constants, one for the regular hourly pay rate and the second for the overtime pay rate.

3. Identify the problems with the following declarations:

    a. `float Sales, float Commission;`
    b. `float Sales, int Commission;`
    c. `float Sales, Commission`

d. `char yes_no; maybe;`

e. `static final NUM_PEOPLE = 18;`

4. For this exercise, you will work with a slightly modified version of the tax computation program that you first saw at the end of Chapter 2. This version conducts a very simple dialog with the user, asking the user to enter the amount of the purchase. Instead of asking for the tax rate, the program works with the tax rate as a constant. If the user were to enter 85.99, then the output in the console window would be:

```
The tax on $85.99 is $6.23.
```

a. Enter (or obtain from your instructor) the source code files in Listing 3.2 and Listing 3.3.

Listing 3.2   tax.java

```java
public class tax
{
    // replace this line with a constant named TAX_RATE
    // replace this line with a floating point variable named Price; initialize
    it to 0.0

    public tax (float iPrice)
    {
        // replace this line with an assignment statement that assigns the
        // value of iPrice to Price
    }

    public float computeTax()
        { return Price * TAX_RATE; }
}
```

b. In Listing 3.2, replace the first comment statement (the first line beginning with //) with a declaration for a constant named **TAX_RATE**. Set the tax rate equal to the sales tax rate in your state; if your state has no sales tax, use 0.05. Replace the second comment statement in the file with a declaration of a variable named **Price**, which should be initialized to 0.0. You must use these exact names, including matching the case of the letters, because they are used elsewhere in the program.

```
import java.awt.*;
import java.io.*;
import java.lang.*;
import text.*;

public class taxApp
{
    public void Run()
    {
        // Replace these lines with the declaration of a variable to point to an
        // object declared from the SystemInput class named sysIn.
        // Create the object, either as part of the declaration or as a
        // separate assignment statement. No input parameters are requied.

        // Replace these lines with the declaration of a floating point
        // variable named iPrice
        iPrice = sysIn.readFloat ("Enter the purchase price of the item:");

        // Replace these lines with the declaration of a variable to point to
        // an object declared from class "tax" named theTax
        theTax = new tax (iPrice);
        float amount = theTax.computeTax();

        System.out.println
            ("The tax is $ " + NumberFormat.floatFormat(4,2,amount));
    }

    public static void main (String args[])
    {
        taxApp theApp = new taxApp();
        theApp.Run();
    }
}
```

Listing 3.3   taxApp.java

c. In Listing 3.3, replace the first four comment lines with the declaration of a variable named sysIn that will point to an object of class SystemInput. Then, create an object from that class using the new operator. Because the constructor requires no parameters, you should use a set of empty parentheses for the parameter list. (*Hint:* You can do this using two separate statements or you can combine the declaration and the creation of the object into one.)

d.   In Listing 3.3, replace the second set of comment lines (the fifth and sixth) with the declaration of a floating point variable named iPrice. Replace the third set of comment lines (the seventh and eighth) with the declaration of a variable named theTax to hold a pointer to an object created from the tax class.

e.   Create a project for the program and add the two source code files to it.

f.   Run the program. Find and correct your errors.

5.   When a doctor asks a patient to monitor his or her own blood pressure, the doctor often suggests that the patient take three readings, each about ten minutes apart, and then compute the average of the readings. For this exercise, you will be finding the errors in a program that asks the user for the three readings and then produces the average. It finishes by telling the user whether his or her blood pressure is high:

```
Your average blood pressure is 166/113
Your blood pressure is high.
```

a.   Enter (or obtain from your instructor) the source code in Listing 3.4 and Listing 3.5.

Listing 3.4   pressure.java

```java
public class pressure
{
    private int systolic1; systolic2, systolic3;
    private diastolic1, diastolic2, diastolic3;

    public pressure (int iSys1, int iSys2, int iSys3, int iDias1, int iDias2,
    int iDias3)
    {
        systolic1 = iSys1;
        systolic2 = iSys2;
        systolic3 = iSys3;
        diastolic1 = iDias1;
        diastolic2 = iDias2;
        diastolic3 = iDias3;
    }

    public int systolicAvg ()
        { return ((systolic1 + systolic2 + systolic3)/3); }

    public int diastolicAvg ()
        { return ((diastolic1 + diastolic2 + diastolic3)/3); }
}
```

Listing 3.5 MedApp.java

```java
import java.lang.*;
import java.awt.*;
import java.util.*;
import text.*;

public class MedApp
{
    private final SYSTOLIC = 140;
    private final int DIASTOLIC = 90;

    public void Run()
    {
        SystemInput sysIn = new SystemInput();

        int iSys1 = sysIn.readInt ("First systolic reading:");
        int iDias1 = sysIn.readInt ("First diastolic reading:");
        int iSys2 = sysIn.readInt ("Second systolic reading:");
        int iDias2 = sysIn.readInt ("Second diastolic reading:");
        int iSys3 = sysIn.readInt ("Third systolic reading:");
        iDias3 = sysIn.readInt ("Third diastolic reading:");

        pressure Readings = new pressure (iSys1, iSys2, iSys3, iDias1, iDias2,
    iDias3);
        int sysAvg = Readings.systolicAvg();
        int diasAvg = Readings.diastolicAvg();

        System.out.println ("Your average blood pressure is " + sysAvg + "/" +
    diasAvg);
        if (sysAvg > SYSTOLIC || diasAvg > DIASTOLIC)
            System.out.println ("Your blood pressure is high.");
        else
            System.out.println ("Your blook pressure is OK.");
    }

    public static void main (String args[])
    {
        MedApp theApp = new MedApp();
        theApp.Run();
    }
}
```

b. Create a project for this program and add the source code files to it.

c. Run the project. The compiler will detect several errors that you must find and correct before the program will execute properly. (*Hint:* All of these errors deal with variable and constant declarations, or the lack thereof.)

Writing and Using Methods (Part I)

OBJECTIVES

In this chapter you will read about:

- Method structure.
- Writing simple methods.
- Passing values into a method as arguments.
- Returning values from methods.
- Performing console I/O.

You can describe a Java program as a collection of classes. However, all the work of the program is performed by the methods that are part of those classes. In this chapter we will look at methods in depth, providing a framework on which the rest of this book is built. By the time you have finished this chapter, you will be able to write complete Java programs that accept data from the keyboard, store the data in an object, and echo that data back to the user in a console window.

Method Structure

As you have read, methods have the following general structure:

```
accesibility return_data_type method_name (parameter_list)
{
    // body of method
}
```

The body of a method can contain comments, declarations, and executable Java statements. Beginning with Chapter 5, almost everything you learn in this book will deal with creating effective methods.

The method header specifies the following:

- The method's accessibility (either `public` or `private`).
- The method's return data type (any data type, simple or complex, or `void`, indicating no return value).
- The method's name.
- The method's parameter list, surrounded by parentheses.

As a first example, we will be looking at a program that asks the user for information about a manager (first name, last name, number of people managed, base salary, and bonus rate). After collecting all the data the program creates a manager object and stores the data in that object. Then, it computes the bonus and produces the following output:

```
The manager's name is Doe Jane.
He or she manages 15 people.
He or she will receive $74750.00 this year.
```

Listing 4.1   manager.java

```
public class manager
{
    private int people_managed;
    private String last_name, first_name;
    float salary;

    public manager (int numb_people, String iLname, String iFname,
        float iSalary)
    {
        people_managed = numb_people;
        last_name = iLname;
        first_name = iFname;
        salary = iSalary;
    }

    public int getPeople_managed()
        { return people_managed; }

    public String getLast_name()
        { return last_name; }

    public String getFirst_name()
        { return first_name; }

    public float getSalary()
        { return salary; }

    public float computeBonus (float bonusPercent)
        { return salary * bonusPercent; }
}
```

The class that stores the data—the **manager** class (see Listing 4.1)—has four variables:

```
    private int people_managed;
    private String last_name, first_name;
    float salary;
```

To compute the bonus to be paid to the manager, the **manager** class includes a method named **computeBonus**:

```
    public float computeBonus (float bonusPercent)
    {
        return salary * bonusPercent;
    }
```

As you can see, the parameter list looks a lot like a variable declaration. In fact, that's exactly what parameter lists are: declarations of variables to hold external data that will be provided to the method when the method is called. Once a parameter is declared in the method header, the parameter's variable can be used in the body of the method as if it were a local variable.

The class's constructor has more than one parameter declaration in its parameter list:

```
public manager (int numb_people, String iLname, String iFname,
    float iSalary)
```

When looking at the preceding method header, keep in mind that a constructor has no return data type and that its name is always the same as the name of its class.

Passing Arguments to Parameters

As you have read, an argument is data that are passed into a method when it is called. To call a method, sending data to into one more of the method's input parameters, you use either the names of variables containing the data you want to pass or literal values. For example, if a manager's bonus rate were stored in a variable named bonus_rate and an object of class manager was named theManager, a class such as the manager application class (Listing 4.2) could call the method to compute the amount of the bonus using:

```
float bonusAmount = theManager.computeBonus (bonus_rate);
```

By the same token, the bonus rate could be passed in as a literal:

```
float bonusAmount = theManager.computeBonus (.15F);
```

The manager class's constructor has four parameters. Therefore, we place each of them in the argument list when we create an object:

```
manager theManager = new manager(people_managed, first_name,
    last_name, salary);
```

The preceding assumes, of course, that the data we want to store in the new object have already been placed in the people_managed, first_name, last_name, and salary variables.

Listing 4.2   ManagerApp.java

```java
import java.io.*;
import java.awt.*;
import java.lang.*;
import text.*;

public class ManagerApp
{
    public void Run()
    {
        // gather the data
        SystemInput sysIn = new SystemInput();
        String first_name = sysIn.readString ("Manager's first name:");
        String last_name = sysIn.readString ("Manager's last name:");
        int people_managed = sysIn.readInt ("How many people managed?");
        private float salary = sysIn.readFloat ("Base salary:");

        // create and initialize the object
        manager theManager = new manager(people_managed, first_name,
            last_name, salary);

        // get bonus rate
        float bonus_rate = sysIn.readFloat
            ("Bonus rate as fractional percentage:");
        // compute bonus
        float theBonus = theManager.computeBonus (bonus_rate) +
            theManager.getSalary();

        // Echo all data to console window
        System.out.println ("The manager's name is " +
            theManager.getFirst_name() +
            " " + theManager.getLast_name() + ".");
        System.out.println ("He or she manages " +
            theManager.getPeople_managed() +
            " people.");
        System.out.println ("He or she will receive $" +
            NumberFormat.floatFormat (8,2,theBonus) + " this year.");
    }

    public static void main (String args[])
    {
        ManagerApp theApp = new ManagerApp();
        theApp.Run();
    }
}
```

If you look back at the method header for the `manager` class's constructor, you will notice that although the variable names of the parameters aren't the same, the data types of the parameters are identical. When a method has multiple parameters, Java matches the arguments in the method call to the parameters in the method header by their position in the parameter list. The specific names of the variables are irrelevant, but the data types must match.

How Arguments Are Passed

Java passes all arguments by value. This means that a *copy* of the argument is sent to the method. Any modifications that the method might make to the argument are therefore not accessible to the calling method, which has access to the original data only.

As simple as the preceding might seem, there is one major twist of which you need to be aware: Some values passed as arguments aren't really data; they're addresses where data are stored. An object variable, for example, contains the main memory address of where the object's data are stored. When you pass an object into a method, you pass a copy of that address, not the data values.

As a result, when a method works with an object that has been passed in as an argument, the method is actually working with the original data. Remember: only the address of the data was duplicated when the parameter was passed.

Note   Array variables also contain the starting address of the array's storage in main memory. Arrays are therefore also passed into methods by sending a copy of their address. As you will see in Chapter 8, from a programmer's point of view, arrays are very similar to objects.

The effect of passing the address of something into a method is what is known in other languages as a *pass by reference*. Not only does this make it possible to modify the original version of data in a method and have those modifications available to the calling method, but as you will see later in this chapter, it provides a way to "return" multiple values from a method.

Writing Simple Constructors

The purpose of a constructor is to perform any initialization needed by the object. In the case of the manager program, the constructor takes data passed in as parameters and assigns those values to the object's variables. The body of the constructor therefore consists of four assignment statements:

```
people_managed = numb_people;
last_name = iLname;
first_name = iFname;
salary = iSalary;
```

The preceding is typical of constructors that are part of data-handling classes. However, if you look back at Listing 4.2, you'll notice that the program's application class have a constructor. If there isn't any initialization to be performed, you can omit a constructor. However, in most cases, the compiler will supply an empty default constructor for you:

```
public class_name()
{
}
```

Data Encapsulation and Variable Access

As you read in Chapter 1, one of the major characteristics of the object oriented paradigm is *data encapsulation* (information hiding), where access to data values describing an object is limited to the object itself. The benefit of data encapsulation is that the representation of data remains independent of external objects that use it.

This does not mean, however, that an external object can never retrieve or modify encapsulated data. To provide access to that data, we commonly include "get" and "set" methods in a class. A get method (an *accessor method*) returns a piece of private data to an external object's method; a set method (a *mutator method*) takes a piece of data as an input parameter and assigns it to a private variable, replacing the variable's original contents.

In most cases, a get or set method acts on only one variable. Why? Because doing so gives you flexibility to control the access and modification of variables individually. For example, there may be some variables that you want external methods to be able to see, but not to modify.

By convention, we name get methods using the format `getXXX`, where XXX is the name of the variable whose contents are returned by the method. By the same token, we name set methods, `setXXX`, where XXX is the name of the variable whose contents are changed by the method.

Writing "set" Methods

You use a constructor to give the variables that contain an object's data their initial values. But what can you do if you need to change those values later in the program run? You can use a set method, a method that does nothing but replace a data value.

A set method has the following general format:

```
public void setVariable_name (data_type parameter_name)
    { object_variable_name = parameter_name; }
```

For example, if we wanted to include set methods in the **manager** class, they would be:

```
public void setPeople_managed (float numb_people)
    { people_managed = numb_people; }

public void setFirst_name (String iFname)
    { first_name = iFname; }

public void setLast_name (String iLname)
    { last_name = iLname; }

public void setSalary (float iSalary)
    { salary = iSalary; }
```

Returning Values: "get" Methods

With only very rare exceptions, the variables that hold the data describing an object are private. Nonetheless, other objects may need access to those values. Rather than make such values public, we include get methods in a class. All a get method does is return a value to the calling method. The manager program, for example, includes for get methods, one for each variable.

A get method has the following basic structure:

```
public return_data_type getVariable_name ()
    { return Variable_name; }
```

The method to return a manager's first name is therefore written:

```
public String getFirst_name ()
    { return first_name; }
```

The `return` statement takes whatever value follows it and sends that value back to the calling method, terminating the execution of the method. The value's data type must match the return data type specified in the method header. The value can be stored in a variable, a literal, or computed as the result of some Java expression. Regardless of the source of the value, `return` can send only one value back to the calling method.

Methods that don't have return values (those with a return data type of `void`) can also use the `return` statement. In that case, the `return` statement simply has no value and acts only to terminate the method. Although a method terminates automatically when it reaches the closing brace at the bottom of its source code, `return` can be used anywhere within the body of a method to force termination before the end is reached. You will see many examples of this use of return throughout this book.

Returning Multiple Values

The truth be told, you *can't* return more than one value from a method. As you read in the preceding section, the `return` statement sends back only a single value. However, you can take advantage of the fact that passing an object to a method passes the object's address rather than a copy of the object to get the same effect as you would if you could actually return multiple values.

The technique requires the following steps:

1. Declare a class that contains variables for each of the values you want to return from the method. The class should also contain one or more set methods to load the object with data and get methods that make its data accessible to objects from other classes.
2. Include an object of that class in the method's parameter list.
3. Create an object from the class and pass it into the method.
4. Inside the method, make whatever changes you need to data.
5. Use the set method(s) to load the object with the modified data.

Because you passed the address of the object into the method, the method operates on the object's original storage rather than a copy of the object's data. This means that when the method finishes, the modified data will be in main memory, accessible to the calling method. Although no values were actually returned, a calling method was actually able to access more than one value modified by a method it called.

To make this technique clearer, let's look at a slightly modified version of the manager program. In this case, we want to see more than just the total amount of pay the manager receives; we want to see the base pay and the bonus amount as well. The output of the modified program is as follows:

```
The manager's name is Dough Jane.
He or she manages 15 people.

Salary info:
      Base pay: $65000.00
  Bonus amount: $ 9750.00
     Total pay: $74750.00
```

The data used for display are captured in the `SalaryData` class. As you can see in Listing 4.3, in addition to its variables, the class has a single set method that places values in all its variables and get methods to send the values back to a calling method.

The `manager` class method `computeBonus` needs to be modified a bit to use an object from the `SalaryData` class. Instead of returning the total pay to the calling method, it loads all its results into the `SalaryData` object that was passed in as an argument:

```
public void computeBonus (float bonusPercent,
    SalaryData theMoney)
    {
        float bonusAmt = salary * bonusPercent;
        float total = salary + bonusAmt;
        theMoney.set (salary, bonusAmt, total);
    }
```

Notice that the method no longer returns a value. (Its return data type has been changed to `void`.) Instead, it relies on the calling method to send it an argument into which it can place values. In this particular example, the input parameter in question is of type `SalaryData` and has the name `theMoney`.

To make use of the `SalaryData` object, the application class manipulating the `manager` object must be modified as well. If you look carefully at Listing 4.4, you will notice that after collecting the bonus rate, the application class's `Run` method creates an object of class `SalaryData`:

Listing 4.3   SalaryData.java

```java
class SalaryData
{
    private float salary, bonus, total_pay;

    public SalaryData()
    {
        salary = OF;
        bonus = OF;
        total_pay = OF;
    }

    public void set (float iSalary, float iBonus, float iTotal_pay)
    {
        salary = iSalary;
        bonus = iBonus;
        total_pay = iTotal_pay;
    }

    public float getSalary ()
        { return salary; }

    public float getBonus ()
        { return bonus; }

    public float getTotal_pay ()
        { return total_pay;}
}
```

```java
            SalaryData theMoney = new SalaryData();
```

Then, when the Run method wants to compute the salary information, it calls the manager class's computeBonus function with both the bonus rate and the SalaryData object as arguments:

```java
        theManager.computeBonus (bonus_rate, theMoney);
```

To gain access to the variables stored in theMoney, the application class's Run method uses the SalaryData class's get methods. For example, the expression

```java
        theMoney.getSalary()
```

returns the value in the salary variable to the Run function.

Listing 4.4   ManagerApp.java modified to use a SalaryData object

```java
import java.io.*;
import java.awt.*;
import java.lang.*;
import text.*;

public class ManagerApp
{
    public void Run()
    {
        // gather the data
        SystemInput sysIn = new SystemInput();
        String first_name = sysIn.readString ("Manager's first name:");
        String last_name = sysIn.readString ("Manager's last name:");
        int people_managed = sysIn.readInt ("How many people managed?");
        float salary = sysIn.readFloat ("Base salary:");

        // create and initialize the object
        manager theManager = new manager(people_managed, first_name,
            last_name, salary);
        // get bonus rate
        float bonus_rate = sysIn.readFloat
            ("Bonus rate as fractional percentage:");
        // create object to hold salary data
        SalaryData theMoney = new SalaryData();
        // compute salary
        theManager.computeBonus (bonus_rate, theMoney);
        // Echo all data to console window
        System.out.println ("The manager's name is " +
            theManager.getFirst_name() +
            " " + theManager.getLast_name() + ".");
        System.out.println ("He or she manages " +
            theManager.getPeople_managed() +
            " people.");
        System.out.println ("\nSalary info:");
        System.out.println ("    Base pay: $" +
            NumberFormat.floatFormat (8,2,theMoney.getSalary()));
        System.out.println (" Bonus amount: $" +
            NumberFormat.floatFormat (8,2,theMoney.getBonus()));
        System.out.println ("    Total pay: $" +
            NumberFormat.floatFormat (8,2,theMoney.getTotal_pay()));
    }

    public static void main (String args[])
    {
        ManagerApp theApp = new ManagerApp();
        theApp.Run();
    }
}
```

Performing Console I/O

The one major topic we haven't discussed to this point is the precise way in which programs such as the manager program perform their input and output. Although Java's console I/O capabilities are severely limited, you will need to use what little is available if you are going to write any meaningful programs before we get a chance to introduce graphic user interface programming.

As an example, we will be looking at a "bucket management" program, a bit of silliness that stores data about the buckets we own and how many holes there are in each bucket. The data handling class (Listing 4.5) contains a constructor that places values in each of the class's variables and two get functions to return data to a calling method. After collecting data about three buckets, the program echoes that data back to the user, producing output similar to the following:

Listing 4.5   bucket.java

```
public class Bucket
{
    private int numbHoles = 0;
    private float capacity = OF;

    public Bucket (int Holes, float Gallons)
    {
        numbHoles = Holes;
        capacity = Gallons;
    }

    public int getNumbHoles()
        { return numbHoles; }

    public float getCapacity()
        { return capacity; }
}
```

```
            Bucket #1 holds 15 gallons and has 6 holes.
            Bucket #2 holds 2 gallons and has 4 holes.
            Bucket #3 holds 5 gallons and has 85 holes
```

Console Input

The Java specifications call for keyboard input one character at a time through an object named System.in. There are two major drawbacks to attempting to use this object. First, performing all keyboard input one character at a time is very clumsy, especially when you want a number rather than a character or string. Second, not all Java development environments support System.in.

Therefore, this book is accompanied by a package of classes that make console input much simpler. To use these classes, place the file *text.zip* in the same folder as *classes.zip*, wherever that happens to be. Then, at the beginning of every file that will use a class from the package, include:

```
import text.*;
import java.awt.*;
```

As you know, the import mechanism tells the Java compiler which files to search when it looks for classes and methods. The wildcard * imports all classes in the package and is much simpler than trying to list the specific classes or methods your program will be using. The first statement imports the classes in *text.zip*. The second imports the classes from the Java class library that support Java's graphic user interface, which are used by *text.zip*.

The methods that support keyboard input are part of the System-Input class. Therefore, before you can perform input, you must create an object of that class. By convention, it is called sysIn:

```
SystemInput sysIn = new SystemInput();
```

The constructor creates a Java window with an edit box into which a user can type a value. A prompt telling the user what to enter can appear above the box (for example, see Figure 4.1).

Figure 4.1   A system input window

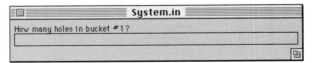

Whenever you want to read a value from the system input window, you call a `SystemInput` method:

- **readFloat**: Reads one floating point value.
- **readDouble**: Reads one double value.
- **readInt**: Reads an integer value.
- **readLong**: Reads a long integer value.
- **readChar**: Reads a character value.
- **readString**: Reads a string value.

Each of these method takes a single parameter, the string that will appear as a prompt above the edit box. Each method returns a value of the appropriate data type. For example, as you can see in the bucket program's application class `Run` method (Listing 4.6), the program calls `readInt` to obtain the number of holes and `readFloat` to get the capacity:

```
iHoles = sysIn.readInt ("How many holes in bucket #1?");
iGallons = sysIn.readFloat
    ("How many gallons does bucket #1 hold?");
```

To capture the value returned by the method call, the program assigns the return value to a variable.

Console Output

To display output in the console window, you call the `println` method of the object `System.out`. The method takes one parameter: the string that should be written to the console window. This is not, however, as restrictive as it might appear.

First, `System.out` is able to convert numbers to strings. Therefore, you can use any type of numeric variable as part of a `println` string. Second, you can combine a variety of values into a single string by using the *concatenation operator*, a + that pastes one string of characters onto the end of another.

System.
out

As a first example, consider the following statement:

```
System.out.println ("Bucket #1 holds " + Bucket1.getCapacity() +
    " gallons and has " + Bucket1.getNumbHoles() + " holes.\n");
```

println   The first element in the argument list is a literal string. (It's a string because it's surrounded by double quotes.) The second element is the result of a call to the **bucket** class's `getCapacity` method, which returns a floating point value

Listing 4.6   bucketApp.Java

```java
import java.awt.*;
import java.io.*;
import java.lang.*;
import text.*;

public class bucketApp
{
    int iHoles;
    float iGallons;

    public void Run()
    {
        // create a system input window object
        SystemInput sysIn = new SystemInput();

        iHoles = sysIn.readInt ("How many holes in bucket #1?");
        iGallons = sysIn.readFloat ("How many gallons does bucket #1 hold?");
        Bucket Bucket1 = new Bucket (iHoles,iGallons);

        iHoles = sysIn.readInt ("How many holes in bucket #2?");
        iGallons = sysIn.readFloat ("How many gallons does bucket #2 hold?");
        Bucket Bucket2 = new Bucket (iHoles,iGallons);

        iHoles = sysIn.readInt ("How many holes in bucket #3?");
        iGallons = sysIn.readFloat ("How many gallons does bucket #3 hold?");
        Bucket Bucket3 = new Bucket (iHoles,iGallons);

        System.out.println ("Bucket #1 holds " + Bucket1.getCapacity() + "
            gallons and has " + Bucket1.getNumbHoles() + " holes.\n");

        System.out.println ("Bucket #2 holds " + Bucket2.getCapacity() + "
            gallons and has " + Bucket2.getNumbHoles() + " holes.\n");

        System.out.println ("Bucket #3 holds " + Bucket3.getCapacity() + "
            gallons and has " + Bucket3.getNumbHoles() + " holes.\n");
    }

    public static void main(String args[])
    {
        bucketApp theBuckets = new bucketApp();
        theBuckets.Run();
    }
}
```

that `System.out.println` converts into a string and concatenates on the first element. The third element is another literal string, which is followed by a call to the `bucket` class's `getNumbHoles` method. The integer returned by the method call is converted into a string and added to the string. The final element is another literal string.

As well as function calls, you can also embed arithmetic operations in a `println` argument list. For example, the following statement is legal:

```
System.out.println ("The total is " + (sum * bonus));
```

However, you may find that some arithmetic expressions give the Java compiler problems, especially those that contain addition operators that the compiler may confuse with the concatenation operator. If the compiler won't accept an embedded arithmetic operation, simply remove the operation from the `println` argument string and assign its result to a variable, which you can then place back in the argument string.

`System.out.println` supports almost no formatting. However, it does add a carriage return and line feed at the end of each line. As a result, each time you call `println`, output begins at the left edge of a new line. You can control this behavior to some extent:

System. out

print

- To prevent the carriage return and line feed at the end of a line, use the `print` method instead of `println`.
- To force a carriage return, place `\n` in the string being printed. For example,

```
System.out.println ("\n\nThis is a test\n");
```

  prints two blank lines, a string of text, and another blank line.

The `\n` is an example of what is known as an *escape character*. The `\` tells Java to ignore the normal meaning of what follows and to treat it in a special way. In this case, Java ignores *n* as a character and interprets it as a request for a carriage return and a line feed. (The carriage return takes the cursor to the left edge of the console window; the line feed moves it down one line.)

Escape characters can be very handy for putting characters in output strings that ordinarily have special meanings. For example, if you need to surround a literal string with double quotes, how can you make a double quote part of your output? The answer is to precede the double quote with `\`, as in `\"`. By the same token, you can include a `\` in your output by using two of them: `\\`. The first removes the special meaning of `\`, while the second is the actual character that appears.

Using the NumberFormat Class

If you look back at the output from the second version of the manager program, you'll notice that the floating point numbers have been formatted so that they are aligned on their right edge with a leading dollar sign and two places to the right of the decimal point. This type of formatting is *not* a part of `System.out.println`. It has been provided through a combination of careful placement of characters in `println`'s argument string and the `NumberFormat` class, which is a part of *text.zip*.

`NumberFormat` contains two static member functions—`floatFormat` and `intFormat`—both of which return the number as a formatted string. Because these are static functions, you don't need to create an object of the `NumberFormat` class to call them. You use the name of the class in place of an object name.

The `intFormat` function has the following general syntax:

```
NumberFormat.intFormat (width, int_value)
```

The first parameter is the number of spaces that you want the number to occupy. The second is the integer value. If the number of places in the integer is smaller than the width, `intFormat` places blanks in front of the number. All integers are therefore right justified. If the number of places in the integer is equal to or larger than the width, the integer is left unmodified.

Because `intFormat` makes it possible to predict the amount of space an integer will occupy, you can use it to make values line up. For example, consider the following code fragment:

```
int value1 = 105, value2 = 99, value3 = 12;
System.out.println ("Value 1: " +
    NumberFormat.intFormat (3, value1));
System.out.println ("Value 2: " +
    NumberFormat.intFormat (3, value2));
System.out.println ("Value 3:" +
    NumberFormat.intFormat (3, value3));
```

The output will be:

```
Value 1: 105
Value 2:  99
Value 3:  12
```

Keep in mind, however, that the three integers line up only because the text that precedes them is the same length in each case.

The `floatFormat` function has the following general syntax:

```
NumberFormat.floatFormat (width, precision, float_value);
```

The first parameter is the overall width of the number, including the decimal point and any digits to the right of the decimal point. If the final number is shorter than the width, it will be padded with blanks on the left, just like an integer. The second parameter is the number of digits to the right of the decimal point. If the input value has more digits, then the number is rounded. If the input value has fewer digits, then the method adds trailing zeros. The third parameter is the value that will be formatted.

The dollar signs that precede the output of the manager program are not part of `floatFormat`. Instead, they are part of the literal string that precedes each number:

```
System.out.println ("       Base pay: $" +
    NumberFormat.floatFormat (8,2,theMoney.getSalary()));
System.out.println ("  Bonus amount: $" +
    NumberFormat.floatFormat (8,2,theMoney.getBonus()));
System.out.println ("      Total pay: $" +
    NumberFormat.floatFormat (8,2,theMoney.getTotal_pay()));
```

In addition, notice how the literal strings that precede each floating point value have be preceded with blanks so that the dollar signs line up. Even if the floating point values are formatted identically, they won't line up unless they are preceded by exactly the same number of characters!

Summary

In this chapter we reviewed the general structure of a Java method. A method's header begins with the method's accessibility (public or private), followed by its return data type, the method's name, and its parameter list. The parameters are declared (given data types and names) in the list.

Methods can send one value back to the calling method with the `return` statement.

Arguments are passed into methods by value. This means that a copy of the argument is sent to the method. Some elements of a Java program, including objects and arrays, are represented by the main memory addresses of their storage locations. When these addresses are sent to a method as input arguments, the method has access to the original copy of the data and can therefore modify the same data to which the calling method has access. This provides the equivalent of a pass by reference for those specific types of program elements. In fact, Java programs often use objects whose sole purpose is to collect multiple values from a called method.

For the purposes of this book, console input is provided by the `SystemInput` class, which is a part of *text.zip*. Console output is provided by the `println` method of the Java object `System.out`.

Exercises

1. Write and test a program that lets a person pick six numbers for playing a biweekly state lottery. Accept the six numbers and a date (use a String variable) from the keyboard. The data handling class for this program is a lottery ticket. You will need to create just one object from this class. The program's application class should collect the input data from the user, create the object, and then call a method that displays the lottery ticket on the screen. The lottery ticket might look something like Figure 4.2.

Figure 4.2   A sample lottery ticket

```
****************************************************
*              Some State Lottery          *
*                 12/21/98                 *
*                                          *
*           4   9  10  11 12   29          *
****************************************************
```

2. Write and test a program that prints sales flyers for a grocery store. Create a class for a grocery store product, including the product name, regular price, and the sale price of the product. The application class should ask the user for information about four products and create the objects as the data are collected. Then, use the data from the objects to display the flyer on the screen. It might look something like Figure 4.3.

3. Write and test a program that displays a calendar like that in Figure 4.4. Ask the user to input the month number and year. Also ask the user to input the day of the week on which the month starts. However, it is up to your program to print the correct number of days for a given month. To make this program work, consider creating a date class and initializing

Figure 4.3 A sample grocery store sales flyer

```
              Jones' Corner Grocery

                   SALE PRICES
            Week of 12/21/98 - 12/27/98

                  REGULAR PRICE    SALE PRICE
  Ground Beef        $1.79/lb      $1.09/lb
  2% Milk             1.75/gal      .99/gal
  Plain Yogurt         .79 each     .49 each
  Lettuce              .99 head     .69 head
```

objects with 28, 29, 30, and 31 days. Then use a `switch` to determine which object you should use to display the calendar, based on the month number. Don't forget to consider whether a year is a leap year when someone enters 2 for the month number!

Figure 4.4 A sample calendar

```
11 1999

Sun   Mon   Tue   Wed   Thur   Fri   Sat

       1     2     3     4      6     6

 7     8     9    10    11     12    13

14    '5    16    17    18     19    20

21    22    23    24    25     26    27

28    29    30
```

4. Write and test a program that stores emergency phone numbers. In this case, the data handling class is an emergency service. It has two variables: the name of the service and the phone number. The application class should gather data and create objects for police, fire, and ambulance. Then, the application class should ask each object to return its data so the application class can display a nicely formatted listing of the telephone numbers.

5. In many medical practices, the diagnoses that are determined for a patient are coded using numeric codes. Write and test a program that handles data about a diagnosis made for a patient. The data handling class should include a patient number, a diagnosis code, and a date (stored as a string). Each run of the program corresponds to the diagnoses for one patient (up to five per patient). Allow the user to enter the patient number and date only once. Then collect the five diagnosis codes. After you've created and initialized objects, display a report that summarizes what the user has entered. Make your own choices about the structure of the classes and their member functions.

6. One of the things that businesses often do is create classes that can be reused throughout many programs. One such class is an address, which is made up of the following pieces of data:

   - Street
   - City
   - State
   - Zip
   - Country

   For this exercise, create an Address class. Store each variable as a string. Include a constructor that accepts data for all variables, accessor methods for each variable, and mutator methods for each variable. Create an application class that tests each method.

7. In a retail business, a commonly used class described a person (a customer or an employee). Your job in this exercise is to begin designing a Person class that can be easily reused.

   Include the following data in the class:

   - Social security number (String)
   - First name (String)
   - Last name (String)
   - Home address (an object of the Address class from Exercise 6)
   - Work address (an object of the Address class from Exercise 6)

- Home telephone (String)
- Work telephone (String)

For this exercise, include a constructor that accepts data for all variables. Also include accessor and mutator methods for all variables. Write an application class that demonstrates that your methods work. (*Hint*: The Address class has its own access and mutator methods, so take advantage of them.)

Writing Methods (Part II)

OBJECTIVES

In this chapter you will read about:

- Using Java operators to perform arithmetic and logical operations.
- Performing selection operations.
- Performing iteration.
- Manipulating strings.

This chapter introduces you to the additional Java elements that you will use to write the bodies of most methods, including selection (making choices between various actions) and iteration (repeating actions). You'll also read more about string manipulations.

Much of Java syntax is virtually identical to that of C and C++. If you are familiar with those languages, you can skim most of this chapter until you reach the section that covers string manipulation. Java string handling is significantly different from C and C++.

Java Operators

Like any high-level language, Java provides operators that manipulate numeric and character values. As you will see in the following sections, many arithmetic operators are similar to what you have used in other high-level languages. However, some arithmetic operators are not found in languages other than C and C++. The syntax of the logical operators is also unique to C, C++, and Java, although the functions that the operators perform are not.

Arithmetic Operators

The Java arithmetic operators are summarized in Table 7.2 in order of precedence. These operators can be used in an assignment statement to place the result of an operation into a variable. For example, the statement

```
average = sum/numbItems;
```

takes the value stored in `sum`, divides it by the value stored in `numbItems`, and stores the result in `average`.

Expressions using arithmetic operations can also be placed in any statement that expects a numeric value. For example, the following is a legal Java statement:

```
return sum/numbItems;
```

However, `System.out.println` *cannot* accept arithmetic expressions. For example, the following statement will cause the Java compiler to report an error:

```
System.out.println (sum/numbItems);
```

Table 7.2   The Java arithmetic operators listed in order of precedence

Operator	Function
+	Positive (preserve sign)
-	Negative (change sign)
++i	Preincrement i
--i	Predecrement i[a]
*	Multiplication
/	Division[b]
%	Modulo
+	Addition
-	Subtraction[c]
i++	Postincrement
i--	Postdecrement[d]

a. Preincrement and predecrement have the same precedence.
b. Multiplication and division have the same precedence.
c. Addition and subtraction have the same precedence.
d. Postincrement and postdecrement have the same precedence.

Embedding arithmetic expressions in other statements saves both storage space and execution time when you don't need to use the result of the arithmetic expression again in the method in which the expression appears. However, if the result is to be used more than once, then it is more efficient to store it in a variable instead of recomputing the value each time it is needed.

Java uses its rules of precedence to decide the order in which expression are evaluated. As with other high-level languages, when an expression contains more than one operator of the same precedence, evaluation proceeds from left to right. You can also override the default precedence with parentheses.

The Increment and Decrement Operators

Java has two arithmetic operators—increment and decrement—that aren't found in languages such as COBOL, Pascal, or Modula-2. The increment operator increases a value by one; the decrement operator decreases a value by one. When the increment or decrement occurs depends on whether the operator precedes or follows the name of the variable whose value is being modified.

To see how the increment and decrement operators work, consider the examples in Table 7.3. In each case, `idx` begins with a value of 10; `sum` contains 100. Notice that when the operator is placed before a variable, the increment or decrement occurs before any other operation is performed in the expression; when the operator follows a value, the increment or decrement occurs after all other operations have been performed.

Table 7.3   The effect of the increment and decrement operators

Statement	Action	Result
`sum = sum + (++idx)`[a]`;`	(Preincrement) Increment `idx`. Add `idx` to sum.	`idx = 11` `sum = 111`
`sum = sum + idx++;`	(Postincrement) Add `idx` to sum. Increment `idx`.	`idx = 11` `sum = 110`
`sum = sum + (--idx)`[b]`;`	(Predecrement) Decrement `idx`. Add `idx` to sum.	`idx = 9` `sum = 109`
`sum = sum + idx--;`	(Postdecrement) Add `idx` to sum. Decrement `idx`.	`idx = 9` `sum = 110`

a. The parentheses have been inserted to make it clear to the Java compiler that the statement includes an addition operator and a preincrement operator rather than any other combination of operations.
b. As with the parentheses surrounding the preincrement operator, those surrounding the predecrement operator are present simply to separate the addition operator from the predecrement operator.

The increment and decrement operators are handy for loop index variables. Instead of writing `index = index + 1`, you can simply use `index++`. As you will see in Chapter 8, this can eliminate a line of code when you are stepping through the elements in an array.

Performing Exponentiation

There is one obvious omission from Table 7.2: There is no operator that performs exponentiation (raising a value to a power). If you need to compute the square of a number, you can always use a statement such as

```
square = number * number;
```

However, trying to perform other exponentiation can be clumsy and difficult. The answer is to use a method from the Math class in the Java class libraries.

Math

pow

Exponentiation is performed with the Math class's pow function. Because pow is a static method, you call it using the class's name, rather than the name of an object created from the class:

```
thePower = Math.pow (value, power);
```

This method takes two parameters, both of type double, and returns a double. The first parameter is the value you want to exponentiate; the second parameter is the power to which it will be raised.

The pow function is very flexible: It can accept fractional and negative powers as well as positive, integer powers. However, if either argument is of a data type other than double, you must typecast to a double:

```
double result = 0;
float base = 109.15;
float power = -0.55;
result = Math.pow ((float) base, (float) power);
```

Using Arithmetic Operators

As an example of a program that performs some simple arithmetic, let's look at a program that conducts a simple survey to find out how casual someone likes to dress. The survey asks the user the following questions:

```
Do you own more than four pairs of jeans?
Do you own a jean jacket?
Do you own more than 10 T-shirts?
Do you own more than four pairs of sneakers?
Do you purposely wear clothes with holes in them?
```

After accepting the answers (1 for *yes* and 0 for *no*), the program displays a count of the number of *yes* responses:

```
You answered 'yes' to 3 questions.
```

Underlying the program is a class named Survey (see Listing 5.1). Each method (with the exception of the constructor) returns a 0 or 1, based on the user's response to a question.

Listing 5.1   survey.java

```
import java.io.*;
import java.awt.*;
import text.*;

public class Survey
{
    private SystemInput sysIn;
    public Survey()
    {
        sysIn = new SystemInput();
        System.out.println ("\nPlease answer questions with 1 for 'yes' and 0
    for 'no'.\n");
    }

    public int Quest1()
        { return sysIn.readInt ("Do you own more than four pairs of jeans?"); }

    public int Quest2()
        { return sysIn.readInt ("Do you own a jean jacket?"); }

    public int Quest3()
        { return sysIn.readInt ("Do you own more than 10 T-shirts?"); }

    public int Quest4()
        { return sysIn.readInt ("Do you own more than four pairs of
    sneakers?"); }

    public int Quest5()
        { return sysIn.readInt ("Do you purposely wear clothes with holes in
    them?"); }
}
```

To figure a user's score on the survey, the application class's Run method (Listing 5.2) creates a local variable named total. It then adds the value returned by a call to one of a Survey object's methods to the total. After all the methods have been called—and all the responses added—the Run method displays the final result.

In Listing 5.2, each function call has been placed in a separate addition statement. However, this isn't the shortest or more efficient way to write this sequence of operations. An alternative is to put all the additions into one statement:

```
total = theSurvey.Quest1() + theSurvey.Quest2() +
    theSurvey.Quest3() + theSurvey.Quest4() +
    theSurvey.Quest5();
```

Listing 5.2   ClothingApp.java

```java
import java.io.*;

public class ClothingApp
{
    public void Run()
    {
        // create a survey object
        Survey theSurvey = new Survey();

        int total = 0; // variable to hold 'yes' responses

        // Call each member function in turn, adding the result to the total
        total = total + theSurvey.Quest1();
        total = total + theSurvey.Quest2();
        total = total + theSurvey.Quest3();
        total = total + theSurvey.Quest4();
        total = total + theSurvey.Quest5();

        System.out.println ("You answered 'yes' to " + total + " questions.");
    }

    public static void main (String args[])
    {
        ClothingApp theApp = new ClothingApp();
        theApp.Run();
    }
}
```

The preceding single statement will execute more quickly than the separate additions because a value is only stored in main memory once.

Logical Operators

The Java logical operators are summarized in Table 5.3. As you can see, there are significant differences between these operators and those used by languages such as COBOL, Pascal, or Modula-2. For example, while many languages use the word NOT for the inversion operator, Java uses an exclamation point (!). By the same token, Java uses != for the not equals operator rather than the more common <>.

Table 5.3   The Java logical operators

Operator	Function
||	OR
&&	AND
!	NOT
|	Bit-wise OR
&	Bit-wise AND
==	Equal to
!=	Not equal to
<	Less than
<=	Less than or equal to
>	Greater than
>=	Greater than or equal to

Notice in Table 5.3 that there are two OR operators and two AND operators. The operators that are made up of two characters (|| and &&) perform the logical operations with which you are familiar. The operators that use only a single character, however, perform operations on the bits in an integer storage location.

Assume, for example, that you have two binary values, 1010 and 0001. If you perform a bit-wise OR using those two integers, the computer takes each pair of bits and performs a logical OR. The result will therefore be 1011, in effect setting the second and fourth bits in the second number and preserving the 1 in the first bit.

Theoretically, a Java compiler shouldn't accept an expression like

```
Value1 > Value2 | Value3 < Value4
```

The two simple expressions evaluate to booleans, which can't be typecast to the integers required for the bit-wise OR. However, you may find that your Java compiler *does* accept such an expression. This means that you must pay special attention to complex logical expressions to make sure that you use *two* |s or &s.

A similar situation exists with the equal to operator. Notice that the logical equal to operator is *two* equal signs (==); the assignment operator is one. Fortunately, most Java compilers will catch a single equal sign in a logical expression as an error.

Assignment Statement Shorthand

Assignment statements often store their results in one of the storage locations used in the expression on the right side of the assignment operator. For example, a program might accumulate a sum with:

```
sum = sum + newNumb;
```

Java provides a shorthand for this type of assignment. The preceding statement can be written

```
sum += newNumb;
```

In this notation, notice that the arithmetic operator precedes the assignment operator. The assignment statement shorthand operators are summarized in Table 7.4.

Table 7.4   Assignment table shorthand

Shorthand	Equivalence
sum += newNumb;	sum = sum + newNumb;
sum -= newNumb;	sum = sum - newNumb;
sum *= newNumb;	sum = sum * newNumb;
sum /= newNumb;	sum = sum / newNumb;
sum %= newNumb;	sum = sum % newNumb;

Assignment, Data Type Conversion, and Typecasting

Unlike languages such as Pascal and Modula-2, Java doesn't have separate operators for integer and floating point division. The type of division that Java performs depends on the data types of the values that are part of the expression. Java performs conversions of numeric values as needed.

For example, assume that you have the following two variables:

```
float value1 = 10.0F;
int value2 = 20;
```

What happens when you perform the division

```
value1 / value2
```

Java examines the expression and notes that there is one floating point value and one integer value. It therefore typecasts the integer to a floating point value and performs a floating point division, producing the result 0.5. If you want to force an integer division, you need to typecast the floating point value:

```
value1 / (int) value2
```

There is a hierarchy of data types that determines how numeric conversions occur:

```
double
float
long
int
short
```

When an expression contains more than one type of numeric data, data types lower in the list are converted to match whichever type is highest in the list.

Java can also typecast character data. When `char` data are used in an expression with integers, Java converts the characters to integer, handling the ASCII codes as if they were numeric values. As you will see later in this chapter, this comes in handy when you want to use a character in a `switch` (`case`) construct.

Another Arithmetic Program

To pull all these arithmetic operations together, let's look at a slightly longer program that performs a variety of operations on two numbers. After accepting two numbers from the user (in this example, 12.5 and 6), the program produces the following output:

```
The sum of these numbers is 18.5
The difference between these numbers is 6.5
The product is 75
The floating point quotient is 2.08333
The integer quotient is 2
The remainder of an integer division is 0
The first number raised to the power of the second number is
    3.8147e+06
The square root of the first number is 3.53553
The square root of the second number is 2.44949
```

The arithmetic is handled by the Numbers class (Listing 5.3). As you can see, each method takes one or two of the values stored in an object and performs some arithmetic manipulation. You should notice three important things as you study these methods:

Listing 5.3 numbers.java

```java
import java.lang.*;

public class Numbers
{
    private float value1;
    private float value2;

    public Numbers (float ivalue1, float ivalue2)
    {
        value1 = ivalue1;
        value2 = ivalue2;
    }

    public float addition()
        { return value1 + value2; }

    public float subtraction()
        { return value1 - value2; }

    public float multiplication()
        { return value1 * value2; }

    public float floatDivide()
        { return value1 / value2; }

    public int intDivide()
        { return (int) value1 / (int) value2; }

    public int modulo()
        { return (int) value1 % (int) value2; }

    public float power ()
        { return (float) Math.pow (value1, value2); }

    public float root1()
        { return (float) Math.sqrt (value1); }

    public float root2()
        { return (float) Math.sqrt (value2); }
}
```

- The result of the arithmetic operation isn't stored in a variable. Instead, the expression is placed directly in the `return` statement. The computer evaluates the expression and then returns the result of the expression directly to the calling method.
- The two functions that perform integer arithmetic (`intDivide` and `modulo`) use explicit typecasting to convert the floating point values stored in an object into integers.

Math

- The two square root methods use a method from the `Math` class, `sqrt`. This method takes a single `double` parameter, the value for which you want to compute the square root. It also returns a `double`.

sqrt

The application class `Run` function that produces program output can be found in Listing 5.4. It begins by accepting the two values from the user and then creating an object from the `Numbers` class. The remainder of the `Run` function is a series of calls to `System.out.println` in which calls to `Number` class member functions have been embedded. Because the function results are for display only, there is no reason to store them in variables.

Selection

As you would expect, Java supports selection. Like other high-level languages, it provides an `if` statement. Java also provides its own version of the `case` statement: `switch`. In addition, Java has a shorthand for a simple `if/else` construct that can be embedded in another statement. This section looks at the syntax for all of these structures.

As a simple example of using selection, we will be examining a program that converts amounts in U.S. dollars to English pounds, French francs, and Japanese yen. The program first asks the user for the conversion rates and whether the amount in dollars should be multiplied by a given rate or divided by the rate. Then, the user can perform any number of conversions by entering the amount in dollars and the country for which the conversion should be performed. The output simply tells the user the conversion amount:

```
$  100.00 =    40.00 Pounds.
```

Listing 5.4   ArithmeticApp.java

```java
import java.awt.*;
import java.io.*;
import java.lang.*;
import text.*;

public class ArithmeticApp
{
    public void Run()
    {
        float ivalue1, ivalue2;

        SystemInput sysIn = new SystemInput();
        ivalue1 = sysIn.readFloat ("Enter the first number:");
        ivalue2 = sysIn.readFloat ("Enter the second number:");

        Numbers theNumbers = new Numbers (ivalue1, ivalue2);

        System.out.println ("\nThe sum of these numbers is " +
            theNumbers.addition());
        System.out.println ("The difference between these numbers is " +
            theNumbers.subtraction());
        System.out.println ("The product is " + theNumbers.multiplication());
        System.out.println ("The floating point quotient is " +
            theNumbers.floatDivide());
        System.out.println ("The integer quotient is " +
            theNumbers.intDivide());
        System.out.println ("The remainder of an integer division is " +
            theNumbers.modulo());
        System.out.println
            ("The first number raised to the power of the second number is " +
            theNumbers.power());
        System.out.println ("The square root of the first number is " +
            theNumbers.root1());
        System.out.println ("The square root of the second number is " +
            theNumbers.root2());
    }

    public static void main (String args[])
    {
        ArithmeticApp theMath = new ArithmeticApp();
        theMath.Run();
    }
}
```

Using the if Statement

The Java `if` statement has the following general syntax:

```
if (logical_expression)
    statement(s) to execute if true;
else
    statement(s) to execute if false;
```

The `else` portion of the statement, of course, is optional. If either `if` or `else` are followed by more than one statement, the statements must be surrounded by braces.

One of the currency convert program's methods uses the following `if` statement to determine which of two arithmetic operations to use to perform a conversion:

```
if (Method == 'm' || Method == 'M')
    return ConversionFactor * Dollars;
else
    return Dollars / ConversionFactor;
```

Notice that there is a semicolon after the statement following `if`, as well as one after the statement following `else`.

As you would expect, `if` statements can be nested. For example, a program that plays a number guessing game with a user that we will be examining later in this chapter uses the following `if` structure to evaluate a user's guess:

```
if (guess == answer)
    return EQ;
else
    if (guess < answer)
        return LO;
    else
        return HI;
```

Because the `if` statement nested after the `else` is a single statement, no braces are required around it.

Using the switch Statement

Although `if` statements can be nested without limit, deeply nested `if`s are difficult to debug and modify. When a program needs to evaluate many possible values for a single variable (for example, deciding what to do based on an option in a menu), it is cleaner to use a `switch` statement. In fact, if you need to take actions based on more than two values of the same variable, you should use a `switch` rather than an `if`.

The `switch` statement (the Java equivalent of the Pascal and Modula-2 `case` statement) takes action based on the value of an integer expression. It has the following general syntax:

```
switch (integer_variable)
{
    case integer_value1:
        statements to execute
        break;
    case integer_value2:
    case integer_value3:
        statements to execute
        break;
:
:

    default:
        statements to execute if no case is matched
}
```

There are several syntax details to which you need to pay attention when writing a `switch` structure:

- The entire body of the `switch` is surrounded in a single set of braces.
- Each `case` is associated with one integer value. However, multiple `case` statements can be associated with the same set of actions, as occurs with *integer_value2* and *integer_value3* in the preceding general syntax.
- The integer variable following `switch` can be any integer variable type or a `char` variable.
- The integer value following `case` can be an integer variable, an integer literal, character variable, or character literal. When the value is a character, Java automatically typecasts it into an integer.
- Each `case` is followed by the statements that are to be executed when the value in the `switch` variable matches the value following `case`.
- The `break` statement at the end of a group of executable statements causes the `switch` to branch to the statement below the closing brace. Although not required as far as a compiler's syntax

checking is concerned, a `break` prevents Java from evaluating any other `case` statements within the `switch`.

Note

The `break` statement causes Java to immediately jump out of the innermost set of braces in which it is contained. As you will see shortly, `break` can also be used to exit from a loop.

- The statements following `default` are executed if the value in the `switch` variable matches none of the preceding `case` values: A `default` statement is optional. If no `default` is present and the value in the `switch` variable doesn't match any `case` values, the `switch` statement simply does nothing.

Using ?

Java has an unusual, but rather useful, shorthand for a simple `if`/`else` construct. The syntax

```
logical_expression ? true_action : false_action;
```

is the same as

```
if (logical_expression)
    true_action;
else
    false_action;
```

The beauty of the ? operator is that you can embed it in another statement. For example, assume that you want to number a list of items and that you want the colons following the numbers to line up, something like this:

```
   ...
 8:
 9:
10:
11:
   ...
```

If you are displaying a number less than 10, then an extra space should be printed in front of the number. You can make that selection using the ? operator:

```
num < 10 ? "  " : " "
```

If the number is less than 10, then you need two spaces; otherwise, you need one. All you have to do is then put the ? statement in an output statement:

```
System.out.println ((num < 10 ? "  " : " ") + num +
    ": " + value);
```

The Currency Converter Program

To see how selection, and in particular switch statements, are used in a Java program, let's now look at the complete currency converter program. Data handling is taken care of by the converter class (Listing 5.5). Objects created from this class contain data about the conversion factor and the method that should be used to perform a conversion (multiplication or division).

Listing 5.5   converter.java

```java
public class converter
{
    private float ConversionFactor = OF;
    char Method;

    public converter (float factor, char iMethod)
    {
        ConversionFactor = factor;
        Method = iMethod;
    }

    public float doConversion (float Dollars)
    {
        if (Method == 'm' || Method == 'M')
            return ConversionFactor * Dollars;
        else
            return Dollars / ConversionFactor;
    }

}
```

The class contains two methods:

- A constructor that initializes an object's variables.
- A method that performs a conversion and returns the result as a floating point value (`doConversion`).

The application class that manipulates `converter` objects can be found in Listing 5.6. The `Run` function begins by collecting data for and creating three `converter` objects. Then it provides the user with a two-option menu: either enter 1 to perform a conversion or 2 to exit the program. This choice forms the control condition for a loop that lets the program perform one than one conversion during the same program run. (You will be introduced to the syntax of the loop in the next section of this chapter.)

Within the loop, there is a `switch` structure that organizes the actions to be taken for each menu option. Although there are only two possible menu options, there are two major advantages to using the `switch` rather than nested `if` statements. First, the code is easier to understand. Second, it is easier to modify. Adding processing for a new menu option requires simply adding another `case` to the `switch`, along with statements that are to be executed when the new menu option is chosen.

As you study the program, notice that the `default` option in this `switch` provides an error message for the user, indicating that he or she has entered a value not in the menu. Notice also that the code following the first menu option choice (a value of 1) includes an embedded `switch`. This is perfectly legal: A `case` can be followed by any executable statement. The inner `switch` structure looks for character literals rather than integer literals. Keep in mind that Java automatically typecasts the character literal to an integer, making its evaluation of the value based on its ASCII code.

If you can't find calls to the `doConversion` method when you first examine the application class, look carefully at the inner `switch`. Each call is embedded in a call to `NumberFormat.floatFormat`, which in turn is embedded in a call to `System.out.println`.

Iteration

Java provides three looping statements: `while`, `do while`, and `for`. Which you use depends on the needs of your program: whether the loop will be executed a fixed or variable number of times and whether the loop must always be executed at least once.

Listing 5.6   converterApp.java

```java
import java.io.*;
import java.awt.*;
import text.*;
class converterApp
{
    public void Run()
    {
        SystemInput sysIn = new SystemInput();

        // create three converter objects
        float factor = sysIn.readFloat ("Conversion factor for England:");
        char iMethod = sysIn.readChar ("Method ( M)ultiply or D)ivide):");
        converter England = new converter (factor, iMethod);

        factor = sysIn.readFloat ("Conversion factor for Japan:");
        iMethod = sysIn.readChar ("Method ( M)ultiply or D)ivide):");
        converter Japan = new converter (factor, iMethod);

        factor = sysIn.readFloat ("Conversion factor for France:");
        iMethod = sysIn.readChar ("Method ( M)ultiply or D)ivide):");
        converter France = new converter (factor, iMethod);

        // Now let the user do conversions
        int choice = sysIn.readInt
            ("You can: 1) Perform a conversion or 2) Quit");
        // This loop continues the program until the user enters a 2 for Quit.
        // You will learn how to write loops in the next section of this
        // chapter.
        while (choice != 2)
        {
            switch (choice)
            {
                case 1:
                    char country = sysIn.readChar
                        ("Country ( E)ngland, F)rance, or J)apan ):");
                    float dollars = sysIn.readFloat
                        ("Dollar amount to be converted:");
                    switch (country)
                    {
                        case 'e':
                        case 'E':
                            System.out.println ("\n$" +
                                NumberFormat.floatFormat(8,2,dollars) + " = " +
                                NumberFormat.floatFormat
                                    (8,2,England.doConversion (dollars)) +
                                " Pounds.");
                            break;
```

Continued next page

Listing 5.6(Continued)   converterApp.java

```
                            case 'f':
                            case 'F':
                                System.out.println ("\n$" +
                                    NumberFormat.floatFormat(8,2,dollars) + " = " +
                                    NumberFormat.floatFormat
                                        (8,2,France.doConversion (dollars)) +
                                    " Francs.");
                                break;
                            case 'j':
                            case 'J':
                                System.out.println ("\n$" +
                                    NumberFormat.floatFormat(8,2,dollars) + " = " +
                                    NumberFormat.floatFormat
                                        (8,2,Japan.doConversion(dollars)) +
                                    " Yen.");
                                break;
                            default:
                                System.out.println
                                    ("\nYou've entered a country I can't handle.");
                        }
                        break;
                    case 2:
                        break;
                    default:
                        System.out.println
                            ("\nYou've entered an unsupported option.");
                }
                choice = sysIn.readInt
                    ("You can: 1) Perform a conversion or 2) Quit");
            }

    }

    public static void main (String args[])
    {
        converterApp theApp = new converterApp();
        theApp.Run();
    }
}
```

Using the while Statement

The `while` statement is the most common Java looping structure. It has the following general syntax:

```
while (logical_expression)
{
    body of loop
}
```

If the body of the loop is only one statement, the surrounding braces aren't needed.

The important thing to remember about a `while` is that the logical expression in parentheses is evaluated at the top of the loop. This means that it is possible that a loop might never be executed. As an example, consider the following:

```
int Option = 9;
while (Option != 9)
{
    // body of loop
}
```

Because the logical expression is false the first time the program encounters the `while`, control passes to the statement below the body of the loop, without ever executing the statements in the loop. This not necessarily a bad thing. Consider, for example, the code in Listing 5.7. The purpose of the code is to move the decimal point in a positive floating point number so that the number is in the format `.XXXX`. It also needs to keep track of how many times the decimal point is moved. If the original number is greater than or equal to 1, it should be multiplied by 0.1; if the number is less than 0l1, it should be multiplied by 10. Listing 5.7 contains two `while` loops, one for each condition. Rather than using an `if` to decide which loop to execute, the code takes advantage of the fact that the original value in `Number` will pass the test of no more than one `while`, ensuring that only the correct transformation is performed. (If the number is already in the correct format, neither loop will execute.)

Listing 5.7   Loops that intentionally may never be executed

```
float Number;
int timesMoved = 0;
  :
  :
while (Number >= 1)
{
    Number *= 0.1;
    timesMoved++;
}
while (Number < .1)
{
    Number *= 10;
    timesMoved++;
}
```

Using the do while Statement

The Java do while is a variation on the while. It has the following general syntax:

```
do
{
    // body of loop
}
while (logical_expression)
```

Notice that the logical expression that controls the loop appears at the bottom of the loop. A do while will therefore always execute at least once, until it reaches the while at the bottom where the control expression is actually evaluated.

Given that the body of a do while is executed at least once, you might be tempted to use it frequently. You might, for example, want to use it to control a main program loop that terminates when a user chooses a Quit option from a main menu. The loop would then have the structure:

```
static final int QUIT = 9;
int Option;
do
{
    Option = sysIn.readInt ("Menu goes here");
    // take action based on value of Option
}
while (Option != QUIT);
```

The advantage of this structure is that you don't have to give Option a value before the loop begins. If you use a while, the code must be written:

```
static final int QUIT = 9;
int Option = 0;
do
{
    Option = sysIn.readInt ("Menu goes here");
    // take action based on value of Option
}
while (Option != QUIT);
```

In this example, Option must be initialized to something other than the value of QUIT so that the loop will execute the first time.

Nonetheless, using do while can make a program harder to understand and debug because the while (*logical_expression*); at the end of the loop looks an awful lot like a while without a body. Many programmers therefore prefer to avoid using do while as much as possible, even if it means remembering to initialize while control values.

Using the for Statement

The for structure is useful when you need a loop that increments a numeric control variable and stops when that variable reaches some predetermined value. In particular, it is convenient when processing an entire array, in order. The for structure has the following general syntax:

```
for (initial_control_value; terminating_condition; increment)
{
    // body of loop
}
```

For example, assume that you have numbItems elements in an array. You want to process each element, beginning with the first. Assuming that the control variable i has not been declared outside a loop, a for structure to control the loop would be written:

```
for (int i = 0; i < numbItems; i++)
{
    // body of loop
}
```

The first statement within the parentheses initializes the control variable. If the control variable has not been declared, you can include the declaration as part of the initialization, as was done in this example.

The second statement within the parentheses is a logical expression. The loop continues as long as the condition is true. The final statement is an arithmetic expression that increments the control variable. In this particular example, the loop continues as long as the control variable is less than the number of items in the array. Each time the loop increments, the control variable is incremented by one. You will see how `for` is used in array processing in Chapter 8.

The break and continue Statements

As you saw earlier, the `break` statement is used within a `switch` to branch out of the `switch` after the program has matched a `case` value and executed the associated statements. The `break` statement, however, can be used in other ways, including branching out of a loop at any time. In particular, `break` can be very useful when there are many conditions that can terminate a loop, too many to put into a single logical expression.

Note

If you are familiar with assembly language, then it might help you to understand the operation of the `break` if you know that its action is to pop the address of the statement below the bottom of the loop of the stack and place that address in the CPU's program counter.

The `continue` statement causes a loop to iterate. Its use can speed up program execution by preventing a program from evaluating `if` statements whose logical expressions can't be true because a preceding `if`'s logical expression is true.

As an example of both `break` and `continue`, consider the `while` in Listing 5.8. Notice that the logical expression for this `while` generates an infinite loop. A loop of this type relies on `if` statements that contain `break`s to terminate the loop.

The first `if` in the body of the loop traps input values greater than 100. In this example, the loop should iterate after performing the multiplication. Although it wouldn't hurt to leave out the `continue`—the value won't meet any of the following `if`'s logical expressions—the program will execute fast if Java doesn't have to evaluate the remaining `if`s.

Listing 5.8   Using break and continue

```
while (1 < 2)
{
    int newValue = 0;
    int someValue = sysIn.readInt ("Enter an integer:");
    if (someValue > 100)
    {
        newValue += someValue * 10;
        continue;
    }
    if (someValue > 50 && someValue <= 100)
    {
        newValue += someValue / 10;
        break;
    }
    if (someValue > 25 && newValue <= 50)
    {
        newValue += someValue - 10;
        break;
    }
    if (newValue < 1)
        break;
}
```

The remaining three if structures in the loop contain logical expressions that terminate the loop. Although the logical expressions in the ifs could have been combined into a single while logical expression, doing so would have created a complicated logical expression that would be hard to understand. The structure in the example is easier to understand.

There is one drawback to placing logical expressions that terminate a loop inside the loop (rather than in the while): The program can be harder to debug and modify because it isn't immediately obvious which conditions in the body of the loop actually stop the loop. Most programmers therefore try to limit the use of break in a while to situations where a while's logical expression would be impractically complicated.

Iteration Example: The Hi/Lo Game

The Hi/Lo game is a number guessing game. The computer chooses a random number between 0 and 100. The player's job is to discover the number in seven or less guesses. As you can see in Figure 5.1, the user enters a guess in a system input window and the program responds in the console output window.

Figure 5.1   The Hi/Lo game in progress

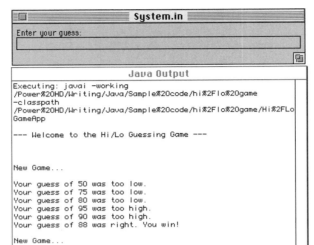

The implementation of the game that appears here also keeps statistics on how well the player is doing. At the end of the game (see Figure 5.2), the programs displays the number of games played, how many have been won, and the winning percentage.

The Game class

The data handling class in the Hi/Lo game program is called `Game` (see Listing 5.9). The application class will create one object from this class.

The `Game` class has three variables: the correct answer, which the player is trying to guess, the current guess made by the player, and an a reference to an object declared from the class `Random`, which provides a random number generator for the program. There are also four methods:

- A constructor: The constructor initializes an object's variables and also creates the random number generator object. To use Java's random number generator, you must be sure to import `java.util.*`.

Figure 5.2   The end of the Hi/Lo game

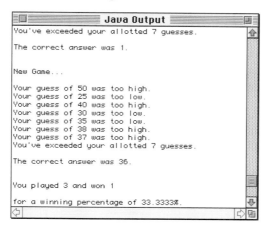

```
Java Output
You've exceeded your allotted 7 guesses.

The correct answer was 1.


New Game...

Your guess of 50 was too high.
Your guess of 25 was too low.
Your guess of 40 was too high.
Your guess of 30 was too low.
Your guess of 35 was too low.
Your guess of 38 was too high.
Your guess of 37 was too high.
You've exceeded your allotted 7 guesses.

The correct answer was 36.


You played 3 and won 1

for a winning percentage of 33.3333%.
```

Random

nextInt

Math

abs

- **InitGame**: The **InitGame** method generates a new answer for the game by calling the **Random** class's **nextInt** method. This method returns a pseudo-random **long**. The Hi/Lo game, however, needs a positive integer in the range 1 to 100. Therefore, the **InitGame** method first ensures that the number is positive by calling the **Math** class's **abs** method, which returns the absolute value of a number. Finally, **InitGame** scales the number—which may have any value in the range of a **long**—by dividing it by the constant **RAND_FACTOR**. (The value of **RAND_FACTOR** was determined by trial and error.)
- **evaluateGuess**: The **evaluateGuess** method contains the nested **if** structure you saw earlier in this chapter to examine one guess made by the user. The constants **HI**, **LO**, and **EQ** are declared in both the **Game** class and the application class.
- **getAnswer**: The **getAnswer** method returns the correct answer to a calling method.

The Application Class

The application class that uses an object created from the **Game** class to play the Hi/Lo game can be found in Listing 5.10. The main driver method (**PlayGame**) creates a new **Game** object and then enters an outer **while** loop

Listing 5.9   game.java

```java
import java.lang.*;
import java.util.*;

public class Game
{
    static final int EQ = 0;
    static final int LO = -1;
    static final int HI = 1;
    static final int MAX_GUESSES = 7;
    static final int RAND_FACTOR = 21000000;

    private int answer;
    private int guess;
    private Random randomNumberGen;

    public Game()
    {
        answer = 0;
        guess = 0;
        randomNumberGen = new Random(); // initialize random number generator
    }

    public void InitGame()
        { answer = Math.abs(randomNumberGen.nextInt()/RAND_FACTOR);}

    public int evaluateGuess (int guess)
    {
        if (guess == answer)
            return EQ;
        else
        if (guess < answer)
            return LO;
        else
            return HI;
    }

    public int getAnswer()
        { return answer; }
}
```

that iterates once for each game played. An inner `while` loop manages game play. It iterates until the user either makes the maximum number of guesses or guesses the correct answer.

Listing 5.10   GameApp.java

```java
import java.awt.*;
import java.io.*;
import java.lang.*;
import text.*;

public class GameApp
{
    static final int EQ = 0;
    static final int LO = -1;
    static final int HI = 1;
    static final int MAX_GUESSES = 7;

    private int games_played;
    private int games_won;

    public GameApp ()
    {
        games_played = 0;
        games_won = 0;
    }

    public void PlayGame()
    {
        int choice, count, result, guesses_made;
        char keep_going = 'Y';
        Game gamePlayed = new Game();

        SystemInput sysIn = new SystemInput();

        System.out.println
            ("\n--- Welcome to the Hi/Lo Guessing Game ---\n\n");
        while (keep_going == 'Y' || keep_going == 'y')
        {
            System.out.println ("\nNew Game...\n");
            count = 0;
            guesses_made = 0;
            result = LO;
            gamePlayed.InitGame();
            incrementPlayed();
            while (guesses_made++ < MAX_GUESSES && result != EQ)
            {
                choice =  sysIn.readInt("Enter your guess: ");
                result = gamePlayed.evaluateGuess (choice);
```

Continued next page

Listing 5.10(Continued)   GameApp.java

```java
            switch (result)
            {
                case EQ:
                    System.out.println
                        ("Your guess of " + choice +
                        " was right. You win!");
                    break;
                case LO:
                    System.out.println
                        ("Your guess of " + choice + " was too low.");
                    break;
                case HI:
                    System.out.println
                        ("Your guess of " + choice + " was too high.");
                    break;
            }
        }
        if (guesses_made > MAX_GUESSES && result != EQ)
        {
            System.out.println ("You've exceeded your allotted " +
                MAX_GUESSES + " guesses.\n");
            System.out.println ("The correct answer was " +
                gamePlayed.getAnswer() + ".\n");
        }
        else
            if (result == EQ)
                incrementWon();

        keep_going = sysIn.readChar ("Another game?");
    }
    displayFinal();
}

private void incrementPlayed()
    { games_played++; }

private void incrementWon()
    { games_won++; }

private void displayFinal()
{
    System.out.println
        ("\nYou played " + games_played + " and won " + games_won);
    System.out.println
        ("\nfor a winning percentage of " +
        (float) games_won/games_played * 100 + "%.");
}
```

Continued next page

Listing 5.10(Continued)   GameApp.java

```
    public static void main (String args[])
{
    GameApp theGame = new GameApp();
    theGame.PlayGame();
    }
}
```

As you study the application class, notice that there is no way to determine exactly which of the two conditions causes the inner loop to stop. The program must therefore use an **if** structure to explicitly test the two conditions and take action based on whichever it finds.

At the end of a game, the user is given the option of continuing to play another game or ending the program. The outer loop uses the value in the **keep_going** variable to decide whether to begin another game. Because the user might enter either an upper- or lowercase letter, the logical expression in the outer **while** contains an OR to test for both possible characters.

After the outer loop terminates, the **PlayGame** method has one more task: it calls the **displayFinal** method to compute the percentage of games won and display the user's statistics. Notice that the algorithm for calculation involves dividing the number of games won by the number of games played and then multiplying by 100. Unfortunately, the **games_played** and **games_won** variables are integers. Unless the player wins every game, the result of the integer division will always be zero. The program therefore typecasts the result into a floating point value.

String Manipulation

Because strings are made up of groups of characters, you can't use the same operators to manipulate them that you would use with simple values. In this section we will look at procedures for comparing strings, for determining their length, and for extracting parts of strings.

Java strings are objects created from the **String** class. This means that when you work with strings, you are working with objects. You therefore handle strings much like you would handle any other object. In particular, this means that when you need to do something with a string, you must call one of the class's methods. The exceptions to this rule involve creating string objects and assigning values to them.

Creating and Assigning Values to Strings

As you saw in Chapter 3, when it comes to creating and assigning values to string objects, you handle the objects as if they were simple data types. For example to create a string object, you declare a variable to hold a reference to the string, just as you would for any object:

```
String theString;
```

However, you don't need to use the new operator to allocate storage. Java takes care of it for you.

To assign a value to a string, you don't need to know anything about a string object's variables or use a set method. You simply assign a value using the assignment operator:

```
theString = "This is a test";
```

Comparing Strings

Comparing two strings to determine which comes alphabetically first is a bit of a tricky proposition because there is no way to guarantee that the strings will be the same length. Java therefore provides two ways to make the comparison, using methods of the String class.

The simplest comparison simply determines whether two strings are identical. (Keep in mind that Java is case sensitive and that all string comparisons take case into consideration.) To compare string A to string B, you could code:

String

```
boolean result = StringA.equals (StringB);
```

The equals function returns true if the strings are equal, false if they are not.

equals   As a simple example, let's look at an application (Listing 5.12) that accepts a string from the user that it stores in an object of class testName (Listing 5.12). After creating an object from testName, the application class's Run function accepts a second name from the user, which is then tested for equality with the name stored in the testName object.

The actual test is performed by the testName class's testOne method. As you can see in Listing 5.12, this method tests the two strings using equals and returns the boolean result to the calling method.

Listing 5.11   whichApp.java

```java
import java.awt.*;
import java.io.*;
import java.lang.*;

public class whichApp
{
    private testName theName;

    public void Run()
    {
        SystemInput sysIn = new SystemInput();
        String iName = sysIn.readString ("Enter the name to test:");

        theName = new testName (iName);

        iName = sysIn.readString ("Enter a name to compare:");
        if (theName.testOne (iName))
            System.out.println ("The two names are the same.");
        else
            System.out.println ("The two names are different.");
    }


    public static void main (String args[])
    {
        whichApp theApp = new whichApp();
        theApp.Run();
    }
}
```

Listing 5.12   testName.java

```java
public class testName
{
    private String name;

    public testName (String iName)
        { name = iName; }


    public boolean testOne (String iName)
        { return name.equals(iName); }
}
```

String

compareTo

If simple equality isn't enough information about the relationship between two strings, you can use the String class's compareTo method, whose integer result indicates the relative alphabetical relationship of two strings. The compareTo method returns the following values:

- 0 if the two strings are equal.
- < 0 if the first string (the string performing the test) alphabetically precedes the second string.
- > 0 if the first string alphabetically follows the second string.

To show you compareTo in action, let's look at a slightly modified version of the name comparison program. As you can see in Listing 5.13. the syntax of compareTo is exactly the same as equals. However, it returns an integer rather than a boolean.

Listing 5.13   testName.java, modified to use compareTo

```
public class testName
{
    private String name;

    public testName (String iName)
        { name = iName; }

    public int testOne (String iName)
        { return name.compareTo(iName); }
}
```

To evaluate the result of the comparison, the application class (Listing 5.14) must be modified as well. Notice that the Run function now tests for the three possible outcomes of a call to compareTo.

Warning

If you use the == to compare two strings, you will simply be comparing the addresses where the strings are stored. (Don't forget that strings are objects and that a variable that represents a string therefore contains the address of the beginning of the string's storage.) Unless the strings share the same storage (and are therefore the same string), using == will never return true.

Listing 5.14   whichApp.java, modified to process the result of compareTo

```java
import java.awt.*;
import java.io.*;
import java.lang.*;

public class whichApp
{
    private testName theName;

    public void Run()
    {
        SystemInput sysIn = new SystemInput();
        String iName = sysIn.readString ("Enter the name to test:");

        theName = new testName (iName);

        iName = sysIn.readString ("Enter a name to compare:");
        if (theName.testOne (iName) == 0)
            System.out.println ("The two names are the same.");
        else if (theName.testOne (iName) < 0)
            System.out.println ("The first name is alphabetically first.");
        else
            System.out.println ("The second name is alphabetically first.");
    }

    public static void main (String args[])
    {
        whichApp theApp = new whichApp();
        theApp.Run();
    }
}
```

Obtaining the Length of a String

String

length

To find out how many characters there are in a string, you use the String class's length method:

```java
String theString = "Jane and Dick";
int numb_char = theString.length();
```

After executing the statement above, the numb_char variable will contain 13.

Extracting Substrings

As you saw in Chapter 3, you can access a single character in a string using the String class's charAt method. When you need chunks of a string, extracting them one character at a time can be somewhat clumsy. Therefore, the String class contains a method that lets you remove any number of characters from a string, creating what is known as a *substring*.

String

substring

The substring method has the following general syntax:

```
string_variable = string_variable.substring
    (first_char_to_take, first_character_not_to_take);
```

For example, if you execute the following code

```
String theString = "Jane and Dick";
String theSubString = theString.substring (0,4);
```

the variable theSubString will contain Jane. Notice that the positions of the characters in the string are numbered from left to right, beginning with 0. In this particular example, the substring includes characters in positions 0 through 3, stopping with position 4.

As an example of substring in action, let's look at a program that accepts a person's name as two separate strings (first name and last name) and then combines them using the concatenation operator into a single string in the format Last, First. The program can then reverse the names in the single variable to generate a second string in the format First Last.

The bulk of the program's work is performed by the names class (Listing 5.15). The class stores the first name, last name, and the combined name in Last, First format. As you can see, the constructor accepts the input strings and uses concatenation to create the combined name.

The application class (Listing 5.16) accepts the first name and last name strings from the user and then creates a Names object. It then displays the contents of the Names object's wholeName variable. The application's last action is to declare a string variable to hold the reversed name and then call the reverse method to reformat the string.

If you look carefully at the reverse method you might think that something very odd is occurring. The application class passes in a string variable. The reverse method makes some changes to the string variable and then returns it to the application class. Why go to all this trouble? Why not simply create the string in the reverse method and then return it? Because if

Listing 5.15   names.java

```java
import java.io.*;
import java.lang.*;

public class Names
{
    private String First;
    private String Last;
    private String wholeName;

    public Names (String iFirst, String iLast)
    {
        First = iFirst;
        Last = iLast;
        wholeName = Last + ", " + First;
    }

    public String getWhole()
        { return wholeName; }

    public String reverse (String reversed)
    {
        int pos = 0;

        while (wholeName.charAt (pos) != ' ')
            pos++;

        String firstHalf = wholeName.substring (pos+1);
        String secondHalf = wholeName.substring (0,pos-1);
        reversed = firstHalf + " " + secondHalf;
        return reversed;
    }
}
```

you create the string in the reverse method, it will be destroyed when the method finishes execution. This means that even if the application class receives the starting address of where the string *was* when the reverse method was working with it, the string won't be there after the reverse method terminates. Therefore, the application class creates a string variable that it can send to the reverse method for the reverse method to use. Because the string variable is local to the application class's Run function, and *not* to the reverse method, it will remain accessible after the reverse method terminates.

Listing 5.16   NamesApp.java

```java
import java.awt.*;
import java.io.*;
import java.lang.*;

public class NamesApp
{
    public void Run()
    {
        SystemInput sysIn = new SystemInput ();

        String iFirst = sysIn.readString ("First name:");
        String iLast = sysIn.readString ("Last name:");
        Names person = new Names (iFirst,iLast);

        System.out.println ("\nThe whole name is " + person.getWhole());
        String reversed = "";
        System.out.println ("The reversed name is " +
            person.reverse(reversed));
    }

    public static void main (String args[])
    {
        NamesApp theNames = new NamesApp();
        theNames.Run();
    }
}
```

Summary

This chapter introduced the structured elements of Java, including details on operators, selection, and iteration.

Java supports the typical set of arithmetic operators found in a high-level programming language. However, there is no exponentiation operator; exponentiation is typically performed using a Java class library method. Java also provides special operators for quickly incrementing and decrementing a value by one. Java supports the logical operators AND, OR, and NOT, along with bit-wise logical operators that perform logical operations on the individual bits in two storage locations.

During arithmetic operations, Java automatically converts data types so that all values in the operation are the same data type. By default, conversion is to the data type with the greatest range and precision. A programmer can override automatic data conversion with explicitly typecasting, which forces a conversion to a specific type of data. Typecasting is the only way to force Java to perform a floating point division with two integers.

Java supports two selection structures: `if` and `switch`. The `if` structure is like that found in other high-level languages. It supports an `else` clause; `if` structures can be nested as needed. The `switch` structure is similar to the `case` statement found in Pascal and Modula-2. Its use is appropriate when a program needs to evaluate and take action on more than two values of the same variable.

Java supports three iteration structures: `while`, `do while`, and `for`. The `while` structure places the test for stopping the loop at the top of the loop. It can therefore be used for all loops, even those that should not be executed under certain circumstances. The `do while` structure places the test for stopping the loop at the bottom of the loop. It is therefore always executed at least once. The `for` loop is a shorthand version of a `while` that bases the condition for stopping the loop on some value that is iterated each time the loop is executed.

Because Java strings are complex values, they cannot be manipulated using standard Java operators. In particular, Java provides `String` class methods to compare strings and to extract portions of strings.

Exercises

1. Write and test a program that computes the total cost for framing a picture. The data handling class should store the following data:

   - Job ticket number (a unique number assigned to each order)
   - The width of the frame in inches
   - The length of the frame in inches
   - The price of the frame per running inch
   - The price of mounting the picture
   - The price of glass
   - The price of labor

   Provide the following methods for the class:

   - A constructor that places data into an object
   - A method to compute the cost of framing (including the frame, glass, mounting, and labor)
   - Get methods to return the contents of each variable

The application class should provide a one-line menu for the user similar to the following:

```
1) Enter data 2) Compute cost 3) Display data 4) Quit
```

Include methods in the application class to implement each of the menu options. Provide a `while` loop that allows the user to continue with the program until he or she enters a 4 for Quit.

2. Write and test a program that computes available storage for an oil tank in an oil tank farm. The data handling class should store the following data:

- Tank number
- Capacity in gallons
- Current number of gallons in the tank

Provide the following methods for the class:

- A constructor that places data into an object
- A method to compute how full the tank is expressed as a percentage of the capacity
- A method to compute the available space in the tank expressed as a percentage of the capacity
- Get functions to return the contents of each variable

The application class should provide a one-line menu for the user similar to the following:

```
1) Enter data 2) Current oil level 3) Available capacity 4) Quit
```

Include methods in the application class to implement each of the menu options. Provide a `while` loop that allows the user to continue with the program until he or she enters a 4 for Quit.

3. Write and test a program that uses a decision tree to identify a living creature that the user describes to the program. The way in which the program should make its decisions is diagrammed in Figure 5.3. The program collects information by asking the user questions such as "How many legs

does the creature have?" and "Does the creature live in water?" Design your own classes for this program. Decide how many objects you will need to create from each class.

Figure 5.3   A decision tree for identifying a living creature

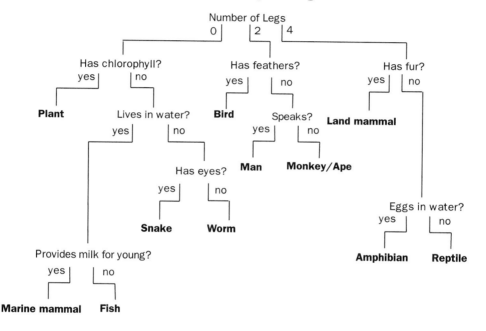

4. Write and test a program that computes the amount of principal in a certificate of deposit, where the interest paid is added to the principal each month. The formula for the principal after interest is paid for a given month is:

```
Principal = Amount of initial deposit *
    (1 + Monthly interest rate)^(Number of months on deposit)
```

Decide what classes are needed for this program. Create any necessary objects.

Give the user the opportunity to enter the *annual* interest rate. (The program should compute the monthly interest rate.) Also give the user the choice of term for the CD (12, 24, or 36 months). Display the amount of principal on deposit for each month during the term of the CD.

5. Create a class that stores information about the costs to produce a product, including the number of units produced in the past month, the direct materials cost per unit, the direct labor cost per unit, and the overhead per unit. Include a method that computes the total cost for all units produced in the past month. Write a program that lets the user enter data for a product and then displays the total cost for that product.

6. Create a class to handle the conversion between 12-hour and 24-hour time. The class should include variables for the time (a four-digit integer) and whether it represents 12- or 24-hour time. Include a method that performs the conversion based on the value in the "12 or 24" variable. Then display the result in an appropriate format. For example, 12-hours time should be displayed as HH:MM PM or HH:MM AM, where HH is the hour and MM is the minutes; 24-hour time should be displayed simply as HH:MM.

7. Create a class that handles the pricing of purchases of athletic uniforms for a uniform supply company. The class should include a product number for the uniform, a price for the top, a price for the bottom, a price for purchasing the combination of top and bottom, and the percentage discount if 50 or more complete uniforms are purchased. Include a method that computes the price of an order for a uniform. Write a program that demonstrates that the class and its methods work, where the user enters the prices and the number of uniforms being purchased.

8. Create a class that holds a string. Include a method that reverses the order of the characters in the string. Write a program that demonstrates that the reversal method works.

9. Assume that you are an industrial spy trying to break the data encryption scheme used by one of your employer's competitors. One of your basic techniques is to examine the frequency of characters in a block of text. Create a class that holds a string of characters. Include a method that scans the

string and counts the frequency with which each letter in the string appears. (Ignore spaces and punctuation marks; treat uppercase and lowercase letters the same.) When the scan is finished, display the frequency counts. Write a program that demonstrates that the method works.

10. Write a program that performs simple arithmetic (add, subtract, multiply, divide) using Roman numerals. The data handling class on which this program is based should include a string for a Roman numeral and an integer for its integer equivalent. The class will need methods to convert from a Roman numeral to an integer and from an integer to a Roman numeral.

    The application class that manipulates data handling objects should let users enter expressions in typical arithmetic format, such as:

    XXX-XV

    The program should then scan the string to find the Roman numerals and the operator. You should consider writing methods that scan a string for a specific character and, once the character has been found, extract parts of a string based on the position of that character in the string. Once the program has performed the arithmetic, it should convert the result back to a Roman numeral for display.

11. In this exercise, you will expand the reusable Person class that you began developing for Exercise 7 in Chapter 4. Add the following capabilities to the class:

    - Add data validation tests to the constructor to verify that the social security number, first name, last name, and home telephone have been entered. (These values are required; the others are optional.)
    - Validate that social security numbers are in the form XXX-XX-XXXX. Add this validation to the constructor and to the social security number variable's mutator method.
    - Validate that telephone numbers are in the form (XXX) XXX-XXXX. Add this validation to the constructor and to both telephone number variables' mutator methods.

    Modify the application class used to test the Person class so that it proves that your validation works.

6

Inheritance

OBJECTIVES

In this chapter you will read about:
- Using inheritance to allow similar classes to share data and methods.
- Where inheritance is appropriate and where it isn't.
- How polymorphism, implemented through abstract methods, allows objects from related classes to react differently to the same method.
- How Java interfaces give classes additional functionality.

This chapter introduces one of the most important features of the object-oriented paradigm: inheritance. Inheritance makes it possible for similar objects to share variable and method definitions. Inheritance also supports *polymorphism*, through which different objects can respond to the same message in different ways. In addition, inheritance is vital to the implementation of a graphic user interface, which in turn is required for creating applets.

Where Inheritance Makes Sense

As you read in Chapter 1, using inheritance creates a hierarchy of classes through which the variables and methods for classes higher in the hierarchy are passed down to classes below. This means that when similar classes share variables and methods, you only need to declare them once, rather than repeating them for each class in which they appear.

The idea of inheritance can be a bit confusing, especially if you've studied data management. Although inheritance initially looks a lot like the relationships between entities in a database system, it is a different concept. To see where inheritance is appropriate and where inheritance hurts rather than helps, let's take a look at the design of a program to manage a retail video store.

The first thing to understand about a video store is that the store needs to store data about the type of merchandise it carries. However, the store doesn't rent a type of merchandise; it rents *copies* of those types. There are therefore two major groups of classes that a video store program must handle: classes about the types of merchandise and classes about merchandise copies.

In Figure 6.1, each box represents a class. (A video store also requires a customer class, which doesn't appear in this particular diagram.) The hierarchy at the top of the diagram, connected by solid lines, describes types of merchandise carried by the store. The hierarchy at the bottom of the diagram, also connected by solid lines, describes the copies of the types of merchandise that are actually rented to customers. The dashed lines in the middle of the diagram indicate where inheritance isn't appropriate. You'll read more about this shortly.

The base class of the type of merchandise hierarchy is a generic `Merchandise Item`. As you can see in Figure 6.1, it contains data that are applicable to movies, other videos, *and* video games. The `Video Game` class inherits all the variables from the `Merchandise Item` class and adds two variables that are specifically applicable to games. The `Video` class also inherits the

Figure 6.1   Merchandise item hierarchy for a video store

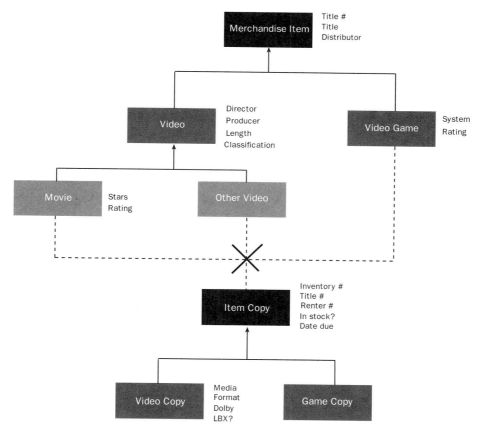

Merchandise Item class's variables and adds variables of its own. However, the **Video** class has two classes derived from it (**Movie** and **Other Video**). **Video** is therefore both a base class and a derived class.

Objects are created from only three of the classes in the merchandise item hierarchy: **Movie**, **OtherVideo**, and **Game**. Notice that these are classes at the bottom of the hierarchy, classes from which no other classes are derived. Although this is not always the case, it is not uncommon for objects to be created only from classes at the bottom of a hierarchy.

The copy hierarchy begins with the base class `Item Copy`. It contains variables that apply to all copies of merchandise items, regardless of the type of item. The `Video Copy` derived class adds variables that apply only to videos. The `Game Copy` class doesn't need any additional data. As with the merchandise item hierarchy, objects are created only from the two classes at the bottom of the hierarchy and never from the `Item Copy` class.

One question arises at this point: If the `Other Video` and `Game Copy` classes don't add any variables to those they inherit from their respective base classes, why include these classes in the design at all? Because the classes behave differently even when they receive the same message. For example, the `Other Video` class behaves differently from the `Movie` class when it receives the messages "write your data to a file."

If you have taken a database course, then you are probably also wondering why the `Item Copy` class and its derived classes aren't part of the merchandise item hierarchy. It is very true that the store stocks many copies of each merchandise item. In fact, a database system would represent this as a one-to-many relationship. Keep in mind, however, that inheritance *copies* all the variables from a base class into a derived class.

If `Video Copy`, for example, was derived from `Movie`, each copy of a given movie would repeat all the data about the movie, including its title, distributor, producer, director, stars, and rating. The result would be a great deal of unnecessary duplicated data. The fact that the extra data waste disk space is the least of the problems. As you may know from your database course, the presence of unnecessary duplicated data sooner or later leads to data inconsistency, a situation in which data that should be the same are not. A search for a movie by title would never find any copy that had even one incorrect letter in its title, perhaps causing someone at the store to believe that no copies of a given title were in stock.

In this situation, inheritance isn't appropriate. Use inheritance where the derived classes actually need every variable from their base classes. (A copy of a merchandise item doesn't need all the data describing the item; it only needs an identifier, such as an item number, that can be used to locate that object that contains the descriptive data.) Use inheritance where the inherited variables don't represent unnecessary duplicated data.

Another way to help determine when inheritance is appropriate is to recognize that in most cases, inheritance represents the special relationship "is a," in which a derived class is a more specific example of its base class. In other words, a `Video` "is a" `Merchandise Item`; a `Movie` "is a" `Video`. If you can express the relationship between classes using the "is a" relationship, then inheritance is probably appropriate.

The Graphing Program

As an example of a program that uses inheritance, we will be looking at a program that creates graphs of the sales made by three salespeople during the four quarters of a year. The output (Figure 6.2) includes two different types of graphs: a bar graph with individual bars for each salesperson for each quarter and a stacked bar graph with one bar for each quarter. The user's input is the sales made by each salesperson.

Figure 6.2   Output of the graph program

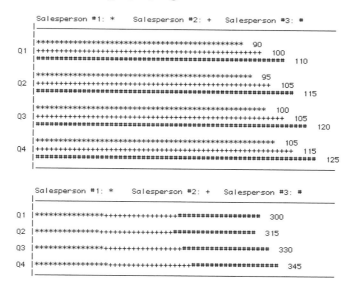

Note

Yes, the graphs drawn from text characters aren't very attractive. Not to worry; we'll be replacing them with real graphics in Chapter 7.

The data on which the graphs are based are taken from an object of class graphData. As you can see in Listing 6.1, the class contains individual variables for each salesperson and quarter. (This program would be much more generic—and somewhat shorter—if it could use arrays, but since we haven't discussed them yet, we'll live with the individual variables.) The methods include two constructors (one that initializes the variables in an object and a default constructor that does nothing) and get methods that supply every piece of data the object contains. The only purpose for an object of this class is to act as a holding place for data and to return it to a graphing class when requested to do so.

The base class (also called the *parent* or *super* class) for the graph hierarchy is salesGraph. However, although the bar graph and stacked bar graph share the same data, the two are drawn in different ways. Therefore, the graphing program contains two classes derived from salesGraph: barGraph and stackedGraph. The relationship between the three classes is diagrammed in Figure 6.3. (Derived classes are also called *child* classes or *subclasses*.)

When barGraph or stackedGraph receive a message to "paint yourself on the screen," they behave somewhat differently. Where barGraph draws one line for each salesperson in each quarter, stackedGraph must draw only one line for each quarter. The message will be the same, but the implementation of the method will be different. Coupled with the fact that both barGraph and stackedGraph are specializations of the more generic class salesGraph—they pass the "is a" test—this makes the graph program a perfect environment for inheritance. You will see the details of this inheritance hierarchy throughout this chapter.

The barGraph and stackedGraph classes inherit both variables and methods from their base class, salesGraph. Along with variables such as those that hold the highest data value (high_value) and the scale factor (scale_factor), they each inherit an object of class graphData that is used to hold the data to be graphed (see Figure 6.4). The derived classes can use these variables as if they were declared within the derived class. They also inherit base class methods. You will read about the details of how variables and methods can be inherited in the next sections of this chapter.

Listing 6.1   graphData.java

```java
class graphData
{
    private int S1Q1, S1Q2, S1Q3, S1Q4;
    private int S2Q1, S2Q2, S2Q3, S2Q4;
    private int S3Q1, S3Q2, S3Q3, S3Q4;

    private String Label1 = "Q1";
    private String Label2 = "Q2";
    private String Label3 = "Q3";
    private String Label4 = "Q4";

    private int labelLength = 2;

    public graphData()
        {}

    public graphData (int i11, int i12, int i13, int i14,
        int i21, int i22, int i23, int i24, int i31, int i32,
        int i33, int i34)
    {
        S1Q1 = i11;
        S1Q2 = i12;
        S1Q3 = i13;
        S1Q4 = i14;
        S2Q1 = i21;
        S2Q2 = i22;
        S2Q3 = i23;
        S2Q4 = i24;
        S3Q1 = i31;
        S3Q2 = i32;
        S3Q3 = i33;
        S3Q4 = i34;
    }

    public int getS1Q1() { return S1Q1; }

    public int getS1Q2() { return S1Q2; }

    public int getS1Q3() { return S1Q3; }

    public int getS1Q4() { return S1Q4; }

    public int getS2Q1() { return S2Q1; }

    public int getS2Q2() { return S2Q2; }

    public int getS2Q3() { return S2Q3; }
```

Continued next page

Listing 6.1(Continued)   graphData.java

```java
    public int getS2Q4() { return S2Q4; }

    public int getS3Q1() { return S3Q1; }

    public int getS3Q2() { return S3Q2; }

    public int getS3Q3() { return S3Q3; }

    public int getS3Q4() { return S3Q4; }

    public String getLabel1() { return Label1; }

    public String getLabel2() { return Label2; }

    public String getLabel3() { return Label3; }

    public String getLabel4() { return Label4; }

    public int getLabelLength() { return labelLength; }
}
```

Figure 6.3   The graph class hierarchy

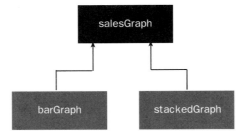

Creating Base Classes

For the most part, a base class looks like any other class. However, there are a few elements that are specific to inheritance. As an example, consider the `salesGraph` class in Listing 6.2. There are two things in that class that we haven't discussed yet: the keywords `protected` and `abstract`.

Figure 6.4   Inherited elements in the graph class hierarchy

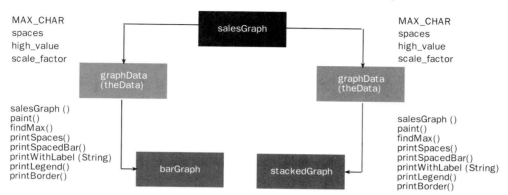

Inheritance and Accessibility

To this point, you have worked with public and private variables and methods. Public items are accessible to all functions; private items are accessible only to members of the class in which they are defined. However, when we are working with inheritance, we would like to be able to share variables and methods among all the classes in a hierarchy. That's where protected access comes in.

A derived class cannot access any private variables and methods of its base class. To get around this problem and still hide the internals of the base class from classes and methods outside the class hierarchy, a base class usually uses protected items rather than private items. Protected items are accessible to methods in all derived class. Notice in Listing 6.2, for example, that all of the salesGraph class's variables are protected. In addition, utility methods that are called by the public paint method are also protected. If salesGraph weren't a base class, all the protected methods would be private.

In general, inheritance means that a derived class has access to public and protected items of its base class. Public items are inherited as public; protected items remain protected. Private items are inaccessible.

Listing 6.2   The salesGraph class

```
public abstract class salesGraph
{
    protected static final int MAX_CHAR = 50;
    protected int spaces;
    protected int high_value;
    protected int scale_factor;
    protected graphData theData = new graphData();

    public salesGraph (graphData iData)
    {
        theData = iData;
        spaces = theData.getLabelLength() + 1; // spaces before axis
        high_value = findMax();
        scale_factor = high_value / MAX_CHAR;
        if (scale_factor < 1)
            scale_factor = 1;
    }

    public abstract void paint(); // abstract method with no implementation

    protected int findMax () // returns maximum data value in graphData object
    {
        int max = theData.getS1Q1();
        if (theData.getS1Q2() > max)
            max = theData.getS1Q2();
        if (theData.getS1Q3() > max)
            max = theData.getS1Q3();
        if (theData.getS1Q4() > max)
            max = theData.getS1Q4();
        if (theData.getS2Q1() > max)
            max = theData.getS2Q1();
        if (theData.getS2Q2() > max)
            max = theData.getS2Q2();
        if (theData.getS2Q3() > max)
            max = theData.getS2Q3();
        if (theData.getS2Q4() > max)
            max = theData.getS2Q4();
        if (theData.getS3Q1() > max)
            max = theData.getS3Q1();
        if (theData.getS3Q2() > max)
            max = theData.getS3Q2();
        if (theData.getS3Q3() > max)
            max = theData.getS3Q3();
        if (theData.getS3Q4() > max)
            max = theData.getS3Q4();
        return max;
    }
```

Continued next page

Listing 6.2(Continued)   The salesGraph class

```
private void printSpaces()
    {
        for (int i = 1; i <= spaces; i++)
            System.out.print (" ");
    }

    protected void printSpacedBar()
    {
        System.out.print ("\n");
        printSpaces();
        System.out.print ("|");
    }

    protected void printWithLabel (String theLabel)
    {
        System.out.print ("\n" + theLabel + " |");
    }

    protected void printLegend()
    {
        System.out.print
        ("\n    Salesperson #1: *    Salesperson #2: +    Salesperson #3: #");
    }

    protected void printBorder()
    {
        printSpacedBar();
        for (int i = 1; i <= MAX_CHAR + 15; i++)
            System.out.print ("_");
    }
}
```

Abstract Methods, Polymorphism, and Abstract Classes

One of the most powerful capabilities of inheritance is its support for polymorphism, the ability to have classes in the same inheritance hierarchy respond differently to the same message. A program is using polymorphism when methods in different classes have the same signature but differ in the content of the method body.

As you will see in the next section of this chapter, classes derived from salesGraph implement their own versions of the paint method. This is known as *overriding* a base class method. When a program is using polymorphism, derived classes override base class methods by including methods with exactly the same signature as the methods in the base class but with separate bodies that act in different ways.

Warning   It's easy to confuse polymorphism and method overloading. With overloading, methods in the same class have the same name but different signatures. With polymorphism, methods in different classes in the same inheritance hierarchy have the same signature but different implementations.

If you look at the `print` method in the `salesGraph` class, you will notice that it has no implementation. It exists only as a method signature, including the keyword `abstract`. An *abstract method* is a method that has no implementation in a base class. Derived classes are then required to override the abstract method.

When should you use an abstract method? When there is no generic implementation of a method that might be used by a derived class. This is indeed the case with the graphing program. There is no generic way to draw a graph; the way in which a graph is produced is specific to the type of graph. Therefore, it's not possible to write generic graphing code and an abstract method makes sense.

Any class that includes at least one abstract method becomes an *abstract class*. Notice in Listing 6.2 that the class header for the `salesGraph` class includes the keyword `abstract`. This presence of this keyword would make the class abstract even if it contained no abstract methods.

Why would you want an abstract class if it didn't contain any abstract methods? Because a program can't create any objects from an abstract class. If you want to require a program to use derived classes, rather than creating objects directly from a base class, simply make the class abstract.

Creating Derived Classes

Derived classes like the `barGraph` and `stackedGraph` classes in Listing 6.3 have much in common with classes that aren't part of an inheritance hierarchy. However, they also have the following peculiarities:

- The class's header must indicate the class from which it is derived, using the keyword `extends`, as in `extends salesGraph`.

Listing 6.3   The barGraph and stackedGraph classes

```java
public class barGraph extends salesGraph
{
    public barGraph (graphData iData)
    {
        super (iData);
    }

    public void paint()
    {
        int i;

        printLegend();

        printBorder();
        printSpacedBar();
        printSpacedBar();
        for (i = 1; i <= (theData.getS1Q1()/scale_factor); i++)
            System.out.print ("*");
        System.out.print ("  " + theData.getS1Q1());
        printWithLabel (theData.getLabel1());
        for (i = 1; i < (theData.getS2Q1()/scale_factor); i++)
            System.out.print ("+");
        System.out.print ("  " + theData.getS2Q1());
        printSpacedBar();
        for (i = 1; i < (theData.getS3Q1()/scale_factor);i++)
            System.out.print ("#");
        System.out.print ("  " + theData.getS3Q1());
        printSpacedBar();
        printSpacedBar();

        for (i = 1; i <= (theData.getS1Q2()/scale_factor); i++)
            System.out.print ("*");
        System.out.print ("  " + theData.getS1Q2());
        printWithLabel (theData.getLabel2());
        for (i = 1; i < (theData.getS2Q2()/scale_factor); i++)
            System.out.print ("+");
        System.out.print ("  " + theData.getS2Q2());
        printSpacedBar();
        for (i = 1; i < (theData.getS3Q2()/scale_factor);i++)
            System.out.print ("#");
        System.out.print ("  " + theData.getS3Q2());
        printSpacedBar();
        printSpacedBar();
        for (i = 1; i <= (theData.getS1Q3()/scale_factor); i++)
            System.out.print ("*");
        System.out.print ("  " + theData.getS1Q3());
        printWithLabel (theData.getLabel3());
```

Continued next page

Listing 6.3(Continued)   The barGraph and stackedGraph classes

```
for (i = 1; i < (theData.getS2Q3()/scale_factor); i++)
        System.out.print ("+");
    System.out.print ("   " + theData.getS2Q2());
    printSpacedBar();
    for (i = 1; i < (theData.getS3Q3()/scale_factor);i++)
        System.out.print ("#");
    System.out.print ("   " + theData.getS3Q3());
    printSpacedBar();
    printSpacedBar();

        for (i = 1; i <= (theData.getS1Q4()/scale_factor); i++)
            System.out.print ("*");
        System.out.print ("   " + theData.getS1Q4());
        printWithLabel (theData.getLabel4());
        for (i = 1; i < (theData.getS2Q4()/scale_factor); i++)
            System.out.print ("+");
        System.out.print ("   " + theData.getS2Q4());
        printSpacedBar();
        for (i = 1; i < (theData.getS3Q4()/scale_factor);i++)
            System.out.print ("#");
        System.out.print ("   " + theData.getS3Q4());

        printBorder();
        System.out.print ("\n\n");
    }
}

public class stackedGraph extends salesGraph
{
    public stackedGraph (graphData iData)
    {
        super (iData);
    }

    public void paint ()
    {
        int i;
        int stackedScale = scale_factor * 3;

        printLegend();
        printBorder();
        printSpacedBar();

    printWithLabel(theData.getLabel1());
        for (i = 1; i <= (theData.getS1Q1()/stackedScale); i++)
            System.out.print ("*");
```

Continued next page

Listing 6.3(Continued)   The barGraph and stackedGraph classes

```
      for (i = 1; i <= (theData.getS2Q1()/stackedScale); i++)
         System.out.print ("+");
      for (i = 1; i <= (theData.getS3Q1()/stackedScale); i++)
         System.out.print ("#");
      System.out.print ("   " +
         (theData.getS1Q1() + theData.getS2Q1() + theData.getS3Q1()));
      printSpacedBar();

      printWithLabel(theData.getLabel2());
      for (i = 1; i < (theData.getS1Q2()/stackedScale); i++)
         System.out.print ("*");
      for (i = 1; i < (theData.getS2Q2()/stackedScale); i++)
         System.out.print ("+");
      for (i = 1; i < (theData.getS3Q2()/stackedScale); i++)
         System.out.print ("#");
      System.out.print ("   " +
         (theData.getS1Q2() + theData.getS2Q2() + theData.getS3Q2()));
      printSpacedBar();

      printWithLabel(theData.getLabel3());
      for (i = 1; i < (theData.getS1Q3()/stackedScale); i++)
         System.out.print ("*");
      for (i = 1; i < (theData.getS2Q3()/stackedScale); i++)
         System.out.print ("+");
      for (i = 1; i < (theData.getS3Q3()/stackedScale); i++)
         System.out.print ("#");
      System.out.print ("   " +
         (theData.getS1Q3() + theData.getS2Q3() + theData.getS3Q3()));
      printSpacedBar();

      printWithLabel (theData.getLabel4());
      for (i = 1; i < (theData.getS1Q4()/stackedScale); i++)
         System.out.print ("*");
      for (i = 1; i < (theData.getS2Q4()/stackedScale); i++)
         System.out.print ("+");
      for (i = 1; i < (theData.getS3Q4()/stackedScale); i++)
         System.out.print ("#");
      System.out.print ("   " +
         (theData.getS1Q4() + theData.getS2Q4() + theData.getS3Q4()));

      printBorder();

      System.out.print ("\n\n");
   }
}
```

- The class doesn't include any methods that are inherited from the base class. In our particular example, this means that all of the protected utility methods in `salesMethod` are implemented only once, in the base class.
- Constructors aren't inherited. Each derived class must include its own constructors. However, as you will see shortly, a derived class can call its base class's constructor. This is the only situation in which a method can call a constructor directly.
- The class implements any abstract methods it needs as well as any methods that are unique to the particular class. The `barGraph` and `stackedBar` classes therefore include an implementation of `paint`. However, neither adds any methods of its own.
- A derived class can also add any variables it needs in addition to those it inherits from its base class. In this particular example, no additional variables are required.
- A derived class can use methods that it inherits from its base class as if they were its own. The `barGraph` and `stackedGraph` classes, for example, call the protected utility method implementations in `salesGraph` (for example, `printSpacedBar`) as if they were their own private methods.

Inheritance and Derived Class Constructors

As just mentioned, constructors aren't inherited. A derived class must therefore implement its own constructors, even if there is only a single constructor that does nothing but call the base class constructor.

In the example we have been considering, a constructor needs to let an object know where the data to be graphed are stored by copying the address of a `graphData` object into one of the object's variables. It also needs to compute a variety of values used to scale the data being graphed. However, all of that work is done in the base class constructor; there's nothing the derived class constructors need to add. Therefore, all the derived class constructors need to do is call the base class constructor.

To reference the base class of a derived class, you use the keyword `super`. Since the name of a constructor is the same as the name of a class, you can call a base class constructor by using that keyword and including any needed parameters in the parameter list. For example, the `salesGraph` constructor requires an object of class `graphData` as an input parameter. Therefore, the derived classes can call that constructor with:

```
super (iData);
```

where `iData` is an object created from the `graphData` class.

Using Derived Classes

A Java program uses a derived class just like it would use a class that is not part of an inheritance hierarchy. As you can see in Listing 6.4, the graph program's application class creates objects from the two derived classes just as it would any other class.

A program using an object created from a derived class can call methods from three sources:

- Methods that are inherited from base classes in the inheritance hierarchy.
- Methods that override base class methods.
- New methods that have been added to the derived class.

A program calls methods of derived class objects exactly in the same way it calls any other method.

Typecasting to Base Classes

One of the useful things you can do with objects created from classes in the same inheritance hierarchy is typecast those objects so that they can be referenced as if they were created from their base class. For example, the following statements are legal:

```
salesGraph theGraph = (salesGraph) new barGraph (theData);
stackedGraph theStackedGraph = new stackedGraph (theData);
theGraph = (salesGraph) theStackedGraph;
```

Why would you want to do this? So you can refer to related objects in a generic way. For example, it makes it possible to keep objects created from different classes in the same data structure. You will see examples of doing so when we talk about arrays of objects in Chapter 8.

Listing 6.4   graphApp.java

```java
import java.io.*;
import java.lang.*;
import java.util.*;
import text.*;

public class graphApp
{
    private graphData theData;
    private barGraph theBarGraph;
    private stackedGraph theStackedGraph;
    public void Run()
    {
        SystemInput sysIn = new SystemInput();
        int S1Q1 = sysIn.readInt ("Salesperson 1, Quarter 1:");
        int S1Q2 = sysIn.readInt ("Salesperson 1, Quarter 2:");
        int S1Q3 = sysIn.readInt ("Salesperson 1, Quarter 3:");
        int S1Q4 = sysIn.readInt ("Salesperson 1, Quarter 4:");
        int S2Q1 = sysIn.readInt ("Salesperson 2, Quarter 1:");
        int S2Q2 = sysIn.readInt ("Salesperson 2, Quarter 2:");
        int S2Q3 = sysIn.readInt ("Salesperson 2, Quarter 3:");
        int S2Q4 = sysIn.readInt ("Salesperson 2, Quarter 4:");
        int S3Q1 = sysIn.readInt ("Salesperson 3, Quarter 1:");
        int S3Q2 = sysIn.readInt ("Salesperson 3, Quarter 2:");
        int S3Q3 = sysIn.readInt ("Salesperson 3, Quarter 3:");
        int S3Q4 = sysIn.readInt ("Salesperson 3,q Quarter 4:");

        theData = new graphData(S1Q1,S1Q2,S1Q3,S1Q4,S2Q1,S2Q2,S2Q3,S2Q4,
            S3Q1,S3Q2,S3Q3,S3Q4);
        theBarGraph = new barGraph(theData);
        theStackedGraph = new stackedGraph (theData);
        theBarGraph.paint();
        theStackedGraph.paint();
    }

    public static void main (String args[])
    {
        graphApp theApp = new graphApp();
        theApp.Run();
    }
}
```

In addition, it allows you to handle an object created from any class as an object of class `Object` (the ultimate class from which all Java objects inherit). Although every Java object must have a class, when you don't know precisely what class a method will need to handle, you can use the `Object` class because every class has `Object` as an ancestor. An example of this usage can be found in Chapter 7.

Interfaces

A Java class can extend exactly one base class. Java doesn't support *multiple inheritance* (deriving a class from more than one base class), but you can achieve the same result by using a Java interface.

An *interface* is a specification of methods that a class will implement and/or variables that a class will use. An interface looks like a class without any data and with only abstract methods. Alternatively, it may include variables but no methods, or it may include both variables and abstract methods. The major characteristic of an interface is that all its methods are abstract; none of the methods are implemented.

The biggest difference between using inheritance and using interfaces is that with inheritance, a derived class doesn't need to override every method declared in its parent class. Methods that are implemented in the base class can be used by a derived class—assuming they are appropriate to the derived class—without including them in the derived class's declaration. An interface, however, has no implementations of its methods. A class that implements an interface must therefore override every method in the interface that it intends to use.

The declaration of an interface looks much like a class declaration. However, the word `class` is replaced with `interface`:

```
interface interfaceName
{
    // variables declarations
    // abstract methods
}
```

For example, the interface that we will be using in Chapter 7 to identify and process a click on a button has nothing but one abstract method

```
interface ActionListener
{
    public void actionPerformed (ActionEvent);
}
```

An implementation of this method accepts one input parameter: an object describing the action that a user has taken (in this case, a mouse click in a button).

When it needs to use the variables and/or methods described by an interface, a class *implements* the interface by including the keyword `implements` followed by the name of the interface on the line that names the class. For example, a class to handle a mouse click might begin as follows:

```
class mouseProcessor implements ActionListener
```

Although a class can only extend one class (have one base class), it can implement any number of interfaces. You will see extensive uses of interfaces beginning in Chapter 7.

Summary

Inheritance provides a mechanism for allowing similar classes to share variables and functions in a hierarchical manner. Inheritance is appropriate when the classes are related by the "is a" relationship: A derived class "is a" more specific instance of a base class.

Derived classes inherit variables and methods from classes above them in the inheritance hierarchy (base classes). Objects created from derived classes call inherited methods and access inherited variables just like methods and variables that are part of the derived class itself.

Not everything can be inherited. In particular, constructors and destructors aren't inherited. However, when an object is created from a derived class, the base class constructor can be called by using the keyword `super`.

Polymorphism provides a way to allow objects created from different classes to respond to the same message in different ways. Polymorphic methods must have the same signature. This is in direct contrast to method overloading, in which methods that are part of the same class have different signatures.

Base classes from which no objects can be created are known as abstract base classes. An abstract base class may contain one or more abstract methods, methods that exist as a signature only, without any implementation. A class that contains an abstract method becomes an abstract class.

Interfaces are Java's way of supporting multiple inheritance. While a derived class inherits variables, implemented methods, and abstract methods from its base class, interfaces have no implemented methods. A class that implements an interface must therefore override every method in the interface that it intends to use.

Exercises

1. Create a class hierarchy that describes a company's employees. The hierarchy should include an employee's name, social security number, and pay rate. There are three types of employees, each of which is paid in a different way:

    *   Hourly employees: An employee's pay rate is expressed as dollars per hour. Weekly gross pay is computed by multiplying hours worked times pay rate. Hours over 40 are paid as time-and-a-half.
    *   Commissioned employee: A commissioned employee's pay rate is expressed as a percentage of sales made in a given week. Weekly gross pay is computed by multiplying the commission rate by total sales made.
    *   Salaried employee: A salaried employee's pay rate is expressed as the total salary paid in a year. Weekly gross pay is computed by dividing the yearly salary by 52.

    Write a program that lets the user enter the type of employee. Then, based on the type of employee, collect the rest of the data needed to determine the person's weekly gross pay. Create an object for that employee from an appropriate derived class. Finish by calling a polymorphic method that computes and returns the gross pay. Display the gross pay for the user.

2. Write a program for a land development company. The land sold by the company comes in lots that may be rectangular, square, or triangular (a rectangle slanted to the side). The program should compute the area of a lot. To support this program, design an inheritance hierarchy for the lots, including polymorphic methods that perform the computations. The program should let a user enter the shape of a lot and the lot's dimensions. Then it should display the area for the user. (*Hint:* Which dimensions are required depend on the shape of the lot.)

3. Write a program for a company that produces food storage containers. The containers come in three shapes: cylindrical, half circle (bowl-shaped), and rectangular. (You may assume that the volume of a bowl is half the volume of a sphere with the same diameter.) The program should compute the volume of a container. To support this program, design an inheritance hierarchy for the containers, including polymorphic methods that perform the computations. The program should let a user enter the shape of the container and then ask the user for the rest of the data needed to perform the computations.

4. Write a program that produces human names in a variety of formats. The program should allow a user to enter the format he or she wants and then request the remaining data needed. Output should be the name in the requested format as a single string. The program should support the following formats (FI = first initial; MI = middle initial):

    - *Last_name, First_name*
    - *Last_name, First_name MI*
    - *First_name Last_name*
    - *First_name MI Last_name*
    - *Last_name, FI MI*
    - *FI MI Last_name*

    Include an inheritance hierarchy that contains a polymorphic method to format the name string. It is up to you to decide how many derived classes you will need.

5. Write a program for a ticket agency that computes the price of a ticket and then prints the ticket on the screen. Output should include the price of the ticket (to be given orally to the purchaser over the telephone) and the printed ticket. The rules for the various types of tickets are as follows:

    - Rock concerts: The ticket price is the face value of the ticket plus a 5 percent service charge, up to a maximum of $7.50. The printed ticket includes the date and location of the concert, the name of the performer, the seat number, and the price of the ticket.
    - Farm team baseball games: The ticket price is the face value of the ticket. (There is no service charge.) The printed ticket includes the

date of the game, the name of the opposing team, and the stadium section (seats are first come, first served within a section).

- Symphony concerts: The ticket price is the face value of the ticket plus a $3.00 service charge. The printed ticket includes the date and location of the concert along with the seat number.

Include an inheritance hierarchy for the tickets. Classes should include polymorphic methods for computing the ticket price and printing the tickets.

6. Implement the class hierarchy for the inventory items of a video store, using the video store classes described in this chapter as a guide to identify base and derived classes and the attributes that need to be stored. Your classes should include constructors to initialize objects and get and set methods for all variables. It is up to you to decide the classes in which specific methods should be implements. Write an application that demonstrates that you can create objects from the derived classes and that your methods work. Use the `SystemInput` class to allow the user to gather data for the objects; display your output in the console window.

7. The Person class that you have been developing can be used as the base class for a retail store's Employee and Customer classes. For this exercise, extend the Person class to an Employee class. Add the following:

- An hourly wage variable (`double`)
- A variable for the number of hours worked per week (`float`)
- Accessor and mutator methods for the new variables.
- A method to compute the worker's typical weekly gross pay.

Also modify the constructor to accommodate the new variables. Also extend the Person class to a Customer class. Add the following:

- The customer's credit card number (`String`)
- The expiration date of the credit card number (MM/YY as a `String`)
- Accessor and mutator methods for the new variables.

Then, write an application class to demonstrate that you can create objects from the derived classes and that their methods work properly.

7

Event-Driven Programming and the Graphic User Interface

OBJECTIVES

In this chapter you will learn about:
- The principles of event-driven programming and how they affect the structure of a program.
- The Java library classes that support a graphic user interface.
- Writing programs that draw windows and simple graphic shapes.

Given the demands of today's computer users, to be well accepted application programs need to have a graphic user interface (GUI). Prior to the introduction of Java, one of the greatest problems with GUI programming was that each operating system had its own proprietary routines—knon as Application Program Interfaces, or APIs—that supported the interface elements (for example, windows and menus). Not only was the look-and-feel of an application different, but the way in which a programmer wrote programs for each environment was not the same. Although the programs may have been written in the same language (usually Pascal, C, or C++), the code that provided windows, menus, and other GUI features was radically different.

Java to a large extent eliminates the problem by providing a package of classes that support a GUI under any operating system that has a Java virtual machine. The virtual machine translates the Java bytecodes into references to the operating system's proprietary GUI toolbox. Therefore, Java programs will look a little different among OS platforms, but the code is compatible.

The drawback to Java's solution is that the GUI classes must take a "lowest common denominator" approach. The GUI elements that you can use in a Java program are those that are found in all GUIs that support Java virtual machines.

Java GUI classes are part of the AWT (Abstract Windowing Toolkit) and are found in the package `java.awt`. In some cases, you can create objects directly from AWT classes. In other cases—in particular, windows—you derive your own class from an AWT class, adding the functionality of the GUI element to your own objects.

Note At the time this book was written, a number of software developers were working on alternatives to AWT. However, so far none of them translate across platforms as well.

In this chapter, you will be introduced to a number of very important concepts. You will learn what it means for a program to be event-driven and how that affects the structure of a program. You will also learn to create windows and many elements that you can place on windows, including buttons, canvases, and panels. In addition, you will learn to draw and fill simple graphic shapes and to draw text in a window. As we explore further aspects of Java in later chapters, we will extend the elements of a GUI that you can use.

What It Means to Be Event-Driven

Programming a GUI means that you must structure your program in a very specific way, primarily because GUI programs are *event-driven*. This means that the program waits for something to happen, identifies what occurred, and then takes action based on what occurred. Events include user actions such as clicking a button with the mouse, pressing a key on the keyboard, or making a choice from a menu.

To some extent, programs that use text menus are event-driven. The program waits for the user to enter a number that represents a menu choice. Then the program uses a `switch` construct to identify which menu option was chosen. However, a program of this type responds to only one event: the press of the Enter key signaling that a value for a menu choice has been entered. A true event-driven program responds to a much wider range of events, including mouse events, disk events, and so on.

Writing program code to detect the occurrence of an event is a complicated process. In practice, events are actually detected by the operating system, which places events intended for application programs in a *queue* (a waiting list accessed in first in, first out order). A program then issues a call to an operating system routine that gives the program the next event.

If you were writing a GUI application from scratch, without the benefit of a Java virtual machine, the main structure in your program would be an "event loop," a loop that retrieved the next event from the queue and then figured out what to do based on the type of event. However, the routines that retrieve events are operating system-specific. That functionality is therefore handled by the Java virtual machine, which retrieves the event and passes it to the Java program.

When an event occurs, the Java virtual machine creates an object from a subclass of the `EventObject` class that corresponds to the type of event. At that point, the job of a Java program is to provide code that watches, or "listens," for events of specific types and then takes the necessary action to respond to those events. For example, if the user performed an action that should close a window, then the program needs to perform that close. The programmer must include code that instructs the window to listen for the type of event object that the virtual machine creates when a user does something that should close a window.

To this point, the Java programs you have written have been relatively self-contained. You can look at a program and trace its execution by hand because all the code you need (with the exception of a few utility routines from class libraries) is included. However, when you first look at an event-driven GUI program, the code will probably seem incomplete. You won't be able to trace the program flow by hand; code to detect events and code to call the methods that identify and handle events won't be present. (Your program will include methods to identify and handle events, but it won't contain direct calls to those methods.) This is because that functionality is built into the Java virtual machine and into classes that are part of Java's AWT. To make matters worse, the code in an event-driven program rarely executes sequentially.

To write event-driven programs, you must be familiar with how classes in the AWT are related, what methods they provide, and which of those methods you need to override in your own classes. You must also know which classes can be used to create objects and which classes must be subclassed. In addition, you must know which events specific parts of the GUI can listen for and how to identify and process those events.

The Structure of a GUI Program

A Java program that uses a GUI begins with a top-level window that is created from a subclass of the AWT class `Frame`. This class replaces the application class that we have been using in programs that use console I/O. Its `main` method creates an object of the class. As a first example, let's look at a very simple program that produces the window in Figure 7.1.

Figure 7.1   A simple Java window

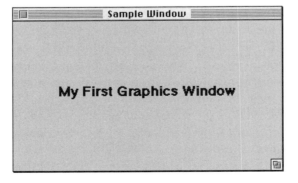

The window has the characteristics of any top-level window. If you are running under Windows, it will have a control menu, minimize box, maximize box, and close box. Under the Macintosh OS (System 7), which is what you see in Figure 7.1, it has a close box and a grow box; Mac OS 8 also adds a rollup box. The controls you will see if you are working in a UNIX environment depend on the particular UNIX GUI you are using. However, you will have at least a close box.

If you run the program that produces this window, you will discover that the only control that is active is the close box. To keep the program short and relatively simple, the only event to which the program responds is a single click in that close box. The additional controls are provided by the AWT `Frame` class. It is up to the programmer, however, to provide code that identifies and processes events involving those controls.

The source code for the simple window program can be found in Listing 7.1. At first glance, it may not look like an executable program. However, because of the functionality inherited from `Frame` and the event trapping provided by the Java virtual machine, the program is complete and will run as written. Here's how it works:

Object

addXXX
Listener

Component

paint

Component

show

- The Java virtual machine executes the `main` method.
- The `main` method creates an object of its own class.
- The Java virtual machine runs the class's constructor. In this example, the constructor gives the window a title. (If you don't do this, the window's title will be "Untitled.")
- The Java virtual machine returns to the `main` method and creates an object from the `windowListener` class, which it adds to the window (`addWindowListener`). The window is now able to listen and respond to a click in its close box. Notice that the code in the `windowListener` class implements a method named `windowClosing`. The Java virtual machine will call this method when the user does something that according to the platform's user interface guidelines should close the window (for example, click the window's close box).
- The `main` method resizes the window.
- The Java virtual machine then runs the `show` method, which draws the window. The call to `show` eventually invokes a call to the `paint` method, which in this example displays a line of formatted text in the middle of the window.

Listing 7.1   simpleWindow.java

```java
import java.awt.*;
import java.io.*;
import java.lang.*;
import java.awt.event.*;

public class simpleWindow extends Frame
{
    private static final String theText = "My First Graphics Window";

    public simpleWindow ()
        { setTitle ("Sample Window"); }

    public void paint (Graphics graphObject)
    {
        Dimension theSize = size(); // dimensions of window
        // Create a new font object
        Font theFont = new Font ("Helvetica",Font.BOLD,18);
        // Get information about the font, including its size
        FontMetrics theFontMetrics = graphObject.getFontMetrics (theFont);
        // Find out width, in pixels, of text using the chosen font
        int textWidth = theFontMetrics.stringWidth (theText);
        // Compute number of pixels on one edge of text when text is centered
        int edge = (theSize.width - textWidth)/2;
        // Use the font object in the window
        graphObject.setFont (theFont);
        // Draw the text
        graphObject.drawString (theText,edge,100);
    }

    static public void main (String args[])
    {
        simpleWindow theWindow = new simpleWindow();
        // add a windowListener object to the main window
        theWindow.addWindowListener (new windowListener());
        theWindow.setSize (350,200);
        theWindow.show();
    }
}

class windowListener extends WindowAdapter
{
    public void windowClosing (WindowEvent theEvent)
    {
        System.exit(0);
    }
}
```

- At this point, the program sits back to wait for an event. Nothing happens until the user clicks in the close box. Then, the Java virtual machine creates an object from the `WindowEvent` class. It passes that event object to the object in which the event occurred (in this example, the program's main window), calling the appropriate listener method to handle the event (`windowClosing`). Note that the object in which the event occurred must be listening for the event. If it isn't, the Java virtual machine won't be able to pass on the event object.
- The listener method calls `System.exit(0)` to quit the program and the Java virtual machine.

Note

If you are working with the Metrowerks CodeWarrior development environment on the Macintosh, you will need to replace the `System.exit(0)` with

```
Window theWindow = (Window) theEvent.getSource();
theWindow.dispose();
```

You should make that substitution throughout all the code in this book. This is because quitting a CodeWarrior Java program doesn't cause the Macintosh Java virtual machine to stop running and return to the operating system, as it does with most other Java development environments.

Warning

Be sure that you include code to close an application's main window in your Java program. If you don't, you will need to use an operating system key sequence to quit the program. For example, under Windows 95 or NT, you'll need to press CTRL-ALT-DEL; under the Macintosh OS, you'll need to press CMD-OPTION-ESC.

The Frame Hierarchy

Before we explore further GUI programming techniques, let's stop for a moment and take a look at the hierarchy of classes that provides windows and window surfaces onto which a Java program can draw and/or place elements. The basic window hierarchy is summarized in Figure 7.2.

Figure 7.2   The basic Java window hierarchy

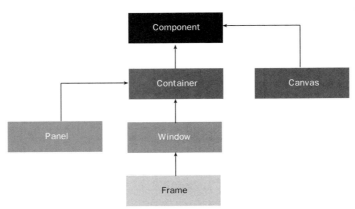

At the top of the hierarchy is the **Component** class. A *component* is a single graphic element in a Java program. A window is a component, but so is a menu, a button, and a check box. The **Component** class contains the original **handleEvent** and **paint** methods, which classes derived from it override.

The **Container** class is derived directly from **Component**. A *container* is a component, such as a window, that can contain other components. This class adds several important methods to those it inherits from its base class, including methods to add and remove components from the container, to determine the size of the container, and to deliver an event to one of the container's components.

The **Window** class is a generic window, without title bar or other controls. Although you might use it directly to implement a popup window, its most common use is as the base class for **Frame**, which provides the typical top-level window.

A Java program can place elements directly into a frame, but doing so makes organizing the frame somewhat awkward. Therefore, we typically place control such as buttons in *panels*. Because a panel can contain other components, its class is derived from **Container**. Graphic elements are drawn onto *canvases*. Canvases are drawing surfaces, not containers, and cannot contain other components; therefore, the class is derived directly from **Component**. Once a Java program creates the necessary panels and canvases, they are added as components to a frame.

Event Handling

As you saw in the simple window example, a part of a Java interface that wants to respond to events sets itself up as a listener by attaching to itself one or more objects created from listener classes. Each listener object has methods containing code to process and handle the events to which its owner object should respond.

Types of Events

There are 14 types of events in Java's event hierarchy (see Figure 7.3). The events that we will use in program throughout the rest of this book include:

Figure 7.3   The event hierarchy

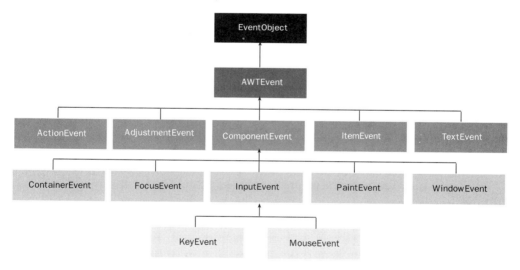

- Action events: Action events are triggered by a number of different user actions, including clicking a button with the mouse, double-clicking an item in a list, and making a selection from a menu.
- Adjustment events: Currently, only scroll bars trigger adjustment events.

- Component events: Component events handle generic component activities, such as moving, resizing, hiding, and showing the components. For example, moving or resizing a window triggers a component event.
- Item events: Item events are triggered when a user makes a change in a component such as a check box, radio button, or popup menu.
- Mouse events: A mouse event occurs whenever the user presses or releases the mouse button or when the user moves the mouse pointer into or out of a component.
- Window events: A window event occurs when a user opens, closes, maximizes, or minimizes a window.

Action, adjustment, item, and text events are known as *semantic events* because they are triggered by a sequence of actions, rather than a single low-level action. For example, mouse events track low-level mouse movements, such as moving the mouse button over a component, pressing the mouse button, releasing the mouse button, and moving the mouse button away from the component. In contrast, an action event in a button includes moving the mouse over the button, pressing the mouse button, and releasing the mouse button. (You need to press and release the mouse button to generate a click.)

Like other classes, event classes have methods your program can use. One that you will use frequently is `getSource`, a method available to all event classes that returns a reference to the object posting the event (class `Object`). You will typically typecast the return type to a specific type of object. For example, assuming that the event object is stored in `theEvent`, to obtain a reference to a window posting a closing event, a program would use:

Event-
Object

getSource

```
Window theWindow = (Window) theEvent.getSource();
```

You can then take whatever actions on the window are needed (in particular, closing it). You will see other event methods throughout this book as we look at handling events for specific GUI components.

Whenever the Java virtual machine receives an event from the operating system's event queue, it creates an object from the appropriate event class and then passes that object to a listener object method, which then acts to handle the event.

Creating and Registering Listener Objects

Listener objects are created from classes that implement the listener interfaces. As you can see in Figure 7.4, there are 11 listener interfaces, all of which are derived from the generic `EventListener`. These interfaces are stored in `java.awt.event.*`, which you must import into your source code when you are working with an event-driven program.

Figure 7.4   The listener interface hierarchy

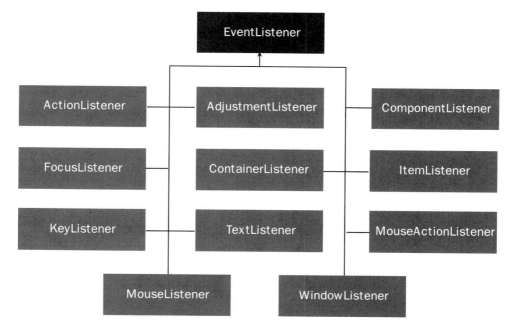

Event-
Listener

addXXX-
Listener

To attach a listener object to the object that will be listening for events, you *register* the listener, using the listening object's registration method, all of which are named using the format `addXXXListener`, where XXX is the type of listener being registered. Each registration method takes a listener object as an input parameter.

For example, to add a listener to the simple window, you use the `addWindowListener` method, which requires an object of some class that implements the `WindowListener` interface as input. Therefore, assuming that we have a class that implements `WindowListener` named `windowListener`, we can register the listener with:

```
theWindow.addWindowListener (new windowListener());
```

The registration methods for the GUI elements that we will be using in this book can be found in Table 7.5.

Table 7.5   Listener registration methods used in this book

GUI Element	Registration Method(s)
Applet	void addMouseListener (MouseListener)
Button	void addActionListener (ActionListener)
Checkbox	void addItemListener (ItemListener)
Choice	void addItemListener (ItemListener)
Component	void addComponentListener (ComponentListener)
List	void addItemListener (ItemListener)[a] void addActionListen (ActionListener)[b]
MenuItem	void addActionListener (ActionListener)
Scrollbar	void addAdjustmentListener (AdjustmentListener)
TextField	void addActionListener (ActionListener)
Window	void addWindowListener (WindowListener)

a. Used to detect a change in the selected item in a list.
b. Used to detect a double-click in a list

Listener Methods

Each listener interface contains methods that the Java virtual machine calls when an event occurs. In Table 7.6, for example, you can see the listener methods that are used in programs throughout this book. (As you become more proficient with Java, you want to experiment with other listener interfaces and methods, such as those in Table 7.7.)

Table 7.6   Listener methods used in this book

Interface	Method(s)
ActionListener	void actionPerformed (ActionEvent)
AdjustmentListener	void adjustmentValueChanged (AdjustmentEvent)
ComponentListener	void componentResized (ComponentEvent) void componentMoved (ComponentEvent)
ItemListener	void itemStateChanged (ComponentEvent)
MouseListener	void mousePressed (MouseEvent)
WindowListener	void windowClosing (WindowEvent) void windowClosed (WindowEvent)

Table 7.7   Additional listener methods

Interface	Method(s)
ComponentListener	void componentShown (ComponentEvent) void componentHidden (ComponentEvent)
MouseListener	void mouseClicked (MouseEvent) void mousePressed (MouseEvent) void mouseReleased (MouseEvent) void mouseEntered (MouseEvent) void mouseExited (MouseEvent)
MouseMotionListener	void mouseDragged (MouseEvent) void mouseMoved (MouseEvent)
TextListener	void textValueChanged (TextEvent)
MouseListener	void mouseClicked (MouseEvent) void mouseReleased (MouseEvent) void mouseEntered (MouseEvent) void mouseExited (MouseEvent)
WindowListener	void windowActivated (WindowEvent) void windowDeactivated (WindowEvent) void windowOpened (WindowEvent) void windowIconified (WindowEvent) void windowDeiconified (WindowEvent)

What can you put in the implementation of a listener method? Anything your program needs to do when the associated event occurs. For example, assume that you place an OK button on a window. Then you register an action listener for that button. When the user clicks on the button, the Java virtual machine generates an actionEvent object and passes it the listener object's `actionPerformed` method, which must contain the code to perform whatever the program should do when the button is clicked. In the case of the OK button, the program probably collects any information it needs from components in the window and then closes the window.

Adapters

One of the problems with interfaces is that because none of their methods have bodies, when you implement an interface you must implement every one of the interface's methods. This becomes rather tedious, for example, if you are only interested in trapping a window closing event and don't want to be bothered with all the other window listener methods.

To make life easier, Java includes *adapters*, listener classes that have an empty implementation for each method. Your program can then extend these classes and override only those methods you really need. For example, if you look at Listing 7.1, you'll see that the listener extends `WindowAdapter`, rather than implementing the `WindowListener` interface directly. (The adapter classes can be found in Table 7.8.)

Table 7.8   Adapter classes

Adapter	Interface
ComponentAdapter	ComponentListener
ContainerAdapter	ContainerListener
FocusAdapter	FocusListener
KeyAdapter	KeyListener
MouseAdapter	MouseListener
MouseMotionAdapter	MouseMotionListener
WindowAdapter	WindowListener

Note

The event-handling model about which you have been reading is new to Java 1.1. The older event model is still supported in version 1.1, but will be phased out in future releases. If you come across Java programs with `handleEvent` and `action` methods instead of listeners, then you are looking at the older event model.

Inner Classes

The biggest problem with implement a listener class is that it doesn't have access to the variables of the object to which it is attached. You could write a constructor for a listener into which you passed any data the listener would need. However, there is a much easier way: inner classes. An *inner class* is a class that is defined within a method of another class.

To see how this works, we'll look at two new versions of the simple window program. The first places the window listener class inside the program's `main` method, where an object of that listener class is attached to the window (see Listing 7.2). The only difference between this program and the original in Listing 7.1 would appear to be the location of the listener class. However, because the listener class is within the `simpleWindow` class, it now has access to any variables that are global to the class. In this example, the only variable that meets that criterion is `theText`, which the listener class doesn't need to use.

Listing 7.2 contains what is known as a *named inner class*, an inner class that has a name like any other class. However, if an inner class is only going to be used once, usually as a listener, then it isn't necessary to give it a name. You can use an *anonymous inner class* instead.

As an example, look closely at Listing 7.3. The entire window listener class is declared as part of the statement that creates an object from the class. The general syntax is:

```
theObject.addXXXListener (new Adapter/Interface ()
{
    // body of listener goes here
} );
```

Notice that the declaration ends with a right parenthesis and semicolon. The parenthesis closes the parameter list of the `addXXXListener` call; the semicolon ends the statement.

Given that you have three alternative places to declare listener classes, which should you use? You can use the following guidelines to help you make your choice:

- If the listener is generic—in other words, it can be resized in other programs—then it makes sense to make it a separate class in its own file.

Listing 7.2   The simple window program with a named inner class

```java
import java.awt.*;
import java.io.*;
import java.lang.*;
import java.awt.event.*;

public class simpleWindow extends Frame
{
    private static final String theText = "My First Graphics Window";

    public simpleWindow ()
    {
        setTitle ("Sample Window");
    }

    public void paint (Graphics graphObject)
    {
        Dimension theSize = size(); // dimensions of window
        // Create a new font object
        Font theFont = new Font ("Helvetica",Font.BOLD,18);
        // Get information about the font, including its size
        FontMetrics theFontMetrics = graphObject.getFontMetrics (theFont);
        // Find out width, in pixels, of text using the chosen font
        int textWidth = theFontMetrics.stringWidth (theText);
        // Compute number of pixels on one edge of text when text is centered
        int edge = (theSize.width - textWidth)/2;
        // Use the font object in the window
        graphObject.setFont (theFont);
        // Draw the text
        graphObject.drawString (theText,edge,100);
    }

    static public void main (String args[])
    {

    // The named inner class
    class windowListener extends WindowAdapter
    {
        public void windowClosing (WindowEvent theEvent)
            { System.exit(0);}
    }

        simpleWindow theWindow = new simpleWindow();
        theWindow.addWindowListener (new windowListener());
        theWindow.setSize (350,200);
        theWindow.show();
    }
}
```

Listing 7.3   The simple window program with an anonymous inner class

```java
import java.awt.*;
import java.io.*;
import java.lang.*;
import java.awt.event.*;

public class simpleWindow extends Frame
{
    private static final String theText = "My First Graphics Window";

    public simpleWindow ()
    {
        setTitle ("Sample Window");
    }

    public void paint (Graphics graphObject)
    {
        Dimension theSize = getSize(); // dimensions of window
        // Create a new font object
        Font theFont = new Font ("Helvetica",Font.BOLD,18);
        // Get information about the font, including its size
        FontMetrics theFontMetrics = graphObject.getFontMetrics (theFont);
        // Find out width, in pixels, of text using the chosen font
        int textWidth = theFontMetrics.stringWidth (theText);
        // Compute number of pixels on one edge of text when text is centered
        int edge = (theSize.width - textWidth)/2;
        // Use the font object in the window
        graphObject.setFont (theFont);
        // Draw the text
        graphObject.drawString (theText,edge,100);
    }

    static public void main (String args[])
    {
        simpleWindow theWindow = new simpleWindow();
        // The anonymous innser class
        theWindow.addWindowListener (new WindowAdapter()
        {
            public void windowClosing (WindowEvent theEvent)
            {
                System.exit(0);
            }
        } );
        theWindow.setSize (350,200);
        theWindow.show();
    }
}
```

- If the listener's code is going to change frequently, then it is easier to find the listener if it is a separate class.

- If the listener is specific to a given program but can be used more than once, then it is most efficient to make it a named inner class.

- If the listener is specific to a given program and is only going to be used once, then an anonymous inner class works well. This also has the advantage of placing event-handling code near the creation of the object that is using the code.

The GUI Version of the Graphing Program

As you were promised in Chapter 6, in this chapter we will prepare a graphic version of the graphing program. A program run of the GUI version begins like the text-based version of the program, where the user enters the data to be graphed. The program then displays a window with two buttons (see Figure 7.5). When the user clicks on the Bar Graph button, the program prepares and displays the data in bar graph format (Figure 7.6). Clicking the Stacked Bar Graph button produces the stacked bar graph (Figure 7.7). The user can switch between the two graphs at any time by clicking the appropriate button.

The GUI version of the program uses the same five classes as the text-based version: the three classes in the graph hierarchy (`salesGraph`, `barGraph`, and `stackedGraph`), the `graphData` class for handling the values to be graphed, and the `graphApp` class for controlling the overall actions of the program. The `graphData` class is unmodified from the original version of the program and won't be duplicated in this chapter. However, the classes in the graph hierarchy and the application class have been significantly modified and you will see them, and the GUI elements they produce, throughout this chapter.

The Top-Level Window

Like any stand-alone GUI Java program, the graphing program begins with a class derived from `Frame`. Although this class isn't truly an application object, as you can see in Listing 7.4 it has retained the name `graphApp` for consistency. (At this point, there may be much in Listing 7.4 that you don't understand. Don't worry: You'll understand the purpose of every line of code by the end of this chapter.)

Figure 7.5   The initial graphing-program window

The **graphApp** class has two methods:

- A constructor that creates a system input window, gathers data needed from the user, creates a **graphData** object for storing the data, and sets the window's title. The constructor also adds all components to the window that should be visible when the window is first displayed. You will be introduced to these components (a panel and two buttons on that panel) shortly. In addition, the constructor contains anonymous inner classes for handling a window closing event and clicks in the window's two buttons.

- A **main** method to create the window, resize it, and display it.

Figure 7.6   The bar graph

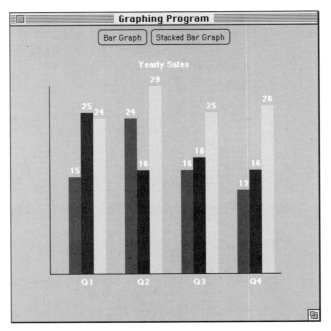

Layout Managers

Although you can place components anywhere in a Java container, you can make positioning easier and more precise by using a *layout manager*, an object that governs the placement of components in a container. There are five layout manager classes:

- FlowLayout (the default for applets): When a container has a flow layout, components are placed horizontally across the container, as many as will fit on one line. The components wrap to additional lines as they are added. If you resize the container, Java reflows the components so that they flow across the entire width of the container. By default, if the width of the components is less than the width of the container, the components will be centered in the container.

- BorderLayout (the default for application windows): A border layout divides the container into five regions (see Figure 7.8). You

Figure 7.7   The stacked bar graph

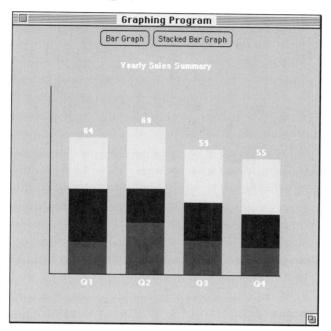

place a component by specifying the region in which it should be located. When the window is resized, the edge regions remain the same size, but the area of the Center region changes.

- GridLayout: A grid layout divides the container into equal-sized cells. When you create the layout, you specify the number of columns and rows. As the window is resized, the cells are resized to maintain the same number of columns and rows at all times.
- CardLayout: A card layout is used to create tabbed properties boxes, which are prevalent in the Windows 95 operating system.
- GridBagLayout: A grid bag layout is made up of small cells that can be combined in any way to make regions of varying sizes.

Specifying a Layout

The graphing program's top-level window uses a border layout. The panel containing the buttons is placed in the North region. A canvas on which a graph is drawn is placed in the South region.

Listing 7.4   graphApp.java (GUI version)

```java
import java.io.*;
import java.lang.*;
import java.util.*;
import java.awt.*;
import text.*;
import java.awt.event.*;

public class graphApp extends Frame
{
    private graphData theData;
    private barGraph theBarGraph;
    private stackedGraph theStackedGraph;
    private salesGraph currentCanvas = null;
    private graphApp thisApp;

    public graphApp()
    {
        thisApp = this; // need this to add things inside inner classes

        addWindowListener (new WindowAdapter () // handle click in close box
        {
            public void windowClosing (WindowEvent theEvent)
            {
                System.exit(0);
            }
        } );

        SystemInput sysIn = new SystemInput();
        int S1Q1 = sysIn.readInt ("Salesperson 1, Quarter 1:");
        int S1Q2 = sysIn.readInt ("Salesperson 1, Quarter 2:");
        int S1Q3 = sysIn.readInt ("Salesperson 1, Quarter 3:");
        int S1Q4 = sysIn.readInt ("Salesperson 1, Quarter 4:");
        int S2Q1 = sysIn.readInt ("Salesperson 2, Quarter 1:");
        int S2Q2 = sysIn.readInt ("Salesperson 2, Quarter 2:");
        int S2Q3 = sysIn.readInt ("Salesperson 2, Quarter 3:");
        int S2Q4 = sysIn.readInt ("Salesperson 2, Quarter 4:");
        int S3Q1 = sysIn.readInt ("Salesperson 3, Quarter 1:");
        int S3Q2 = sysIn.readInt ("Salesperson 3, Quarter 2:");
        int S3Q3 = sysIn.readInt ("Salesperson 3, Quarter 3:");
        int S3Q4 = sysIn.readInt ("Salesperson 3, Quarter 4:");

        theData = new graphData(S1Q1,S1Q2,S1Q3,S1Q4,S2Q1,S2Q2,S2Q3,S2Q4,
            S3Q1,S3Q2,S3Q3,S3Q4);
```

Continued next page

Listing 7.4(Continued)   graphApp.java (GUI version)

```java
        setTitle ("Graphing Program");
        setLayout (new BorderLayout());
        Panel thePanel = new Panel();
        thePanel.setLayout (new FlowLayout());

        Button theButton = new Button ("Bar Graph");
        // handle click on Bar Graph button
        theButton.addActionListener (new ActionListener ()
        {
            public void actionPerformed (ActionEvent theEvent)
            {
                if (currentCanvas != null)
                    thisApp.remove (currentCanvas); // remove existing graph
                theBarGraph = new barGraph (theData);
                // typecast to base class pointer
                currentCanvas = (salesGraph) theBarGraph;
                thisApp.add ("Center",theBarGraph);
                thisApp.show();
            }
        } );
        thePanel.add (theButton);

        theButton = new Button ("Stacked Bar Graph");
        // handle click on Stacked Bar Graph button
        theButton.addActionListener (new ActionListener ()
        {
            public void actionPerformed (ActionEvent theEvent)
            {
                if (currentCanvas != null)
                    thisApp.remove (currentCanvas); // remove existing graph
                theStackedGraph = new stackedGraph (theData);
                currentCanvas = (salesGraph) theStackedGraph;
                thisApp.add ("Center",theStackedGraph);
                thisApp.show();
            }
        } );
        thePanel.add (theButton);
        add ("North",thePanel);
    }

    public static void main (String args[])
    {
        Frame theWindow = new graphApp();
        theWindow.setSize (400,400);
        theWindow.show();
    }
}
```

Figure 7.8   The regions in a border layout

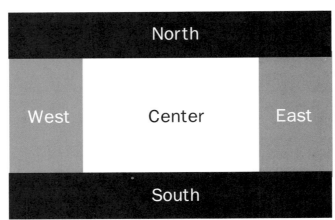

Before you can place something in a layout, you must create a layout manager object and install a reference to that object in the container to which it applies. (The exception is the default flow layout, which you can use without creating an object for it.)

To create a new layout manager object, you use the new operator, just as you would if you were creating an object from a class you wrote yourself:

```
new BorderLayout()
```

The reference to the new layout manager object can then be used as an input parameter to the setLayout method, which inserts the reference into a container object. You can save the reference to the layout manager object in a variable. However, unless you are using something complicated like a grid bag layout, it is unlikely that you will ever need to reference that object again directly. We therefore usually embed the creation of the layout manager object in the call to setLayout:

Container

setLayout

```
setLayout (new BorderLayout());
```

The syntax above doesn't contain a reference to the container object. This means that it must be used within a method of that container, exactly as it is found in the constructor for the graphApp class.

If you need to set the layout for an object that isn't the current object, you must indicate the object to which the new layout applies. For example, to set the layout for the panel that contains the graphing program's buttons, the program uses

```
thePanel.setLayout (new FlowLayout());
```

In this case, `thePanel` is a variable that holds a reference to the object whose layout is being set.

By default, components are centered in a flow layout. If you want to left or right align components, you specify the alignment when you create the flow layout object:

```
new FlowLayout (RIGHT) // right aligns components
new FlowLayout (LEFT) // left aligns components
```

Creating Panels

A panel is a container that holds user interface components, such as buttons, radio buttons, popup menus, or check boxes. You place the interface elements in the panel, and then place that panel into another container.

Although you can create a subclass from the `Panel` class, there is no requirement that you do so. The graphing program creates a panel for its buttons directly from the class:

```
Panel thePanel = new Panel();
```

Then, the program can give the panel its flow layout, using the syntax you saw in the preceding section. At this point, the panel is ready to receive its contents.

Adding Components to a Container: Buttons and Panels

There are two basic steps to adding a component to a container:

- Create an object for the component.
- Call the container's **add** method to add the component to the container's list of components.

Note

Typically a program adds components to a container before displaying the container for the first time. This does not preclude you from adding or removing components later in the program run. Keep in mind, however, that you will need to issue a call to a method that forces the program to redraw the window to which you have added or removed components (for example, **show**); otherwise, you won't see them.

Buttons are usually created directly from the Button class, without preparing a subclass. The constructor requires one parameter: a string containing the button's label.

The graphing program uses two button objects, one for a bar graph and one for a stacked bar graph:

```
Button barButton = new Button ("Bar Graph")
Button stackedButton = new Button ("Stacked Bar Graph")
```

As with any object, creating a new button returns a reference to the button object. You will need to save this reference to add a listener to the button and to add the button to a container.

Container

add

To a component to a container, you use the **add** method:

```
thePanel.add (barButton);
thePanel.add (stackedButton);
```

Notice that the **add** method takes one parameter: a reference to a component object.

Note

If you look closely at Listing 7.4, you'll notice that references to both buttons are stored in the same variable. You can get away with this when you don't need to reference a component directly once it has been set up. In the graph program, for example, once a button has been created, been given a listener, and added to a panel, the program never needs to reference it again. There is therefore no need to take up extra memory with a separate variable for each button.

Once the buttons have been added to the panel, the panel can be added to the graphApp object:

```
add (thePanel);
```

Because the panel is being added to the current object (the graphApp object), the program can call **add** without indicating a specific object. An equivalent syntax would be

```
this.add (thePanel);
```

because this always refers to the current object.

The `Container` class contains several overloaded implementations of the `add` method. You will therefore see additional syntax for that method throughout the rest of this book.

Note

Making Buttons Work

Creating button objects and adding them to a container isn't enough to make the buttons respond to a user's click. A program must give each button a listener object that provides code that is to be executed whenever a click occurs.

Clicking in a button generates an action event. The Java virtual machine creates an object from the `ActionEvent` class and passes it to the listener registered with the button that was clicked. The `ActionListener` interface has only one method—`actionPerformed`—that the virtual machines then calls. The action event object becomes an input parameter to this method.

Although every listener method takes an event object as an input parameter, there's no reason you have to use that object within listener method implementations.

Note

Action-
Listener

action-
Performed

The graph program uses two anonymous inner classes, one for each button. They have the following general structure:

```
theButton.addActionListener (new ActionListener ()
{
    public void actionPerformed (ActionEvent theEvent)
    {
        // Code to be executed when button is clicked.
        // goes here.
    }
} );
```

You will implement the `actionPerformed` method of the `Action-Listener` interface each time you want to provide code to be executed when a button is clicked. Keep in mind that you can implement the listener as a separate class, a named inner class, or an anonymous class, as long as you register the listener with its object.

Inner Classes and the this Variable

There is one important characteristic of inner classes that should be mentioned at this point. Although the inner classes have access to all their parent class's private variables (for example, `currentCanvas`), they are nonetheless distinct classes. If you attempt to use the keyword `this` within an inner class, it refers to an object of the listener, not to the listener's parent class. What makes this such a problem is that you often need to refer to the parent class object (for example, the graph window, an object of class `graphApp`) within the listener.

There are at least two ways around the problem. The most generic (and perhaps the most elegant), is to use a series of method calls that obtain the source of the event, the container of the event source, the container of the counter, and so on, until you reach the parent object. However, it is much easier simply to save a reference to the parent object in a variable that is global to its class, so that the reference is available to the inner class. The graph program, for example, defines a variable `thisApp` as a reference to an object of class `graphApp` and initializes it with

```
thisApp = this;
```

in the class's constructor. Then an inner class that needs to affect an object of its parent class can simply use the `thisApp` reference variable.

As an example, consider the listener class for the Bar Graph button:

```
theButton.addActionListener (new ActionListener ()
{
    public void actionPerformed (ActionEvent theEvent)
    {
        if (currentCanvas != null)
            thisApp.remove (currentCanvas);
        theBarGraph = new barGraph (theData);
        // typecast to base class pointer
        currentCanvas = (salesGraph) theBarGraph;
        thisApp.add ("Center",theBarGraph);
        thisApp.show();
    }
} );
```

Notice that the last two lines in the `actionPerformed` method add a component to the application window and then show the window. Both method calls require a reference to the application window object because they are contained within a method of another class.

Canvases

A canvas is a component in which you can draw text or graphic shapes. Because you draw in a canvas by overriding the `Canvas` class's `paint` method, you will always need to create a subclass of `Canvas`. As you can see in Listing 7.5, the graphing program derives its base graph class—`salesGraph`—from `Canvas`. The two classes that inherit from `salesGraph`—`barGraph` (Listing 7.6) and `stackedGraph` (Listing 7.7)—inherit all the functionality of the `Canvas` class through their parent. (Yes, there's a lot of code in these three listings that you don't understand yet. But don't panic; all will become clear, just as we've been explaining everything in Listing 7.4.)

Creating a Canvas

To create a canvas, you create an object from a class that has been derived from `Canvas`. The `graphApp` class maintains two private variables—`theBar-Graph` and `theStackedGraph`—to hold references to the canvases. Therefore, to create the canvases, the program uses the following two statements within its `action` method:

```
theBarGraph = new BarGraph (theData);
theStackedGraph = newStackedGraph (theData);
```

The `action` method then typecasts the reference to the new canvas to the base class `salesGraph`:

```
currentCanvas = (salesGraph) theBarGraph;
currentCanvas = (salesGraph) theStackedGraph;
```

The `currentCanvas` variable provides a common place for storing a reference to whichever canvas happens to be installed on the `graphApp` window at any time. (If `currentCanvas` has a value of `null`, then there is no canvas on the window.)

Adding a Canvas to a Container

Container

To add a canvas to a container, you use the container's `add` method, just as you would with any other component:

add

```
add ("Center",theBarGraph);
add ("Center",theStackedGraph);
```

Listing 7.5   The salesGraph base class

```java
public abstract class salesGraph extends Canvas
{
    protected static final int SPACER = 25;
    protected static final int EDGE = 50;
    protected int high_value;
    protected float scale_factor;
    protected graphData theData = new graphData();
    protected int canvasHeight, canvasWidth;
    protected Font theFont;
    protected FontMetrics theFontMetrics;

    public salesGraph (graphData iData)
    {
        theData = iData;
        high_value = findMax();
        theFont = new Font ("Helvetica",Font.BOLD,10);
    }

    protected int findMax () // returns maximum data value in graphData object
    {
        int max = theData.getS1Q1();
        if (theData.getS1Q2() > max)
            max = theData.getS1Q2();
        if (theData.getS1Q3() > max)
            max = theData.getS1Q3();
        if (theData.getS1Q4() > max)
            max = theData.getS1Q4();
        if (theData.getS2Q1() > max)
            max = theData.getS2Q1();
        if (theData.getS2Q2() > max)
            max = theData.getS2Q2();
        if (theData.getS2Q3() > max)
            max = theData.getS2Q3();
        if (theData.getS2Q4() > max)
            max = theData.getS2Q4();
        if (theData.getS3Q1() > max)
            max = theData.getS3Q1();
        if (theData.getS3Q2() > max)
            max = theData.getS3Q2();
        if (theData.getS3Q3() > max)
            max = theData.getS3Q3();
        if (theData.getS3Q4() > max)
            max = theData.getS3Q4();
        return max;
    }
```

Continued next page

Listing 7.5(Continued)   The salesGraph base class

```
protected void findSize()
    {
        Dimension theSize = getSize(); // dimensions of canvas
        canvasHeight = theSize.height;
        canvasWidth = theSize.width;
    }

    protected void findScale() // allow fractional scale values
    {
        scale_factor = (float) high_value / (float) (canvasHeight-(EDGE * 2));
    }

    protected int scaleY(int Y)
    {
        if (Y < scale_factor)
            return (int) (Y * scale_factor);
        else
            return (int) (Y / scale_factor);
    }
}
```

Notice that in this case, the **add** method has two parameters: a position within the window's border layout and a reference to the component being added. When a container uses a border layout, you specify the region into which you want a component to be added by using the region's name as the **add** method's first parameter. Because the parameter is a literal string, it must be surrounded by double quotes.

Making a Canvas Visible

Like other components, a canvas isn't drawn when you add it to a container. You must do something that forces the Java virtual machine to redraw the container's contents. In the graphing program, the **graphApp** class's action event listeners for its two buttons call **show**, ensuring that the entire window—including the newly added canvas—will be redrawn.

Removing a Canvas from a Container

Container When switching between graphs, the graphing program removes the current canvas from the window prior to adding a new one. To remove a component from a container, you use the **remove** method:

remove
```
remove (currentCanvas);
```

Listing 7.6   The barGraph class

```
public class barGraph extends salesGraph
{
    public barGraph (graphData iData)
    {
        super (iData);
    }

    public void paint (Graphics graphObject)
    {
        findSize(); // find current size of canvas
        graphObject.drawLine (EDGE,EDGE,EDGE,canvasHeight-EDGE); // y axis
        graphObject.drawLine (EDGE,canvasHeight-EDGE,
            canvasWidth-EDGE,canvasHeight-EDGE); // x axis

        // used for centering labels
        theFontMetrics = graphObject.getFontMetrics (theFont);
        graphObject.setFont (theFont);
        // draw title
        graphObject.setColor (Color.white);
        String title = "Yearly Sales";
        int labelWidth = theFontMetrics.stringWidth (title);
        int labelStart = canvasWidth/2 - labelWidth/2;
        graphObject.drawString (title,labelStart,EDGE/2);
        findScale();
        // size bars for four groups of three bars each
        int barWidth = ((canvasWidth - (EDGE*2)) - (SPACER * 4))/12;
        // draw the bars and write values above them
        drawLabeledBar (theData.getS1Q1(),0,1,barWidth,graphObject);
        drawLabeledBar (theData.getS2Q1(),1,1,barWidth,graphObject);
        drawLabeledBar (theData.getS3Q1(),2,1,barWidth,graphObject);
        drawLabeledBar (theData.getS1Q2(),3,2,barWidth,graphObject);
        drawLabeledBar (theData.getS2Q2(),4,2,barWidth,graphObject);
        drawLabeledBar (theData.getS3Q2(),5,2,barWidth,graphObject);
        drawLabeledBar (theData.getS1Q3(),6,3,barWidth,graphObject);
        drawLabeledBar (theData.getS2Q3(),7,3,barWidth,graphObject);
        drawLabeledBar (theData.getS3Q3(),8,3,barWidth,graphObject);
        drawLabeledBar (theData.getS1Q4(),9,4,barWidth,graphObject);
        drawLabeledBar (theData.getS2Q4(),10,4,barWidth,graphObject);
        drawLabeledBar (theData.getS3Q4(),11,4,barWidth,graphObject);

        // add labels on X axis
        graphObject.setColor (Color.white);
        drawLabel (theData.getLabel1(),0,1,barWidth,graphObject);
        drawLabel (theData.getLabel2(),3,2,barWidth,graphObject);
        drawLabel (theData.getLabel3(),6,3,barWidth,graphObject);
        drawLabel (theData.getLabel4(),9,4,barWidth,graphObject);
    }
```

Continued next page

Listing 7.6(Continued)   The barGraph class

```
private void drawLabeledBar (int value, int barNumb, int barGroup, int
    barWidth, Graphics graphObject)
    {
        int barHeight = scaleY (value);
        int Y = canvasHeight - barHeight - EDGE;
        int X = EDGE + SPACER*barGroup + barWidth*barNumb;
        switch (barNumb % 3) // three bars per group
        {
            case 0: graphObject.setColor (Color.red); break;
            case 1: graphObject.setColor (Color.blue); break;
            case 2: graphObject.setColor (Color.yellow);
        }
        graphObject.fillRect (X,Y,barWidth,barHeight);
        int labelWidth = theFontMetrics.stringWidth (Integer.toString(value));
        int labelStart = barWidth/2 - labelWidth/2;
        graphObject.setColor (Color.white);
        graphObject.drawString (Integer.toString(value),X+labelStart,Y-5);
    }

    private void drawLabel (String Label, int barNumb, int barGroup, int
    barWidth, Graphics graphObject)
    {
        int labelWidth = theFontMetrics.stringWidth (Label);
        int labelStart = (barWidth * 3)/2 - (labelWidth/2);
        graphObject.drawString (Label,EDGE + SPACER*barGroup +
            barWidth*barNumb + labelStart,canvasHeight-EDGE+15);
    }
}
```

The method's single parameter is a reference to the component being removed. Don't forget to show the container again after removing a component so the container is redrawn without the component you've removed.

Note

You technically don't need to remove a canvas if you are going to draw another one on top of it. By default, when Java draws it overwrites anything already on the screen. However, if you don't remove the canvas first, there may be a bit of flicker as Java redraws the screen with the new canvas. Although we won't always remove components before redrawing, you should pay attention to how smoothly your version of Java redraws. If you see any flickering on the screen, you may want to remove a component before drawing again in the area occupied by that component.

Listing 7.7   The stackedBar class

```
public class stackedGraph extends salesGraph
{
    private int total1, total2, total3, total4;
    public stackedGraph (graphData iData)
        { super (iData);}

    public void paint (Graphics graphObject)
    {
        findSize(); // find current size of canvas
        graphObject.drawLine (EDGE,EDGE,EDGE,canvasHeight-EDGE); // y axis
        // x axis
        graphObject.drawLine
            (EDGE,canvasHeight-EDGE,canvasWidth-EDGE,canvasHeight-EDGE);
        // used for centering labels
        theFontMetrics = graphObject.getFontMetrics (theFont);
        graphObject.setFont (theFont);
        // draw title
        graphObject.setColor (Color.white);
        String title = "Yearly Sales Summary";
        int labelWidth = theFontMetrics.stringWidth (title);
        int labelStart = canvasWidth/2 - labelWidth/2;
        graphObject.drawString (title,labelStart,EDGE/2);
        findScale();
        // size bars for four bars
        int barWidth = ((canvasWidth - (EDGE*2)) - (SPACER * 4))/4;
        int oldY = drawLabeledBar
            (theData.getS1Q1(),0,0,1,barWidth,graphObject);
        oldY = drawLabeledBar
            (theData.getS2Q1(),oldY,1,1,barWidth,graphObject);
        oldY = drawLabeledBar (
            theData.getS3Q1(),oldY,2,1,barWidth,graphObject);
        oldY = drawLabeledBar (theData.getS1Q2(),0,3,2,barWidth,graphObject);
        oldY = drawLabeledBar
            (theData.getS2Q2(),oldY,4,2,barWidth,graphObject);
        oldY = drawLabeledBar
            (theData.getS3Q2(),oldY,5,2,barWidth,graphObject);
        oldY = drawLabeledBar (theData.getS1Q3(),0,6,3,barWidth,graphObject);
        oldY = drawLabeledBar
            (theData.getS2Q3(),oldY,7,3,barWidth,graphObject);
        oldY = drawLabeledBar
            (theData.getS3Q3(),oldY,8,3,barWidth,graphObject);
        oldY = drawLabeledBar (theData.getS1Q4(),0,9,4,barWidth,graphObject);
        oldY = drawLabeledBar
            (theData.getS2Q4(),oldY,10,4,barWidth,graphObject);
        oldY = drawLabeledBar
            (theData.getS3Q4(),oldY,11,4,barWidth,graphObject);
    }
```

Continued next page

Listing 7.7(Continued)   The stackedBar class

```
private int drawLabeledBar (int value, int previousY, int blockNumb, int
   barNumb, int barWidth, Graphics graphObject)
{
   int X, Y = 0;
   int blockHeight = scaleY (value)/3;
   int labelWidth, labelStart;
   X = EDGE + SPACER*barNumb + barWidth*(barNumb-1);
   switch (blockNumb % 3)
   {
      case 0:
         // Draw bar labels
         String Label = null;
         graphObject.setColor (Color.white);
         switch (barNumb)
         {
            case 1:
               Label = theData.getLabel1();
               total1 = value;
               break;
            case 2:
               Label = theData.getLabel2();
               total2 = value;
               break;
            case 3:
               Label = theData.getLabel3();
               total3 = value;
               break;
            case 4:
               Label = theData.getLabel4();
               total4 = value;
               break;
         }
         labelWidth = theFontMetrics.stringWidth (Label);
         labelStart = (barWidth/2) - (labelWidth/2);
         graphObject.drawString (Label,EDGE + SPACER*barNumb +
            barWidth*(barNumb-1) + labelStart,canvasHeight-EDGE+15);

         Y = canvasHeight - blockHeight - EDGE;
         graphObject.setColor (Color.red);
         break;
      case 1:
         Y = previousY - blockHeight;
         switch (barNumb)
         {
            case 1: total1 += value; break;
            case 2: total2 += value; break;
            case 3: total3 += value; break;
```

Continued next page

Listing 7.7(Continued)   The stackedBar class

```
            case 4: total4 += value;
        }
        graphObject.setColor (Color.blue);
        break;
    case 2:
        Y = previousY - blockHeight;
        // Draw value above completed bar
        String total = null;
        switch (barNumb)
        {
            case 1: total = Integer.toString(total1 + value); break;
            case 2: total = Integer.toString(total2 + value); break;
            case 3: total = Integer.toString(total3 + value); break;
            case 4: total = Integer.toString(total4 + value);
        }
        labelWidth = theFontMetrics.stringWidth (total);
        labelStart = (barWidth/2) - (labelWidth/2);
        graphObject.setColor (Color.white);
        graphObject.drawString (total,EDGE + SPACER*barNumb+
            barWidth*(barNumb-1) + labelStart,Y-5);
        graphObject.setColor (Color.yellow);
    }
    graphObject.fillRect (X,Y,barWidth,blockHeight);
    return Y;
    }
}
```

Drawing and Filling Simple Shapes

At this point, we've discussed all the code in the **graphApp** class. Now it's time to look at the graph classes, which take care of actually drawing the graphs. The graphs are actually made up of two simple shapes—lines and rectangles—and text. Drawing the shapes and text is actually very simple. Most of the complexity in the code comes from figuring out exactly *where* drawing should occur!

Coordinate Systems for Drawing

When you draw in a canvas (or directly in a frame, for that matter), the position at which you draw is expressed in terms of an XY coordinate system that is relative to the object. Each point in the coordinate systems represents one pixel on the screen. The origin (0,0) is in the top left corner of the object. The value of the X coordinate increases as you move to the right; the value of the Y coordinate increases as you move down.

Notice in Figure 7.9 that when you place a canvas in a frame, the two objects have independent coordinate systems. Locations that you give for drawing in the canvas are relative to the top left corner of the canvas rather than the frame.

Figure 7.9   Coordinate systems for drawing

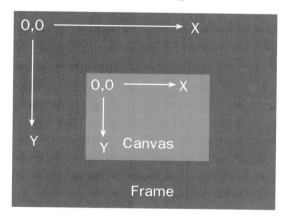

Graphics Objects

When a Java program needs to redraw an object on the screen, it eventually calls the object's `paint` method, which is the sole location for drawing text or graphics. This method takes a single object of the `Graphics` class as a parameter.

The `Graphics` class, from which your program never creates objects directly, acts as a base class for all graphic elements. The graphic element being painted is therefore typecast to a `Graphics` object. All calls to methods that draw text or graphics shapes do so using this object.

Drawing Lines

To draw a line, you specify the starting and ending coordinates of the line:

Graphics

```
Graphics_object.drawLine (x1, y1, x2, y2);
```

For example, if the `Graphics` object parameter is called `graphObject`, then a line from 5,5 to 100,125 can be drawn with:

drawLine

```
graphObject.drawLine (5,5,100,125);
```

The axes on the graphs in the graphing program are drawn with the `drawLine` method. To get them the correct length, the program first decides to leave a 50-pixel border around the graph, regardless of the size of the window. This value is stored in the constant `EDGE`. Drawing should therefore start at 50,50 and stop at 50 (the height of the canvas - 50). The trick here is to find the size of the canvas.

Component

getSize

To find the size of a component, you use the `getSize` method, which returns an object of class `Dimension`. A `Dimension` object has two variables: `width` and `height`. The size of the canvas can therefore be determined with

```
Dimension theSize = getSize();
```

To make it easier to reference the size, the graphing program stores the height and width of the canvas in two variables:

```
canvasHeight = theSize.height;
canvasWidth = theSize.width;
```

Now that the size is available, the Y-axis can be drawn with

```
graphObject.drawLine (EDGE,EDGE,EDGE,canvasHeight-EDGE);
```

The X-axis runs along the bottom of the canvas, 50 pixels up from the bottom. It begins 50 pixels from the left edge and ends 50 pixels short of the width of the canvas. The call to `drawLine` is therefore

```
graphObject.drawLine
    (EDGE,canvasHeight-EDGE,canvasWidth-EDGE,canvasHeight-EDGE);
```

Drawing Open and Filled Shapes

Java's AWT provides a collection of methods that draw open and filled shapes (for example, rectangles, round-cornered rectangles, and circles). As you will see, once you've learned to draw one type of shape, adapting your code to draw others is quite straightforward.

Rectangles

To draw a rectangle you need to know four things, which are passed in order as parameters to the `drawRect` method:

- The X-coordinate of the rectangle's top left corner
- The Y-coordinate of the rectangle's top left corner

- The width of the rectangle (in pixels)
- The height of the rectangle (in pixels)

Graphics

drawRect

We can therefore visualize the drawing of a rectangle as starting at the rectangle's top left corner and the proceeding across and down. For example, if you want to draw a 100-pixel square shape with a top-left coordinate of 25,50, you could program that drawing with

Graphics

fillRect

```
graphicObject.drawRect (25, 50, 100, 100);
```

The `drawRect` method draws the outline of an open rectangle. If you want the rectangle filled with the current color, all you need to do is substitute the `fillRect` method:

```
graphicObject.fillRect (25, 50, 100, 100);
```

The shapes that `drawRect` and `fillRect` produce are drawn from the top left corner down and across. This presents a challenge to a program like the graphing program because conceptually the bars in a bar graph are drawn from the bottom up. The program therefore not only needs to figure out the height of a bar, but where the top-left corner will be as well. The process involves some simple arithmetic that varies slightly between the bar graph and the stacked bar graph. As an example, we'll look closely at the bar graph, which draws each bar with a call to its method `drawLabeledBar`. You can then examine the code for the stacked bar graph on your own.

The height of a bar in the bar graph is determined by scaling an actual data value so it will fit within the number of pixels allocated by the height of the graph. (See the `scaleY` method in the `salesGraph` class. Notice that the scale factor is computed in the `findScale` method based on the height of the canvas.) The Y-coordinate for the top left corner of a bar is the height of the canvas minus the height of the bar, minus the border (the 50 pixels stored in `EDGE`):

```
Y = canvasHeight - barHeight - EDGE;
```

Positioning the X-coordinate is a bit trickier. Each bar takes up `barWidth` pixels, which is equal to the length of the X-axis minus the space around the groups of bars, divided by the total number of bars. The space around the groups of bars must also be considered when considering where to place a given bar. Therefore, each bar is identified not only by its bar number (counting bars from 0), but by the group to which it belongs (numbered beginning with 1). Given that the number of pixels between a group is stored in the constant **SPACER**, the top-left X-coordinate for a bar is

```
X = EDGE + SPACER*barGroup + barWidth*barNumb;
```

The value in **EDGE** moves right to the position of the Y-axis. The **SPACER*barGroup** moves **SPACER** pixels to the right for each group of bars. (There will be **SPACER** pixels between the Y-axis and the rightmost bar.) The computation **barWidth*barNumb** takes into account all bars already present on the graph. Because the first bar is numbered 0, that bar will have its right edge at **EDGE+SPACER**. The second bar will have its right edge at **EDGE+SPACER+barWidth**, and so on.

Once the X- and Y- coordinates have been determined, **drawLabeled-Bar** can do the drawing:

```
graphObject.fillRect (X,Y,barWidth,barHeight);
```

Note   Does graphics programming with Java seem very tedious? If you think so, then you're not alone. At this point in time, there are few tools available for doing graphics programming in any other way. You must painstakingly figure out where every shape should be drawn and then issue an explicit command to draw it.

Graphics **Ovals**

drawOval

To draw an oval, you use the **Graphics** class method **drawOval** or **fillOval**. The oval, whether open or filled, is drawn within an imaginary rectangle that completely encloses the shape. Both methods require the following four parameters:

Graphics

fillOval

- The X-coordinate of the top left corner of the bounding rectangle.
- The Y-coordinate of the top left corner of the bounding rectangle.
- The width of the bounding rectangle.
- The height of the bounding rectangle.

If you want a circle, the height and width of the bounding rectangle should be the same.

For example, the outline of an oval that is 80 pixels high at its center and 100 pixels wide at its center could be drawn with:

```
graphicObject.drawOval (50,50,100,80);
```

In this example, the top left corner of the bounding rectangle is anchored at coordinates 50,50.

Rounded Rectangles

A rounded rectangle is a rectangle with round rather than right-angle corners. To draw it, you must not only specify the location and size of the shape, but the angle of the corners. The six parameters needed for the **drawRoundRect** and **fillRoundRect** methods are:

- The X-coordinate of the top left corner.
- The Y-coordinate of the top left corner.
- The width of the rectangle.
- The height of the rectangle.
- The horizontal diameter of the arc (see Figure 7.10).

Figure 7.10   The dimensions of an arc

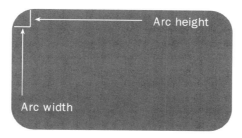

- The vertical diameter of the arc (see Figure 7.10).

To draw a rounded rectangle similar to that in Figure 7.10, you might use the following:

```
graphicObject.fillRoundRect (50, 50, 150, 90, 25, 25);
```

Adding Color

When you draw a shape or text, Java uses the current color. This means that you must identify the color you want to use before you issue the command to draw.

Each color with which you can draw is created as an object of the class `Color`. Java creates 13 color objects for you (see Table 7.9), which you can reference using the name of the class and the name of the object (for example, `Color.white`).

Table 7.9   Standard Java color objects

black	gray	orange	yellow
blue	green	pink	
cyan	lightGray	red	
darkGray	magenta	white	

Color

new

If you aren't satisfied with the default colors, you can create your own color object by specifying the red, green, and blue values for the color, in that order. (The values must be between 0 and 255.) For example, you could create a new color with

```
Color purple = new Color (128, 128, 255);
```

The red value is set to 128 (50% red), the green value to 128 (50% green), and the blue value to 255 (100% blue), producing a bright purple.

Once an appropriate color object exists, you can then make the color the current foreground color of whatever component you will be drawing:

```
graphicObject.setColor (Color.white);
```

Graphics

setColor

The `setColor` method takes one parameter: an object of class `Color`.

Any color that you set stays in effect until you set the color again. All drawing uses whatever color was last installed with `setColor`.

The graphing program draws bars in red, yellow, and blue. All the text is displayed in white. If you look at the `drawLabeledBar` method in the `barGraph` class, you will notice that the color is set prior to drawing each bar. (The modulo division of the bar number by three determines whether a bar is the first, second, or third in a group.)

Background Color

Component

setBack-
ground-
Color

If you want to change the background color of a component rather than changing the color of objects you draw in the component (in particular, the background color of a panel, canvas, or window), use the `setBackgroundColor` method. Like `setColor`, it requires a color object as a parameter. For example, to give the canvas on which we are drawing a background color of light gray, we could use:

```
setBackgroundColor (Color.lightGray);
```

The preceding syntax assumes that the statement appears in a method of one of the graphing classes.

Working with Text

Displaying text in a graphics programming environment is very different from formatting text in a word processor or page layout program. The text must be treated like any other graphics object, with a height and width in pixels. What makes dealing with text a bit complicated is that the dimensions of the text depend upon the font, size, and style of the text. The method that draws text is very easy to use. However, a program may need to expend some effort to determine the coordinates where text drawing should begin.

Much of the text in the graphing program is centered. The title of the graph is centered in the canvas; the numbers above the bars are centered on the bars; the X-axis labels are centered on groups of bars. To center text, you must figure out the width of the area in which the text will appear and the width of the text in the chosen font, size, and style. The X-coordinate for the start of the text is therefore half the difference between the width of the area and the width of the text, plus the X-coordinate for the beginning of the area.

For example, if text is to be centered on a bar in a bar graph, then the X-coordinate for the left edge of the text is

```
(width_of_bar - width_of_text)/2 + left_X-coordinate_of_bar
```

To make centering possible, you must therefore know not only the width in pixels of the area in which the text will be centered, but the width of the text itself.

In this section we will look at how Java represents fonts and at where a program can obtain the information it needs for centering or other precise placements.

Creating Font Objects

When you want to set type characteristics for display, you first create an object of class Font. The class's constructor requires three parameters:

- The name of the font, such as "Helvetica" or "Times"
- The type style (see Table 7.10)

Table 7.10   Type style constants

Constant	Usage	Effect
PLAIN	Font.PLAIN	Plain text; no styles
BOLD	Font.BOLD	Boldface text
ITALIC	Font.ITALIC	Italic text
BOLD,PLAIN	Font.BOLD + Font.ITALIC	Bold and italic text

- The size of the type, expressed in points

Font

new

For example, if you want to create a font object for 10-point Helvetica bold, your program would include:

```
Font theFont = new Font ("Helvetica",Font.BOLD,10);
```

A program defines one Font object for each unique combination of typeface, style, and size it needs to use. However, any given component will have at most one current Font object with which it will draw at any given time.

Although a Java program can use any font installed on your computer, keep in mind that Java programs are supposed to be platform-independent. It is usually safe to stick to Helvetica or Times, which are available on most Windows, UNIX, and Mac OS systems.

Note

Setting the Font for Drawing

To instruct Java to draw text in a component using a specific Font object, you use the Graphics class's setFont method:

Graphics

setFont

```
graphObject.setFont (theFont);
```

The method's sole parameter is a reference to a Font object.

Java will draw with the type specifications in the current Font object until you replace it with another.

Obtaining Font Information

The characteristics of a font in a specific style and size are stored in an object of class FontMetrics. To obtain a reference to a FontMetrics object that holds data about a specific font, use the getFontMetrics method, passing it a reference to a Font object:

Graphics

getFont-
Metrics

```
theFontMetrics = graphObject.getFontMetrics (theFont);
```

Font-
Metrics

In this example, the result of the method call is assigned to a variable so that it can be used to call methods belonging to the FontMetrics class.

Once the FontMetrics object contains information about the size of characters in a specific font, you can ask the object to tell you how many pixels a given string of text will occupy. If the text in question is stored in the variable title, then you can retrieve its width with:

string-
Width

```
int labelWidth = theFontMetrics.stringWidth (title);
```

One the graphing program knows the width of a particular string of text, it can use that value to figure out the X-coordinate where text drawing should occur. For example, a graph's title is centered between the left and right edges of the canvas. Therefore, the X-coordinate of the beginning of the title will be:

```
int labelStart = canvasWidth/2 - labelWidth/2;
```

When centering a value over a bar in the bar graph, the X-coordinate of the label is relative to the X-coordinate of the bar. If the bar began at the left edge of the canvas, the starting position of the value would be:

```
barWidth/2 - labelWidth/2
```

However, because the program needs to take the X-coordinate of the bar into account, the starting position for drawing is actually:

```
barWidth/2 - labelWithd/2 + left_X-coordinate_of_bar
```

Drawing the Text

Assuming that you know the coordinates for the left edge of a string of text, you can instruct Java to draw the text with the `Graphics` class's `drawString` method, which takes the following three parameters:

Graphics

draw-
String

- The text to be drawn
- The X-coordinate where drawing should begin
- The Y-coordinate where drawing should begin

The graphing program can draw the graph's title with:

```
graphObject.drawString (title,labelStart,EDGE/2);
```

Notice that in this case, the Y-coordinate is half the distance of the graph's border.

By the same token, the graphing program can draw a value over a bar with the following:

```
graphObject.drawString
        (Integer.toString(value),X+labelStart,Y-5);
```

In this case, the Y-coordinate is five pixels above the top of the bar.

Summary

An event-driven program is a program that sits and waits for the user to take some action. When the action occurs, the program identifies the action and responds to the action in some appropriate way. Java programs that use a graphic user interface must be event-driven.

A GUI-based Java application begins with a class that inherits from the class `Frame`. The `main` method of this class creates the top-level window object and draws it on the screen with a call to the `show` method. The remaining methods include `paint`, which actually does the drawing.

The event trapping, and the creation of an event object, is handled by the Java virtual machine. The event object is then passed to the object in which the event occurred. To be able to respond to the event, an object must have registered an event listener object for the correct type of event. Event listener classes are implementations of a collection of event listener interfaces, some of which have been implemented as base classes known as adapters. The methods within a listener class provide the code that is to be executed when a specific event occurs.

To draw in a window, you use methods from the Abstract Windowing Toolkit (AWT). Although it is possible to draw directly in a window, you will usually draw in a canvas (an object created directly from `Canvas` or a subclass of `Canvas`). Controls such as buttons are usually placed in panels (objects created directly from `Panel` or a subclass of `Panel`).

The placement of objects in a window is governed by the window's layout. Layouts are also objects.

Anything you can place in a window is known as a *component*. Something that can contain other components is a *container*. A canvas is a component but not a container. A panel, like a window, is a container.

Exercises

In these exercises you will get your first chance to prepare programs with a graphic user interface.

1. Write an event-driven program that asks the user for his or her name and then displays the name with a message in a window.

   • Use the system input window that we have been using for input throughout this book to accept the name.
   • The message to the user should read: "Hello, *user's name*."
   • Make sure that the window responds to a click in its close box so that the user can close the window and exit the program.

2. Write an event-driven program that draws a series of rectangles in a window.

   • Using the system input window, ask the user how many rectangles to draw.
   • Begin the first rectangle at coordinates 10,10. Make the rectangle 30 pixels wide by 20 pixels high.

- Offset each remaining rectangle 5 pixels from the first. For example, the second rectangle will start at 15,15.
- Include code that stops drawing rectangles either when the program has drawn the number requested by the user or when the next rectangle won't fit in the window. (You'll need to find the window's dimensions to do this.)
- Choose any colors you want for the rectangles. Whether you use filled rectangles or open rectangles is up to you. (You could even give the user a choice.)

3. Write an event-driven program that draws labeled shapes in a window.

- Include buttons in a panel that choose between circles and rectangles.
- When the user clicks a button, draw the chosen shape and display a label that identifies the shape (for example, "Circle" or "Rectangle"). For this program, the height of a rectangle and the radius of a circle should be half the size of the canvas on which you are drawing. The shape should be centered on the canvas.
- Place the shape label 10 pixels above the shape. Center the text in the canvas in which you are drawing.
- Use any colors you want. It is up to you whether you use filled or open shapes.
- Be sure that the program responds to a click in its close box.

4. Write an event-driven program that collects sales information from a salesperson, computes the person's commission, and draws the result of the computation in a window.

- Use a system input window to gather the salesperson's total sales, the commission rate, and the month for which the computation is being performed.
- Produce output in a window that appears something like the following:

    Month: January
    Commission rate: 10%
    Sales: $10000
    Commission: $1000

The challenge here is to figure out how you are going to intermix bold and plain text. (*Hint:* You are going to need two font objects, one in each style.)

- Be sure that the program responds to a click in its close box.

5. Write an event-driven program that prepares a quotation for the price of custom-configured computer system.

  - Use a system input window to allow the user to enter the name and price of each component that will be added to the system. You may add more than one of a given component to a system, so it makes sense to ask the user how many of each component will be used. *However, do not ask the user the total number of components in the system; Use an end-of-data-flag (a value that the program recognizes as indicating that no more input follows).*
  - Create a nicely formatted output display that shows each component, how many of that component will be used, the price for one of that component, and the cost for the number of the component being added. At the bottom of the window, show the total price for the entire system.
  - If you want to experiment with drawing, draw boxes around the display to make it look like the display was created by filling in a form.

6. Write an event-driven program that displays a sales slip for a retail store in a window.

  - Use a system input window to gather the name and address of the customer along with the date of the sale.
  - Use a system input window to collect the description and price of each item purchased. *Do not ask the user how many items are being purchased; Use an end-of-data-flag (a value that the program recognizes as indicating that no more input follows).*
  - Produce an output window that contains a nicely formatted sales slip, with the customer information at the top and each item purchased on a separate line in the body. At the end of the line items, display the total amount of the sale.

- If you feel like experimenting with the AWT drawing methods, draw a simple logo for the store in the upper left corner of the sales slip.

7. The Arctic Ski Company has noticed for some time that their sales go up when the weather is cold. They want to plot sales against daily high temperatures to see if this relationship holds true. Write a program for this company that will plot the necessary data.

- Accept pairs of data (a temperature and a sales figure) for seven days using a system input window.
- Create a graph in an output window that plots sales on the X-axis and temperature on the Y-axis. Display a dot (a small filled circle) at each position where a temperature and sales figure pair intersect. Then draw a line from each dot to the other. (*Hint:* Consider creating a class for the pairs of data that includes not only the raw data, but the coordinates where they are plotted.) Be sure to label the axes and add a title to the graph.
- Use color to make it easy to see both the dots and the lines.

8. Write an event-driven program that lets the user change the type characteristics of a string.

- Create an output window that displays the string "This is a font test." Use 10-point plain text for the initial display. Use any typeface that looks nice on the screen.
- Place the following buttons on the window and write code so that clicking the buttons performs the indicated actions:

  - Larger (Make the size of the font 2 points larger, up to 36 points)
  - Smaller (Make the size of the font 2 points smaller, down to 8 points)
  - Red (Make the text red)
  - Blue (Make the text blue)
  - Black (Make the text black)
  - White (Make the text white)

- Bold (Make the text boldface)
- Italic (Make the text italic)
- Plain (Make the text plain)

(*Note:* If the text already has the property corresponding to a clicked button, resetting the property will have no effect.)

8

Arrays and Vectors

OBJECTIVES

In this chapter you will learn about:
- Creating one- and two-dimensional arrays.
- Using arrays that are class variables.
- Sorting arrays.
- Creating simple dialog boxes.
- Vectors, a data structure that is similar to a resizeable array.

Arrays provide a way to organize and access values through a data structure that is often viewed as a list or table. Although most programming languages, including Java, support arrays with many dimensions, programmers commonly use only one- and two-dimensional arrays.

An object-oriented program can use arrays in three different ways. The first is as a local variable in methods. This is the way in which you have probably used arrays in whichever structured programming language you know. Local variable arrays are accessible to the method in which they are defined and any method into which they are passed.

The second way in which an array can be used in an object-oriented program is as a class variable. In this case, an array is defined as a variable for a class. Each object created from the class has its own copy of the array and can manipulate that array with its methods.

The third way in which object-oriented programs use arrays is with arrays of objects. The array is maintained by a special class known as a *container class* because its purpose is to contain other objects. You will learn about arrays of objects and the way in which container classes handle them in Chapter 9.

The syntax for defining and accessing all three types of arrays is the same. However, because you are familiar with local variable arrays, this chapter specifically looks at the second type of arrays: those that are class variables.

As promised, this chapter also introduces a bit more of Java's graphics user interface. You will learn to create simple dialog boxes that provide messages to the user. You will also learn about how you can change a button's label while a program is running and how to identify that button in a situation where labels are neither unique nor constant.

Declaring One-Dimensional Arrays

The simplest type of array is a one-dimensional array, which can most easily be thought of as a single-column list where every row has the same data type. To declare a one-dimensional Java, use the following general syntax:

```
data_type[] variable_name;
```

Like any other variable declaration, the data type is followed by the name of the variable. In this case, however, the data type is followed by a pair of square brackets ([and]). You also use the brackets to surround an array index when accessing individual elements of an array.

For example, in the yearly sales average program that you will see shortly, the variable to hold 12 months' worth of sales is declared with:

```
float[] Sales;
```

Notice that the declaration contains no indication of the number of elements that will be in the array.

It is important to realize that declaring an array does not set aside storage for the array; it only sets aside a variable to hold a reference to where the array's storage will begin in main memory. This is exactly what happens when you declare a variable to hold a reference to an object.

To actually allocate storage, you use the new operator, just as you would if you were creating an object:

```
array_variable = new data_type [number_of_elements];
```

Assuming that the constant NUM_MON equals 12, then storage for an array to hold a year's sales totals can be created with:

```
Sales = new float [NUM_MON];
```

Note

It is a good programming practice to define constants to use for the total number of elements when declaring arrays. It makes the program easier to read because the name of the constant tells you something about the meaning of the array. It also makes the program easier to modify because you don't have to go hunting through the program to find the array definition; you only need to change the constant, which is typically located at the beginning of the class using it.

Initializing Arrays

Once you have allocated space for an array, you can initialize its elements. You must do this one element at a time, usually using a for loop:

```
for (int i = 0; i < NUM_MON; i++)
    Sales[i] = 0.0F;
```

If you aren't familiar with C or C++, then something may seem a bit odd about the preceding loop: The array indexes go from 0 to 11, rather than from 1 to 12. Java, like C and C++, numbers array elements beginning with 0, not 1! Although you allocate space for the array using the total number of elements in the array, the index of the last value in the array is one less than the total number of elements. (Forgetting that array indexes begin with 0 is a common mistake programmers make when learning a language like Java.)

Java will warn you if you attempt to use an array element for which you haven't allocated space. In this way, Java prevents an array from accidentally encroaching on space in use by other variables and objects.

Warning

The name of an array represents the address in main memory where the array begins, just as the name of an object represents the address of the object's storage. This means that you can't initialize an array by assigning a single value to the array name; you must initialize each element, one at a time. In fact, if you try something like

```
Sales = 0.0F;
```

you will probably cause your computer to crash sometime during the program run. The preceding assignment statement changes the location of the array to main memory address 0, a location that the operating system almost always uses. When the program assigns a value to the relocated array, it will be overwriting something needed by the operation system!

Using a One-Dimensional Array

To explore how an array defined as a class variable can be used, we'll be looking at a program that computes average monthly sales over a one-year period when given total sales for 12 individual months. The program lets the user enter the 12 sales values and then computes the average (Figure 8.1). It also displays the entire contents of the array (Figure 8.2).

Figure 8.1   Average sales display

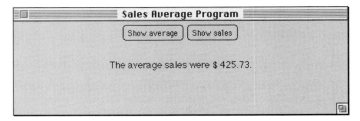

Figure 8.2   Sales listing display

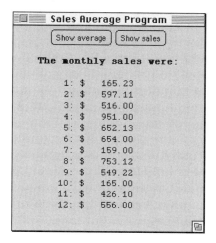

The data for the sales average program are stored in a class named yearlySales. As you can see in Listing 8.1, it has only one variable, an array named Sales that holds 12 floating point values. There are three methods:

Listing 8.1   yearlySales.java

```java
public class yearlySales
{
    public static final int NUM_MON = 12;
    private float[] Sales;

    public yearlySales()
    {
        Sales = new float[NUM_MON];
        for (int i = 0; i < NUM_MON; i++)
            Sales[i] = 0;
    }

    public void InitSales (int i, float Amount)
        { Sales[i] = Amount; }

    public float getSales(int i)
        { return Sales[i]; }
}
```

- The constructor allocates storage for the array and initializes those storage locations
- The `InitSales` method that places one value in a specific array element. This method requires two parameters: the value to be inserted into the `Sales` array and the index of the element into which the value should be placed. The method uses these parameters to simply assign the value to the correct element in the array. Values are therefore inserted into the array one at a time.

Note

There is one alternative to the procedure used by `InitSales`. The object manipulating the `yearlySales` object could accept all 12 values into an array of its own and then pass the array into the method. Even in this case, however, the values would have to be transferred from the array used as an input parameter to the object's array one element at a time.

- The `getSales` method that returns the value of a specific element to a calling method. It accepts an index value as its single parameter and returns the value stored in the element.

Note

It is important to realize that the `yearlySales` class does no I/O; its entire purpose is to store and return data. The classes that manipulate and format data for output are completely separate. When you structure a program in this way, you make the classes more independent. You can then modify the I/O interface without needing to make any changes to internal data storage, producing a program that is easier to modify and classes that are easier to reuse.

The sales average's top level window is managed by the `salesApp` class in Listing 8.2. The window contains a panel with the "Show average" and "Show sales" button. When the user clicks on a button, the `action` method creates a canvas from a class that manipulates sales data and produces formatted output.

The average sales display, which you saw in Figure 8.1, is produced by the `averageCanvas` class. As you can see in Listing 8.3, the class's constructor requires an object of class `yearlySales` as an input parameter. The constructor assigns the address of the input parameter to its own variable:

```
theSales = inputSales;
```

Listing 8.2   salesApp.java

```java
import java.awt.*;
import java.io.*;
import java.lang.*;
import java.awt.*;
import text.*;
import java.awt.event.*;

public class salesApp extends Frame
{
    private static final int NUM_MON = 12;
    private float oneMonth;
    private yearlySales SalesObject = new yearlySales(); // sales object
    private salesApp thisApp;

    public salesApp()
    {
        thisApp = this; // need this for adding stuff in inner classes

        addWindowListener (new WindowAdapter ()
        {
            public void windowClosing (WindowEvent theEvent)
            {
                Window window = (Window) theEvent.getSource();
                window.dispose();
                //System.exit(0);
            }
        } );

        SystemInput sysIn = new SystemInput();

        for (int idx = 0; idx < NUM_MON; idx++)
        {
            oneMonth = sysIn.readFloat ("Enter sales for month " +
                Integer.toString(idx+1) + ":");
            SalesObject.InitSales(idx, oneMonth);
        }

        setTitle ("Sales Average Program");
        setLayout (new BorderLayout());
        Panel thePanel = new Panel(); // panel for buttons
```

Continued next page

Listing 8.2(Continued)   salesApp.java

```
        Button theButton = new Button ("Show average");
        theButton.addActionListener (new ActionListener ()
        {
            public void actionPerformed (ActionEvent theEvent)
            {
                averageCanvas theCanvas = new averageCanvas (SalesObject);
                thisApp.add ("Center",theCanvas);
                thisApp.show();
            }
        } );
        thePanel.add (theButton);

        theButton = new Button ("Show sales");
        theButton.addActionListener (new ActionListener ()
        {
            public void actionPerformed (ActionEvent theEvent)
            {
                listCanvas theCanvas = new listCanvas (SalesObject);
                thisApp.add ("Center", theCanvas);
                thisApp.show();
            }
        } );
        thePanel.add (theButton);
        add ("North",thePanel); // add panel to container
    }

    public static void main (String args[])
    {
        salesApp theApp = new salesApp();
        theApp.setSize (400,300);
        theApp.show ();
    }
}
```

It is important to recognize that the preceding assignment statement does *not* make a copy of the input object. Instead, it allows two different variables to reference the same storage location in main memory.

Once the averageCanvas object knows where the data are stored, its constructor calculates the average. The data are retrieved from the yearly-Sales object, one value at a time, using the getSales method.

The class's second method, paint, is called when the salesApp object issues a call to show. (The show method calls the repaint method for each component a container contains, which in turn calls the paint method.)

Listing 8.3   averageCanvas.java

```java
import java.awt.*;
import java.io.*;
import java.lang.*;
import java.awt.*;
import text.*;

public class averageCanvas extends Canvas
{
    private static final int NUM_MON = 12;
    private yearlySales theSales;
    private float average;

    public averageCanvas (yearlySales inputSales)
    {
        theSales = inputSales;
        float sum = 0.0F;
        for (int i = 0; i < NUM_MON; i++)
            sum += theSales.getSales(i);
        average = sum/(float) NUM_MON;
    }

    public void paint (Graphics graphObject)
    {
        // create output string
        String theResult = "The average sales were $" +
            NumberFormat.floatFormat (7,2,average) + ".";

        Dimension theSize = getSize(); // Find size of canvas
        // Create font and get font metrics
        Font theFont = new Font ("Helvetica",Font.PLAIN,12);
        FontMetrics theFontMetrics = graphObject.getFontMetrics (theFont);
        graphObject.setFont (theFont);

        // computations for centering
        int resultWidth = theFontMetrics.stringWidth (theResult);
        int resultHeight = theFontMetrics.getHeight ();

        int widthOffset = (theSize.width - resultWidth) / 2;
        int heightOffset = (theSize.height - resultHeight) / 2;

        // draw the text
        graphObject.drawString (theResult,widthOffset, heightOffset);
    }
}
```

Font-
Metrics

getHeight

The `paint` method in Listing 8.3 contains one AWT method you have not seen before: `FontMetrics.getHeight`. This method returns the height of a typical line of text (in pixels) in the font described by the font metrics object. As long as the font doesn't contain any characters that extend unusually high or low, you can use the results of this method to gauge the amount of vertical space to leave for a line of text.

The display of the contents of the array is handled by the `listCanvas` class in Listing 8.4. Like the `averageCanvas` class, its constructor accepts an object of the `yearlySales` class, whose location it assigns to a local variable. The `paint` method uses a `for` loop to step through the entire array that belongs to the `yearlySales` object, retrieving the contents of the array one element at a time using the `getSales` method. Notice that the display code spaces the listing by placing each successive line of text (font height + 3) pixels below the preceding

Declaring and Allocating Space for Two-Dimensional Arrays

A two-dimensional array can be visualized as a table with columns and rows. Each element in the array is referenced by the combination of its row number and column number. For example, assume that you have an array that is three rows down by three columns across, like a tic-tac-toe board. The top left element has the coordinates 0,0; the bottom right element has the coordinates 2,2. (Don't forget that Java arrays start array index numbers with 0 rather than 1.)

To declare a variable to reference such an array, a Java program contains a statement with the following general syntax:

```
data_type [][] array_name;
```

Notice that as with a one-dimensional array, the declaration does not include any reference to the number of elements in the array.

If the elements in the array are characters, then the array could be declared with:

```
char [][] grid;
```

To allocate space for the array, you must then use the `new` operator, specifying the number of elements needed:

```
grid = new char [3][3];
```

Listing 8.4   listCanvas.java

```java
import java.awt.*;
import java.io.*;
import java.lang.*;
import java.awt.*;
import text.*;

public class listCanvas extends Canvas
{
    private static final int NUM_MON = 12;
    private yearlySales theSales;
    private float average;

    public listCanvas (yearlySales inputSales)
        { theSales = inputSales; }

    public void paint (Graphics graphObject)
    {
        String firstLine = "The monthly sales were:";
        Dimension theSize = getSize(); // find size of canvas
        // Create fonts
        Font boldFont = new Font ("Courier",Font.BOLD,12);
        Font plainFont = new Font ("Courier",Font.PLAIN,12);
        FontMetrics boldMetrics = graphObject.getFontMetrics (boldFont);
        FontMetrics plainMetrics = graphObject.getFontMetrics (plainFont);

        // computations for centering first line
        int theWidth = boldMetrics.stringWidth (firstLine);
        int widthOffset = (theSize.width - theWidth)/2;
        // draw first line 20 pixels from top of canvas, centered in the width
        graphObject.setFont (boldFont);
        graphObject.drawString (firstLine, widthOffset, 20);

        // now draw the monthly sales data
        graphObject.setFont (plainFont);
        // leave 3 pixels between lines
        int lineHeight = plainMetrics.getHeight() + 3;
        // leave one line between first line and data; left offset 20 pixels
        int Y = lineHeight * 2 + 20;
        widthOffset += 20;
        for (int i = 0; i < NUM_MON; i++)
        {
            graphObject.drawString ((i < 9 ? "  " : " ") +Integer.toString(i+1)
            +  ": $" + NumberFormat.floatFormat
            (9,2,theSales.getSales(i)),widthOffset,Y);
            Y += lineHeight;
        }
    }
}
```

The tic-tac-toe program you are going to see shortly uses one array whose elements are actually button objects. (The user clicks on a button to place a marker on the playing field.) Therefore, the data type of the array is Button:

```
Button [][] grid;
```

The program allocates space for the button objects with:

```
grid = new Button [ROWS][COLS];
```

(ROWS and COLS are both constants containing 3.) Note that each element in this array has now been declared to hold a reference to a button object. We will be able to use these references to identify and manipulate the buttons, even if we don't know the button labels.

Sorting a One-Dimensional Array

One of the things that we need to do frequently with data stored in arrays is to place those data in some sort of order, usually numeric, alphabetical, or chronological. There a many ways to sort the contents of an array. One of the easiest to understand and program is the *bubble sort*. It is also relatively efficient when the values originally are more in order than out of order (only a few values need to be rearranged) and when the number of values to be sorted are relatively few.

A bubble sort looks at successive pairs of values and swaps their position in the array if they are in the wrong order. For example, if the value in array element 2 is greater than the value in array element 3, the bubble sort swaps the values in those two elements. The sort then proceeds to examine elements 3 and 4, 4 and 5, and so on to the end of the array. Reaching the bottom of the array, the sort returns to the top to begin examining pairs of values again. Once the program makes a scan through the entire array without swapping any values, the array is in the correct low-to-high order.

As an example, consider the array in Figure 8.3. In the first pass through the array, a sort method makes four swaps (exchanges four pairs of elements). Notice that the effect is to move the largest element into place at the bottom of the array.

During the second pass, only two pairs of elements are out of order. Again, the effect is to percolate the largest values to the bottom. Pass three makes one swap to place the array in correct order. However, the sort method must make one more pass without swaps to detect that fact.

Figure 8.3   Performing a bubble sort

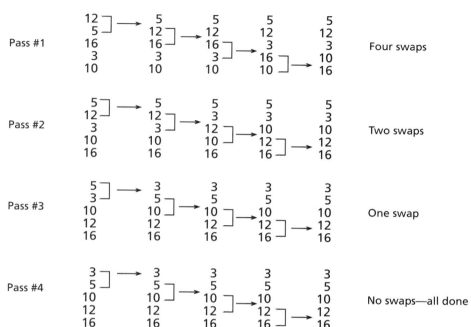

As an example, we'll add a sort method to the sales average program's yearlySales class. The new method, which can be found in Listing 8.5, is called by the listCanvas class's paint method before values are displayed.

To perform the sort, the method uses two loops. The outer—a while—keeps going until the swap_made variable indicates that no swaps have been made (swap_made = false). The inner loop—a for—makes one pass through the array.

Each time the program begins a pass through the array, it makes the assumption that no swaps have been made (in other words, that the array is in the correct order). It therefore sets the swap_made variable to false just before entering the for loop.

Within the for loop, the sort method retrieves a value from an array element (value) and from the value below it (valueBelow). Then, it compares the two elements. If value is greater than valueBelow, the elements are out of order and must be swapped.

Listing 8.5   Coding a bubble sort

```
public void sort ()
{
    boolean swap_made = true;
    float value, valueBelow, temp;

    while (swap_made)
    {
        swap_made = false;
        for (int i = 0; i < NUM_MON - 1; i++)
        {
            value = Sales[i];
            valueBelow = Sales[i+1];
            if (value > valueBelow)
            {
                // put current data into temporary variable
                temp = value;
                // copy data from element below into current element
                Sales[i] = Sales[i+1];
                // copy from temporary storage into element below
                Sales[i+1] = temp;
                swap_made = true;
            }
        }
    }
}
```

Whenever the need for a swap is detected, the bubble sort copies the array element with the lower index into a temporary storage location (in this case, the variable named `temp`). The program can then copy the value below into the location of the value being held in temporary storage. Finally, the value in temporary storage can be copied into its new location in the array (one array element below where it was originally located). The method finishes the swap process by changing the value in `swap_made` to TRUE, ensuring that at least one more pass will be made through the array.

Notice that if all the values in the array are in order, the expression that compares `value` and `valueBelow` will never be true. This means that the program won't reach the block of code that performs a swap, and—more important—changes the value of `swap_made` from FALSE to TRUE. This means that the program will exit the `for` loop without making any swaps, in which case the `while` will also stop.

Note There is one drawback to sorting we have just done: It destroys the original array. In other words, we no longer know which value was entered first, and so on. Therefore, in many cases where you want to preserve the original ordering of your data, you may want to create a second array into which you copy the original values. You can then sort the second array, leaving the original intact.

Using a Two-Dimensional Array: The Tic-Tac-Toe Game

The array of button references named `grid` is used as the playing field for a tic-tac-toe game in which a human plays against the computer. Play begins with the user choosing to play X or O by clicking on the appropriate button (see Figure 8.4).

Figure 8.4 The tic-tac-toe game playing field

The player then makes a move by clicking in a button on the playing field. The player's marker appears in the clicked button, followed quickly by the computer's chosen move. The player and the computer continue to alternate button choices, as in Figure 8.5, until a winner is found or the game ends in a draw. A simple dialog box appears to let the player know the result of the game (Figure 8.6).

Once the user clicks the OK button to dismiss the dialog box, the Play X and Play O buttons are disabled and the New Game button is enabled. Clicking the New Game button clears the playing field and reenables the marker buttons so the user can began playing again.

Figure 8.5   Markers on the tic-tac-toe game playing field

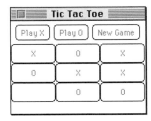

Figure 8.6   The end of a tic-tac-toe game

The Data Handling Class

The tic-tac-toe game is built from three classes. The first, tttGame in Listing 8.6, manages the two-dimensional array that keeps track of which markers have been placed in which button in the playing field. It also makes the computer's move and evaluates that status of the playing field at the end of every move.

Notice first that this class does no I/O. It manages game play, but is completely independent of how the playing environment appears to the user. This means that a programmer can change the user interface at will, without having to worry about the underlying function of game play.

Game Setup

The tic-tac-toe game uses only one object of the tttGame class. The class's constructor simply initializes a random number generator (used to make the computer's move) and allocates space for an array of characters that will keep track of where markers have been placed.

Whenever a new game begins, the program calls the InitGame method. This code was implemented separately from the constructor so that a user could play many games without needing to create a new tttGame object. As you can see in Listing 8.6, the method assigns a blank to each element in the

Listing 8.6   tttGame.java

```java
import java.io.*;
import java.lang.*;
import java.util.*;

public class tttGame
{
    static final int ROWS = 3;
    static final int COLS = 3;
    static final int WIN = 1;
    static final int TIE = 0;
    static final int PLAY_ON = -1;
    static final int PLAYER = 1;
    static final int COMPUTER = 0;
    static final long RAND_FACTOR = 720000000;

    private char[][] grid;
    private int row, column;
    private int player_moves;
    private int computer_moves;
    private char player, computer;
    private Random randomNumberGen;

    public tttGame()
    {
        randomNumberGen = new Random();
        grid = new char[ROWS][COLS];
    }

    public void InitGame()
    {
        int x,y;

        for (x = 0; x < ROWS; x++)
            for (y = 0; y < COLS; y++)
                grid [x][y] = ' ';
        row = 0;
        column = 0;
        player_moves = 0;
        computer_moves = 0;
    }
```

Continued next page

Listing 8.6(Continued)   tttGame.java

```java
    public void chooseMarker (char marker)
    {
        if (marker == 'X')
        {
            player = 'X';
            computer = 'O';
        }
        else
        {
            player = 'O';
            computer = 'X';
        }
    }

    public boolean playerMove (int prow, int pcol)
    {
        if (grid[prow][pcol] != ' ')
            return false;
        grid[prow][pcol] = player;
        player_moves++;
        return true;
    }

    public String computerMove()
    {
        int row, column;

        row = (int) Math.abs(randomNumberGen.nextInt() / RAND_FACTOR);
        column = (int) Math.abs(randomNumberGen.nextInt() / RAND_FACTOR);

        while (grid[row][column] != ' ')
        {
            row ++;
            if (row == ROWS) row = 0;
            if (grid[row][column] != ' ')
            {
                column++;
                if (column == COLS) column = 0;
            }
        }
        grid[row][column] = computer;
        computer_moves++;
        return Integer.toString(row) + Integer.toString(column);
    }
```

Continued next page

Listing 8.6(Continued)   tttGame.java

```
public int checkGrid()
{
    int x, y;

    for (x = 0; x < ROWS; x++)  // look for winner across rows
        if (grid[x][0] != ' ' && grid[x][0] == grid[x][1] &&
            grid[x][1] == grid[x][2])
                return WIN;
    for (y = 0; y < COLS; y++) // look for winner down columns
        if (grid[0][y] !=+ ' ' && grid[0][y] == grid[1][y] &&
            grid[1][y] == grid[2][y])
                return WIN;
    // check for diagonal win
    if ((grid[0][0] == grid[1][1] && grid[1][1] == grid[2][2] &&
        grid[0][0] != ' ') || (grid[0][2] == grid [1][1] &&
        grid[1][1] == grid[2][0] && grid[0][2] != ' '))
            return WIN;
    / 9 moves mean grid is full
    if (player_moves + computer_moves == 9) return TIE;  /
    return PLAY_ON;
}

public int whoWon()
{
    if (player_moves > computer_moves)
        return PLAYER;
    else
        return COMPUTER;
}
}
```

grid. Notice that just as with one-dimensional arrays, the only way to insert values is to access each element individually. In the case of a two-dimensional
array, we frequently use nested for loops, as was done in this method.

When a player clicks either the Play X or Play O button, the class that
provides the tic-tac-toe game's playing field window calls the tttGame method
chooseMarker. This method assigns the chosen marker to the player and the
unused marker to the computer. Because the Play X and Play O buttons are
disabled after a marker is chosen, this method will be executed only once for
each new game.

Making Moves

Each time the player clicks on a button in the playing field, the playing field window class identifies the button that was clicked and passes its grid coordinates to the `playerMove` method. This method assigns the player's marker to the appropriate array element and increments the number of moves made by the player, which is used in determining the status of the game.

The computer's move (handled by `computerMove`) is a bit more complex because the computer must generate the move itself. For this program, the computer generates two random numbers between 1 and 3 and then subtracts 1 from each to bring the values into the correct range for the `grid` array's indexes. If the array element indicated by the random values is unoccupied (in other words, it contains a blank), then the computer inserts its marker and increments the number of moves it has made.

If the randomly selected element is occupied, the computer looks in the next row. If the next row is occupied, it looks in the next column. The process repeats until the computer finds an open element. Notice that the method detects when the "next" index is 3 and resets it to 0 so the index values don't exceed those available in the array.

Note

There are certainly better strategies for picking moves in a tic-tac-toe game. (This one might be described as somewhat brain dead.) However, strategies that analyze the current position of markers on the board require much more code than the random strategy. Since the purpose of this program is to demonstrate how to use two-dimensional arrays, buttons with changeable labels, and dialog boxes, rather than to make the computer a good game player, the random strategy has been used.

Integer

parseInt

Notice that the `computerMove` method returns the coordinates of the computer's move as a string in the format XY. When the application class receives this value, it can turn it back into an integer and then separate it into two values using the `Integer` class's `parseInt` method:

```
integer_variable = Integer.parseInt (string);
```

For example, if the grid coordinates are stored as the string "02", then they could be translated back to the integer 02 with:

```
int coordinates = Integer.parseInt ("02");
```

Why go to all this trouble? Because a method can only return one value with the `return` statement and this method needs to send back two. Rather than creating an entire class just to hold two coordinates, it's easier to combine them into a single value that can be easily returned and separated into its constituent parts.

Finding Winners and Ties

Immediately after a move is made, the computer checks to see if the game is over using the `checkGrid` method. The method's first job is to look for a winner, a process for which there is no simple algorithm. The method therefore first checks each row to see if the elements aren't blank and that they contain the same marker. If there is no winner across the rows, the method checks down the columns. If there is no winner down the columns, then the function looks diagonally. When the computer finds a winner, it returns a flag indicating that either the computer or player has won.

Assuming there is no winner, the method then checks for a tie. If the sum of the number of moves made by the computer and the player is 9, then the grid is full and the game is a draw. Otherwise, play continues.

The `checkGrid` method doesn't detect whether the computer or the player has won. That is performed by the `whoWon` method, which looks to see which of the two has made more moves. Whoever has made more moves in the winner.

The Playing Field Window

The tic-tac-toe game's playing field window is provided by the `tttApp` class (Listing 8.7). This class maintains an object of the `tttGame` class, a panel for the three command buttons (Play X, Play O, New Game), and an array for the grid of buttons that makes up the playing field.

The class's constructor creates a game object, initializes the first game, allocates space for the array of buttons, and then calls the `setUpWindow` method to place visual elements in the top-level window. The `setUpWindow` method also contains listeners for closing the window and clicks in all the buttons that are placed in the window.

Listing 8.7   tttApp.java

```java
import java.awt.*;
import java.io.*;
import java.lang.*;
import java.awt.event.*;

public class tttApp extends Frame
{
    static final int ROWS = 3;
    static final int COLS = 3;
    static final int PLAY_ON = -1;
    static final int WIN = 1;
    static final int TIE = 0;
    static final int PLAYER = 1;
    static final int COMPUTER = 0;

    private int keepPlaying;
    private int goes_first;
    private tttGame inPlay;
    private Button[][] gridButtons;
    private Button X_button;
    private Button O_button;
    private Button New_button;
    private String player;
    private String computer;

    public tttApp()
    {
        keepPlaying = PLAY_ON;
        goes_first = COMPUTER;

        inPlay = new tttGame();
        inPlay.InitGame(); // initialize first game
        gridButtons = new Button[ROWS][COLS];
        setUpWindow();
    }
    private void setUpWindow()
    {
        addWindowListener (new WindowAdapter ()
        {
            public void windowClosing (WindowEvent theEvent)
            {
                Window theWindow = (Window) theEvent.getSource();
                theWindow.dispose();
                //System.exit(0);
            }
        } );
        setTitle ("Tic Tac Toe");
```

Continued next page

Listing 8.7(Continued)   tttApp.java

```java
setBackground (Color.white);
setLayout (new BorderLayout());
Panel buttonPanel = new Panel();
X_button = new Button ("Play X");
X_button.addActionListener (new ActionListener ()
{
    public void actionPerformed (ActionEvent theEvent)
    {
        inPlay.chooseMarker ('X');
        player = " X ";
        computer = " O ";
        X_button.setEnabled(false);
        O_button.setEnabled(false);
    }
} );
buttonPanel.add (X_button);
O_button = new Button ("Play O");
O_button.addActionListener (new ActionListener ()
{
    public void actionPerformed (ActionEvent theEvent)
    {
        inPlay.chooseMarker ('O');
        player = " O ";
        computer = " X ";
        X_button.setEnabled(false);
        O_button.setEnabled(false);
    }
} );
buttonPanel.add (O_button);
New_button = new Button ("New Game");
New_button.addActionListener (new ActionListener ()
{
    public void actionPerformed (ActionEvent theEvent)
    {
        inPlay.InitGame();
        New_button.setEnabled(false);
        X_button.setEnabled(true);
        O_button.setEnabled(true);
        for (int i = 0; i < ROWS; i++)
            for (int j = 0; j < COLS; j++)
            {
                gridButtons[i][j].setLabel ("       ");
                gridButtons[i][j].setEnabled(true);
            }
        repaint();
    }
} );
```

Continued next page

Listing 8.7(Continued)   tttApp.java

```java
        buttonPanel.add (New_button);
        New_button.setEnabled(false);     // This is disabled until end of game
        add ("North",buttonPanel);

        Panel gamePanel = new Panel();
        gamePanel.setLayout (new GridLayout(3,3));
        for (int i = 0; i < ROWS; i++)
            for (int j = 0; j < COLS; j++)
            {
                gridButtons[i][j] = new Button ("         ");
                gridButtons[i][j].addActionListener (new ActionListener ()
                {
                    public void actionPerformed (ActionEvent theEvent)
                    {
                        Button theButton = (Button) theEvent.getSource();
                        for (int k = 0; k < ROWS; k++)
                            for (int m = 0; m < COLS; m++)
                                if (theButton == gridButtons[k][m])
                                    processMove (k,m);
                        repaint();
                    }
                } );
                gamePanel.add (gridButtons[i][j]);
            }
        add ("Center", gamePanel);
    }

    public void processMove (int x, int y)
    {
        inPlay.playerMove (x, y);
        gridButtons[x][y].setLabel(player);
        gridButtons[x][y].setEnabled(false);
        keepPlaying = inPlay.checkGrid();
        if (keepPlaying != PLAY_ON)
        {
            gameEnd();
            New_button.setEnabled(true);
            return;
        }
        String move = inPlay.computerMove();
        int theMove = Integer.parseInt (move);
        x = theMove / 10;
        y = theMove % 10;
        gridButtons[x][y].setLabel(computer);
        gridButtons[x][y].setEnabled(false);
        keepPlaying = inPlay.checkGrid();
```

Continued next page

Listing 8.7(Continued)   tttApp.java

```
if (keepPlaying != PLAY_ON)
        {
            gameEnd();
            New_button.setEnabled(true);
        }
    }

    private void gameEnd()
    {
        tttDialog theDialog;
        if (keepPlaying == WIN)  // find out who won the game
            if (inPlay.whoWon() == PLAYER)
                theDialog = new tttDialog
                    (this,"Congradulations!  You've won the game!");
            else
                theDialog = new tttDialog
                    (this, "The computer won this one. So it goes...");
        else // it's got to be a tie
            theDialog = new tttDialog (this, "This one ended in a draw.");
        theDialog.show();
    }

    public static void main (String args[])
    {
        tttApp mainWindow = new tttApp();
        mainWindow.setSize (175,125);
        mainWindow.show();
    }
}
```

Note

The code in this method could just as easily been part of the constructor. However, the program is a bit cleaner if the code is separated into its own method.

The Button Panel

The "North" section of the playing field window's border layout is occupied by a panel containing three buttons: Play X, Play O, and New Game. As you look at Listing 8.7, notice that each button is given an action listener with a call to `addActionListener`. The code that is to be executed when a user clicks on one of those buttons is included in the `addActionListener` call as an anonymous inner class.

Disabling and Enabling Buttons

In any program, there may be buttons that shouldn't be available all the time. For example, in the tic-tac-toe game, the New Game button should be available only after a game is completed. The Play X and Play O buttons should be available only at the start of a new game. Therefore, although the buttons remain visible throughout the program run, they should be *disabled* (grayed-out so that clicking them has no effect) when their use is inappropriate and *enabled* (made available) when the user can choose them. For example, when the tic-tac-toe game begins, the Play X and Play O buttons are enabled (the default when a button is first created). In contrast, the New button is disabled.

Button

set-
Enabled

To disable a button, you use the `Button` class's `setEnabled` method, passing an input parameter of `false`:

```
New_button.setEnabled(false);
```

To enable the button so that clicking it generates an event that the program can process, you use the same method with an input parameter of `true`:

```
New_button.setEnabled(true);
```

The Tic-Tac-Toe Grid Panel and Grid Layouts

The playing field window has a second panel installed in its "Center" section. This panel, which contains the nine buttons of the tic-tac-toe grid, has a grid layout. To create a grid layout, you specify how many columns and rows the layout will have:

GridLayout

new

```
object_reference = new GridLayout (#_rows, #_columns)
```

Because the tic-tac-toe program doesn't need to use the reference to the layout once it has been attached to the panel, the call to the `new` method can be embedded as a parameter of the `setLayout` method:

```
gamePanel.setLayout (new GridLayout (3,3));
```

Keep in mind that a grid layout creates cells of equal size. When a panel using a grid layout is placed in a container that changes size—such as the "Center" region of a border layout—the size of the cells change as the size of the container changes. This means that the buttons we place in the grid layout's cells will also change sizes as the window is resized.

Setting up the buttons that will form the playing grid is a two-step process. First, the program must create a button object and store a reference to that object in the `gridButtons` array. (Each button is given a label made up of blanks.) Then, the button must be added to the layout. Notice in Listing 8.7 that these steps have been placed in two nested `for` loops.

Container

add

Java adds elements to a grid layout in order, beginning with the top left cell. It fills the first row across, and then drops to the leftmost cell in the second row, continuing in this way until all elements have been added. As a result, you don't need to specify which cell you want when you add an element to the layout:

```
panel_reference.add (element_reference);
```

The tic-tac-toe program can therefore use:

```
gamePanel.add (gridButtons [i][j]);
```

where `i` and `j` are array indexes.

Identifying Clicked Buttons

Once a game is in play (the user has chosen to play either X or O), the tic-tac-toe program waits for the user to click on one of the nine buttons in the grid. At that point, the Java virtual machine passes an action event object to the button that was clicked and calls the action listener's `actionPerformed` method.

If you look back at Listing 8.7, you'll notice that all nine of the buttons in the grid receive an object from the same listener class. (Because the grid buttons are created in a loop, the listener can be implemented as an anonymous inner class.) Nonetheless, during program execution only one clicked button receives an event object and a call to its `actionPerformed` method at a time. This means that there is no question which button was clicked; you can get a reference to the button by calling the `getSource` method. In this particular case, however, that isn't enough: The program needs to know the grid coordinates of the clicked button to process the move.

The grid button action event listener's `actionPerformed` method therefore begins by using the `getSource` method to obtain a reference to the clicked button. (Notice how the result of `getSource` is typecast to the `Button` class.) Then the `actionPerformed` method uses nested `for` loops to compare the clicked button to each element in the two-dimensional grid array.

When a match is found, the method knows that it has located the correct grid position. It can then pass the array indexes to the application object's `pro-cessMove` method, where the move is handled. This includes adding Xs and Os to the buttons as needed.

Warning

Inner classes can generate unexpected problems with method accessibility. The `processMove` method isn't used outside the application class. Like most other methods used internally, you would ordinarily want to give it `private` access. However, the action listener used by the grid buttons needs to call that method. Even though the listener class is physically inside the application class, it is still a distinct class. It won't be able to call `processMove` unless the method has `public` access.

Changing Button Labels

To change the text that appears in a command button (the button's label), you use the `setLabel` method:

Button

setLabel

```
button_reference.setLabel (string);
```

In this program, the player's marker is set with:

Component

repaint

```
gridButtons[x][y].setLabel(player);
```

After a label has been changed, the program must force the window to redraw itself so the change will be visible. Therefore, it calls the `repaint` method, which calls `paint`.

The Dialog Box

When a tic-tac-toe game ends, the program displays a dialog box that tells the user the result of the game. A dialog box, an object created from a subclass of the AWT class `Dialog`, is a window that exists as the child of a top level window (its parent window). The `Dialog` class is itself a subclass of the `Window` class.

A dialog box may be *modal*, in which case the user must close the dialog box before performing any other actions with the program, or it may be *mode-less*, in which case it acts like any other window, permitting a full range of actions with the program while the dialog box is on the screen. Modal dialog boxes are usually used to inform or warn the user; modeless dialog boxes are typically used to collect information from the user.

Because the tic-tac-toe game needs to inform the user of the result of a game, it uses a modal dialog box. As you can see in Listing 8.8, a dialog box class isn't all that different from a window class derived directly from `Frame`. The constructor adds components to the window. It uses a window listener to take care of clicks in its close box (if it has one) and an action listener to handle a click in its OK button.

The dialog box class's constructor requires two parameters: a reference to the dialog box's parent window and a string containing the text that is to be displayed in the dialog box. The text, of course, depends on how the game ended. The use of the reference to the parent window, however, isn't quite so intuitive.

If you look at Listing 8.8, you'll notice that the first line of the constructor contains the word `super`. This is a call to one of the base class's constructors, which has the following general syntax:

```
super (parent_window_reference, title_string, modal/modeless);
```

The third parameter is a boolean that indicates whether the dialog box is modal (TRUE) or modeless (FALSE). Therefore, the tic-tac-toe game call is written:

```
super (parent,"Game's Over",true);
```

Label

new

The dialog box could include a `paint` method to display its text message. However, there is a simpler way to achieve the same end when all you need to do is draw a single line of text: create an object of class `Label` and add it to a container. A label object needs only a string of text as an input parameter (the text of the label). Therefore, the following statement creates the label (stored in the string variable `message`) and adds it to a panel that will be placed in the dialog box:

```
messagePanel.add (new Label(message));
```

Window

dispose

When the user clicks the dialog box's OK button, the Java virtual machine calls the `actionPerformed` method in the button's action listener object. In this particular example, all the listener needs to do is close the window. To close a window of any kind, you use its dispose method, which requires no parameters:

```
thisDialog.dispose();
```

Listing 8.8 tttDialog.java

```java
import java.awt.*;
import java.io.*;
import java.lang.*;
import java.awt.event.*;

public class tttDialog extends Dialog
{
    private Dialog thisDialog;

    public tttDialog (Frame parent, String message)
    {
        super (parent,"Game's Over",true);

        addWindowListener (new WindowAdapter ()
        {
            public void windowClosing (WindowEvent theEvent)
                { thisDialog.dispose(); }
        } );

        Panel messagePanel = new Panel();
        messagePanel.add (new Label(message));
        add ("Center",messagePanel);

        Panel buttonPanel = new Panel();
        Button theButton = new Button("OK");
        theButton.addActionListener (new ActionListener ()
        {
            public void actionPerformed (ActionEvent theEvent)
                { thisDialog.dispose(); }
        } );
        buttonPanel.add (theButton);

        add ("South",buttonPanel);
        resize (300,75);
        thisDialog = this;
    }
}
```

Notice that the dialog box's constructor needs to save a reference to the dialog box itself (`thisDialog`) so that its listener classes can reference the dialog box in a call to `dispose`.

Vectors

The biggest drawback to an array is that it has a fixed size. If a program doesn't use all the elements in the array, then you're wasting memory. Even worse, if a program runs out of room in the array, then there is nothing the program can do. One alternative is a Java class called `Vector`, which provides the equivalent of a one-dimensional array that can grow and shrink in size during program execution. A vector holds references to objects of class `Object` and, like an array, provides direct access to its elements.

As an example of a vector, we'll be looking at a new version of the sales average program that you saw earlier in this chapter. It uses a vector instead of an array to store sales figures. In addition, because the vector can grow as the program runs, the user can enter as many sales values as needed. The program therefore continues to accept input until the user enters a 0.

To use a vector rather than a one-dimensional array, changes have been made to the `yearlySales` class (Listing 8.9) and the `salesApp` class (Listing 8.10). The only modification to the `salesApp` class is the `while` loop for input, which uses a 0 as an end-of-data flag; the `yearlySales` class contains support for the vector.

Creating Vectors

Vector

new

Because a vector is an object, you create it using the **new** operator:

```
Vector reference_variable = new Vector (arguments);
```

There are three constructors for the `Vector` class, differentiated by the number of input parameters:

- If you pass no arguments to a constructor, Java initializes a vector with 10 elements. Whenever the vector runs out of unused elements, Java will add new elements by doubling the vector's current size.
- If you pass a single integer to a constructor, Java initializes a vector using the input value as the number of initial elements. When the vector runs out of unused elements, Java will add new elements by doubling the vector's current size. For example, the `yearlySales` class uses

```
Sales = new Vector (INIT_SIZE);
```

Listing 8.9   The yearlySales class, modified to use a vector

```
import java.util.*;
import java.lang.*;

public class yearlySales
{
    private Vector Sales;
    private  static final int INIT_SIZE = 12;

    public yearlySales()
    {
        Sales = new Vector (INIT_SIZE);
        for (int i = 0; i < INIT_SIZE; i++)
            Sales.addElement (new Float (0));
    }

    public void InitSales (int i, float Amount)
    {
        if (i >= Sales.size())
            Sales.addElement (new Float (Amount));
        else
            Sales.setElementAt (new Float (Amount), i);
    }

    public float getSales(int i)
        { return ((Float) Sales.elementAt (i)).floatValue(); }

    public int getSize ()
        { return Sales.size(); }
}
```

where **INIT_SIZE** contains an integer representing the initial size of the vector.

- If you pass two integers to a constructor, Java uses the first value as the vector's initial size and the second as the increment by which the vector should grow. For example new Vector (10,20) creates a vector with 10 elements that has 20 elements added each time the vector needs to grow.

Listing 8.10   the salesApp class, modified to allow an unlimited number of
               inputs

```
import java.awt.*;
import text.*;
import java.awt.event.*;
import text.*;

public class salesApp extends Frame
{
    private float oneMonth;
    private yearlySales SalesObject = new yearlySales(); // sales object
    private salesApp thisApp;

    public salesApp()
    {
        thisApp = this; // need this for adding stuff in inner classes
        addWindowListener (new WindowAdapter ()
        {
            public void windowClosing (WindowEvent theEvent)
            {
                Window window = (Window) theEvent.getSource();
                window.dispose();
                //System.exit(0);
            }
        } );

        SystemInput sysIn = new SystemInput();
        int idx = 0;
        oneMonth = sysIn.readFloat ("Enter sales for month " +
            Integer.toString(idx+1) + ":");
        while (oneMonth != 0)
        {
            SalesObject.InitSales(idx++, oneMonth);
            oneMonth = sysIn.readFloat ("Enter sales for month " +
                Integer.toString(idx + 1) + ":");
        }

        setTitle ("Sales Average Program");
        setLayout (new BorderLayout());
        Panel thePanel = new Panel(); // panel for buttons
```

Continued next page

Listing 8.10(Continued) the salesApp class, modified to allow an unlimited number of inputs

```
    Button theButton = new Button ("Show average");
    theButton.addActionListener (new ActionListener ()
    {
        public void actionPerformed (ActionEvent theEvent)
        {
            averageCanvas theCanvas = new averageCanvas (SalesObject);
            thisApp.add ("Center",theCanvas);
            thisApp.show();
        }
    } );
    thePanel.add (theButton);

    theButton = new Button ("Show sales");
    theButton.addActionListener (new ActionListener ()
    {
        public void actionPerformed (ActionEvent theEvent)
        {
            listCanvas theCanvas = new listCanvas (SalesObject);
            thisApp.add ("Center", theCanvas);
            thisApp.show();
        }
    } );
    thePanel.add (theButton);
    add ("North",thePanel); // add panel to container
}

public static void main (String args[])
{
    salesApp theApp = new salesApp();
    theApp.setSize (400,300);
    theApp.show ();
}
}
```

Adding Elements

Creating a vector object only initializes the vector object itself; it doesn't add any elements to the object. Therefore, when you want to store something in a vector for the first time, you must add an element:

Vector
add-
Element

vectorVariable.addElement (*objectReference*)

If you add an element that will take the total number of elements in the vector beyond the vector's current size, then Java automatically increases the size of the vector. As you read in the preceding section, the amount of the increase is determined by the way in which vector the object was created.

Storing Numbers in Vector Elements

An element added to a vector is stored as an object of class Object. When you add an element (or change an element's contents), Java typecasts the object from its original class to that of Object. (Remember that all Java classes inherit from Object.) However, this presents a major problem if you want to store numbers, which are simple values not typically stored as object.

Integer
Long
Float
Double

new

The solution is to create an object for a number, using one of the numeric wrapper classes (Integer, Long, Float, Double). For example, to store a sales figure in a new element, the yearly sales program uses:

```
Sales.addElement (new Float (0));
```

To create an object from a wrapper class, you use the name of the class, followed by a single input argument representing the value to be stored in the object.

Changing Element Contents

Vector

set-
ElementAt

To change the contents of an existing vector element, you specify which element and the reference of an object that is to replace the current contents of the element and call the setElementAt method. For example, the sales average program changes the value in its vector with:

```
Sales.setElementAt (new Float (Amount), i);
```

The setElementAt method takes two parameters. The first is the object reference to be stored; the second is the index of the element. Like arrays, vector indexes begin with 0.

Getting the Size of a Vector

When the sales average program creates its vector, it initializes the vector size to 12. However, the user can enter more sales values if he or she wants. This presents a bit of a problem to the program. If the InitSales method tries to

Vector

size

modify the value of a non-existing element by calling `setElementAt` with an index that is smaller than the number of elements in the vector, the program will stop with an "array out of bounds" runtime error.

The solution is for the `InitSales` method to check to see whether the index of the element being modified is a new or existing element. To do this, it can obtain the number of elements in the vector by calling its `size` method:

```
int numberOfElement = Sales.size();
```

Keep in mind when using the `size` method that although the elements are numbered beginning with 0, `size` returns a count of the elements beginning with 1.

Note

Once the `InitSales` method knows the number of elements in the vector, it can add a new element if the index is greater than or equal to the last index currently in the vector or modify an existing element:

```
if (i >= Sales.size())
    Sales.addElement (new Float (Amount));
else
    Sales.setElementAt (new Float (Amount), i);
```

Retrieving Data from a Vector

Vector

Element-
At

Because a vector is an object, instead of a language element like an array, you can't access the elements in a vector simply by giving their indexes: You must use the `elementAt` method. For example, the following statement will retrieve a button reference from a vector of buttons:

```
Button theButton = (Button) theVector.elementAt (index);
```

Although Java takes care of typecasting an object reference to class `Object` when you store an item in a vector, the reverse isn't true. You need to explicitly typecast from `Object` to the correct class when you retrieve an object.

Warning

The `Vector` class doesn't check to make sure that you are typecasting an object reference back to a valid class. For example, it might be valid to typecast an object that came from the `Dialog` class to `Dialog` or `Window`, but not to `Button`. It is up to your program to make sure that typecasts out of a vector are valid.

Note

One implication of a vector's storing everything as an object of class `Object` is that all the elements in a vector don't need to be from the same class. However, if you begin mixing different types of objects in the same vector, it is up to your program to keep track of which type of object has been stored in which element so that typecasting out of the vector will work properly. Given that this is rather cumbersome to implement, it's usually much wiser to stick to a single class within a vector.

Integer
Long
Float
Double

When you want to retrieve a numeric value from a vector, you must use the `xValue` method—where `x` is `integer`, `float`, `long`, or `double`—to extract the number. For example, the sales average program extracts a floating point value from its vector with:

xValue

```
(Float) Sales.elementAt (i)).floatValue()
```

This expression first retrieves element `i` from the vector and typecasts it to class `Float`. Then it calls the `floatValue` method of the `Float` class to extract the floating point value from the `Float` object.

Shrinking a Vector

Vector

Although vectors grow automatically, they don't shrink automatically, even if elements remain unused. However, you can trim a vector to its last used element with the `trimToSize` method:

trimTo-
Size

```
theVector.trimToSize();
```

Most programmers don't trim a vector until they are sure that it isn't going to grow any more because increasing the size of a vector may mean moving it around in memory, a process that slows down the execution of a program.

Adding Elements to and Removing Elements from the Middle of a Vector

The `addElement` and `trimToSize` methods add and remove elements from the end of a vector. You can also add elements to and remove elements from anywhere in a vector.

Vector

insert-
ElementAt

To add an element in the middle of a vector, call the `insertElement-At` method:

```
theVector.insertElementAt (index);
```

The new element will occupy position `index`. All existing elements at that index and above will be shifted one position up (to a higher index) to make room for the new element.

Vector

remove-
ElementAt

To remove an element from the middle of a vector, call the `removeElementAt` method:

```
theVector.removeElementAt (index);
```

The element at position `index` is removed from the vector. The remaining elements are shifted one position down (to a lower index) to cover the hole left by the element that was removed.

Summary

An array is a complex variable that groups more than one value of a single data type. Arrays can be used as class variables or local variables. They can hold data of simple variable types (integers, floating point values, and so on), or they can hold references to objects declared from the same class.

To declare a one-dimensional (one column, many rows) array, place a pair of braces ([ ]) after the data type in the declaration. A two-dimensional array (many columns, many rows) requires two sets of brackets, one for the array index of each dimension. Use the `new` operator to allocate space for a specific number of elements.

The elements in a Java array are numbered beginning with 0. Although the array declaration requires the total number of elements in the array, the index of the highest element in the array is one less than the total number of elements.

To assign a value to an array, a program uses the name of the array followed by brackets containing the index of the element to which the value is to be assigned.

A variable that represents an array contains a reference to the array, the main memory address of the beginning of the array.

A vector is an object of class `Vector` that holds references to objects of the `Object` class. A vector is similar to a one-dimensional array in that it holds an ordered list of elements. However, a vector can grow and shrink in size while a program is running. Because a vector is an object, manipulation of it requires use of class methods. In addition, to store numbers in a vector, a program must create objects from them using the number wrapper classes.

Exercises

1. Write a program with a GUI that analyzes Dow Jones Averages. The program should include a class that stores the closing Dow Jones Averages for a two-week period using a one-dimensional array. Allow the user to enter the averages and then initialize an object of the data handling class with those values. Provide buttons for the user to choose between two methods, one that shows all the averages and another that computes and displays the overall average.

2. Rewrite the program that you wrote for Exercise 1 using a vector rather than an array.

3. Write a program with a GUI that uses a two-dimensional array to store data about the credit-card purchases made by one employee during a seven-day period. The rows in the array should represents the seven days; the columns should represent the purchase amounts made during a given day. Ask the user to enter the data and then use that data to initialize a data handling object. Provide buttons that allow the user to calculate the purchases made on one day (ask the user to indicate which day), the total for each day, and the grand total of the purchases made.

4. You have been asked to keep track of the number of people attending a computer trade show that runs for seven days. Write a program with a GUI that does the following:

    *   Lets the user enter attendance values and uses them to initialize a data handling object that stores the values in an array or a vector.
    *   Display the values in the order in which they were entered.
    *   Computes and displays the average attendance.
    *   Sorts the values and displays them in sorted order.

5. Modify the program you wrote for Exercise 3 so that it makes a copy of the array or vector of attendance figures and sorts the copy, rather than the original. (*Hint:* To copy data from one data structure to another, use a `for` loop. You must copy the elements one at a time!)

6. Write a program that evaluates a poker hand. The program should use a two-dimensional array to store the five-card hand. In one column, store the suit (1 = Diamonds, 2 = Hearts, 3 = Clubs, 4 = Spades); in the other column, store the card value (11 = Jack, 12 = Queen, 13 = King). After the use has entered the contents of the hand, the program should evaluate the hand and report in a dialog box whether the hand contains a flush (all the same suit), a straight (all five cards in numeric order), four of a kind, a full house (three of a kind plus two of a kind), three of a kind, two pair, one pair, or nothing.

7. Objects of the Person class that you have been developing (most recently modified in Exercise 11 at the end of Chapter 5) are most commonly going to be handled by some type of container class. For this exercise, develop an array manager class that handles Person objects.

   Add an ID number (a `long`) to the Person class. Modify the class's constructor to accommodate the new variable. Add accessor and mutator methods. The array manager should keep track of the last ID number used. When a new Person object is created, add 1 to the last ID number used to generate an ID number for the new object.

   Modify your application class to demonstrate that you can add and retrieve objects through an array manager object.

8. Create a class that describes a Student and his or her current course enrollments. Include the following data about the student:

   - Student ID (`long`)
   - First name (`String`)
   - Last name (`String`)
   - Courses in which student is enrolled (`Vector`)

Each course is represented as an object of a class named CourseSection that includes the course number, section, and instructor. Because a student typically takes more than one course, use a vector to contain the multiple courses. The variable that describes a student's courses that is part of the Student class will therefore be a vector object.

Include constructors, accessor, and mutator methods for each class. Write an application class that demonstrates that your classes work.

9. Create an array manager class to handle multiple objects of the Student class you developed for Exercise 8. Modify the application class to demonstrate that you can enter multiple students and display course enrollments for a student when given the student's ID number.

10. Consider the algorithm for the bubble sort that you learned about in this chapter. One of the drawbacks of the process is that a program must make an extra pass through an array when the array is completely sorted to determine that the array is in order and that sorting should stop. What other means could a program use to determine when an array is completely sorted? Your strategy should avoid making the extra pass through the array without requiring the program to do too much extra work.

11. The bubble sort isn't a very efficient sort algorithm. In fact, unless the array is mostly in order, it performs very poorly. Investigate another type of sort (for example, a shell sort). Modify the sort routine in the sales average program so that it implements your more efficient sort.

9 Containers

OBJECTIVES

In this chapter you will learn about:

- Using array managers to handle arrays containing references to multiple objects of the same class.
- Using arrays as method parameters.
- Sorting an array of objects
- Creating and using popup menus.
- Using a hash table to contain references to multiple objects of the same class.

Business information systems usually deal with data that describe many objects of a single class rather than just a single object. For example, a program to manage a pharmacy's prescriptions must handle many customers, many types of drugs, and many prescriptions.

One of the strategies you can use to handle multiple objects of the same class (or objects derived from the same base class) is to place references to the objects in an array. Such arrays are usually managed by a class designed specifically for the purpose, hiding the details of array manipulation from the object using the array. For example, if the pharmacy program mentioned in the previous paragraph used an array to store all its customer objects, then the array would be declared in an array manager class. An array manager object would take care of inserting object references into the array, finding objects in the array, and removing objects from the array. The program's application object would create one array manager object and then request array services from the array manager.

Classes like array managers are known as *container classes* because their sole purpose is to contain and manage objects of another class. In the example we will use in this chapter, the container class also performs computations on data in the array, totally isolating the array from other classes. As you might expect, the benefit of this strategy is that you can change a container class's behavior without needing to modify any classes that use the container class.

In this chapter you will see how a container class is used to isolate other classes from the details of a data structure. While exploring the array manager, you will also learn how to handle arrays when they are used as method parameters, and to create and use popup menus. After looking at the details of an array manager, you will be introduced to a hash table, a container class provided by Java that stores and retrieves elements based on a key value.

Note

To be strictly correct, vectors, which you learned about in Chapter 8, are also container classes, in that the vector object contains and manages elements that are other objects.

The Survey Analysis Program

As an example of a program that handles an array of objects, we will be looking at a program that analyzes the results of a survey about footwear purchasing habits. Participants in the survey were asked how many pairs of different types of footwear they owned and purchased in the past year.

The program's interface is relatively simple. As you can see in Figure 9.1, the top level window contains two popup menus and two buttons. The left popup menu chooses the type of analysis the user wants performed (overall average, average by gender, or frequency distribution). The right popup menu chooses the data value that is to be analyzed (for example, athletic shoes owned, boots purchased).

Figure 9.1   The survey analysis program's user interface

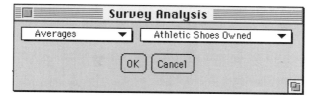

To perform an analysis, the user makes choices from both menus and clicks the OK button. (The Cancel button acts just like the window's close box to end the program.) The results appear in a dialog box. For example, in Figure 9.2 you can see a frequency distribution of the number of pairs of boots owned by survey respondents.

The survey analysis program uses seven classes:

- Survey: The Survey class holds the data from one survey. Notice in Listing 9.1 that with the exception of the class's constructors, all of the methods are "get" methods that return a single piece of data to a calling method. The Survey class therefore acts only as a repository for data. It is totally independent of the program's user interface.

Note   The survey analysis program loads data from a text file. (The assumption is that the text file was produced by scanning mark-sense forms.) We will be covering text I/O in Chapter 12. Until that time, you should ignore the constructor that reads an object's data from a file.

Figure 9.2   Sample survey analysis output

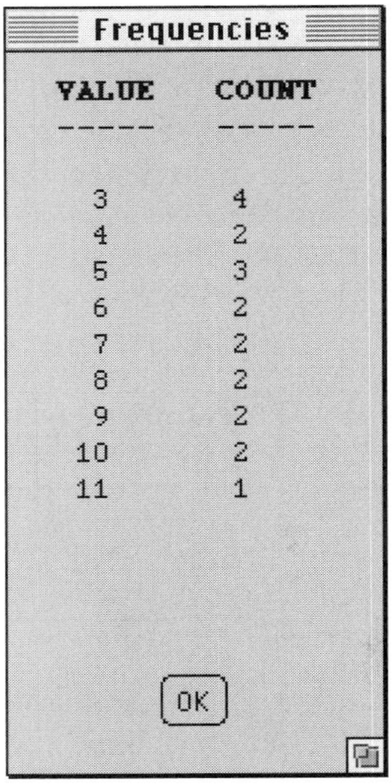

```
╔══════════════════════════╗
║ ▦▦▦  Frequencies  ▦▦▦     ║
╟──────────────────────────╢
║   VALUE      COUNT        ║
║   ─────      ─────        ║
║                           ║
║     3          4          ║
║     4          2          ║
║     5          3          ║
║     6          2          ║
║     7          2          ║
║     8          2          ║
║     9          2          ║
║    10          2          ║
║    11          1          ║
║                           ║
║                           ║
║                           ║
║                           ║
║                           ║
║          ┌────┐           ║
║          │ OK │           ║
║          └────┘           ║
║                        ▣  ║
╚══════════════════════════╝
```

- ArrayMgr: The ArrayMgr class, which we will examine in great detail shortly, contains an array of references to Survey objects. It handles inserting new object references into the array and performs computations on data in the array, returning the results of the computations to a calling method. Like the Survey class, the array manager is totally independent of the program's user interface.

- SurveyApp: The SurveyApp class provides the program's top level user interface. It generates a top level window containing the popup menus and buttons. It traps buttons clicks and, based on the currently selected popup menu items, asks an array manager object to perform computations. Once computations have been performed, the application object creates objects to display results.

- averageDialog: The averageDialog class displays the results of the computation of an average. As you can see in Listing 9.2, this class uses techniques to which you were introduced in Chapter 8.

- GaverageDialog: The GaverageDialog class (Listing 9.3) displays the results of the computation of averages by gender. Like

Listing 9.1   survey.java

```java
import java.awt.*;
import java.io.*;
import java.lang.*;
import java.util.*;

public class Survey
{
    private int Survey_numb = 0;
    private char Gender;
    private int Age = 0;
    private int AthleticOwned = 0;
    private int AthleticBought = 0;
    private int DressOwned = 0;
    private int DressBought = 0;
    private int BootsOwned = 0;
    private int BootsBought = 0;
    private int SandalsOwned = 0;
    private int SandalsBought = 0;

    public Survey ()
    {
        // for use when creating temporary object
    }

    // Loads data from a text file; ignore for now
    public Survey (DataInput inS) throws IOException
    {
        // get a line of data from the file
        String inputLine = inS.readLine();
        // create tokenizer; use space as delimiter
        StringTokenizer theTokenizer = new StringTokenizer (inputLine," ");

        Survey_numb = Integer.parseInt (theTokenizer.nextToken());
        Gender = (theTokenizer.nextToken()).charAt(0);
        Age = Integer.parseInt (theTokenizer.nextToken());
        AthleticOwned = Integer.parseInt (theTokenizer.nextToken());
        AthleticBought = Integer.parseInt (theTokenizer.nextToken());
        DressOwned = Integer.parseInt (theTokenizer.nextToken());
        DressBought = Integer.parseInt (theTokenizer.nextToken());
        BootsOwned = Integer.parseInt (theTokenizer.nextToken());
        BootsBought = Integer.parseInt (theTokenizer.nextToken());
        SandalsOwned = Integer.parseInt (theTokenizer.nextToken());
        SandalsBought = Integer.parseInt (theTokenizer.nextToken());
    }
```

Continued next page

Listing 9.1(Continued)   survey.java

```java
    public char getGender()
        { return Gender; }

    public int getAge()
        { return Age; }

    public int getAthleticOwned()
        { return AthleticOwned; }

    public int getAthleticBought()
        { return AthleticBought;}

    public int getDressOwned()
        { return DressOwned; }

    public int getDressBought()
        { return DressBought; }

    public int getBootsOwned()
        { return BootsOwned; }

    public int getBootsBought()
        { return BootsBought; }

    public int getSandalsOwned()
        { return SandalsOwned; }

    public int getSandalsBought()
        { return SandalsBought; }
}
```

averageDialog, it uses programming techniques with which you are familiar.

- freqsDialog: The freqsDialog class (Listing 9.4) displays a frequency distribution. Because the output requires a listing rather than just one or two lines of text, this dialog box contains a canvas.
- freqsCanvas: The freqsCanvas class (Listing 9.5) takes care of displaying the frequency distribution listing.

The array manager and application classes of the survey analysis program illustrate most of the concepts that will be covered in the rest of this chapter. Nonetheless, the program is far from complete. It should do many more things, including computing standard deviations, medians, modes, and statistics based on groupings of respondents by age. (You will get a chance to add some of the missing pieces in the exercises at the end of this chapter.)

Listing 9.2   averageDialog.java

```java
import java.awt.*;
import java.io.*;
import java.lang.*;
import text.*;
import java.awt.event.*;

public class averageDialog extends Dialog
{
    private averageDialog thisDialog;

    public averageDialog (Frame parent, float average)
    {
        super (parent,"Overall average",true);
        thisDialog = this;

        addWindowListener (new WindowAdapter ()
        {
            public void windowClosing (WindowEvent theEvent)
                { thisDialog.dispose(); }
        } );

        setLayout (new BorderLayout());

        Panel messagePanel = new Panel();
        messagePanel.add (new Label ("The average is " +
            NumberFormat.floatFormat(5,3,average) + "."));
        add ("Center",messagePanel);

        Panel buttonPanel = new Panel();
        Button theButton = new Button ("OK");
        theButton.addActionListener (new ActionListener ()
        {
            public void actionPerformed (ActionEvent theEvent)
                { thisDialog.dispose(); }
        } );
        buttonPanel.add (theButton);
        add ("South",buttonPanel);
        setSize (300,75);
        setLocation (50,50);
    }
}
```

Listing 9.3   GaverageDialog.java

```java
import java.awt.*;
import java.io.*;
import java.lang.*;
import text.*;
import java.awt.event.*;

public class GaverageDialog extends Dialog
{
    private GaverageDialog thisDialog;

    public GaverageDialog (Frame parent, float averageM, float averageF)
    {
        super (parent,"Gender-based Averages",true);
        thisDialog = this;

        addWindowListener (new WindowAdapter ()
        {
            public void windowClosing (WindowEvent theEvent)
                { thisDialog.dispose(); }
        } );

        setLayout (new BorderLayout());

        Panel messagePanel = new Panel();
        messagePanel.add (new Label ("The average for men is " +
            NumberFormat.floatFormat(5,3,averageM) + "."));
        messagePanel.add (new Label ("The average for women is " +
            NumberFormat.floatFormat(5,3,averageF) + "."));
        add ("Center",messagePanel);

        Panel buttonPanel = new Panel();
        Button theButton = new Button ("OK");
        theButton.addActionListener (new ActionListener ()
        {
            public void actionPerformed (ActionEvent theEvent)
                { thisDialog.dispose(); }
        } );
        buttonPanel.add (theButton);
        add ("South",buttonPanel);
        setSize (300,125);
        setLocation (50,50);
    }
}
```

Listing 9.4   freqsDialog.java

```java
import java.awt.*;
import java.io.*;
import java.lang.*;
import java.awt.event.*;

public class freqsDialog extends Dialog
{
    private freqsDialog thisDialog;

    public freqsDialog (Frame parent, int[][] freqsArray, int count)
    {
        super (parent,"Frequencies",true);
        thisDialog = this;

        addWindowListener (new WindowAdapter ()
        {
            public void windowClosing (WindowEvent theEvent)
                { thisDialog.dispose(); }
        } );

        setLayout (new BorderLayout());

        freqsCanvas theCanvas = new freqsCanvas(freqsArray, count);
        add ("Center",theCanvas);

        Panel buttonPanel = new Panel();
        Button theButton = new Button ("OK");
        theButton.addActionListener (new ActionListener ()
        {
            public void actionPerformed (ActionEvent theEvent)
                { thisDialog.dispose(); }
        } );
        buttonPanel.add (theButton);
        add ("South",buttonPanel);
        setSize (150,300);
        setLocation (50,50);
    }
}
```

Listing 9.5   freqsCanvas.java

```java
import java.awt.*;
import java.io.*;
import java.lang.*;
import text.*;

public class freqsCanvas extends Canvas
{
    private int[][] freqsArray;
    private int count;

    public freqsCanvas (int[][] inputArray, int inputcount)
    {
        freqsArray = inputArray;
        count = inputcount;
    }

    public void paint (Graphics graphObject)
    {
        String firstLine = "VALUE    COUNT";
        String secondLine = "-----    -----";
        Dimension theSize = getSize(); // find size of canvas
        // Create fonts
        Font boldFont = new Font ("Courier",Font.BOLD,12);
        Font plainFont = new Font ("Courier",Font.PLAIN,12);

        FontMetrics boldMetrics = graphObject.getFontMetrics (boldFont);
        FontMetrics plainMetrics = graphObject.getFontMetrics (plainFont);

        // draw first line 20 pixels from top left corner of canvas
        int Y = 20;
        graphObject.setFont (boldFont);
        graphObject.drawString (firstLine, 20, Y);
        // draw second line below; leave 3 pixels between lines
        int lineHeight = plainMetrics.getHeight() + 3;
        Y += lineHeight;
        graphObject.drawString (secondLine, 20,Y);
        graphObject.setFont (plainFont);
        // leave one line between second line and data
        Y += lineHeight * 2;
        for (int i = 0; i <= count;i++)
        {
            graphObject.drawString
                (NumberFormat.intFormat (3,freqsArray[i][0]) + "      " +
                    NumberFormat.intFormat(3,freqsArray[i][1]),20,Y);
            Y += lineHeight;
        }
    }
}
```

The survey analysis program contains some error messages that display in a console output window. This keeps the program a bit shorter, since displaying error messages dialog boxes would require additional classes.

Declaring Arrays of Objects

In principle, an array of object references isn't much different from any other array. (In fact, you saw a simple use of such an array in Chapter 8, where we used an array of `Button` object references for the tic-tac-toe playing grid.) You therefore declare an array of objects in the same way you declare an array whose elements are from a simple data type:

```
clas[] array_variable_name;
```

The array manager class, for example, sets up a variable to reference survey objects with:

```
Survey[] theSurveys;
```

Once the array variable is declared, a program must then allocate space for the array:

```
array_variable_name = new class[#_of_elements];
```

The survey array can therefore be given space with:

```
theSurveys = new Survey[NUMB_SURVEYS];
```

where **NUMB_SURVEYS** is a constant containing the maximum number of surveys the program can handle.

Array Manipulation by an Array Manager

The entire array manager class can be found in Listing 9.6. As you study the code (ignoring the `load` method for now), there are two important things to notice about the way it works and interacts with the objects it manages:

- Because the array of objects is declared as a private variable of the array manager class, only an object of that class has direct access to the contents of the array. Nonetheless, the array manager *doesn't*

Listing 9.6   ArrayMgr.java

```java
import java.awt.*;
import java.io.*;
import java.lang.*;

public class ArrayMgr
{
    public static final int NUMB_SURVEYS = 50;

    private int lastIndex;
    Survey[] theSurveys;
    int[][] freqsArray;   // used to store frequency table

    public ArrayMgr()
    {
        theSurveys = new Survey[NUMB_SURVEYS];
        // column 1 for value; column 2 for count
        freqsArray = new int [NUMB_SURVEYS][2];
        lastIndex = -1;
    }

    // Performs file I/O; ignore for now
    public void load ()
    {
        try
        {
            DataInputStream InS =
                new DataInputStream (new FileInputStream ("Survey"));
            String inputLine = InS.readLine();
            lastIndex = Integer.parseInt(inputLine); // get lastIndex from file

            for (int i = 0; i <= lastIndex; i++)
                theSurveys[i] = new Survey (InS);
        }
        catch (IOException e)
        {
            System.out.println ("Couldn't open input file");
        }
    }
```

Continued next page

Listing 9.6(Continued)   ArrayMgr.java

```java
public void sort (int whichField)
{
    Survey tempSurvey = new Survey();
    int result, Value, ValueBelow, i;
    boolean swap_made = true;

    while (swap_made)
    {
        swap_made = false;
        for (i = 0; i < lastIndex; i++)
        {
            Value = getValue (i, whichField);
            ValueBelow = getValue (i+1, whichField);
            if (Value > ValueBelow)
            {
                tempSurvey = theSurveys[i];
                theSurveys[i] = theSurveys[i+1];
                theSurveys[i+1] = tempSurvey;
                swap_made = true;
            }
        }
    }
}

public int generateFreqs (int whichField, int [][] freqsArray)
{
    sort (whichField);
    int value, valueBelow, index = 0;
    value = getValue (0, whichField);
    freqsArray[index][0] = value;
    freqsArray[index][1] = 1;
    for (int i = 1; i <= lastIndex; i++)
    {
        valueBelow = getValue (i, whichField);
        if (valueBelow == value)
            freqsArray[index][1]++;
        else
        {
            value = valueBelow;
            index++;
            freqsArray[index][0] = value;
            freqsArray[index][1] = 1;
        }
    }
    return index;
}
```

Continued next page

Listing 9.6(Continued)   ArrayMgr.java

```java
public float generateAverage (int whichField)
{
    int sum = 0;

    for (int i = 0; i <= lastIndex; i++)
        sum += getValue (i, whichField);
    return ((float) sum / (float) (getCount() + 1));
}

public void generateGAverages (int whichField, float[] resultArray)
{
    int i, sumM = 0, sumF = 0, countM = 0, countF = 0;
    char Lgender;
    for (i = 0; i <= lastIndex; i++)
    {
        Lgender = getGender(i);
        if (Lgender == 'M')
        {
            countM++;;
            sumM += getValue (i, whichField);
        }
        else
        {
            countF++;
            sumF += getValue (i, whichField);
        }
    }
    resultArray[0] = (float) sumM / countM;
    resultArray[1] = (float) sumF / countF;
}

public int getValue (int index, int whichField)
{
    int Value = 0;
    switch(whichField)
    {
        case 0: Value = theSurveys[index].getAthleticOwned(); break;
        case 1: Value = theSurveys[index].getAthleticBought(); break;
        case 2: Value = theSurveys[index].getDressOwned(); break;
        case 3: Value = theSurveys[index].getDressBought(); break;
        case 4: Value = theSurveys[index].getBootsOwned(); break;
        case 5: Value = theSurveys[index].getBootsBought(); break;
        case 6: Value = theSurveys[index].getSandalsOwned(); break;
        case 7: Value = theSurveys[index].getSandalsBought(); break;
    }
    return Value;
}
```

Continued next page

Listing 9.6(Continued) ArrayMgr.java

```
public char getGender (int index)
    { return theSurveys[index].getGender(); }

public int getCount ()
    { return lastIndex; }
}
```

have access to the contents of the Survey objects. It must call Survey class "get" methods, just like any other class. For example, in each of the methods that perform computations (generate-Average, generateGAverages, and generateFreqs), the array manager calls its own getValue method, which uses an identifier for the type of data being analyzed to decide which Survey class "get" method to call.

- Like most array managers, the ArrayMgr class needs a counter to keep track of the last index used in its array (lastIndex). Although an array is initialized with a fixed number of elements, there is no requirement that they all be filled.

Sorting an Array of Objects

One of the most commonly performed types of statistical analysis is the generation of frequency distributions. Typically, frequency distributions list all the unique values in a given group of data, ordered from low to high, along with the number of times each value occurs.

Probably the easiest way to produce a frequency distribution is to sort the values and then scan them from low to high, counting how many times each value occurs. The generateFreqs method must therefore ask the array manager to sort the array by any of the eight types of data stored. To implement the sort, we'll use the bubble sort method that you first read about in Chapter 8, but although decisions on whether to perform a swap are made based on data values, what actually gets swapped are object references.

Note

Although the generateFreqs method is currently the only array manager method that sorts data, sorting is performed by the separate sort method so that if the program is expanded later, sorting will be available to any method that needs it.

As you look at the `sort` method in Listing 9.6, notice that the logic of the sort is exactly the same as that used when sorting the array of sales values in Chapter 8. The major differences lies in what is compared and what is swapped. Comparisons are based on values in the variable corresponding to the type of data on which the array is being sorted. However, when it comes time to make a swap, the method moves object references rather than individual pieces of data.

Keep in mind that when a swap is performed, the objects themselves aren't being moved. They remain in their original main memory locations. The values being swapped are simply the addresses where the objects can be found. This is a much faster way to sort objects than actually attempting to order the objects' storage in main memory. It also helps avoid memory fragmentation by leaving objects in their original locations.

Arrays as Method Parameters

The `generateGAverages` and `generateFreqs` methods present a small problem: They need to return more than one value to a calling method. Although we could create special objects to contain the results of the methods, when a method needs to return multiple values of the same data type, it is usually easier to use an array for that purpose.

Like objects, arrays are always passed by reference. This means that when you send an array to a method as an input parameter, you are sending the main memory address of where the array's storage begins in main memory. Therefore, the method is working with the original array and any changes made to that array in the called method will be accessible to the calling method.

The strategy for using arrays to return multiple values from a method is as follows:

1.   Create an array to hold the result values in the calling method.
2.   Place the name of the result array in the method call.
3.   Let the called method perform its manipulation of the result array.
4.   When the called method terminates, use the modified result array as needed.

When you write a method that includes an array as an input parameter, you include the array declaration by placing brackets after the data type. For example, the `generateGAverages` result array appears as:

```
float[] resultArray
```

The size of the array is determined by the calling method, which actually allocates the space for the array.

The `generateFreqs` method requires a two-dimensional result array (one column for the data value and a second for the count):

```
int [][] freqsArray
```

If you look back at Listing 9.6, you will see that both `generate-GAverages` and `generateFreqs` load their result arrays with data. However, neither method contains a `return` statement. The `return` is unnecessary because the calling method already has a reference to the single copy of the result arrays.

Warning You can declare and allocate space for an array in a method, and then return a reference to that array with a `return` statement. However, a local variable is destroyed when its method terminates. Unless you make the array `static`, it will be destroyed before the calling method can use it. If you make the array `static`, it will remain in memory as long as the program is running, which may take up memory space that could otherwise be reused. Therefore, it is more efficient to let the calling method create the array and pass a reference to a called method. The result array can then be destroyed without a problem when the calling method is through with it.

Using an Array Manager

Now that you have seen how an array manager handles the data in its array of objects, we can turn to an application object that uses an array manager object. The `SurveyApp` class (Listing 9.7) is typical of such an application class.

To use the array manager, the application class must create an object of the array manager class. In our example, that means declaring and allocating space for an object of the `ArrayMgr` class:

```
private ArrayMgr theArray;
   :
theArray = new ArrayMgr(); // occurs in the constructor
```

Once the array manager object exists, the application object can request services from it. In the survey analysis program, the first thing the application object does is ask the array manager to load data:

```
theArray.load();
```

Listing 9.7   SurveyApp.java

```java
import java.awt.*;
import java.io.*;
import java.lang.*;
import java.awt.event.*;

public class SurveyApp extends Frame
{
    private ArrayMgr theArray;
    private int theAnalysis = 0, theField = 0;
    private Choice AnalysisType, Field;
    public static final int NUMB_SURVEYS = 50;
    private SurveyApp thisApp;

    public SurveyApp()
    {
        theArray = new ArrayMgr();
        theArray.load();
        thisApp = this;
        setUpWindow();
    }

    private void setUpWindow()
    {
        addWindowListener (new WindowAdapter () // handle closing of window
        {
            public void windowClosing (WindowEvent theEvent)
            {
                thisApp.dispose();
                // System.exit(0);
            }
        } );
        setTitle ("Survey Analysis");
        setLayout (new BorderLayout());

        Panel menuPanel = new Panel();
        AnalysisType = new Choice();
        AnalysisType.addItem ("Averages");
        AnalysisType.addItem ("Gender Averages");
        AnalysisType.addItem ("Frequencies");
        AnalysisType.addItemListener (new ItemListener ()
        {
            public void itemStateChanged (ItemEvent theEvent)
                { theAnalysis = AnalysisType.getSelectedIndex(); }
        } );
        menuPanel.add (AnalysisType);
```

Continued next page

Listing 9.7(Continued)   SurveyApp.java

```java
Field = new Choice();
Field.addItem ("Athletic Shoes Owned");
Field.addItem ("Athletic Shoes Purchased");
Field.addItem ("Dress Shoes Owned");
Field.addItem ("Dress Shoes Purchased");
Field.addItem ("Boots Owned");
Field.addItem ("Boots Purchased");
Field.addItem ("Sandals Owned");
Field.addItem ("Sandals Purchased");
Field.addItemListener (new ItemListener ()
{
    public void itemStateChanged (ItemEvent theEvent)
        { theField = Field.getSelectedIndex(); }
} );
menuPanel.add (Field);
add ("North",menuPanel);

Panel buttonPanel = new Panel();
Button theButton = new Button("OK");
theButton.addActionListener (new ActionListener ()
{
    public void actionPerformed (ActionEvent theEvent)
    {
        if (theField < 0)
            System.out.println ("Please choose a field to analyze.");
        else switch (theAnalysis)
        {
            case 0:
                float average = theArray.generateAverage (theField);
                averageDialog firstDialog =
                    new averageDialog (thisApp,average);
                firstDialog.show();
                break;
            case 1:
                float[] resultArray = new float [2];
                theArray.generateGAverages (theField, resultArray);
                GaverageDialog secondDialog = new GaverageDialog
                    (thisApp, resultArray[0], resultArray[1]);
                secondDialog.show();
                break;
            case 2:
                int[][] freqsArray = new int [NUMB_SURVEYS][2];
                int count = theArray.generateFreqs
                    (theField, freqsArray);
                freqsDialog thirdDialog = new freqsDialog
                    (thisApp, freqsArray, count);
```

Continued next page

Listing 9.7(Continued)　SurveyApp.java

```
                        thirdDialog.show();
                        break;
                }
            }
        } );
        buttonPanel.add (theButton);

        theButton = new Button("Cancel");
        theButton.addActionListener (new ActionListener ()
        {
            public void actionPerformed (ActionEvent theEvent)
            {
                thisApp.dispose();
                // System.exit (0)
            }
        } );
        buttonPanel.add (theButton);
        add ("South",buttonPanel);
    }

    public static void main (String args[])
    {
        SurveyApp theWindow = new SurveyApp();
        theWindow.setSize(400,75);
        theWindow.show();
    }
}
```

Note

The code to load data from a text file could have been placed in the array manager's constructor. However, by keeping the loading separate, the program can more easily be modified to support interactive input as well.

After the data have been loaded and the top-level window has been displayed on the screen, the application object sits and waits for events to occur. When the user clicks the OK button, the application object uses a switch statement in its action method to determine which type of analysis the user is requesting (stored in the theAnalysis variable).

Regardless of the type of analysis, the procedure for generating and displaying results is the same:

1.　Ask the array manager to perform the analysis by calling the appropriate array manager method. (Note that this may mean creating an array to hold the results of the analysis prior to calling the array manager method.) The application object is totally isolated from the way in which the array manager works.

2. Create an object from the appropriate dialog box class, passing in the result of the analysis. The application object is totally isolated from the mechanics of the display.

3. Show the dialog box.

The logic of the application program therefore remains quite simple and consistent. This program will be easy to modify in that new types of analyses can be easily added into the existing structure with only minor modifications to the application class.

Creating and Using Popup Menus

The `SurveyApp` class contains a method named `setUpWindow` that takes care of initializing the program's top-level window. If you look back at Listing 9.7, you will notice that there are two panels on the window, one containing the OK and Cancel buttons (`buttonPanel`) and one containing the popup menus (`menuPanel`). Since you already know how to create command buttons, we'll now turn our attention to the popup menus.

A popup menu is an object of the class `Choice` (a direct descendant of `Component`). To build a popup menu, you must create an object from `Choice` and then individually add items to the menu. You must also add a listener object to the popup menu so that a program can respond whenever a user makes a choice from the menu.

Creating Popup Menus

Choice

To create a popup menu, you declare a variable to hold a reference to a `Choice` object and then create with object with the `new` operator:

```
private Choice AnalysisType, Field;
:
AnalysisType = new Choice ();
```

new

Notice that in this case you don't need any input parameters for the new object's constructor.

Choice

addItem
Container

add

You add items to a popup menu in the order in which you want them to appear using the **addItem** method. The method's single parameter is the text of the menu item, as in:

```
Field.addItem ("Dress Shoes Owned");
```

Once all items have been attached to the popup menu, you add it to the panel where it should appear:

```
menuPanel.add (AnalysisType);
```

Trapping Popup Menu Events

Each time a user makes a selection from a popup menu, Java generates an event object. This means that a program should take action immediately based on the selection, even if that action is simply identifying which menu item has been selected.

A change in the selected item in a popup menu generates an item event. You must therefore register an object that implements the **ItemListener** interface with a **Choice** object. This interface has only one method—**item-StateChanged**—which is called by the Java virtual machine whenever a user changes the selected item. Like the other listener methods that you have seen to this point, **itemStateChanged** requires one input parameter: an event object, in this case, an object created from the **ItemEvent** class.

Choice

Because the survey analysis program performs its calculations only after the user has clicked the OK button, all the program needs to do when a popup menu generates an event is to store the chosen item. Items in a popup menu are numbered beginning with 0. You therefore can get the numeric position of the selected option with the **getSelectedIndex** method:

get-
Selected-
Index

```
theAnalysis = AnalysisType.getSelectedIndex();
```

Note

The only close coupling between the array manager and the application class relates to the positions of the items in the Field popup menu. If you look at the array manager's **getValue** method, you'll notice that it uses field numbers that are the same as the fields' positions in their popup menu. However, it is important to realize that the array manager was written first, and that the application object's popup menus were written to conform to it, rather than the other way around.

Working with Hash Tables

A hash table is an object that stores references to other objects in random order based on a key value. A program retrieves an element from a hash table by supplying the same key that was used to store it. To see how this works conceptually, assume that you have a hash table with room for 12 elements (Figure 9.3). Although this particular example shows the table as a 3 by 4 grid to make it easier to visualize what is occurring, a real hash table usually occupies consecutive memory locations.

Figure 9.3   A hash table

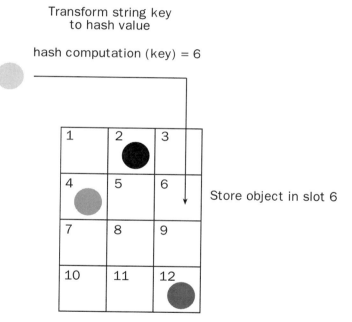

When a program wants to store a reference to an object in the table, it gives the table object a value for the key. The table then takes that key and transforms it into an integer that represents one storage location within the table. (We'll call it a "slot" for want of a better word. The location of a slot is a *hash code*.) The main memory address of the object being stored is placed in whatever location is produced by the key transformation.

The formula that translates a key into a location within the hash table is known as a *hashing algorithm*. To be effective, it must generate locations that are randomly and relatively evenly scattered throughout the table. However, as hash tables begin to fill up—in particular, become more than 75% full—most hashing algorithms begin to produce duplicate locations. Objects whose keys produce the same location in the hash table are said to have collided. When a *collision* occurs, the hash tables stores the objects that collided in the same slot, linking them together in a list (see Figure 9.4). Java's hash table class takes care of managing collision lists, including returning the correct object when you present a key for retrieval.

Figure 9.4   Hash table collisions

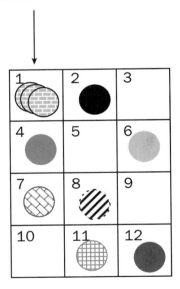

Objects generating the same hash
key are stored in the same slot

As long as there aren't too many collision lists, storage in and retrieval from a hash table is very fast. However, as the length of collision lists goes up, a program must search those lists sequentially to find the correct object, slowing down overall performance. Java's hash table class keeps track of its "load factor," the percentage of filled slots. When the load factor goes above a given level, the hash table reallocates more space for itself by doubling in size. The default load factor is 75%, a good value that you can nonetheless change if you want.

Note

Hashing is not unique to Java. It has been used since the 1960s to physically place records in data files.

Java hash tables store objects of class `Object`. This means, as with a vector, that when you are storing an object in a hash table Java automatically typecasts it to `Object`. However, when you are retrieving objects from the table, it is up to your program to typecast them back to the correct class.

Hash Keys

The keys that you supply to the hash table class for storing an object must be objects themselves. When you specify a key object, the hash table class automatically calls the object's `hashCode` method. The `String` class's `hashCode` method, for example, generates a storage location in the hash table from the characters in the string. In fact, all Java classes that have `hashCode` methods use the contents of the object.

However, those classes that don't have `hashCode` methods have a default hash code based on the object's location in main memory rather than any of the object's contents. The problem with this is that two objects with the same contents but different locations in memory won't generate the same hash code.

Why is it important that hash codes be built from object contents rather than object storage locations? The hash table class is built on the assumption that if you provide a hash key that already exists in the table, storing the new object reference *replaces* the old. If you are using main memory locations, then it is highly unlikely that a replacement will succeed because although the two objects may have the same contents, the hash code generated based on their storage locations will probably be different.

String

hashValue

You will also run into the same problem if you create a class of your own and want to use a key that is something other than an object created from a Java class with a `hashCode` method. In that case, you will need to write a `hashCode` method for your class that returns an integer based on the portion of the contents of the object that are being used as the key. The actual arithmetic doesn't matter, as long as the process does something with the data values that generates a relatively random and spread-out set of integers. To help, you can use the `String` class's `hashValue` method, which returns a string's hash code.

Object

hashCode

For example, assume that you have a catalog that provides quantity pricing for products. You want to use both the catalog number and the quantity as the key because the catalog numbers aren't unique. Your `hashCode` method might look like:

```
public int hashCode()
{
    return catalogNumb.hasValue() + quantity * 12;
}
```

To complete tailoring your class for storing in a hash table, you need to give the hash table class a method for comparing the keys of objects of your class by overriding the `Object` class's `equals` method. Your method needs to compare all elements that make up the hash key:

```
public boolean equals (thisClass otherObject)
{
    return (catalogNumb == otherObject.getCatalogNumb()
        && quantity == otherObject.getQuantity());
}
```

The Sample Hash Table Program

As an example of building and using a hash table, we'll be looking at a simple application that maintains a list of customers. The program's main window serves as a data entry form (see Figure 9.5). When the user clicks the Store button, the program takes the data, creates a customer object, and stores a reference to that object in the hash table using the ID number as the key. If the user clicks the Find button, the program uses just the value of the ID number field to retrieve the customer object. Clicking the list button produces an ordered list of all elements in the table.

The `Customer` class (Listing 9.8) contains a constructor that accepts values for all of an object's variables in its parameter list. The remaining methods are all get methods.

The `CustomerList` class (Listing 9.9) takes care of building the contents of the window, trapping events in the buttons, and maintaining the hash table. This particular window uses one GUI element you haven't seen: a text field. Although we'll leave an in-depth discussion of text fields until Chapter

Figure 9.5   The customer list input window

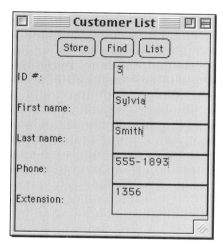

11, it will make it easier for you to follow this code if you know that the `get-Text` method retrieves the text from a text field and the `setText` method replaces the visible text with a new value.

To keep the program relatively short, the output for the customer list program appears in the console window. It has the format:

```
Customer #X: FirstName LastName
             XXX-XXXX XXX
```

Creating a Hash Table

Hash tables are objects of the `Hashtable` class. (Notice that the word "table" begins with a lowercase letter!) To work with one, you must import `java.util.Hashtable` into your source code.

You can create a hash table by invoking one of three constructors:

- `Hashtable()`: The default constructor, which requires no input parameters, creates a hash table without any elements. Each time the table fills up past the load factor, Java doubles the size of the table to provide more space.
- `Hashtable (int initialCapacity)`: If you have some idea of the maximum number of elements you want to place in a hash table, then you can prevent Java from repeatedly spending time

Listing 9.8   Customer.java

```java
import java.lang.*;

public class Customer
{
    private String ID, firstName, lastName, phone, extension;
    public Customer (String inID, String inFirstName, String inLastName,
        String inPhone, String inExtension)
    {
        ID = inID;
        firstName = inFirstName;
        lastName = inLastName;
        phone = inPhone;
        extension = inExtension;
    }

    public String getID ()
        { return ID; }

    public String getFirstName ()
        { return firstName; }

    public String getLastName ()
        { return lastName; }

    public String getPhone ()
        { return phone; }

    public String getExtension ()
        { return extension; }
}
```

resizing the table by giving the table an initial capacity of about 150% of the number of elements.

- `Hashtable(int initialCapacity, float loadFactor)`: To change the load factor, you must use the constructor that also requires a value for the initial capacity. A load factor is expressed as the decimal equivalent of a percentage. For example, 75% would be passed into this constructor as 0.75.

Because there is no way to predict how many customers will be entered into the customer list program, the application's constructor simply creates an empty hash table:

```java
theTable = new Hashtable();
```

Listing 9.9   CustomerList.java

```java
import java.lang.*;
import java.awt.*;
import java.awt.event.*;
import java.util.Hashtable;
import java.util.Enumeration;

public class CustomerList extends Frame
{
    private CustomerList thisWindow;
    private Hashtable theTable;
    private TextField IDField, firstField, lastField, phoneField,
    extensionField;

    public CustomerList ()
    {
        thisWindow = this;
        setTitle ("Customer List");
        theTable = new Hashtable();
        setUpWindow();
    }

    public void setUpWindow()
    {
        addWindowListener (new WindowAdapter ()
        {
            public void windowClosing (WindowEvent theEvent)
            {
                thisWindow.dispose();
                //System.exit(0);
            }
        } );
        Panel buttonPanel = new Panel();
        Button storeButton = new Button ("Store");
        storeButton.addActionListener (new ActionListener ()
        {
            public void actionPerformed (ActionEvent theEvent)
            {
                // Grabbing text from window; ignore for now
                String ID = IDField.getText();
                String first = firstField.getText();
                String last = lastField.getText();
                String phone = phoneField.getText();
                String ext = extensionField.getText();

                Customer theCustomer = new Customer (ID,first,last,phone,ext);
                // add to table
                theTable.put (theCustomer.getID(), theCustomer);
```

Continued next page

Listing 9.9(Continued) CustomerList.java

```
            // Clean out data entry fields; ignore for now
            IDField.setText ("");
            firstField.setText ("");
            lastField.setText ("");
            phoneField.setText ("");
            extensionField.setText ("");
        }
    } );
    buttonPanel.add (storeButton);
    Button findButton = new Button ("Find");
    findButton.addActionListener (new ActionListener ()
    {
        public void actionPerformed (ActionEvent theEvent)
        {
            String theID = IDField.getText(); // grab ID
            Customer theCustomer = (Customer) theTable.get (theID);
            System.out.println ("\nCustomer #" + theID + ": " +
                theCustomer.getFirstName() + " " +
                theCustomer.getLastName() + "\n                " +
                theCustomer.getPhone() + " Extension " +
                theCustomer.getExtension ());
            IDField.setText ("");  // clean out field
        }

    } );
    buttonPanel.add (findButton);
    Button listButton = new Button ("List");
    listButton.addActionListener (new ActionListener ()
    {
        public void actionPerformed (ActionEvent theEvent)
        {
            Customer theCustomer;
            Enumeration theEnumerator = theTable.elements();
            System.out.println ("\n\n");
            while (theEnumerator.hasMoreElements())
            {
                theCustomer = (Customer) theEnumerator.nextElement();
                System.out.println ("Customer #" +
                    theCustomer.getID() + ": " +
                    theCustomer.getFirstName() + " " +
                    theCustomer.getLastName() + "\n                " +
                    theCustomer.getPhone() + " Extension " +
                    theCustomer.getExtension ());
            }
        }
    } );
    buttonPanel.add (listButton);
```

Continued next page

Listing 9.9(Continued)   CustomerList.java

```
    // Fields and labels for data entry; Ignore for now
    Panel dataPanel = new Panel();
    dataPanel.setLayout (new GridLayout (5,2));
    dataPanel.add (new Label ("ID #:"));
    dataPanel.add (IDField = new TextField("",10));
    dataPanel.add (new Label ("First name:"));
    dataPanel.add (firstField = new TextField ("",20));
    dataPanel.add (new Label ("Last name:"));
    dataPanel.add (lastField = new TextField ("", 20));
    dataPanel.add (new Label ("Phone:"));
    dataPanel.add (phoneField = new TextField ("",15));
    dataPanel.add (new Label ("Extension:"));
    dataPanel.add (extensionField = new TextField ("",5));

    add ("North",buttonPanel);
    add ("Center",dataPanel);
  }

  public final static void main (String args[])
  {
    CustomerList theApp = new CustomerList();
    theApp.setSize (200,200);
    theApp.show();
  }
}
```

Adding an Element

Hashtable To add an element to a hash table, you "put" the element into the table:

put

```
        hashTable.put (keyObject, dataObject);
```

For example, to add a customer object to its table, the customer list program uses:

```
        theTable.put (theCustomer.getID(), theCustomer);
```

The put method returns null if an object with the same key was not already present in the table. However, if an object with the key already existed, then Java replaces the old object with the new and returns a reference to the old object.

Retrieving an Element Using Its Key

To retrieve an element from a hash table, you supply its key and "get" the element:

Hashtable

get

```
Element = (ElementClass) hashTable.get (keyObject);
```

For example, to retrieve a single customer object reference from the table—based on an ID number typed by a user—the customer list program uses:

```
Customer theCustomer = (Customer) theTable.get (theID);
```

where `theID` is a string whose value has been retrieved from the ID text field.

Listing Hash Table Contents

Although a hash table is excellent for randomly retrieving elements based on a key value, it doesn't lend itself easily to retrieving its contents in key order. A programmer has no idea where the "first" and "next" elements can be found. Nonetheless, the hash table class does make it possible for you to retrieve the elements in order, using an object known as an *enumerator*. An enumerator is an object whose class implements the `Enumeration` interface.

Hashtable

elements

The job of an enumerator is to produce the "next" element in key order. The hash table class provides an enumerator for each hash table object that a program can retrieve with a call to the `elements` method. For example, the customer list program obtains an enumerator object with:

```
Enumeration theEnumerator = theTable.elements();
```

Hashtable

next-
Element

To retrieve hash table elements using an enumerator, a program calls the enumerator's `nextElement` method. The `hasMoreElements` method returns a boolean that lets a program know when the retrieval process has finished. You put both method calls together in a `while` loop:

Hashtable

hasMore-
Elements

```
while (theEnumerator.hasMoreElements())
{
    theObject = (theClass) theEnumerator.nextElement();
    // process the retrieved object
}
```

Notice that you must typecast the result of the call to `nextElement` to the correct class, just as you do when retrieving an element with `get`.

Summary

One strategy for handling multiple objects of the same class is to create an array to hold the objects. In an object-oriented program, an array of objects is handled by an array manager object. The array manager takes take of initializing objects in its array and returning data from objects in the array.

The name of an array is the address of the beginning of the array in main memory. When an array is passed into a method, the array's address is passed, rather than a copy of the array's contents. Because arrays are always passed by reference in this way, modifying the contents of an array in a method changes the array in main memory.

Sorting an array of objects uses the same methodology as sorting an array containing values of a simple data type. However, while comparisons between array elements are usually made on data values within the object, object references rather than the objects themselves are moved when reordering the array.

A hash table is a collection of object references that are randomly scattered throughout the table based on a location generated by a mathematical transformation of a key value. Hash tables provide fast retrieval based on the key. With the aid of an enumerator, a program can also list the elements in a hash table in key order.

Exercises

1. Write a program with a GUI that lets a person summarize his or her financial accounts. Include a class that represents an account, including the account name, type of account (for example, NOW account, CD, passbook savings), account number, and current value. Use an array manager to handle multiple accounts.

   Your completed program should:

   - Allow interactive data input. (Use the `SystemInput` class.)
   - Compute the user's total worth by combining all the account values.
   - Compute the total worth for each type of account.

2. Rewrite the program from Exercise 1 so that it uses a hash table rather than an array of objects to manage the accounts.

3. Write a program that manages data about the salespeople for a cosmetics company. The data handling class should include the salesperson's name and the dollar value of sales made during each of the past five weeks (one month). Your program should compute the amount paid to each salesperson for the month, based on the following rules:

    *   Base pay is $250 a week plus 10% of sales.
    *   If a salesperson sells over $10,000 in the month, he or she receives a bonus of $500.

    The program should include an array of objects that store data entered interactively. Once the data are in the array, compute and display the number of salespeople receiving pay in the following ranges:

    *   Less than $1000
    * $1000–$2499.99
    * $2500–$4999.99
    * $5000 or more

4. Write a program that analyzes the results of a political survey. Each data handling object that you create should store at least the number of voters surveyed who will be voting for a particular candidate. Include the candidate's name in the data handling class. Use an array manager to hold multiple candidates.

    Create a popup menu that provides users with the following options:

    *   Enter survey data.
    *   Compute the total people surveyed and then compute the percentage voting for each candidate. The method that does this analysis will need to return multiple values. It is up to you to decide whether you can do it with an array or whether you will need a special object for that purpose.
    *   Sort the array of objects by number of voters and display the results of the survey in descending order (most votes first). Show the candidate's name, number of voters, and percentage of voters voting for each candidate. (*Hint:* You're going to need to make a very simple

change to a logical condition in the bubble sort to sort in descending rather than ascending order.)

5. Write a program that tracks which rooms in a hotel are currently occupied. Base the program on a class that describes a room (room number, maximum number of occupants, and a boolean indicating whether the room is occupied). Include methods to indicate when a room becomes occupied and when a room becomes unoccupied. Create an array manager class to handle an array of room objects. When completed, the program should do the following:

    • Allow interactive entry of data to initialize room objects.
    • Display the total number of unoccupied rooms.
    • Display the number of unoccupied rooms of each size (size = maximum number of occupants).
    • Find an unoccupied room of a given size and set that room as occupied.
    • Set a room as occupied.

6. Create at least one class hierarchy to manage a corporation's office furniture and equipment, which includes items such as desks, chairs, file cabinets, computers, copiers, and fax machines. (Consider carefully whether there should be one or two class hierarchies.) Classes should include variables for the name of an item, its manufacturer, a description of the item (using as many variables as necessary), an internal identification number, the date of purchase, purchase price, and current value. Use an array of objects to manage the inventory. Include methods to enter new items and to display data describing items of a given type (for example, desks). In addition, include methods to compute the total current value of all assets of a given type, of all assets, and of all assets organized by type (a control break report).

7. Write a program that keeps track of a retail store's inventory. Assign each type of merchandise item a unique code (something like a UPC code) and store the inventory in a hash table. Store a description, current inventory level, and reorder point for each item. The program should allow users to

enter a key value (using the `SystemInput` class) and obtain the price and inventory level of the object. The program should also display a list of all items that need to be reordered (inventory level less than reorder point).

8. Expand the skeletal video store program you began for Exercise 5 at the end of Chapter 6. Create a hash table to hold the item copies that are being rented. (Consider carefully the class to which you need to typecast objects when you retrieve them from the table.) Use an array of objects to hold video titles. Extend your program to demonstrate that you can store and retrieve item copies by their inventory number. Also demonstrate that you can sort the video objects in alphabetical order by title and list them in that order.

9. As you know, the survey data analysis program that was used as an example isn't complete. To finish the program, add the following:

   • Interactive I/O: Add code that accepts data for new objects from the keyboard and inserts them into the array of objects. Be sure to check that the array isn't full. You might add a button to the top level window to trigger the interactive data entry.

   Standard deviation: The standard deviation is a measure of the degree of spread of data values around the average. It has the formula:

   $$s = \sqrt{\frac{\Sigma(X_i - \bar{X})^2}{N - 1}}$$

   In this formula, X is a data value, $\bar{X}$ is the average (mean) of all data values, and N is the total number of data values. The symbol Σ means to sum all the values. The formula therefore tells you first to compute the mean. Then subtract the mean from each data value and square that difference. Add up all the differences and divide them by the total number of values minus 1. Finally, take the square root. (*Hint:* Use the `Math` class's `sqrt` method.)

Add computations and display of the standard deviation to the `generateAverages` and `generateGAverages` methods. (*Hint:* This is going to change the number of values returned from these methods as well as their display.)

- Median and mode: The median is a data value chosen so that half the values are above it and below it. The mode is the data value (or values) that have the highest frequency. Add code that generates and displays median and mode to the `generateFreqs` method.(*Hint:* This is going to change the number of values returned from this method as well as its display.)

- Statistics grouped by age: Add a method that creates groups of objects based on the age of the respondent. For example, age ranges might be defined as all people under 16, 17–21, 22–30, 31–40, and so on. Then, compute means, medians, and modes for each age group. Consider carefully what classes you will need to add to the program to support age groupings.

10. The survey analysis program displays its error messages in the console output window. Modify the program so that error messages appear in dialog boxes.

10

Applets

OBJECTIVES

In this chapter you will learn about:
- The security challenges presented by an applet.
- The differences between stand-alone Java applications and applets.
- Writing HTML to invoke an applet.

As you know, an applet is a Java program that runs within a World Wide Web browser rather than a Java virtual machine. Applets are typically stored on a web server and downloaded to a user's machine when the user displays an HTML document containing an HTML tag that invokes the applet.

Note   You can test applets using a simple HTML document and a web browser. However, your Java development software may have its own applet viewer that you can use without needing to write any HTML.

By themselves, World Wide Web browsers are not able to interpret and execute Java bytecodes. To make a browser capable of running Java, you must have a *plug-in*, a stand-alone piece of code that adds functionality to a program Plug-ins are used extensively to enhance the abilities of web browsers, including providing support for real-time audio (in particular, the RealAudio plug-ins) and QuickTime movies.

Note   Plug-ins are also available for other types of programs. For example, Adobe Photoshop accepts a variety of plug-ins that add image filtering functions.

Applets require a graphic user interface. Beyond that, they are very similar to stand-alone applications. Nonetheless, there are some simple changes you will need to make to a stand-alone application to transform it into an applet. Some of those changes are dictated by security restrictions that affect what an applet can and cannot do.

This chapter begins by looking at applet security issues. It then turns to transforming an application into an applet and shows you the HTML tags you will need to make applets work in a web browser.

Note   This chapter assumes that you are familiar with basic HTML tags and that you have a Java-enabled web browser available for testing code. If you don't have a Java plug-in, you can download it from Netscape's web site (`http://www.netscape.com`).

Applet Security Issues

Because an applet is downloaded over the web from a server to a user's machine, there are some restrictions on an applet's behavior designed to protect both the source and the recipient:

- An applet cannot access files on a user's machine. It cannot open, read, or write local files.
- An applet cannot access any web server other than the one from which it originated.
- An applet cannot run a program on the user's machine.
- An applet can determine the version of Java under which it is running, the operating system under which it is running, the characters used to separate elements in a path name, and the characters used to terminate lines. However, it cannot gather any other information about the user's machine. This ensures, for example, that an applet cannot take the user's e-mail address and send it back to the server from which the applet came.

In addition, some web browsers want to make certain that users don't confuse applets with local applications. Therefore, whenever an applet opens a child window, such as a dialog box, the child window contains a message across the bottom that reads "Untrusted Java Applet Window." This is disconcerting to many users, so a well-designed applet should avoid opening windows other than the top-level window in which the applet appears.

Applications Versus Applets

An applet's structure is very similar to a stand-alone application. However, there are a few differences to which you must pay attention:

- An applet's application class is derived from `Applet` rather than `Frame`. The `Applet` class is derived from `Panel`, which is a container, just like a frame. If you are converting a stand-alone application to an applet, change the word after `extends` in the class declaration.

Note

Because Applet is derived from Panel, its default layout manager is a flow layout. If you need to use a border layout, be sure to explicitly set the layout.

- An applet has no main method. When you load an applet into a web browser, the browser constructs the applet's frame. The size of the frame is set by the HTML tag that invokes the applet. If you are converting a stand-alone application to an applet, simply delete the main method.
- An applet cannot have a menu bar. If your application uses a menu bar, you must replace menu options with command buttons or other elements that can be contained within a panel. (This isn't an issue with any program you've seen so far because we've delayed the discussion of pull-down menus until Chapter 11.)
- An applet has no constructor. Instead, replace the constructor with a method named init. (If you're converting a stand-alone application, just change the name of the constructor and add a return data type of void. If you're writing an applet from scratch, use an init method in place of a constructor.)

There are actually four methods that you can override when creating an applet. Each runs at a specific time in an applet's life:

- init: As you have just read, the init method replaces a constructor. It is executed just once, when the user initially downloads the applet from the web server.
- start: The start method is run after the init method completes and each time the user returns to the same web page during a single web browsing session. For example, if a user loads an applet, switches to another page, and then returns to the first page, the web browser automatically runs the start method. You can therefore use a start method to reinitialize or redraw anything that should be reset whenever the user redisplays an applet.
- stop: A web browser runs the stop method whenever a user moves away from a page displaying an applet during a single web browsing session. You should therefore use the stop method to perform any necessary cleanup activities. However, keep in mind that an applet can't write to local files, so you won't be able to retain the

state of applet variables. Each time the user returns to a page containing an applet, the applet begins anew.

- `destroy`: A web browser runs the `destroy` method when the user closes the web browser window. In most cases, you don't need to explicitly override this method, as the web browser will take care of shutting down the applet.

A Sample Applet

To help you see the difference between an applet and a stand-alone Java application, let's transform the tic-tac-toe game into an applet. As you can see in Figure 10.1, the results of the game appear below the playing grid rather than in a dialog box. Otherwise, the applet appears just like the stand-alone application. Keep in mind, however, that the size of the applet is set by the HTML code that loads it into the web browser. The playing field cannot be resized as it can when the game runs as an independent application in a standard document window.

Figure 10.1   The tic-tac-toe game running in a web browser

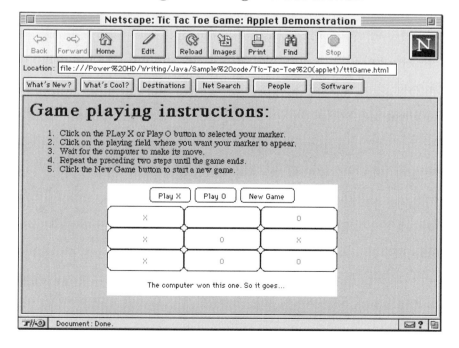

Note

An applet viewer (for example, Figure 10.2) runs an applet in a standard window that can be resized. The applet viewer does allow you to run an applet without a web browser. However, because the size of an applet in a web browser is fixed, the applet view may not necessarily present the applet as it would appear in a browser.

Figure 10.2   The tic-tac-toe game running in an applet viewer

Because the applet version of the tic-tac-toe game doesn't use a dialog box to display the results of a game, the program has only two classes: tttGame and tttApp. The former is unmodified from the version you saw in Chapter 8 because the game class itself is totally divorced from the user interface. The changes needed to turn the program into an applet have all been made in the application class, which handles the user interface.

The source code for the modified tttApp class can be found in Listing 10.1. As you study the code, be sure to notice the following:

- The class is now derived from Applet rather than Frame.
- Code to support applets is found in the package java.applet. The class file therefore includes the line:

      import java.applet.*;

- The constructor's name has been changed to init. Unlike a constructor the init method does require a return data type (in this case, void).

Listing 10.1   tttApp.java modified to run as an applet

```java
import java.awt.*;
import java.io.*;
import java.lang.*;
import java.applet.*;
import java.awt.event.*;

public class tttApp extends Applet
{
    static final int ROWS = 3;
    static final int COLS = 3;
    static final int PLAY_ON = -1;
    static final int WIN = 1;
    static final int TIE = 0;
    static final int PLAYER = 1;
    static final int COMPUTER = 0;

    private int keepPlaying;
    private int goes_first;
    private tttGame inPlay;
    private Button[][] gridButtons;
    private Button X_button;
    private Button O_button;
    private Button New_button;
    private String player;
    private String computer;
    private String message;
    private Panel messagePanel;
    private Label theMessage;

    public void init()
    {
        keepPlaying = PLAY_ON;
        goes_first = COMPUTER;

        inPlay = new tttGame();
        inPlay.InitGame(); // initialize first game
        gridButtons = new Button[ROWS][COLS];
        setUpWindow();
    }

    private void setUpWindow()
    {
        setBackground (Color.white);
        setLayout (new BorderLayout());
```

Continued next page

Listing 10.1(Continued)   tttApp.java modified to run as an applet

```java
        Panel buttonPanel = new Panel();
        X_button = new Button ("Play X");
        X_button.addActionListener (new ActionListener ()
        {
            public void actionPerformed (ActionEvent theEvent)
            {
                inPlay.chooseMarker ('X');
                player = " X ";
                computer = " O ";
                X_button.setEnabled(false);
                O_button.setEnabled(false);
            }
        } );
        buttonPanel.add (X_button);
        O_button = new Button ("Play O");
        O_button.addActionListener (new ActionListener ()
        {
            public void actionPerformed (ActionEvent theEvent)
            {
                inPlay.chooseMarker ('O');
                player = " O ";
                computer = " X ";
                X_button.setEnabled(false);
                O_button.setEnabled(false);
            }
        } );
        buttonPanel.add (O_button);

        New_button = new Button ("New Game");
        New_button.addActionListener (new ActionListener ()
        {
            public void actionPerformed (ActionEvent theEvent)
            {
                inPlay.InitGame();
                New_button.setEnabled(false);
                X_button.setEnabled(true);
                O_button.setEnabled(true);
                for (int i = 0; i < ROWS; i++)
                    for (int j = 0; j < COLS; j++)
                    {
                        gridButtons[i][j].setLabel ("        ");
                        gridButtons[i][j].setEnabled(true);
                    }
                theMessage.setText (" ");
                repaint();
            }
        } );
```

Continued next page

Listing 10.1(Continued)   tttApp.java modified to run as an applet

```
        buttonPanel.add (New_button);
        New_button.setEnabled(false);    // This is disabled until end of game
        add ("North",buttonPanel);

        Panel gamePanel = new Panel();
        gamePanel.setLayout (new GridLayout(3,3));
        for (int i = 0; i < ROWS; i++)
            for (int j = 0; j < COLS; j++)
            {
                gridButtons[i][j] = new Button ("        ");
                gridButtons[i][j].addActionListener (new ActionListener()
                {
                    public void actionPerformed (ActionEvent theEvent)
                    {
                        Button whichButton = (Button) theEvent.getSource();
                        for (int m = 0; m < ROWS; m++)
                            for (int n = 0; n < COLS; n++)
                                if (whichButton == gridButtons[m][n])
                                processMove (m,n);
                        repaint();
                    }
                } );
                gamePanel.add (gridButtons[i][j]);
            }
        add ("Center", gamePanel);

        messagePanel = new Panel();
        theMessage = new Label
            ("                                                      ");
        messagePanel.add (theMessage);
        add ("South",messagePanel);
    }

    public void processMove (int x, int y)
    {
        inPlay.playerMove (x, y);
        gridButtons[x][y].setLabel(player);
        gridButtons[x][y].setEnabled(false);
        keepPlaying = inPlay.checkGrid();
        if (keepPlaying != PLAY_ON)
        {
            gameEnd();
            New_button.setEnabled(true);
            return;
        }
```

Continued next page

Listing 10.1(Continued)   tttApp.java modified to run as an applet

```
        String move = inPlay.computerMove();
        int theMove = Integer.parseInt (move);
        x = theMove / 10;
        y = theMove % 10;
        gridButtons[x][y].setLabel(computer);
        gridButtons[x][y].setEnabled(false);
        keepPlaying = inPlay.checkGrid();
        if (keepPlaying != PLAY_ON)
        {
            gameEnd();
            New_button.setEnabled(true);
        }
    }

    private void gameEnd()
    {
        if (keepPlaying == WIN)  // find out who won the game
            if (inPlay.whoWon() == PLAYER)
                message = "Congratulations!  You've won the game!";
            else
                message = "The computer won this one. So it goes...";
        else // it's got to be a tie
            message = "This one ended in a draw.";

        theMessage.setText (message);
        messagePanel.repaint();
    }
}
```

- The very end of the `setUpWindow` method includes a third panel (`messagePanel`) that is installed in the "South" region of the applet's border layout. This panel is used to display the results of a game using a `Label` object whose text is changed when the game ends.
- The code that changes the message to the user occupies the last two lines of the `GameEnd` method.

Label

setText

To change the text in the message panel's label, the program uses the `Label` class's `setText` method. This method requires only one input parameter: the text to which the label should be changed:

```
        theMessage.setText (message);
```

If you look back at the `setUpWindow` method, you will notice that the label object is initialized with a long string of blanks to set the maximum size of the label. If you are running only in an applet viewer, then it isn't necessary to pre-set the size of the label. The label will display as many characters as it can, based on the current size of the viewer's window. However, when running the applet in a browser, the maximum size of the label is established when the label object is first created.

Changing the contents of the label object isn't enough to make the new text visible. A Java program needs to be told to redraw the changed component. Therefore, the tic-tac-toe applet calls `repaint`, which calls `paint`. If the method is called with simply:

```
repaint()
```

then the entire applet is repainted. However, since the only change that has been made is to the message panel, there's no point in repainting everything. The program will run a bit faster if it just redraws the portion that has been modified. Therefore, the program asks just to have the affected panel repainted with:

```
messagePanel.repaint()
```

(Keep in mind that `repaint` is inherited from the `Component` class and that anything that is derived from `Component` has access to that method.)

Component

repaint

The HTML Tag for Applets

The web page in Figure 10.2 was produced by the HTML in Listing 10.2. To load an applet, you include an **APPLET** tag in an HTML file.

The **APPLET** tag has the following required elements:

```
<APPLET CODE=applet_file.class WIDTH=width_of_applet
    HEIGHT=height_of_applet></APPLET>
```

The **CODE** element is the name of the compile applet file; it will always have an extension of `.class`. By default this file is assumed to be in the same directory as the web page containing the **APPLET** tag. The **WIDTH** and **HEIGHT** elements set the size of the applet's frame in pixels.

If the compiled applet file isn't in the same directory as the web page that downloads it, then you can direct a web browser to look elsewhere by including a **CODEBASE** element, which specifies a subdirectory of the current directory.

Listing 10.2   HTML code for an applet

```
<TITLE>Tic Tac Toe Game: Applet Demonstration</TITLE>
<BODY>
<H1>Game playing instructions:</H1>
<P>
<OL>
<LI>Click on the PLay X or Play O button to selected your marker.
<LI>Click on the playing field where you want your marker to appear.
<LI>Wait for the computer to make its move.
<LI>Repeat the preceding two steps until the game ends.
<LI>Click the New Game button to start a new game.
</OL>
<P><P>
<CENTER>
<APPLET codebase=Java%20Classes CODE="tttApp.class" WIDTH=300 HEIGHT=150
    ALIGN=MIDDLE></APPLET>
</CENTER>
</BODY>
```

As you can see in Listing 10.2, the **CODEBASE** element uses the special HTML characters **%20** to indicate a space in the name of the directory in which the **class** file is located.

The **APPLET** tag can also specify how the applet should be aligned relative to surrounding text with the **ALIGN** element, which works exactly like alignment in the **IMG** tag.

When you create a web page that includes an applet, you can't be certain that the browser used by everyone who downloads the page will have a Java plug-in. You should therefore include some text that will display when Java isn't available, placing it between the **<APPLET>** and **</APPLET>** tags:

```
<APPLET CODE="myapplet.class" WIDTH=300 HEIGHT=300>
    We're sorry, but your browser can't show this Java
    applet.</APPLET>
```

Summary

An applet is a Java program that runs in a World Wide Web Browser. It is downloaded from a web server to a user's computer. For security reasons, applets have limited access to a user's machine that prevents them from accessing local files and applications, and gathering identifying information about the user's machine.

An applet must have a graphic user interface, although it cannot have a menu bar. Applets are derived from `Applet`, rather than from `Frame` as are stand-alone applications. Applets also have no `main` methods and use an `init` method instead of a constructor.

Applets can open child windows. However, some browsers consider windows opened by applet to be insecure and display a message to the effect to the user. Because users may find this disconcerting, applets should not open child windows.

Exercises

1. Write an applet that lets a user see the prices of magazine subscriptions. Place a popup menu on the applet that contains the names of 5 to 10 of your favorite magazines. Also include a button that says something like "How Much?" When the user clicks the button, figure out which magazine is selected in the popup menu and then display its subscription price on the applet.

2. Write an applet that performs temperature conversions. Give the user a popup menu from which he or she can select a temperature. Also provide two buttons ("Convert to Fahrenheit" and "Convert to Celsius"). When the user clicks a button, perform the conversion and display the result at the top of the applet, providing enough text so that the user can understand what has occurred. For example, if the user chose 32 from the popup menu and clicked the Convert to Celsius button, the applet might display:

   ```
   32 dregrees Fahrenehit is 0 degrees Celsius
   ```

3. Write an applet that takes an order for sports team T-shirts. The applet should offer T-shirts from 5 to 10 teams in a popup menu. Use another popup menu to select the size (L, XL, XXL, or XXXL) and a third popup for the quantity (1 through 10). Include a button that says "Add to Order" and a button that says "Done." Each time the user clicks the Add to Order button, read the three popup menus and compute the cost of the user's selections. (L and XL cost $12.95; XXL and XXXL cost $14.95.) Display the items ordered in the applet's window below any previously ordered items. When the user clicks the Done button, add shipping costs ($1 per shirt) and display the order total.

4. Write a program that provides a calculator applet. The calculator should have at least 15 buttons (0 through 9, +, -, /, *, and =). When the user clicks on a button, display the button's label at the top of the button grid. Be sure to accumulate the arithmetic expression in your program as the user clicks buttons. Then, when the user clicks =, calculate and display the result. (*Hint:* It's OK to use a 4 by 4 grid layout for the buttons and leave one of the buttons blank.)

5. Write an applet that displays a randomly chosen text message to a user each time the user views the web browser page on which the applet appears. Create an array or vector of strings to hold a collection of your favorite sayings. Whenever the applet appears, use a random number generator to pick one array/vector element and display its contents. (*Hint:* To make this work each time the page appears rather than only when the applet is first downloaded, you'll need to place the code for displaying text in a `start` method instead of an `init` method. The applet will still need an `init` method.)

6. Write an applet that draws a variety of small shapes in a variety of colors at randomly chosen places on a canvas. Give the user two popup menus: one for the shape (for example, square or circle) and one for color. Whenever the user makes a choice from one of the menus, draw the indicated shape. (*Hint:* Be sure to get the size of the canvas and scale the random numbers you use for the top left corner of a shape so that the applet doesn't attempt to draw off the visible area of the canvas.)

7. Write an applet that lets a user play the child's game of matching pairs:

   - Load a 6 by 6 grid (a two-dimensional array) with pairs of uppercase letters, randomly scattered throughout the grid. (To make this a bit easier, begin by loading the array using assignment statements. This means that your applet will always play the same game. However, once you get the applet running, you can explore using a random number generator to select 18 letters and scatter them about the array to create a new game solution each time the game is played.)
   - Load another 6 by 6 with references to button objects. The buttons should have just a space for their labels.

- Display the grid to the user. Add a "Next Move" button and a "New Game" button.
- To play the game, the user clicks on two buttons. Do not respond to the user until two clicks have been made. Then show the letters on the buttons that were clicked.
- Wait until the user clicks the "Next Move" button. At that time, if the two visible letters are a pair, replace the letters with an asterisk (*). If the two letters are different, replace the letters with a space.
- Score the game by counting the number of moves it takes the user to identify the locations of all the pairs. When all pairs have been found, display the user's score.
- When the user clicks the "New Game" button, reset the grid so all buttons show a space and reset the move counter.

11 Enhancing the GUI

OBJECTIVES

In this chapter you will learn to:

- Create hierarchical pull-down menus and trap user selections in those menus.
- Accept input from a user in a dialog box.
- Create scrolling output.

In this chapter you will be introduced to some additional major elements of a graphic user interface, including hierarchical pull-down menus, accepting input from a user through a dialog box, and scrolling output. Once you can use these elements, you can create Java applications and applets that are completely divorced from console I/O.

The Loan Calculator Program

The major example we will be using in this chapter is a program that produces loan repayment tables for three types of loans (fixed payment, variable payment, and mortgage). The loan calculator has a hierarchical pull-down menu that lets a user create a specific type of loan and then display the repayment table. Notice in Figure 11.1 (Windows 95) that the typical menus you would expect in a menu bar (File and Edit, in particular) aren't present. They aren't provided by the Java virtual machine; if you want them in a Java program you will need to add them yourself. In contrast, the Macintosh virtual machine used to develop the code for this book *does* provide those menus (see Figure 11.2). The presence of File and Edit menus notwithstanding, the program is identical regardless of the platform on which it is running.

The user's first task is to enter data describing a loan. (If the user attempts to display the repayment table before a loan has been initialized, the user sees a dialog box stating that a loan must be created first.) For example, if a Windows user wants to create a fixed payment loan, then he or she sees the dialog box in Figure 11.3; a Macintosh user sees something like Figure 11.4. The user fills in the dialog box and clicks the OK button. The program then initializes a loan object.

To create and display a repayment table, the user chooses the Display Repayment Table menu option. The table appears in the body of the Loan Calculator window (Figure 11.5 for Windows and Figure 11.6 for the Macintosh). If the table is too large to fit in the window, the user can manipulate the vertical scroll bar to bring additional parts of the listing into view. The scrolling adjusts as the size of the window is adjusted.

The Data Handling Classes

Objects for the three types of loans, which are completely independent of the program's user interface, are created from classes that inherit from a generic class named Loan (Listing 11.1). The Loan class provides the two variables all

Figure 11.1   The loan calculator's hierarchical menu (Windows 95)

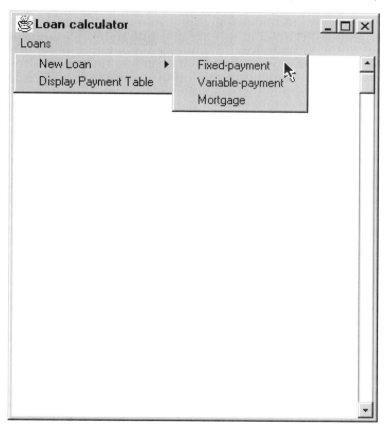

types of loans have in common (the principal and the interest rate) as well as a virtual method for creating the payment table and a utility method for formatting floating point values as currency.

Fixed payment loans (Listing 11.2) add the amount the user will be paying each month. The `Fixed_Payment` class also includes its own implementation of the `CreatePaymentTable` method. Notice that the payment table is a two-dimensional array that is passed in by the calling method. The method returns the number of payments and leaves the payment details in the payment table array.

Figure 11.2   The loan calculator's hierarchical menu (Macintosh)

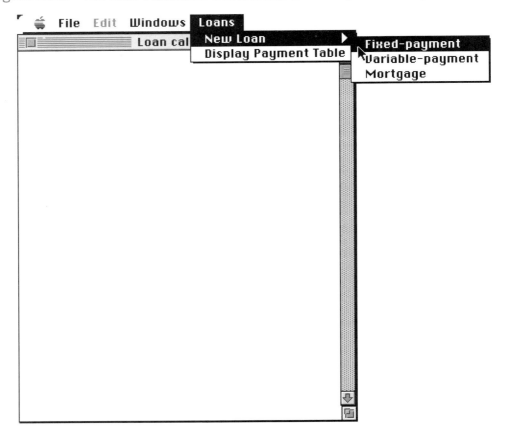

Figure 11.3   Creating a fixed payment loan (Windows 95)

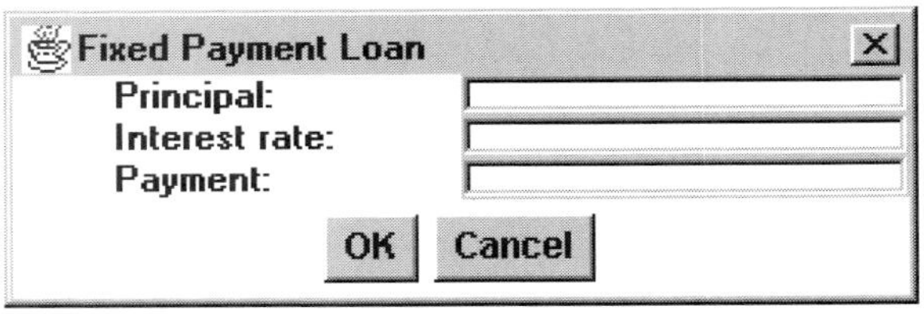

Figure 11.4   Creating a fixed payment loan (Macintosh)

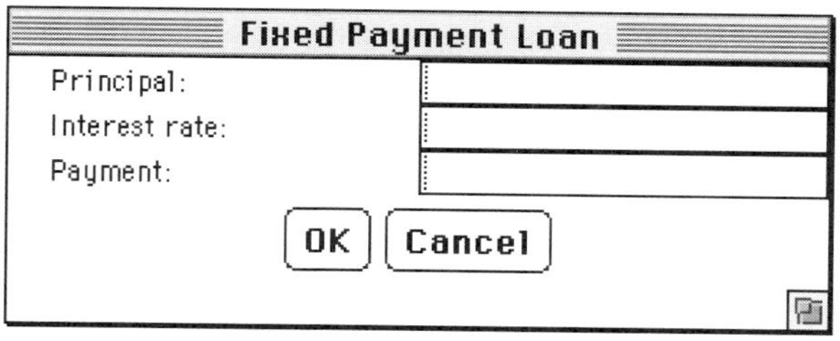

Figure 11.5   A loan repayment table (Windows 95)

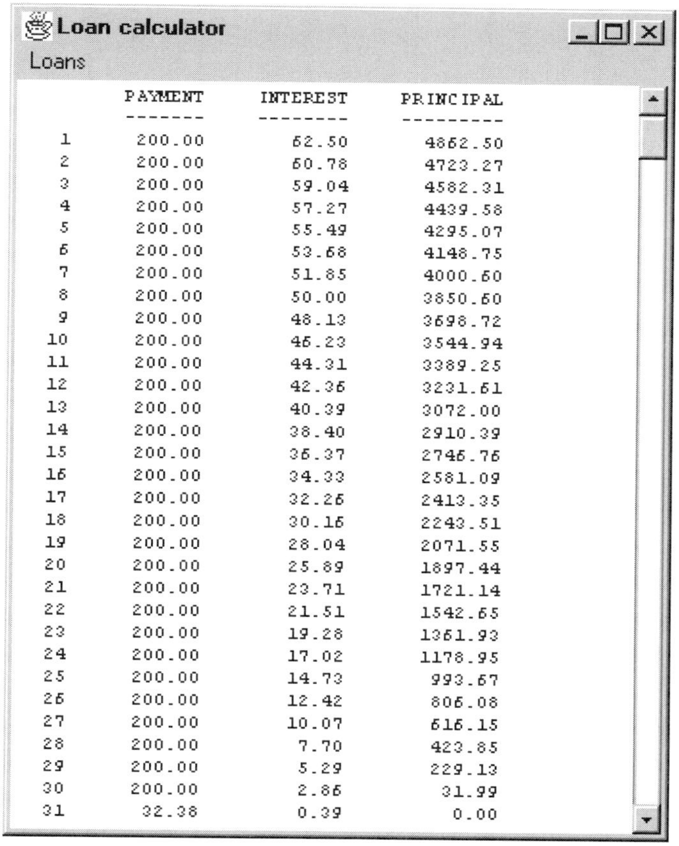

Figure 11.6   A loan repayment table (Macintosh)

PAYMENT	INTEREST	PRINCIPAL
	Loan calculator	
1	200.00	62.50	4862.50
2	200.00	60.78	4723.27
3	200.00	59.04	4582.31
4	200.00	57.27	4439.58
5	200.00	55.49	4295.07
6	200.00	53.68	4148.75
7	200.00	51.85	4000.60
8	200.00	50.00	3850.60
9	200.00	48.13	3698.73
10	200.00	46.23	3544.96
11	200.00	44.31	3389.27
12	200.00	42.36	3231.63
13	200.00	40.39	3072.01
14	200.00	38.40	2910.41
15	200.00	36.38	2746.79
16	200.00	34.33	2581.12
17	200.00	32.26	2413.38
18	200.00	30.16	2243.53
19	200.00	28.04	2071.57
20	200.00	25.89	1897.46
21	200.00	23.71	1721.17
22	200.00	21.51	1542.68
23	200.00	19.28	1361.96
24	200.00	17.02	1178.98
25	200.00	14.73	993.71
26	200.00	12.42	806.13
27	200.00	10.07	616.20
28	200.00	7.70	423.90
29	200.00	5.29	229.18
30	200.00	2.86	32.03
31	32.43	0.40	0.00

Variable payment loans (Listing 11.3), which are like most credit cards, need to know the percentage of the balance that will be paid each period, the minimum payment (used when the principal is low), and the minimum interest rate (also used when the principal is low). Mortgage loans (Listing 11.4) are somewhat more flexible, in that they allow the user to specify either the amount of the loan or a maximum payment.

Listing 11.1 Loan.java

```java
public abstract class Loan
{
    static final int PAYMENT = 0;
    static final int INTEREST = 1;
    static final int PRINCIPAL = 2;
    static final int MAX_TERM = 360;
    static final int NUM_COLUMNS = 3;

    protected float principal;
    protected float interest_rate;

    public Loan (float i_principal, float i_interest_rate)
    {
        principal = i_principal;
        interest_rate = i_interest_rate;
    }

    public abstract int CreatePaymentTable (float payment_table[][]);

    public float formatDollars (float theNumber)
    {
        int tempInt = (int)(theNumber * 100);
        return (float)tempInt/(float)100;
    }
}
```

Error Messages

Whenever the user makes an error, such as attempting to display a repayment table before a loan has been created or leaving out both the payment and principal for a mortgage loan, the loan calculator program displays a dialog box containing an error message. This dialog box is produced by the simple class in Listing 11.5.

You can use this dialog box in any Java program, anywhere an error message that requires only a single OK button is appropriate. Its only parameter is the text of the error message that is to be displayed.

Working with Pull-Down Menus

To add a menu bar and pull-down menus to a Java program, you will need a menu bar object along with objects for all the menus and their items. You will also need an action listener object for each menu item whose `actionPerformed` method is called whenever the user chooses a specific menu item.

Listing 11.2 Fixed_Payment.java

```java
public class Fixed_Payment extends Loan
{
    private float payment;   /* amount customer will be paying each month */

    public Fixed_Payment (float i_principal, float i_interest_rate,
        float i_payment)
    {
        super (i_principal, i_interest_rate); // call base class constructor
        payment = i_payment;
    }

    public int CreatePaymentTable (float payment_table[][])
    {
        int i = 0;
        float monthly_interest;

        while (principal >= payment)
        {
            payment_table[i][PAYMENT] = payment;
            monthly_interest = formatDollars(principal *
                (float) (interest_rate/12.0));
            payment_table[i][INTEREST] = monthly_interest;
            principal = formatDollars
                (principal - (payment - monthly_interest));
            payment_table[i++][PRINCIPAL] = principal;
        }
        if (principal > 0.0)
        {
            payment_table[i][INTEREST] =
                formatDollars(principal * (float) (interest_rate/12.0));
            payment_table[i][PAYMENT] =
                formatDollars(principal + payment_table[i][INTEREST]);
            payment_table[i][PRINCIPAL] = (float) 0.0;
        }
        return i;
    }
}
```

When you add the menu bar object to an object created from the Frame class or any class that is derived from Frame, the menu bar appears in the appropriate place for a menu bar, given the operating system under which the program is running. For example, under Windows 95, the menu bar is attached to the window. On the Macintosh, the menu bar appears at the top of the start-up monitor. Nonetheless, the Java code to produce the menu bar and its menu is the same regardless of platform.

Listing 11.3 Variable_Payment.java

```
public class Variable_Payment extends Loan
{
    private float payment_percent;  /* % of principal to be paid each month */
    private float minimum_payment;  /* minimum payment
    private float minimum_interest;  /* minimum interest assessed */

    public Variable_Payment (float i_principal, float i_interest_rate,
        float i_payment_percent, float i_minimum_payment,
        float i_minimum_interest)
    {
        super (i_principal, i_interest_rate);
        payment_percent = i_payment_percent;
        minimum_payment = i_minimum_payment;
        minimum_interest = i_minimum_interest;
    }

    public int CreatePaymentTable (float payment_table[][])
    {
        int i = 0;
        float interest, payment;

        while (principal >= minimum_payment)
        {
            interest = principal * (float) (interest_rate/12.0);
            if (interest < minimum_interest) interest = minimum_interest;
            payment_table[i][INTEREST] = formatDollars(interest);
            principal = principal + interest;
            payment = principal * payment_percent;
            if (payment < minimum_payment) payment = minimum_payment;
            principal = principal - payment;
            payment_table[i][PRINCIPAL] = formatDollars(principal);
            payment_table[i++][PAYMENT] = formatDollars(payment);
        }
        if (i == 0)
            payment_table[i][INTEREST] = 0;
        else
        {
            payment_table[i][INTEREST] =
                formatDollars(principal * (float) (interest_rate/12.0));
            if (payment_table[i][INTEREST] < minimum_interest)
                payment_table[i][INTEREST] = minimum_interest;
        }
        payment_table[i][PAYMENT] =
            formatDollars(principal + payment_table[i][INTEREST]);
        payment_table[i][PRINCIPAL] = (float) 0.0;
        return i;
    }
}
```

Listing 11.4   Mortgage.java

```java
public class Mortgage extends Loan
{
    private int num_periods;
    private int periods_per_year;
    private float payment;

    public Mortgage (float i_principal,float i_interest_rate,
        int i_num_periods, int i_periods_per_year, float i_payment)
    {
        super (i_principal, i_interest_rate);
        num_periods = i_num_periods;
        periods_per_year = i_periods_per_year;
        payment = i_payment;
    }

    public int CreatePaymentTable (float payment_table[][])
    {
        int i = 0;
        float period_interest_rate, PVIFA;

        period_interest_rate = interest_rate/periods_per_year;

        PVIFA = (float)((1/period_interest_rate) -
            (1/(period_interest_rate * Math.pow((double) 1 +
            period_interest_rate,(double) num_periods))));

        if (payment == 0)
            payment = principal/PVIFA;
        else
            if (principal == 0)
                principal = payment * PVIFA;
            else
            {
                errorDialog theDialog =
                    new errorDialog ("Enter either principal or payment");
                theDialog.show();
                return (0);
            }
        while (principal > payment)
        {
            payment_table[i][INTEREST] =
                formatDollars(principal * period_interest_rate);
            payment_table[i][PAYMENT] = formatDollars(payment);
            principal = principal - (payment - payment_table[i][INTEREST]);
            payment_table[i++][PRINCIPAL] = formatDollars(principal);
        }
```

Continued next page

Listing 11.4(Continued)   Mortgage.java

```
payment_table[i][INTEREST] =
        formatDollars(principal * period_interest_rate);
      payment_table[i][PAYMENT] =
        formatDollars(principal + payment_table[i][INTEREST]);
      payment_table[i][PRINCIPAL] = (float) 0.0;
      return i;
   }
}
```

Creating a Menu Bar

Creating a menu bar and accompanying menus requires the following steps:

1. Create a menu bar object (an object of class MenuBar).
2. Create a menu object (an object of class Menu).
3. Add an item to the menu object (an object of class MenuItem).
4. Register an action listener with the menu option (an object of a class that implements the ActionListener interface).
5. Repeat Steps 3 and 4 for all items to be added to the menu.
6. Add the menu to the menu bar.
7. Repeat Steps 2 through 5 for any other menus you need.
8. Add the menu bar to its parent window.

You must add menus to the menu bar in the order in which you want them to appear, beginning at the left edge of the menu bar. By the same token, you add menu items to menus in order from the top down. To create a sub-menu, you add a menu object with items to another menu object.

The loan calculator program's menus are created in the application class's constructor. (The entire application class, LoanApp can be found in Listing 11.6. We will be discussing various aspects of this class throughout the rest of this chapter.) The procedure closely follows the general steps outlined above:

MenuBar

new

1. Create the menu bar object, storing a reference to it in the variable mbar. Notice that the constructor for the menu bar class requires no input parameters:

```
MenuBar mbar = new MenuBar();
```

Listing 11.5 errorDialog.java

```java
import java.awt.*;
import java.lang.*;
import java.awt.event.*;

public class errorDialog extends Frame
{
    private Font systemFont = new Font ("System",Font.BOLD,12);
    private errorDialog thisDialog;

    public errorDialog (String message)
    {
        thisDialog = this;
        setTitle ("Status");
        setBackground (Color.white);
        Panel messagePanel = new Panel();
        messagePanel.add (new Label(message));
        add ("Center",messagePanel);

        Panel buttonPanel = new Panel();
        buttonPanel.setFont (systemFont);
        Button theButton = new Button("OK");
        theButton.addActionListener (new ActionListener ()
        {
            public void actionPerformed (ActionEvent theEvent)
                { thisDialog.dispose(); }
        } );
        buttonPanel.add (theButton);

        add ("South",buttonPanel);
        setSize (300,75);

        addWindowListener (new WindowAdapter ()
        {
            public void windowClosing (WindowEvent theEvent)
                { thisDialog.dispose(); }
        } );
    }
}
```

Menu

new

2. Create a menu object for the Loans menu. The constructor requires the name of the menu as an input parameter:

```java
theMenu = new Menu ("Loans");
```

3. Create a menu object for the New Loan submenu:

```java
Menu subMenu = new Menu ("New Loan");
```

Listing 11.6   LoanApp.java

```java
import java.awt.*;
import java.io.*;
import java.lang.*;
import text.*;
import java.awt.event.*;

interface DialogProcessor     // for getting data from dialog boxes
{
    public void processDialog (Dialog theDialog, Object theObject);
}

public class LoanApp extends Frame implements DialogProcessor
{
    static final int PAYMENT = 0;
    static final int INTEREST = 1;
    static final int PRINCIPAL = 2;
    static final int MAX_TERM = 500;
    static final int NUM_COLUMNS = 3;

    private Loan theLoan; // base class object for use throughout program
    private float [][] payment_table;
    private FixedData fixed_payment_data;
    private VariableData variable_payment_data;
    private MortgageData mortgage_data;
    private boolean loanCreated = false;  // for error checking
    private int num_payments;
    private int dy = 0;
    private Scrollbar vertical;
    private outputCanvas theCanvas;
    private LoanApp thisApp;
    private MenuItem fixed, variable, mortgage, display;

    public LoanApp()
    {
        thisApp = this;

        addWindowListener (new WindowAdapter ()  // handles window closing
        {
            public void windowClosing (WindowEvent theEvent)
            {
                System.exit (0);
            }
        } );
```

Continued next page

Listing 11.6(Continued)   LoanApp.java

```java
    addComponentListener (new ComponentAdapter ()  // handles window moving
    {
        public void componentResized (ComponentEvent theEvent)
        {
            Dimension theSize = theCanvas.getSize();
            vertical.setValues (vertical.getValue(),theSize.height,0,5000);
            vertical.setBlockIncrement (theSize.height);
        }
    } );

    setLayout (new BorderLayout());

    // create payment table
    payment_table = new float [MAX_TERM][NUM_COLUMNS];
    fixed_payment_data = new FixedData(0,0,0);
    variable_payment_data = new VariableData(0,0,0,0,0);
    mortgage_data = new MortgageData (0,0,0,0,0);

    // handles menu events
    class menuItemListener implements ActionListener
    {
        public void actionPerformed (ActionEvent theEvent)
        {
            MenuItem theItem = (MenuItem) theEvent.getSource();
            if (theItem == fixed)
            {
                FixedPaymentDialog theDialog =
                    new FixedPaymentDialog (thisApp);
                theDialog.show();
                loanCreated = true;
            }
            else if (theItem == variable)
            {
                VariablePaymentDialog theDialog =
                    new VariablePaymentDialog (thisApp);
                theDialog.show();
                loanCreated = true;
            }
            else if (theItem == mortgage)
            {
                MortgageDialog theDialog = new MortgageDialog (thisApp);
                theDialog.show();
                loanCreated = true;
            }
```

Continued next page

Listing 11.6(Continued)   LoanApp.java

```
            else if (theItem == display)
            {
                if (!loanCreated)
                {
                    errorDialog theDialog = new errorDialog
                        ("You must create a loan first.");
                    theDialog.show();
                }
                else
                {
                    num_payments =
                        theLoan.CreatePaymentTable (payment_table);
                    theCanvas.init (num_payments,payment_table);
                    theCanvas.repaint();
                }
            }
        }
    }
}

MenuBar mbar = new MenuBar(); // create the menu bar

menuItemListener theMenuListener = new menuItemListener();
Menu theMenu = new Menu ("Loans");
Menu subMenu = new Menu ("New Loan");
subMenu.add (fixed = new MenuItem("Fixed-payment"));
fixed.addActionListener (theMenuListener);
subMenu.add (variable = new MenuItem("Variable-payment"));
variable.addActionListener (theMenuListener);
subMenu.add (mortgage = new MenuItem("Mortgage"));
mortgage.addActionListener (theMenuListener);
theMenu.add (subMenu);

theMenu.add (display = new MenuItem("Display Payment Table"));
display.addActionListener (theMenuListener);
mbar.add (theMenu);

setMenuBar (mbar); // attach menu bar to window

setBackground (Color.white);
setTitle ("Loan calculator");

add ("East",vertical = new Scrollbar(Scrollbar.VERTICAL));
vertical.setBlockIncrement (400);
```

Continued next page

Listing 11.6(Continued)   LoanApp.java

```java
    class scrollBarListener implements AdjustmentListener
    {
        public void adjustmentValueChanged (AdjustmentEvent theEvent)
        {
            theCanvas.translate (0,vertical.getValue());
            repaint();
        }
    }
    / handle scolling
    vertical.addAdjustmentListener (new scrollBarListener ());   /

    theCanvas = new outputCanvas();
    add ("Center",theCanvas);
}

public void setVisible()
{
    super.show();
    Dimension theSize = theCanvas.getSize();
    vertical.setValues (0,theSize.height,0,5000);
}

public void processDialog (Dialog theDialog, Object theData)
{
    if (theDialog instanceof FixedPaymentDialog)
    {
        fixed_payment_data = (FixedData) theData;
        Fixed_Payment newLoan = new Fixed_Payment
            (fixed_payment_data.principal,fixed_payment_data.interest_rate,
            fixed_payment_data.payment);
        theLoan = (Loan) newLoan; // typecast to base class pointer
    }
    else if (theDialog instanceof VariablePaymentDialog)
    {
        variable_payment_data = (VariableData) theData;
        Variable_Payment newLoan = new Variable_Payment
            (variable_payment_data.principal,
            variable_payment_data.interest_rate,
            variable_payment_data.payment_percent,
            variable_payment_data.minimum_payment,
            variable_payment_data.minimum_interest);
        theLoan = (Loan) newLoan;
    }
```

Continued next page

Listing 11.6(Continued)   LoanApp.java

```
    else if (theDialog instanceof MortgageDialog)
    {
        mortgage_data = (MortgageData) theData;
        Mortgage newLoan = new Mortgage (mortgage_data.principal,
            mortgage_data.interest_rate,
            mortgage_data.num_periods,mortgage_data.periods_per_year,
            mortgage_data.payment);
        theLoan = (Loan) newLoan;
    }
}

public static void main (String args[])
{
    Frame mainWindow = new LoanApp();
    mainWindow.setSize (350,400);  // width, height
    mainWindow.show();
}
}
```

MenuItem

new

4. Add the first item to the submenu object by creating an object of the **MenuItem** class, using the menu option's name as an input parameter:

```
subMenu.add (new MenuItem (fixed = "Fixed-payment"));
```

Notice that creating the menu item has been placed inside the call to the **add** method. This means that we are not saving references to the menu item objects. The program will therefore need to use the names of the items to identify which item has been chosen by the user.

5. Register a listener object with the menu item object.

In this program, the listener for menu objects has been implemented as a named inner class (**menuItemListener**). At the very least, this means that each menu item could be registered with an object created from the same class. However, if you look at the **actionPerformed** method in **menuItemListener** class, you will see that it handles *all* the menu items in the program. Therefore, the program needs only one object of this listener class, which it can then register with all the menu items:

```
menuItemListener theMenuListener = new menuItemListener();
    :
fixed.addActionListener (theMenuListener);
```

What do you gain by this strategy? All the menu handling is in one method, making it easier to modify the program's menu structure. The alternative to this organization is to give each menu item its own listener class (perhaps using a separate anonymous inner class for each method) that contains just the code for the menu item with which it is registered. The advantage to this latter strategy is that menu handling code is kept with the menu item to which it belongs. You should therefore choose whichever structure makes the most sense for your particular program.

Menu

add

6. Add the remaining items to the submenu and register listeners for them:

```
subMenu.add (variable = new MenuItem("Variable-payment"));
variable.addActionListener (theMenuListener);
subMenu.add (mortgage = new MenuItem("Mortgage"));
mortgage.addActionListener (theMenuListener);
```

7. Add the submenu to the Loans menu as the first menu option:

```
theMenu.add (subMenu);
```

8. Add the final menu item to the Loans menu and register its listener:

```
theMenu.add (display = new MenuItem("Display Payment Table"));
display.addActionListener (theMenuListener);
```

MenuBar

add

9. Add the menu to the menu bar:

```
mbar.add (theMenu);
```

Trapping Menu Selections

When a user makes a choice from a pull-down menu, the Java virtual machine detects an action event, generates an action event object, and passes that object to the **actionPerformed** method of the listener registered with the menu item that was chosen.

At that point, the **actionPerformed** method must identify which menu item was selected. It therefore begins by obtaining a reference to the item that incurred the event:

```
MenuItem theItem = (MenuItem) theEvent.getSource();
```

(Notice in this case that the result of the call to `getSource` has been typecast to an object of class `menuItem`.) Then the method compares the reference to the selected menu item with the menu item references that were stored when the menu item objects were created. As you can see in Listing 11.6, the `menu-ItemListener` class's `actionPerformed` method uses a nested `if` statement. (A `switch` would be cleaner, but can't be used here because the Java compiler doesn't interpret an object reference as the integer required by a `switch`.) When a match is found, the program executes code specific to the selected menu item.

Additional Menu Considerations

MenuItem

In most cases, the text of a menu item stays the same throughout a program run. In some circumstances, however, a program does change menu item text. For example, in a graphics program a menu item Hide Grid appears whenever the grid is displayed; when the user chooses the option to hide the grid, the

setLabel item text changes to Show Grid. In that case, a Java program will need to keep a reference to the menu item option to identify it in an `action` method.

MenuItem

To change a menu item's text, use the `setLabel` method:

```
menuItem_reference.setLabel ("new item text");
```

getLabel

If you need to retrieve the current text of a menu item, use the `getLabel` method:

```
string_variable = menuItem_reference.getLabel();
```

It is not always appropriate to make every menu item available at every moment a program is running. For example, a program should disable an Edit

MenuItem menu's Cut option when nothing is selected for cutting. You therefore need to be able to disable and enable menu options:

*set-
Enabled*

```
To disable: menuItem_reference.setEnabled(false);
To enable:  menuItem_reference.setEnabled(true);
```

When all of the menu items in a menu are disabled, the entire menu is disabled. (Enabling one menu item enables the menu itself.)

Implementing Scrolling Output

When an entire loan repayment table won't fit in the current size of the loan calculator's display canvas, the user can bring additional portions of the table into view using the application window's vertical scroll bar. (You can also use a horizontal scroll bar, but in this particular application only a vertical scroll bar was necessary.)

Handling the scroll bars is a cooperative effort between a frame, a canvas whose contents are being scrolled, a component listener, and an adjustment listener. The scroll bars are attached to the frame. A component listener registered with the frame takes care of readjusting scrolling when the window is resized. The adjustment listener takes care of scrolling when the user drags the scrollbar's thumb. However, the decision as to what portion of the canvas can be seen at any given time, based on the position of the scroll bars, is handled by the canvas class. (A program paints the entire canvas, but only shows part of it.)

Creating and Installing Scroll Bars

To create and install a scroll bar, a class derived from **Frame** creates a scroll bar object:

ScrollBar

```
Scrollbar vertical = new ScrollBar (ScrollBar.VERTICAL);
```

new

The constructor takes a constant as a parameter to indicate whether this is a vertical (ScrollBar.VERTICAL) or horizontal (ScrollBar.HORIZONTAL) scroll bar.

You then add the scroll bar object to the frame. Assuming the frame has a border layout, you place a vertical scroll bar in the "East" region:

```
add ("East",vertical);
```

ScrollBar

setBlock-
Increment

Set the number of pixels to be scrolled when the user presses the page or page down keys with the **setPageIncrement** method, passing in the number of pixels to be scrolled:

```
vertical.setBlockIncrement (400);
```

Assuming that the scrolled area is a canvas, not the frame itself, a program also needs to set the amount of the canvas that will be visible at any time. One of the easiest ways to do this is to override the application class's `show` method so you can obtain the size of the canvas and then use the height variable as the height of the visible region:

ScrollBar

setValues

```
public void show()
    {
        super.show();
        Dimension theSize = theCanvas.getSize();
        vertical.setValues (0,theSize.height,0,5000);
    }
```

The `setValues` method takes four parameters: the current position of the scroll bar (0 to place it at the top of the window), the height of visible area (equal to the height of the canvas), the minimum value of the scroll bar (usually 0), and the maximum value of the scroll bar (in this case, the arbitrary value 5000, which will provide an area far larger than needed to display the loan repayment table).

Trapping and Performing Scrolling

In our particular example, output is drawn by the `outputCanvas` class (Listing 11.7). There are two elements in this class that have been included specifically to handle the scrolling in response to events in the vertical scroll bar.

The first element is the `translate` method. In the canvas class, the purpose of this method is to store the scroll offsets (the number of pixels by which the window has been scrolled). As you can see in Listing 11.7, the method simply stores the number of pixels passed in as input parameters and then calls `repaint` to redraw the canvas.

As you read in Chapter 7, user actions in scroll bars generate adjustment events. To trap them, a program creates a class that implements the `AdjustmentListener` interface and the interface's single method: `adjustmentValueChanged`. In the `LoanApp` class, the adjustment listener class is a named inner class (`scrollBarListener`).

When the Java virtual machine detects an adjustment event, it generates an adjustment event object and then calls the adjustment listener object's `adjustmentValueChanged` method. The method begins with a call to the canvas's `translate` method, obtaining the input parameter for the vertical scroll bar using the scroll bar object's `getValue` method:

```
theCanvas.translate (0, vertical.getValue());
```

Listing 11.7   outputCanvas.java

```java
public class outputCanvas extends Canvas
{
    static final int PAYMENT = 0;
    static final int INTEREST = 1;
    static final int PRINCIPAL = 2;
    static final int MAX_TERM = 500;
    static final int NUM_COLUMNS = 3;

    private int num_payments;
    private float[][] payment_table = new float[MAX_TERM][NUM_COLUMNS];
    private boolean do_paint = false;
    int dx, dy;
    private Font systemFont = new Font ("System",Font.BOLD,12);

    public outputCanvas()
    {
        setBackground (Color.white);
    }

    public void init (int iPayments,float[][] iTable)
    {
        num_payments = iPayments;
        payment_table = iTable;
        do_paint = true;
    }

    public void translate (int x, int y)
    {
        dx = x;
        dy = y;
        repaint();
    }

    public void paint (Graphics graphObject)
    {
        if (do_paint)
        {
            graphObject.translate (-dx, -dy);

            Font theFont = new Font ("Courier",Font.PLAIN,10);
            graphObject.setFont (theFont);
            int base = 12;
```

Continued next page

Listing 11.7(Continued) outputCanvas.java

```
        graphObject.drawString (" PAYMENT",50,base);
        graphObject.drawString ("INTEREST",125,base);
        graphObject.drawString ("PRINCIPAL",200,base);
        base +=12;
        graphObject.drawString (" -------",50,base);
        graphObject.drawString ("--------",125,base);
        graphObject.drawString ("---------",200,base);
        base += 12;
        for (int i = 0; i <= num_payments; i++)
        {
            graphObject.drawString (NumberFormat.intFormat(3,i+1),10,base);
            graphObject.drawString (NumberFormat.floatFormat
                (8,2,payment_table[i][PAYMENT]),50,base);
            graphObject.drawString (NumberFormat.floatFormat
                (8,2,payment_table[i][INTEREST]),125,base);
            graphObject.drawString (NumberFormat.floatFormat
                (9,2,payment_table[i][PRINCIPAL]),200,base);
            base += 12;
        }
    }
    graphObject.setFont (systemFont);
    }
}
```

In this case, because there is no horizontal scroll bar, the program simply passes 0 for the X coordinate.

The canvas's `paint` method always draws the entire repayment table based on the assumption that coordinate 0,0 is at the top left edge of the visible region of the canvas. However, when the window is scrolled, we want drawing to begin at a different position so that the appropriate section of the output will be visible. Therefore, a program needs to shift the coordinate system of the graphics object used for drawing by the amount of the scroll (those values stored by the canvas's `translate` method).

To see what is needed, take a look at Figure 11.7. Assume that the total scroll distance is 5000 and the vertical scroll bar is scrolled 25 percent. In that case, we want the canvas's 0,0 coordinate to actually be at 0, -1250 in the graphics object where drawing takes place.

The `Graphics` class has its own `translate` method that shifts the origin of a graphics object up and to the left. Because we really need to move the original down and to the right, we pass the *negative* of the scroll position:

```
        graphObject.translate (-dx, -dy);
```

Figure 11.7   Shift graphics object coordinates for scrolling

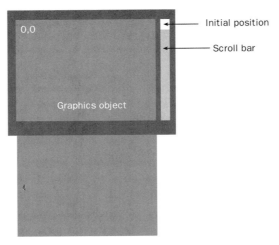

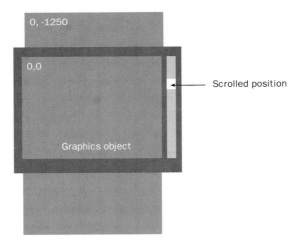

In this particular example, the effect of calling `translate` is to associate the canvas's coordinate 0,0 with the graphics object's coordinates 0,-1250.

Once the graphics object has been shifted, the program can draw the entire canvas. The visible region will be that portion of the graphics object with coordinates 0,0 at its top left corner.

Scrolling and Window Resizing

When an application window is resized, the scroll bar's values need to be set again. The frame must therefore register a component listener object—created from a class that implements the componentListener interface—to handle window resized events. The componentListener interface contains methods that are called when a component is moved, resized, shown, or hidden. To avoid having to implement all four methods, a program can extend the componentAdapter class rather than implementing the componentListener interface directly. The loan program, for example, implements just the componentResized method in an anonymous inner class.

The first task of the componentResized method is to get the size of the canvas after the window's size has changed. It then calls the setValues method. In this case, the first parameter in the call will be scroll bar's current position, returned by the getValue method:

ScrollBar

getValue

```
vertical.setValues (vertical.getValue(),theSize.height,0,5000);
```

Finally, the method also needs to reset the page up and page down increment:

```
vertical.setBlockIncrement (theSize.height);
```

Collecting Information in Dialog Boxes

Using a window or dialog box to collect information from a user is a common feature of programs with graphic user interfaces. As you will see in this section and the section that follows, you can provide the user with a variety of elements for specifying input:

- Text field: A text field provides a space for entering one line of data. You will learn to use text fields in this section.
- Check box: A check box is a square that can contain an X or be empty.
- Check box group: A check box group is actually a group of round radio buttons. Only one radio button in a group can be selected at a time. Clicking one button selects the button and deselects whichever button was previously selected.
- Drop-down list (popup menu): A drop-down list (alias popup menu), which you have already learned to use, provides a static list

from which the user can choose one option. Only one option is visible at a time.

- List: A list is a scrolling list of options from which a user can choose one or more.

You will see examples of the remainder of these input elements in the next section of this chapter.

Adding Text Fields

The dialog boxes that collect data for the loan calculation program uses text fields in which the user can type data. As you can see in Listing 11.8, each dialog box uses a panel with a grid layout that is two columns across. The left column contains label objects to identify what the user is to enter. The right column contains text fields.

TextField

new

To create a text field, you create an object of the `TextField` class:

```
objectReference = new TextField (inital_text, size);
```

This size parameter sets the number of characters that will appear at any one time in the text field. However, because most of the fonts we use today have variable character widths, this measurement isn't very precise. All you can do is make your best guess. Note that this size doesn't limit the number of characters the user can enter. If the user enters more characters than will fit, the text field scrolls to the left.

Once a program has created text field objects, it can add them to a panel. The loan calculator program's dialog boxes perform both actions in one step:

```
thePanel.add (principal = new TextField ("",8));
```

Getting Data from a Text Field

TextField

getText

To retrieve data from a text field, use the field's `getText` method:

```
stringVariable = textFieldReference.getText();
```

Regardless of the characters typed in the text field, the `getText` method always returns a string. This means that if you need a number, you must convert the text.

Listing 11.8   Dialog box classes for collecting input data

```
public class FixedPaymentDialog extends Dialog
{
    private TextField principal;
    private TextField interest_rate;
    private TextField payment;
    private Font systemFont = new Font ("System",Font.BOLD,12);
    private Button theButton;
    private FixedPaymentDialog thisDialog;

    public FixedPaymentDialog (LoanApp parent)
    {
        super (parent, "Fixed Payment Loan",true);
        thisDialog = this;
        addWindowListener (new WindowAdapter()
        {
            public void windowClosing (WindowEvent theEvent)
                { thisDialog.dispose(); }
        } );

        setBackground(Color.white);
        Panel thePanel = new Panel();
        thePanel.setLayout (new GridLayout (3,2)); // rows,columns
        thePanel.add (new Label ("      Principal:"));
        thePanel.add (principal = new TextField ("",8));
        thePanel.add (new Label ("      Interest rate:"));
        thePanel.add (interest_rate = new TextField ("",8));
        thePanel.add (new Label ("      Payment:"));
        thePanel.add (payment = new TextField ("",8));
        add ("Center",thePanel); // add panel to dialog box

        thePanel = new Panel();
        thePanel.setFont (systemFont);

        theButton = new Button ("OK");
        theButton.addActionListener (new ActionListener ()
        {
            public void actionPerformed (ActionEvent theEvent)
            {
                thisDialog.dispose();
                float f_principal =
                    new Float((principal.getText()).trim()).floatValue();
                float f_interest_rate =
                    new Float((interest_rate.getText()).trim()).floatValue();
                float f_payment =
                    new Float((payment.getText()).trim()).floatValue();
```

Continued next page

Listing 11.8(Continued)   Dialog box classes for collecting input data

```
                ((DialogProcessor)getParent()).processDialog (thisDialog,
                    new FixedData (f_principal,f_interest_rate,f_payment));
            }
        } );
        thePanel.add (theButton);

        theButton = new Button ("Cancel");
        theButton.addActionListener (new ActionListener ()
        {
            public void actionPerformed (ActionEvent theEvent)
                { thisDialog.dispose(); }
        } );
        thePanel.add (theButton);

        add ("South",thePanel);
        setSize (300,100);
    }
}

public class VariablePaymentDialog extends Dialog
{
    private TextField principal;
    private TextField interest_rate;
    private TextField payment_percent;
    private TextField minimum_payment;
    private TextField minimum_interest;
    private Font systemFont = new Font ("System",Font.BOLD,12);
    private Button theButton;
    private VariablePaymentDialog thisDialog;

    public VariablePaymentDialog (LoanApp parent)
    {
        super (parent, "Fixed Payment Loan",true);
        thisDialog = this;
        addWindowListener (new WindowAdapter ()
        {
            public void windowClosing (WindowEvent theEvent)
                { thisDialog.dispose(); }
        } );

        setBackground(Color.white);
        Panel thePanel = new Panel();
        thePanel.setLayout (new GridLayout (5,2)); // rows,columns
        thePanel.add (new Label ("     Principal:"));
        thePanel.add (principal = new TextField ("",8));
```

Continued next page

Listing 11.8(Continued)   Dialog box classes for collecting input data

```
thePanel.add (new Label ("      Interest rate:"));
thePanel.add (interest_rate = new TextField ("",8));
thePanel.add (new Label ("      Payment percentage:"));
thePanel.add (payment_percent = new TextField ("",8));
thePanel.add (new Label ("      Minimum monthly payment:"));
thePanel.add (minimum_payment = new TextField ("",8));
thePanel.add (new Label ("      Minimum monthly interest:"));
thePanel.add (minimum_interest = new TextField ("",8));
add ("Center",thePanel); // add panel to dialog box

thePanel = new Panel();
thePanel.setFont(systemFont);

theButton = new Button ("OK");
theButton.addActionListener (new ActionListener ()
{
    public void actionPerformed (ActionEvent theEvent)
    {
        thisDialog.dispose();
        float f_principal = (float)
            new Double((principal.getText()).trim()).doubleValue();
        float f_interest_rate = (float) new
            Double((interest_rate.getText()).trim()).doubleValue();
        float f_payment = (float) new
            Double((payment_percent.getText()).trim()).doubleValue();
        float f_min_pay = (float) new
            Double((minimum_payment.getText()).trim()).doubleValue();
        float f_min_int = (float) new
            Double((minimum_interest.getText()).trim()).doubleValue();
        ((DialogProcessor)getParent()).processDialog
            (thisDialog, new VariableData (f_principal,f_interest_rate,
            f_payment,f_min_pay,f_min_int));
    }
} );
thePanel.add (theButton);

theButton = new Button ("Cancel");
theButton.addActionListener (new ActionListener ()
{
    public void actionPerformed (ActionEvent theEvent)
        { thisDialog.dispose(); }
} );
thePanel.add (theButton);
add ("South",thePanel);
setSize (325,150);
    }
}
```

Continued next page

Listing 11.8(Continued)   Dialog box classes for collecting input data

```java
public class MortgageDialog extends Dialog
{
    private TextField principal;
    private TextField interest_rate;
    private TextField num_periods;
    private TextField periods_per_year;
    private TextField payment;
    private Font systemFont = new Font ("System",Font.BOLD,12);
    private Button theButton;
    private MortgageDialog thisDialog;

    public MortgageDialog (LoanApp parent)
    {
        super (parent, "Mortgage Loan",true);
        thisDialog = this;
        addWindowListener (new WindowAdapter ()
        {
            public void windowClosing (WindowEvent theEvent)
                { thisDialog.dispose(); }
        } );

        setBackground(Color.white);
        Panel thePanel = new Panel();
        thePanel.setLayout (new GridLayout (5,2)); // rows,columns
        thePanel.add (new Label ("     Principal (0 to compute):"));
        thePanel.add (principal = new TextField ("",8));
        thePanel.add (new Label ("     Payment (0 to compute):"));
        thePanel.add (payment = new TextField ("",8));
        thePanel.add (new Label ("     Yearly interest rate:"));
        thePanel.add (interest_rate = new TextField ("",8));
        thePanel.add (new Label ("     Payment Periods in loan:"));
        thePanel.add (num_periods = new TextField ("",8));
        thePanel.add (new Label ("     Payment Periods per year:"));
        thePanel.add (periods_per_year = new TextField ("",8));
        add ("Center",thePanel); // add panel to dialog box

        thePanel = new Panel();
        thePanel.setFont (systemFont);
        theButton = new Button ("OK");
        theButton.addActionListener (new ActionListener ()
        {
            public void actionPerformed (ActionEvent theEvent)
            {
                thisDialog.dispose();
                float f_principal = (float) new
                    Double((principal.getText()).trim()).doubleValue();
```

Continued next page

Listing 11.8(Continued)   Dialog box classes for collecting input data

```
}                          float f_payment = (float) new
                              Double((payment.getText()).trim()).doubleValue();
                           float f_interest_rate = (float) new
                              Double((interest_rate.getText()).trim()).doubleValue();
                           int i_num_periods = (int)
                              Integer.parseInt((num_periods.getText()).trim());
                           int i_periods_per_year = (int)
                              Integer.parseInt((periods_per_year.getText()).trim());
                           ((DialogProcessor)getParent()).processDialog (thisDialog,
                              new MortgageData (f_principal,f_interest_rate,
                              i_num_periods,i_periods_per_year,f_payment));
                        }
                     } );
                     thePanel.add (theButton);

                     theButton = new Button ("Cancel");
                     theButton.addActionListener (new ActionListener ()
                     {
                        public void actionPerformed (ActionEvent theEvent)
                           { thisDialog.dispose(); }
                     } );
                     thePanel.add (theButton);
                     add ("South",thePanel);
                     setSize (375,150);
      }
}
```

Integer   If you want an integer, you can use the `Integer` class's `parseInt`

method:

```
integerVariable = Integer.parseInt (string);
```

parseInt   A comparable method exists in the `Long` class (`parseLong`).

If you look at the dialog box classes, you will notice a call to the `String` class's
`trim` method for every string retrieved from a text field. The purpose of this
Note   method is to remove leading and trailing blanks from a string.

String

However, there is no simple way to convert strings to real numbers. To
get either a `float` or `double` you must create an object of either the `Float`
or `Double` class and then call a method that converts the string representation
trim   of the number to a numeric value (`floatValue` for a `float`, `doubleValue`
for a `double`).

The constructor for an object of the `Float` class accepts the string representation of the number as an input parameter. The loan calculator program can use the string retrieved from a text field, after it has been trimmed. When you put all of this together, you get a statement like:

```
value = new Float((payment.getText()).trim()).floatValue();
```

The Problem with Sharing Dialog Box Data

When the user makes a change to input elements like text fields that have been placed in a window (as opposed to a dialog box), Java sends an event to the component that is that source of the user's actions. You can then either process the input immediately or simply store the value of the input element for later processing. However, when you place input elements in a dialog box, you are faced with the problem of sending the input back to the dialog box's parent window.

Assume, for example, that you are working with the dialog box in Figure 11.3 or Figure 11.4. (Both are created by exactly the same code.) The process for creating the dialog box is to create an object from the dialog box class and then call `show` to make the dialog box appear:

```
FixedPaymentDialog theDialog =
    new FixedPaymentDialog (thisApp);
theDialog.show();
```

Now that the dialog box is on the screen, what should you do to get data from it? Well, you might think that you should include some "get" methods in the dialog box class, one for each input element in the dialog box. You could then follow the call to `show` with something like:

```
principal = theDialog.getPrincipal();
interest = theDialog.getInterest();
payment = theDialog.getPayment();
```

Unfortunately, it won't work. Why? Because the `show` method finishes immediately after drawing the dialog box on the screen. The program then executes the three lines that retrieve data from the dialog box. This means that the program won't wait for the user to enter data and click the dialog box's OK button. If you use the preceding code, there won't be any values in `principal`, `interest`, or `payment`. (That is, unless the user can type at computer processing speeds!)

To solve the problem, you need to provide a means for the dialog box to call a method belonging to its parent window that processes the data in the dialog box when the user clicks the dialog box's OK button. The key is to give the parent window the characteristics of a class whose purpose is to process dialog box data. As you will see, this will allow you to write the dialog box class in a generic way, without needing to know the class from which its parent class has been created.

The trouble with this strategy is that the parent window already inherits from `Frame`, and therefore can't inherit the characteristics of another class. Therefore, the solution is to create a custom interface that will process the dialog box data, loading an object with the settings in the dialog box. The parent window can then implement the interface, as well as inheriting from `Frame`.

Using an Interface to Send Dialog Box Data to Its Parent Window

The interface that we add to the `LoanApp` class has nothing but one abstract method

```
interface DialogProcessor // for getting data from dialog boxes
{
    public void processDialog (Dialog theDialog,
        Object theObject);

}
```

An implementation of this method accepts two input parameters: the dialog box from which data are being collected and an object containing the data. Because we want to be able to use this interface when collecting data from any dialog box in any program, we can't specify the name of the class in which the result data will be stored. For example, the loan calculator program uses three classes to hold input data, all of which inherit from a single base class (see Listing 11.9). Therefore, the second parameter is of class `Object`, the ultimate base class from which all objects inherit.

The process for sending dialog box data back to a parent window is as follows:

1. Trap the event that occurs when the user clicks the dialog box's OK button by registering an action event listener with that button.

Listing 11.9   Classes for holding dialog box data

```
class DialogData
{
    float principal;
    float interest_rate;

    public DialogData (float i_principal, float i_interest_rate)
    {
        principal = i_principal;
        interest_rate = i_interest_rate;
    }
}

class FixedData extends DialogData
{
    float payment;  // amount customer will be paying each month

    public FixedData (float i_principal, float i_interest_rate, float
    i_payment)
    {
        super (i_principal, i_interest_rate); // call base class constructor
        payment = i_payment;
    }
}

class VariableData extends DialogData
{
    float payment_percent;  /* percentage of principal to be paid each month */
    float minimum_payment;  /* minimum payment to be used when principal gets
    low */
    float minimum_interest;  /* minimum interest assessed */

    public VariableData (float i_principal, float i_interest_rate, float
    i_payment_percent, float i_minimum_payment, float i_minimum_interest)
    {
        super (i_principal, i_interest_rate);
        payment_percent = i_payment_percent;
        minimum_payment = i_minimum_payment;
        minimum_interest = i_minimum_interest;
    }
}
```

Continued next page

Listing 11.9(Continued)   Classes for holding dialog box data

```
class MortgageData extends DialogData
{
    int num_periods;
    int periods_per_year;
    float payment;

    public MortgageData (float i_principal,float i_interest_rate, int
    i_num_periods, int i_periods_per_year, float i_payment)
    {
        super (i_principal, i_interest_rate);
        num_periods = i_num_periods;
        periods_per_year = i_periods_per_year;
        payment = i_payment;
    }
}
```

2. In the listener object's `actionPerformed` method, begin by clos-
    ing the dialog box with a call to `dispose`.

    ```
    thisDialog.dispose();
    ```

3. Then store the data from the dialog box in local variables.

    ```
    float f_principal = new
        Float((principal.getText()).trim()).floatValue();
    float f_interest_rate = new
        Float((interest_rate.getText()).trim()).floatValue();
    float f_payment = new
        Float((payment.getText()).trim()).floatValue();
    ```

4. Next create an object to hold all the data collected from the dialog
    box, initializing it with the values collected in Step 3.

Dialog

getParent

5. Get a reference to the dialog box's parent window using the `get-`
    `Parent` method. Typecast the parent window to an object of the
    `DialogProcessor` interface and finish by calling the `process-`
    `Dialog` method. The loan calculation program performs Steps 4
    and 5 with a single statement.

    ```
    ((DialogProcessor)getParent()).processDialog (this,
        new FixedData (f_principal,f_interest_rate,f_payment));
    ```

By using the `DialogProcessor` interface and typecasting to it when retrieving the dialog box's parent window, the dialog box class avoids needing to know the exact class from which the parent window was created. We could do without the interface by typecasting to the `LoanApp` class, but then the dialog box would be closely tied to the `LoanApp` class. Using the interface creates code that is more generic and therefore is better programming.

Other GUI Elements for Dialog Boxes

There are three major GUI input elements that you have not seen demonstrated: check boxes, radio buttons, and lists. In this section we will look at a simple demonstration program that uses all three in a dialog box and displays the settings of the input elements when the user closes the dialog box.

The program's top-level window contains two buttons: one to display a dialog box containing the input elements (Figure 11.8) and one to display the results of the user's selections in the dialog box (Figure 11.9). Because the program won't draw results without initializing the output canvas with valid data, no error is generated if a user clicks the Show Results button before displaying the dialog box and making choices in it. Instead, the button simply does nothing.

Figure 11.8   The input element sample dialog box

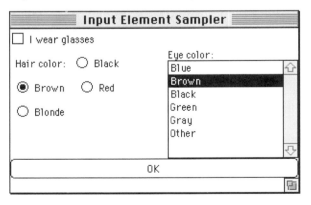

The GUI element test program uses four classes:

- `GUITestApp`: The application class for the top-level window (Listing 11.10) that traps events in its two buttons. The procedures

Figure 11.9   Output of the input element sample program

for displaying the dialog box and getting results from the dialog box to pass to the display canvas are conceptually the same as that used in the loan calculator program. Notice, however, that the `processDialog` method is considerably simpler: All `processDialog` has to do in this program is copy the reference to an object holding the results into a local variable, which can then be used to initialize the display canvas.

- `resultHolder`: The class for passing data between the dialog box and the application (Listing 11.11).
- `displayCanvas`: The canvas that displays the results stored in a `resultHolder` object (Listing 11.12).
- `sampleDialog`: The dialog box that collects data from a check box, a group of radio buttons, and a list (Listing 11.13). This is where the code for the input elements can be found.

Using Check Boxes

Checkbox

new

Check boxes are boolean entities that represent TRUE when they contain an X and FALSE when they are empty. To place a check box in a window, you create an object of class `Checkbox`, supplying the check box's label as an input parameter:

```
checkboxReference = new Checkbox (labelString);
```

Listing 11.10   GUITestApp.java

```java
public class GUITestApp extends Frame implements DialogProcessor
{
    private displayCanvas theCanvas;
    private resultHolder resultObject;
    private GUITestApp thisApp;

    public GUITestApp()
    {
        thisApp = this;
        setTitle ("GUI Element Test");
        setBackground (Color.white);

        addWindowListener (new WindowAdapter()
        {
            public void windowClosing (WindowEvent theEvent)
            {
                System.exit(0);
            }
        });

        theCanvas = new displayCanvas();
        add ("Center",theCanvas);

        Panel buttonPanel = new Panel();
        Button dbButton = new Button ("Show Dialog Box");
        dbButton.addActionListener (new ActionListener ()
        {
            public void actionPerformed (ActionEvent theEvent)
            {
                sampleDialog theDialog = new sampleDialog (thisApp);
                theDialog.show();
            }
        });
        Button resultsButton = new Button ("Show Results");
        resultsButton.addActionListener (new ActionListener ()
        {
            public void actionPerformed (ActionEvent theEvent)
            {
                theCanvas.init (resultObject);
                theCanvas.repaint();
            }
        });

        buttonPanel.add (dbButton);
        buttonPanel.add (resultsButton);
        add ("North",buttonPanel);
    }
```

Continued next page

Listing 11.10(Continued)   GUITestApp.java

```
    public void processDialog (Dialog theDialog, Object theData)
    {
        resultObject = (resultHolder) theData;
    }

    public static void main (String args[])
    {
        GUITestApp theApp = new GUITestApp();
        theApp.setSize (200,200);
        theApp.show();
    }
}
```

Listing 11.11   resultHolder.java

```
class resultHolder
{
    private boolean glassesState;
    private String theEyeColor, theHairColor;

    public resultHolder (boolean iglasses, String ieye, String ihair)
    {
        glassesState = iglasses;
        theEyeColor = ieye;
        theHairColor = ihair;
    }

    public boolean getGlasses()
        { return glassesState; }

    public String getEyes()
        { return theEyeColor; }

    public String getHair()
        { return theHairColor; }
}
```

The check box appears without an X and with its label to the right of the box, as in Figure 11.8.

When a user clicks in a check box, the Java virtual machine creates an object from the ItemEvent class. To make a program respond to an item event in a check box, you must therefore register an item listener with the check box object:

Listing 11.12   displayCanvas.java

```java
import java.awt.*;
import java.lang.*;
import java.io.*;

public class displayCanvas extends Canvas
{
    private boolean glasses;
    private String eyeColor, hairColor;
    private boolean do_paint = false;

    public displayCanvas()
    {
        setBackground (Color.white);
    }

    public void init (resultHolder theResult)
    {
        glasses = theResult.getGlasses();
        eyeColor = theResult.getEyes();
        hairColor = theResult.getHair();
        do_paint = true;
    }

    public void paint (Graphics graphObject)
    {
        if (do_paint)
        {
            graphObject.drawString
            (glasses ? "You wear glasses." : "You don't wear glasses.",15,20);
            graphObject.drawString
                ("Your eyes are " + eyeColor.toLowerCase() + ".",15, 40);
            graphObject.drawString
                ("Your hair is " + hairColor.toLowerCase() + ".",15, 60);
        }
    }
}
```

```java
            glasses.addItemListener (new ItemListener ()
            {
                public void itemStateChanged (ItemEvent theEvent)
                {
                    // event handling code goes here
                }
            } );
```

As you can see, the `ItemListener` interface has only one method—`item-StateChanged`—for you to implement.

Listing 11.13   sampleDialog.java

```java
import java.awt.*;
import java.lang.*;
import java.io.*;
import java.awt.event.*;

public class sampleDialog extends Dialog
{
    private Checkbox glasses;
    private boolean glassesState = false;
    private Checkbox black, brown, red, blonde; // hair color
    private List eyeColor;
    private String theHairColor = "brown", theEyeColor = "brown";
    private Button OKButton;
    private sampleDialog thisDialog;
    private resultHolder theResults;

    public sampleDialog(GUITestApp parent)
    {
        super (parent,"Input Element Sampler",true);

        theResults = new resultHolder
            (glassesState, theEyeColor, theHairColor);
        setBackground (Color.white);
        Panel thePanel = new Panel();
        thePanel.setLayout (new BorderLayout());

        // Check box for whether you wear glasses
        thePanel.add ("North",glasses = new Checkbox ("I wear glasses"));
        glasses.addItemListener (new ItemListener ()
        {
            public void itemStateChanged (ItemEvent theEvent)
            {
                Checkbox box = (Checkbox) theEvent.getSource();
                theResults.setGlasses(box.getState());
            }
        });

        // Radio buttons for hair color
        // Using name inner class because it is used several times
        class hairListener implements ItemListener
        {
            public void itemStateChanged (ItemEvent theEvent)
            {
                Checkbox box = (Checkbox) theEvent.getSource();
                theResults.setEyes ((box.getLabel()).toLowerCase());
            }
        }
    }
```

Continued next page

Listing 11.13(Continued)   sampleDialog.java

```java
Panel hairPanel = new Panel();
hairPanel.setLayout (new FlowLayout(FlowLayout.LEFT));
hairPanel.add (new Label("Hair color:"));
CheckboxGroup hairColor = new CheckboxGroup();
hairPanel.add (black = new Checkbox ("Black",hairColor,false));
black.addItemListener (new hairListener());
hairPanel.add (brown = new Checkbox ("Brown",hairColor,true));
brown.addItemListener (new hairListener());
hairPanel.add (red = new Checkbox ("Red",hairColor,false));
red.addItemListener (new hairListener());
hairPanel.add (blonde = new Checkbox ("Blonde",hairColor,false));
blonde.addItemListener (new hairListener());
thePanel.add ("Center",hairPanel);

// List for eye color
Panel eyePanel = new Panel();
eyePanel.setLayout (new BorderLayout());
eyePanel.add ("North",new Label ("Eye color:"));
// six items; multiple selection not allowed
eyeColor = new List (6 ,false);
eyeColor.addItem ("Blue");
eyeColor.addItem ("Brown");
eyeColor.addItem ("Black");
eyeColor.addItem ("Green");
eyeColor.addItem ("Gray");
eyeColor.addItem ("Other");
// make brown hair the default; Item numbering begins with 0
eyeColor.select (1);
eyeColor.addItemListener (new ItemListener()
{
    public void itemStateChanged (ItemEvent theEvent)
    {
        List theList = (List) theEvent.getSource();
        theResults.setHair (theList.getSelectedItem());
    }
});

eyePanel.add ("Center",eyeColor);
thePanel.add ("East",eyePanel);

thePanel.add ("South",OKButton = new Button ("OK"));
OKButton.addActionListener (new ActionListener ()
{
    public void actionPerformed (ActionEvent theEvent)
    {
        thisDialog.dispose();
```

Continued next page

Listing 11.13(Continued)   sampleDialog.java

```
            ((DialogProcessor)thisDialog.getParent()).processDialog
                (thisDialog, theResults);
        }
    } );

    add ("Center",thePanel);
    setSize (300,175);

    thisDialog = this;
    }
}
```

Typically, when a check box event occurs, a program tests the check box to see if it is checked or unchecked with the `getState` method:

Checkbox

getState

```
boolean variable = checkboxReference.getState();
```

If you want to control the state of a check box, for example to give it an initial value of checked, then you can use the `setState` method:

Checkbox

```
checkboxReference.setState (booleanValue);
```

For example, to place an X in the `glasses` check box used in the demonstration program:

setState

```
glasses.setState (true);
```

Using Check Box Groups (Radio Buttons)

Java views radio buttons as a group of check boxes. For each group of radio buttons, you create one object of the class `CheckboxGroup`. Then, as you add check box objects to a panel, you specify that they are part of a group. Any check box associated with a group appears as a round radio button, just like the hair color radio buttons in Figure 11.8.

Java radio buttons behave as you would expect: When the user clicks a button in the group, the previously selected button becomes unselected. All your program needs to do is create the check box group, add the check boxes to the group, and then let the check box group class take care of the rest.

Checkbox-Group

To begin the process, create the check box group object:

new

```
CheckboxGroup checkboxGroupReference = new CheckboxGroup();
```

Be sure to store the object reference returned by the call to new. You'll need it when adding check boxes to the group.

To add the check boxes to the group so they will appear as radio buttons, you create objects of the Checkbox class but use a different constructor from the one you used when creating a stand-alone check box:

```
checkboxReference = new Checkbox (label,checkboxGroupReference,
    initialState);
```

For example, to create the radio button for black hair, the demonstration program uses:

```
black = new Checkbox ("Black",hairColor,false);
```

Note that the variable hairColor contains a reference to the check box group with which this check box object is to be associated.

There are several things to keep in mind when creating radio buttons:

- You can place a radio button anywhere you want in a window. The grouping of radio buttons occurs when you create the check box object, not when you add the object to a panel. There is theoretically no reason why all the radio buttons in a group must be physically located next to one another.
- Only one check box object in a check box group can have a state of TRUE at any one time. Be sure that you initialize only one object in each group to TRUE; make sure the rest are FALSE.
- Although each radio button appears with its own label, there is no way to label the check box group. Therefore, the demonstration program places the check boxes and a label object in their own panel (hairPanel), which is then added to the dialog box's panel (thePanel). This method of using panels with different layout managers, one within the other, makes it easier to place elements where you want them. In this particular case, it makes it possible to place the label object on top of the group of radio buttons.

Any time the user clicks a radio button, Java generates an item event. This means that you must register an item listener with *each* check box object in the group. In most cases, the listener will be the same for each radio button. It therefore makes sense to use a named class (in the sample GUI program, a named inner class) from which objects can be created repeatedly.

Inside the item listener's `itemStateChanged` method, a program usually stores something to indicate which radio button in the group is currently selected. You could, for example, store a reference to the button:

Checkbox

getLabel

```
Checkbox currentButton = (Checkbox) theEvent.getSource();
```

Because the result of calling **getSource()** is of class **Object**, you must remember to typecast it to the correct class for the assignment to work.

Alternatively, you can retrieve the label assigned to the radio button. (This is particularly useful if you intend to display that label at some point.) For example, the demonstration program uses:

String

toLower-Case

```
Checkbox box = (Checkbox) theEvent.getSource();
theResults.setEyes ((box.getLabel()).toLowerCase());
```

String

toUpper-Case

These statements actually do three things. First, they typecast the source of the event to a check box object. Then they call the **Checkbox** class method **get-Label**, which returns the object's current label string. Then, they convert all characters in that string to lowercase so they will appear more naturally when used in an output sentence. (The string class also includes a **toUpperCase** method, which converts all characters in a string to uppercase characters.)

Using Lists

To create a list from which users can choose one or more options, you create an object of class **List** and then add items to the list, just as you add items to a pull-down menu:

List

new

```
List listReference = new List
    (#itemsToShow,allowMultipleSelections?);
```

The first parameter is an integer indicating the number of items in the list that should always be visible. (The list will scroll if it contains more items.) The second parameter is a boolean that is set to TRUE if multiple selections are allowed in the list or FALSE if they are not. The demonstration program creates its list object with:

```
eyeColor = new List (6 ,false);
```

where **eyeColor** has been previously declared to hold a reference to an object of class **List**.

List

addItem

You add items one by one to the list with the **addItem** method:

```
listReference.addItem (itemText);
```

For example, the GUI demonstration program adds its list items with:

```
eyeColor.addItem ("Blue");
eyeColor.addItem ("Brown");
eyeColor.addItem ("Black");
eyeColor.addItem ("Green");
eyeColor.addItem ("Gray");
eyeColor.addItem ("Other");
```

When a user selects an item in a list by clicking on the item to highlight it, the Java virtual machine generates an item event. However, if a user double-clicks on an item, the Java virtual machine generates an action event. If you want a user to be able to make a selection from a list and signal a click on an OK button at the same time by double-clicking on the list, then you will register an action listener with the list object. However, if you simply want to allow the user to select with a single click, then you will register an item listener. You can support both types of interaction by simply giving the list two listener objects, one for each type of event.

The GUI sample application traps only single clicks on list items and therefore registers only an item listener. The code for handling a list selection therefore appears in the listener object's **itemStateChanged** method.

List

get-
Selected-
Item

Within that method, you typically want to store the text of whichever item or items were selected. If multiple selections are not allowed (as is the case with the demonstration program), then you can retrieve the single selected item text with the method **getSelectedItem**:

List

get-
Selected-
Items

```
String theItem = listReference.getSelectedItem();
```

If you have allowed multiple selections, then you need to provide an array of strings to hold all the selections and use the **getSelectedItems** method instead:

```
String[] theItems = new String[#maximumItems];
theItems = listReference.getSelectedItems();
```

Summary

In this chapter you learned to add many common user interface elements to a Java program, including pull-down menus, scrolling output, and dialog boxes for data entry.

Each pull-down menu is a separate object that is added to either a menu bar object (in which case it becomes a menu in the menu bar) or to another menu object (in which case it becomes a submenu). A menu bar object is added to a window object. Where the menu bar appears when the program is running, however, depends on the current operating system.

Scrolling output is provided by scroll bar objects. When an event occurs in a scroll bar, the program detects the amount of movement and uses that value to offset the origin of the graphics object in which drawing will take place. Although the program always redraws the entire output, only that portion of it that has its top left corner at graphics object's coordinates of 0,0 will be visible.

Dialog boxes, which are commonly used to gather input from users, present a problem to a Java programmer because once the dialog box is displayed, the program doesn't automatically wait for the user to work with the dialog box and click the OK button to signal that data should be processed. The solution is to have the dialog box's event handling code call a method from the dialog box's parent window that processes the contents of the dialog box. This is accomplished by using a Java interface to give the parent window the characteristics of a class in addition to the one from which it inherits.

Exercises

1. Write a program that displays a formatted check in an output window. Use a dialog box to collect data for the check (for example, date, payee, amount). Draw the check using lines, rectangles, and text as appropriate.

2. Write a program that displays a single text of string that the user enters. Give the user popup menus and/or scrolling lists from which he or she can pick the text style (for example, plain, boldface, or italic) and the type size in points. Whenever the user makes a selection, redraw the text string in the window using the user's new choice.

3. Write a program that prepares a sales slip for a retail store customer. Use a dialog box to collect data about each item on a purchase. Then, display the sales slip in a scrolling window. The sales slip should show the name of each item, the quantity purchased, the cost of each item, the total cost for an item of a given type, and the total cost of the entire purchase. The sales slip should also display the name of the store and the current date. (*Tip:* You can get the current system date by creating an object of the class `Date` with `Date today = new Date();`. You can convert the date to a string for output with `today.toString()`.)

4. Write the program described in Exercise 3 as an applet rather than an application. Consider carefully how the change from an application to an applet will affect the design of the program's user interface.

5. Write a program that stores and outputs a customer mailing list. Give the user a dialog box into which he or she can enter data about a single customer. As you create customer objects, store them in an array or a vector. Allow the user to view the entire mailing list at any time, nicely formatted as if for mailing labels, in a scrolling list in the program's top-level window. Use one or more pull-down menus to let the user choose what action to perform.

6. Write a program that conducts and scores an on-line multiple choice exam. The exam should present each question to the user in a dialog box. When the user chooses an answer, store the answer. Then, when all questions have been asked, score the exam, reporting the result in the top-level window as both the total number correct and the percentage correct. (*Hint:* Consider creating an object to hold each question and its possible answers. Then use an array or vector to hold the objects, which can then be used as the source for text for display in the dialog box.)

7. Write the program described in Exercise 6 as an applet rather than an application so that students could take their exam over the World Wide Web. Consider carefully how the change from an application to an applet will affect the design of the program's user interface.

8. Write a program that provides an on-line help system for a data entry program. Use pull-down menus to give the user access to each "page" (output screen) in the help system. The pages should contain the following content:

   - A description of the program.
   - The program's three menu options ("Enter employees," "Enter managers," "Enter hours worked").
   - Instructions for entering employee data.
   - Instructions for entering manager data.
   - Instructions for entering the number of hours worked each week.

   Use a scrolling output window to display the text of each page. (*Hint:* There are two strategies you can use here. One is to create a separate canvas for each page and then remove and install canvases as the user makes menu selections. The second is to reinitialize a single output canvas each time the user makes a menu selection.) If you want to be creative, draw shapes in your output canvases to simulate what the user's data entry forms look like.

9. Modify the survey analysis program that was used as an example in Chapter 10 so that it uses pull-down menus for its interface. Also provide a dialog box for users to perform interactive data entry. A user should be able to enter the data for an entire survey in one dialog box.

12 File I/O and Exception Handling

OBJECTIVES

In this chapter you will read about:

- How stream I/O underlies all Java I/O.
- To read data from and write data sequentially to delimited text files.
- To read data from and write data to random access files.
- To use the standard Open File and Save File dialog boxes.
- How exception handling can be used to handle file I/O errors.
- How you can define your own exceptions to trap and handle errors.

Java views all of its I/O as if the data were traveling in single file, as if it were the water flowing down a stream one byte wide. When you are working with screen and keyboard I/O, however, for the most part you don't have to worry about I/O streams; you just take advantage of the capabilities of the AWT. However, sometimes you need to perform I/O directly, especially when working with files.

At the lowest level, Java reads and writes data as unformatted streams of bytes, leading to the terminology *stream I/O*. In this chapter, you will be introduced to several important concepts surrounding the use of Java's stream I/O. The first is the process for reading data from and writing data to delimited text files. The second is using exception handling—an advanced programming concept—to trap and deal with I/O errors. In addition, you'll see how to store and retrieve data from random access files. At the end of this chapter, you'll learn to create your own exceptions so you can trap and handle errors that your programs might generate.

Note   Most programming texts at the level of this book don't mention exception handling. However, you can't do file I/O using Java without it. Therefore, we'll go into it just enough so you understand what is happening when you work with text files. You'll also learn to create your own exceptions for trapping program-specific errors. Knowing a bit about exception handling will also be useful if you plan to explore Chapter 13, which deals with images and multithreading.

Note   Yes, it's true that we don't program using data files much anymore. Applets can't access local files, and many business application programs interact with database management systems rather than directly with data files. Nonetheless, it is important that you understand the concepts of basic file I/O so you can use it if it becomes necessary.

The Stream I/O Classes

Java provides a large collection of classes that support I/O. As you can see in Figure 12.1, there are actually two inheritance hierarchies, one for input and one for output. In addition to the classes in the illustration, there are also two interfaces (`DataInput` and `DataOutput`) implemented by the `DataInputStream`, `DataOutputStream`, and `RandomAccessFile` classes.

When working with data files, you will be using five of these classes:

- `DataInputStream`: A data input stream reads "primitive" Java data types. In this context, the term primitive refers to simple data types, such as integers, floating point numbers, characters, and booleans. A data input stream exists in main memory and isn't connected with any physical device. You must therefore attach it to a another stream (such as file input stream) that is directly connected to an input source.
- `FileInputStream`: A file input stream connects an input stream with a data file. Because a file stream handles data one byte at a time, you can attach it to a data input stream to make data handling easier. We will use the combination of a data input stream and a file input stream to read data from sequential text files.
- `PrintStream`: A print stream writes formatted text output to a stream. You "print" individual values (for example, integers, floating point numbers, characters, and strings) to the stream. Like a data input stream, it needs to be connected to another type of stream that talks to some output device, such as a disk file or a print buffer.
- `FileOutputStream`: A file output stream writes one byte at a time to a disk file. You will commonly combine a file output stream with a print stream so a program can work with Java data types, rather than having to convert everything to a stream of bytes. The combination of a print stream and a file output stream is therefore useful for writing to sequential text files.
- `RandomAccessFile`: A random access file lets you read and/or write data anywhere in a file. Each opened file maintains a location pointer that you move before you begin reading or writing. In most cases, you write undifferentiated streams of bytes to a random access file. You must therefore know how much space each piece of data occupies so you can locate it accurately.

Figure 12.1 The stream I/O class hierarchies

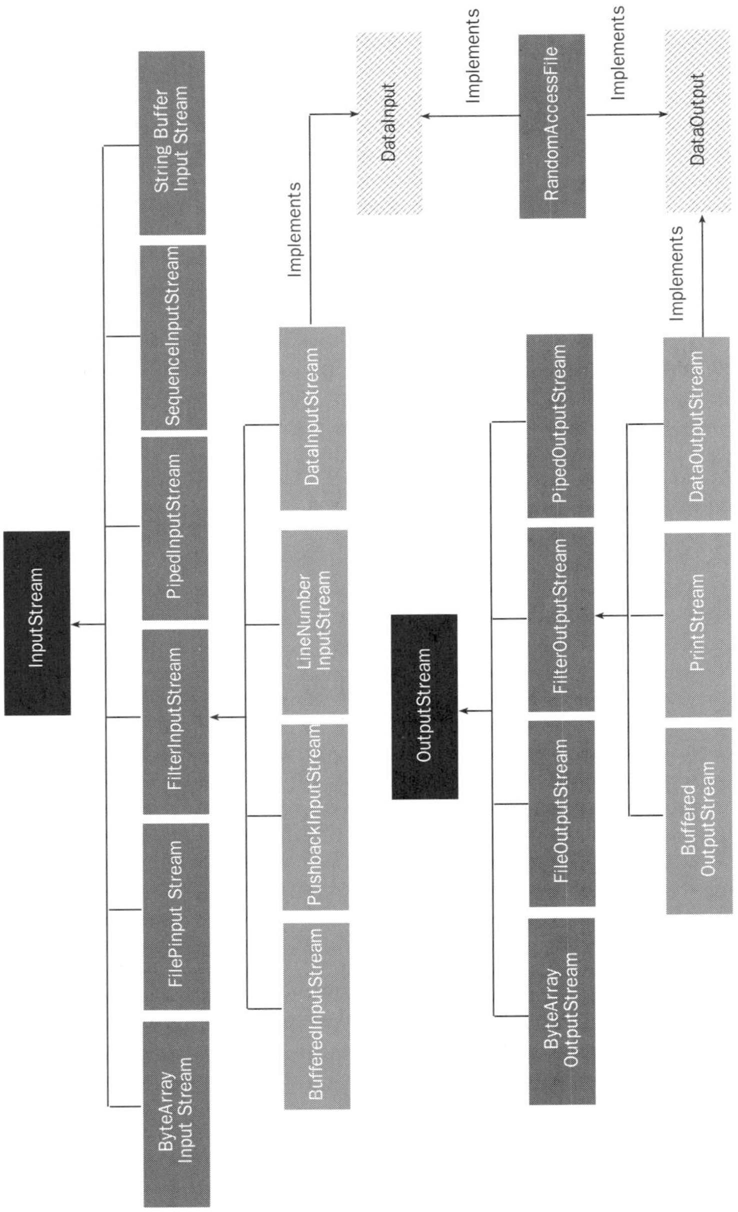

The Basics of Exception Handling

An *exception* is an error that occurs while a program is running that causes the program to stop if the error isn't trapped and handled. It is a runtime error from which a program can't recover on its own. Such errors include:

- Hardware errors: Hardware errors occur when a disk drive can't be found, a disk file can't be opened, a printer isn't available, and so on. A hardware error can also occur if a program runs out of main memory or a disk drive is full.
- Program errors: Program errors occur, for example, when a program attempts to divide by zero or to access an array element beyond the declared size of the array. When such errors occur, normal processing can't continue. Other program errors, such as encountering the end of a file when reading, aren't really errors, but signals of conditions that a program wants to recognize. In the case of an end-of-file exception, a program typically knows that all data have been read and that the file input process can stop.
- User errors: User errors occur when a user enters invalid data. With Java, the most common user error that generates an exception is an illegally formed URL.

When an errors occurs, a program *throws an exception*. The exception can be *caught* and handled by the program, in which case program execution can probably continue. However, if the exception isn't caught, an error message describing the exception shows up in the Java console output window and program execution terminates.

All Java exceptions are objects created from a subclass of the class `Throwable` (in other words, something a program can "throw"). As you can see in Figure 12.2, the inheritance hierarchy splits into two branches, represented by the classes `Error` and `Exception`.

The `Error` class handles truly abnormal occurrences, such as running out of main memory or other internal system problems. As a rule, a program should not attempt to throw an error from this side of the hierarchy, particularly because there is almost nothing a program can do to recover. However, you can deal directly with exceptions that are subclasses of `Exception`.

The `Exception` portion of the hierarchy splits into two subclasses, `IOException` for problems dealing with I/O, and `RuntimeException` for

Figure 12.2   The Java exception hierarchy

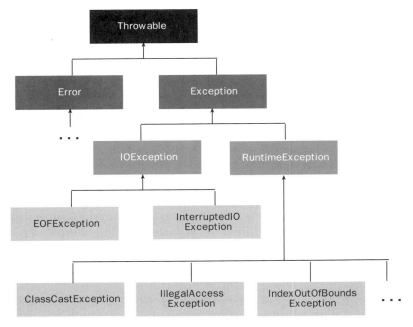

all other runtime errors. Sample subclasses of both appear in Figure 12.2. (There are too many to show in the diagram.) As you write file I/O code, you will need to alert Java that an IOException is possible and include code that handles an exception if it occurs.

The try/catch Structure

When you are writing code that can throw an exception, you *try* to perform an action and then *catch* an exception if it occurs. The general syntax of this structure is:

```
try
{
    // attempt to do something here
}
catch (exception_class)
{
    // error handling code goes here
}
```

The code in the `catch` block is executed if an exception of the specified class is thrown by an attempt to do something inside the `try` block. Otherwise the program simply skips over the `catch` code.

A method that includes code that might throw an exception needs to tell the compiler the type of exception that is expected. For example, a method that writes to a text file might throw an `IOException` and therefore indicates that possibility in its first line:

```
class someClass extends someClass throws IOException
```

Working with Sequential Files

The sequential text files that programs normally write are known as *delimited text files* because they use special characters to indicate the end of each *field* of data (a single number, characters, or string) and a different character to indicate the end of each *record* (all the fields that belong to a single object).

The separation characters (*delimiters*) can be any characters that aren't used in the data. If a file contains no strings, then a blank is often used as the field delimiter and a new line as the record delimiter. However, if a file needs to store strings, then tabs can be used as field delimiters.

Note Most DBMSs can load data into a database from space- or tab-delimited text files. Although you can use just about any character that isn't part of the data as a delimiter, if there is any chance that your files will be used by a DBMS, you should stick with the standard space and tab field delimiters.

Delimiters don't appear in a file by themselves. As you will see shortly, a program needs to write them along with the data. By the same token, the program reading the text files needs to know what characters are used as delimiters so it can separate the data back into distinct values.

Getting File Names

Although you can embed a file name as a constant in a program statement that opens a file stream, in terms of the user interface it is much better to present the user with the standard Open File and Save File dialog boxes so he or she can choose files and file locations. Java makes it easy to work with those dialog boxes through the `FileDialog` class.

As a first example, let's expand the very simple "bucket management" program that we used earlier in this book. (It stores the capacity and number of holes in three buckets.) The code for presenting an Open File dialog box can be found in Listing 12.1. The process is as follows:

Listing 12.1 Working with an Open File dialog box

```
FileDialog theDialog = new FileDialog
    (this,"Choose bucket data file:",FileDialog.LOAD);
theDialog.setDirectory (".");
theDialog.show();
String filename = theDialog.getFile();
if (filename == null)
{
    errorDialog message = new errorDialog ("You haven't chosen an input file");
    message.show();
    System.exit(0);
}
```

FileDialog

new

FileDialog

set-
Directory

FileDialog

getFile

1. Create an object of the `FileDialog` class. Pass three parameters to the constructor: a reference to the parent window (usually the current class), a title for the dialog box (a string), and a constant indicating whether you want the Open File (`FileDialog.LOAD`) or Save File (`FileDialog.SAVE`) dialog box.

2. If you want, set the default directory by calling the `setDirectory` method.

3. Display the dialog box by calling `show`. Unlike the other dialog boxes with which we have been working, the file dialog box freezes the program until the user closes the dialog box in some way. Therefore, `show` doesn't finish running until the user either chooses a file or cancels.

4. Retrieve the chosen file name by calling the `getFile` method. If the user cancels, the string returned by `getFile` will be null.

5. Check to see if you have a valid file name. If not, take any appropriate action. In this case, the program displays an error dialog telling the user that data can't be loaded and then stops execution. Otherwise, go ahead and open the file and read data.

Warning

The strategy described in Step 5 fails if you are running a program for the first time and there is no existing data file. If you are working from scratch, the program will not be able to run because you can't get around the Catch-22 of there being no initial file! You can get around the problem by adding extra code to ask the user if he or she wants to either quit the program or create a new data file.

FileDialog

setFile

Getting a file name from the Save File dialog box is very similar (see Listing 12.2). In this case, you use the constant `FileDialog.SAVE` to indicate a Save File dialog box. You can also include a default file name by calling the `setFile` method and passing the file name as a string.

Listing 12.2 Working with a Save File Dialog box

```
theDialog = new FileDialog (this,"Save the bucket data as",FileDialog.SAVE);
theDialog.setDirectory (".");
theDialog.setFile ("bucket.data"); // default file name
theDialog.show();
filename = theDialog.getFile();
if (filename == null)
{
    errorDialog message = new errorDialog ("Can't save data");
    message.show();
    System.exit(0);
}
```

Opening File Output Streams

Print-
Stream

new

To open a file for writing, you will need two streams. The first is an object of class `FileOutputStream` that makes the connection with a disk file. The second is an object of class `PrintStream`, which gives you the ability to work with Java data types rather than individual bytes.

You can do the process in two steps:

```
FileOutputStream theFile = new FileOutputStream (filename);
PrintStream inS = new PrintStream (theFile);
```

Alternatively, you can put it all together into one statement:

DataOutput-
Stream

new

```
PrintStream outS =
    new PrintStream  (new FileOutputStream (filename));
```

In either case, notice that the `PrintStream` object takes another stream as an input parameter for its constructor. This is because the print stream needs to know where to send its output (in this case, another stream).

Because opening I/O streams can fail, you must put the statements that create the streams in a `try` block, along with the statements that trigger methods to actually do the writing (see Listing 12.3). Notice that the `Bucket` class has a method named `write` that actually contains the code that sends data to the file. The application object calls this method, passing the reference to the output stream as an input parameter. Notice also that the `catch` block traps any type of I/O exception and displays an error message indicating that the output file isn't available.

Listing 12.3   The try/catch structure for writing to a file

```
try
{
    PrintStream outS = new PrintStream (new FileOutputStream (filename));
    Bucket1.write (outS);
    Bucket2.write (outS);
    Bucket3.write (outS);
}
catch (IOException theException)
{
    errorDialog message = new errorDialog ("Couldn't open output file.");
    message.show();
    System.exit (0);
}
```

Writing to a Delimited Text File

To write to a print stream, you use either the stream's `print` method, which writes a single data value, or its `println` method, which writes a data value followed by a new line character (`\n`). If the method containing the calls to `print` or `println` doesn't include a `try/catch` structure, then the method must indicate that it can throw an exception.

As an example, take a look at Listing 12.4. The method's first line indicates that it might throw an I/O exception. The body of the method writes data to the file with successive calls to `print`. It places a tab character (`\t`) between the two data values and a new line character at the end.

Note

Although tab and new line are invisible characters, nonetheless they are characters with ASCII codes, just like any visible character. If you open a tab-delimited text file with a text editor, whether you see the effect of the tabs depends on whether the text editor recognizes the ASCII code for a tab.

Listing 12.4   Writing to a delimited text file

```
public void write (PrintStream outS) throws IOException
{
    outS.print (numbHoles);
    outS.print ("\t");
    outS.print (capacity);
    outS.print ("\n");
}
```

You can "print" any single data value. What this means is that you can't simply write an entire object to a print stream, although you can write its individual data values, including integers, floating point values, booleans, characters, and strings. For example, in the case of the bucket program, we wrote each object's two data values separately.

Warning

It's often handy to open a text file with a text editor or word processor to check that it has been written properly. However, be very, very careful that you don't save the opened file. Many text editors replace tab characters with blanks; word processors include formatting codes in their files. In either case, if you save such a file, you won't be able to read it back in with your Java program because its layout will have changed.

Opening File Input Streams

DataInput-
Stream

new

Opening a file for reading is similar to opening a file for writing. The only difference is in the type of streams you create. The following statement, for example, creates a file input stream that is connected to a data input stream:

```
DataInputStream inS =
    new DataInputStream  (new FileInputStream (filename));
```

FileInput-
Stream

new

Like the output streams, the code that creates input streams must be placed within a `try/catch` structure to handle any I/O exception that might arise. As you can see in Listing 12.5, a reference to the data input stream object is passed as a parameter to a `Bucket` object constructor, where the actual file reading takes place.

Listing 12.5 The try/catch structure when reading from a text file

```
try
{
    DataInputStream inS =
        new DataInputStream (new FileInputStream (filename));

    Bucket1 = new Bucket (inS);
    Bucket2 = new Bucket (inS);
    Bucket3 = new Bucket (inS);

    System.out.println ("\nThe current bucket data are:\n");
    showData();

    System.out.println ("\nNow you can change the data:\n");
}
catch (IOException theException)
{
        errorDialog message = new errorDialog ("Couldn't open input file.");
        message.show();
        System.exit (0);
}
```

Reading from a Delimited Text File

Reading from a delimited text file is a bit more involved than writing to a file because not only do you need to physically get a stream of bytes from a file, but you need to break the stream into its constituent fields. The process is as follows:

DataInput-
Stream

readLine

1. Read a line of text from the file. A "line" is defined as a string of characters terminated by a new line character. Assuming that you have used the new line character to terminate the data for one object, then a line of text will contain all the data for a single object. As you can see in Listing 12.6, you can do this with the data input stream readLine method, which returns a string.

2. Create a string tokenizer object that knows that *tokens* (fields) in the input string are delimited by tab characters.

3. Extract the tokens from the string and convert them to the correct data types.

Listing 12.6   Reading from a delimited text file

```
public Bucket (DataInput inS) throws IOException
{
    String inputLine = inS.readLine(); // get an entire line from the file
    StringTokenizer theTokenizer = new StringTokenizer (inputLine,"\t");
    numbHoles = Integer.parseInt (theTokenizer.nextToken());
    capacity = new Float(theTokenizer.nextToken()).floatValue();
}
```

The tricky part here is the idea of pulling the input string apart into its separate fields. Java contains a class named StringTokenizer that searches a string of text and extracts successive characters that are separated by some known delimiter. (You can use a tokenizer to search any string, not just one that you read from a file.)

String-
Tokenizer

new

To begin the process, you create an object of the StringTokenizer class, initializing it with the string and the Delimiter:

```
StringTokenizer theTokenizer = new StringTokenizer
        (string_to_tokenize, delimiter_string);
```

If there is more than one delimiter character, you can include multiple characters in the delimiter string. In Listing 12.6, for example, the single delimiter is a tab character.

String-
Tokenizer

nextToken

Then you can ask the tokenizer to feed you tokens, in order from left to right across the string, using the nextToken method:

```
String aToken = theTokenizer.nextToken();
```

Once you have the token, you can convert it to the correct data type. In Listing 12.6, the retrieval of the token and its conversion to the correct data type are handled in a single statement.

Warning

String-
Tokenizer

hasMore-
Tokens

If there are no more tokens in the string, calling nextToken throws an exception. Although when reading from a text file you will know how many tokens there are, if you are parsing a string that a user has typed from the keyboard, you run the risk of throwing an exception. You can avoid it by calling the tokenizer method hasMoreTokens before each call to nextToken. The hasMoreTokens method returns true if there are tokens left in the string.

Dealing with Multiple Objects

In the case of the bucket management program, we knew exactly how many objects were represented by the data file. However, in practice the number of objects may vary from one run of the program to another. Consider, for example, the survey analysis program that you saw in Chapter 10. That program is designed to analyze survey data that have been scanned into a text file. There is therefore no way to predict how many objects are represented in any given data file.

There are two ways to handle this problem. The first is to keep reading data until an I/O exception occurs. If the exception is an end-of-file exception, then you know that all data have been read. The second strategy is to write the number of records in the file as the first piece of data. The survey analysis program uses this latter approach.

If you look at Listing 12.7, you can see that the array manager's `load` method first opens the necessary input streams. Then, it reads the first line in the file, which contains only one value: the number of objects represented in the file. (Since there is only one value in the line, there is no need to use a tokenizer.) The number of objects retrieved from the file can then be used in a loop that creates new survey objects, reading their data from the file.

Listing 12.7   Controlling the reading of an unknown number of objects

```
public void load ()
{
    try
    {
        DataInputStream InS = new DataInputStream
            (new FileInputStream ("Survey"));
        String inputLine = InS.readLine();
        lastIndex = Integer.parseInt(inputLine); // get lastIndex from file

        for (int i = 0; i <= lastIndex; i++)
            theSurveys[i] = new Survey (InS);
    }
    catch (IOException theException)
        { System.out.println ("Couldn't open input file");}
}
```

Notice in Listing 12.7 that the array manager's `load` method recreates the array of objects as it reads from the data file. The array of objects contains the main memory addresses of objects. We don't write these addresses to a data file. We only write object data. Why? Because each time a program is run, the objects may be loaded into memory in different locations. Therefore, the contents of the array won't be valid from one program run to another. A program must recreate each of its main memory data structures each time it loads its data into memory.

Just as with the bucket program, the survey analysis program does the actual reading of data in the data handling class (Survey). The process, which you can see in Listing 12.8, is to read a line of data, create a tokenizer, and then retrieve successive tokens from the input string. Because we know exactly how many tokens there are, there is no need to verify that additional tokens exist.

Listing 12.8   Reading a survey object full of data

```
public Survey (DataInput inS) throws IOException
{
    // get a line of data from the file
    String inputLine = inS.readLine();
    // create tokenizer; use space as delimiter
    StringTokenizer theTokenizer = new StringTokenizer (inputLine," ");

    Survey_numb = Integer.parseInt (theTokenizer.nextToken());
    Gender = (theTokenizer.nextToken()).charAt(0);
    Age = Integer.parseInt (theTokenizer.nextToken());
    AthleticOwned = Integer.parseInt (theTokenizer.nextToken());
    AthleticBought = Integer.parseInt (theTokenizer.nextToken());
    DressOwned = Integer.parseInt (theTokenizer.nextToken());
    DressBought = Integer.parseInt (theTokenizer.nextToken());
    BootsOwned = Integer.parseInt (theTokenizer.nextToken());
    BootsBought = Integer.parseInt (theTokenizer.nextToken());
    SandalsOwned = Integer.parseInt (theTokenizer.nextToken());
    SandalsBought = Integer.parseInt (theTokenizer.nextToken());
}
```

Note

It is essential to recognize that you must read a delimited text file in exactly the same way you wrote it. The token extraction and conversion to the correct data types won't work unless you extract and convert the fields in precisely the same order in which they were written. This close coupling between a program and its data file can be a problem when the program changes: Data files may become invalid and must then be rewritten completely to match the modified program. This is one of the reasons that so much IS work today involves database systems, which isolate programs from file structures by allowing a DBMS to translate logical data requests into physical storage access routines.

Working with Random Access Files

Sequential text files are acceptable if the amount of data stored in the files can be loaded into main memory all at once. However, as data files grow larger, it isn't practical to maintain all of the data in RAM. Therefore, we need to be able to read and write selected portions of a file while a program is running. Random access files provide this capability by giving a program control over a location pointer. Reading and writing begin at the pointer's current position. A program therefore moves the pointer to the correct place in the file before beginning an I/O operation.

The trick, of course, is knowing where to position the pointer. To make that easier, most random access files use fixed field lengths. In other words, each field takes up the same amount of space in every record, regardless of the amount of meaningful data in the field. For example, a first name field might be allocated 15 characters. Even if a person's first name is only six characters, the first name field still takes up space for 15.

Assuming that we number records beginning with 1, the start of a record in a random access file is determined by the following algorithm:

```
(record_number - 1) * record_length
```

The record length is expressed in bytes. This means that to calculate the record length you need to know exactly how many bytes each field in the record occupy. The space occupied by basic Java data types can be found in Table 12.1. In particular, notice that characters occupy *two* bytes rather than the one byte storage typical of ASCII characters. Java uses Unicode, a two-byte character code that provides non-Roman characters for languages such as Japanese or Russian. (ASCII is actually a subset of Unicode.)

Table 12.1   Space occupied by Java data types

Data Type	Space in Bytes
int	4
long	8
float	4
double	8
char	2

As an example of a program that uses random file access, we will be exploring a program that maintains a telephone directory for a large company. The end user can enter a person's first and last names and find their office location and telephone extension. The data stored about an employee are laid out as follows:

- ID number: A four-character string (8 bytes).
- First name: A 15-character string (30 bytes).
- Last name: A 15-character string (30 bytes).
- Office number: A five-character string (10 bytes)
- Telephone extension: An integer (4 bytes).

The total length of the record is therefore 8 + 30 + 30 + 10 + 4 or 82 bytes. Each time the program needs to read information about an employee, it converts the ID number to an integer, subtracts one, and multiplies it by the record length. Then it moves the file pointer to the computed number of bytes from the beginning of the file.

Indexing a Random Access File

A question you might be asking at this point is: "How does a program figure out which record it wants in a random access file?" There are several strategies for doing so. You might, for example, require the user to enter a record number. This is easy to do, but not terribly intuitive for the user. In the case of the telephone directory program, it makes more sense for a user to enter an employee's name. Then the program can use the name to find the record ID.

What we are actually describing here is maintaining an index to the records in the random access file that a program can search based on a key value entered by the user. A hash table therefore makes an ideal data structure to use as an index to the random access file. The index objects contain the user's first and last names (concatenated for the hash key) and the ID number of the record in the random access file. When the user enters the first and last names, the program can then use them to look up the record number in the hash table, making it easy to find the record in the random access file that contains complete employee information (see Figure 12.3).

Figure 12.3 Using a hash table as an index to a random access file

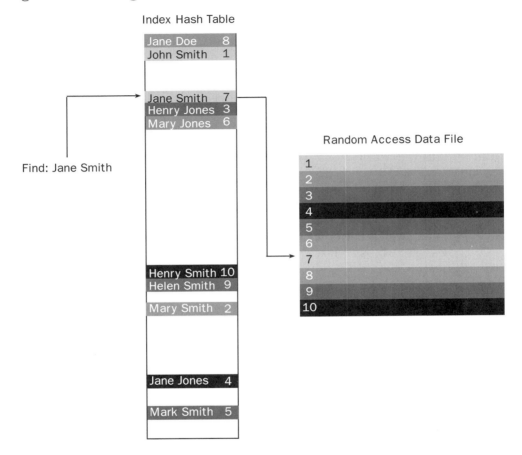

Indexes usually contain just a search key value and a record number. This means that they are much smaller than complete data files and are much more likely to fit into available RAM. We can therefore store the index to the telephone directory in a sequential text file and read it back into main memory, rebuilding the hash table, each time the program is run.

The Telephone Directory Program

The telephone directory program presents the user with a simple three-option menu (Figure 12.4). To add a new entry, the user fills in the text fields in a dialog box (Figure 12.5). Searching for information about a a single employee also begins with a dialog box (Figure 12.6). Output for one employee and the list of all employees appears in the program's main window (Figure 12.7).

Figure 12.4   The telephone directory program's menu

Figure 12.5   Entering a new employee

Employee Input	
First name:	Emily
Last name:	Jones
Office number:	170
Extension:	8871

OK   Cancel

Figure 12.6   Searching for an employee

Search	
First Name:	John
Last Name:	Doe

OK   Cancel

The foundation for the program in the Employee class (Listing 12.9 on page 383). Unlike most of the programs you have seen so far, the telephone directory program will never use more than one object of this entity class at a time. Its purpose is to hold the data for one employee when the user enters data from the keyboard or when data are read from the file. Given an ID number,

Figure 12.7   Telephone directory listings

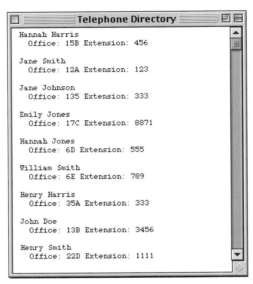

the class takes care of positioning the file pointer as well as reading data from and writing data to a file. As you will see throughout the rest of this discussion, the **Employee** class is the only class that knows anything about the layout of the random access data file. This design means that a programmer can change the layout of the file (for example, changing the number of bytes allocated to a field) without modifying any other classes, making programs that use this class easier to maintain. We will examine the methods used to read and write the file in depth shortly.

The hash table used as an index to the random access data file contains objects created from the **Index** class (Listing 12.10 on page 386). Index objects can write themselves to a sequential text file and read themselves from the file. They can also return their key (the concatenation of first and last name) and the associated record ID.

The two dialog boxes that collect input (**InputDialog** in Listing 12.11 on page 387 and **FindDialog** in Listing 12.12 on page 389) use techniques that you have seen before in this book. Notice that processing of a **FindDialog** object makes use of an object from the class **KeyHolder** to pass the first and last names from the dialog box back to the application object that is the dialog box's parent.

Listing 12.9 Employee.java

```java
import java.io.*; import java.lang.*;

public class Employee
{
    private String ID, firstName, lastName, officeNumb;
    private int extension;  // 4 bytes
    private static final int ID_SIZE = 4;
    private static final int NAME_SIZE = 15;
    private static final int FIRST_OFFSET = (ID_SIZE * 2);
    private static final int LAST_OFFSET = (ID_SIZE + NAME_SIZE) * 2;
    private static final int OFFICE_SIZE = 5;
    private static final int OFFICE_OFFSET = (ID_SIZE + (NAME_SIZE * 2)) *2;
    private static final int EXTENSION_OFFSET =
        (ID_SIZE + (NAME_SIZE * 2) + OFFICE_SIZE) * 2;
    private static final int RECORD_LEN = 82;

    public Employee ()
    {
        ID = "";
        firstName = "";
        lastName = "";
        officeNumb = "";
        extension = 0;
    }

    public Employee (String inFirstName, String inLastName,
        String inOfficeNumb, int inExtension)
    {
        ID = "";
        firstName = inFirstName;
        lastName = inLastName;
        officeNumb = inOfficeNumb;
        extension = inExtension;
    }

    public String readID (RandomAccessFile fin, String inID) throws IOException
    {
        fin.seek ((Long.parseLong(inID) - 1) * RECORD_LEN);
        return readString (fin, ID_SIZE);
    }

    public String readFirstName (RandomAccessFile fin, String inID) throws
    IOException
    {
        fin.seek (((Long.parseLong(inID) - 1) * RECORD_LEN) + FIRST_OFFSET);
        return readString (fin, NAME_SIZE);
    }
```

Continued next page

Listing 12.9(Continued)   Employee.java

```java
public String readLastName (RandomAccessFile fin, String inID)
    throws IOException
{
    fin.seek (((Long.parseLong(inID) - 1) * RECORD_LEN) + LAST_OFFSET);
    return readString (fin, NAME_SIZE);
}

public String readOfficeNumb (RandomAccessFile fin, String inID)
    throws IOException
{
    fin.seek (((Long.parseLong(inID) - 1) * RECORD_LEN) + OFFICE_OFFSET);
    return readString (fin, OFFICE_SIZE);
}

public int readExtension (RandomAccessFile fin, String inID)
    throws IOException
{
    fin.seek (((Long.parseLong(inID) - 1) RECORD_LEN) + EXTENSION_OFFSET);
    return fin.readInt();
}

private String readString (RandomAccessFile fin, int howLong)
    throws IOException
{
    String theString = "";
    for (int i = 1; i <= howLong; i++)
        theString += fin.readChar();
    return theString.trim();
}

public String getFirstName()
    { return firstName; }

public String getLastName()
    { return lastName; }

public void setID (String inID)
    { ID = inID; }

public void write (RandomAccessFile fout) throws IOException
{
    fout.seek (((Long.parseLong(ID) - 1) * RECORD_LEN));
    fout.writeChars (padString (ID_SIZE,ID));
    fout.writeChars (padString (NAME_SIZE,firstName));
    fout.writeChars (padString (NAME_SIZE,lastName));
    fout.writeChars (padString (OFFICE_SIZE,officeNumb));
    fout.writeInt (extension);
}
```

Continued next page

Listing 12.9(Continued)　Employee.java

```
private String padString (int howLong, String theString)
    {
        for (int i = theString.length()+1; i <= howLong; i++)
            theString += " ";
        return theString;
    }
}
```

The scrolling output that appears in the telephone directory's main window is handled by the `OutputCanvas` class (Listing 12.13 on page 391). Notice that the same `paint` method handles displaying one employee's information or information about all employees. The choice is made by setting the boolean `all` in the canvas's constructors. To obtain its data, the canvas uses the hash table to retrieve one or more record numbers and then reads the necessary data from the file. Because all of the file I/O is handled by the `Employee` class, the canvas class doesn't need to know anything about the file; it only needs to call methods that ask for data to be read.

Program control is provided by the application class, `DirectoryApp` (Listing 12.14 on page 392). Like most control classes in an event-driven program, the action isn't at all sequential. The program begins by creating an object of its own class. The class's constructor, the listeners defined as inner classes, and the implementation of the dialog processing interface then take over.

In the `DirectoryApp` class's constructor you will find:

- A window listener that writes the contents of the index hash table to a text file when the user closes the main program window to end the program run.
- Code that sets up the main window's menu bar. Each menu item has its own action listener, implemented as an inner class.
- An "Add New Employee" menu item action listener that creates an instance of the input dialog box and shows the child window.
- A "Find a Telephone Number" menu item action listener that creates an instance of the find dialog box and shows the child window.
- A "List Complete Telephone Directory" menu item action listener that creates a new output canvas, adds it to the window, adjusts the scroll bars, and triggers a repaint of the window.

Listing 12.10   Index.java

```java
import java.lang.*;
import java.io.*;
import java.util.*;

class Index
{
    private String ID, firstName, lastName;

    public Index (DataInput fin) throws IOException
    {
        String inputLine = fin.readLine();
        StringTokenizer theTokenizer = new StringTokenizer (inputLine,":");

        ID = theTokenizer.nextToken();
        firstName = theTokenizer.nextToken();
        lastName = theTokenizer.nextToken();
    }

    public Index (String inID, String inFirstName, String inLastName)
    {
        ID = inID;
        firstName = inFirstName;
        lastName = inLastName;
    }

    public String getID()
        { return ID; }

    public String getKey()
        { return (firstName + " " + lastName); }

    public void write (PrintStream fout)
    {
        fout.print (ID);
        fout.print (":");
        fout.print (firstName);
        fout.print (":");
        fout.print (lastName);
        fout.print ("\n");
    }
}
```

The initialize method takes care of opening the index file and reading its contents. As data for the index objects are read from the file, they are inserted into the hash table being used as an index. This method also opens the random access data file that contains the employee data.

Listing 12.11   InputDialog.java

```java
import java.lang.*;
import java.awt.*;
import java.awt.event.*;

public class InputDialog extends Dialog
{
    private InputDialog thisDialog;
    private TextField first, last, office, ext;
    private Button theButton;
    private Font systemFont = new Font ("System",Font.BOLD,12);

    public InputDialog (DirectoryApp parent)
    {
        super (parent, "Employee Input",true);
        thisDialog = this;
        addWindowListener (new WindowAdapter ()
        {
            public void windowClosing (WindowEvent theEvent)
                { thisDialog.dispose(); }
        } );
        setBackground(Color.white);
        Panel thePanel = new Panel();
        thePanel.setLayout (new GridLayout (4,2));
        thePanel.add (new Label ("     First name:"));
        thePanel.add (first = new TextField ("",15));
        thePanel.add (new Label ("     Last name:"));
        thePanel.add (last = new TextField ("",15));
        thePanel.add (new Label ("     Office number:"));
        thePanel.add (office = new TextField ("",10));
        thePanel.add (new Label ("     Extension:"));
        thePanel.add (ext = new TextField ("",10));
        add ("Center",thePanel);
        thePanel = new Panel();
        thePanel.setFont (systemFont);

        theButton = new Button ("OK");
        theButton.addActionListener (new ActionListener ()
        {
            public void actionPerformed (ActionEvent theEvent)
            {
                int extension = (int)Integer.parseInt ((ext.getText()).trim());
                ((DialogProcessor) getParent()).processDialog (thisDialog,
                    new Employee (first.getText(), last.getText(),
                    office.getText(), extension));
                thisDialog.dispose();
            }
        } );
```

Continued next page

Listing 12.11(Continued)   InputDialog.java

```
thePanel.add (theButton);

      theButton = new Button ("Cancel");
      theButton.addActionListener (new ActionListener ()
      {
         public void actionPerformed (ActionEvent theEvent)
            { thisDialog.dispose(); }
      } );
      thePanel.add (theButton);
      add ("South", thePanel);
      setSize (375,125);
   }
}
```

To handle data coming from dialog boxes, the `DirectoryApp` class implements the `DialogProcessor` interface. The `processDialog` method does the following:

- Identifies which dialog box is being processed.
- Handles a new employee by generating a record ID, creating an index object and storing it in the index hash table, and appending the new employee record to the end of the employee data file.
- Handles finding an employee by finding the record ID in the hash table and using that ID to read the record from the employee data file. It then creates a new output canvas to display the data, adjusts the scroll bars, and triggers a repaint of the main window.

Opening a Random Access File

Opening a random access file is actually easier than opening a sequential text file. A file can be opened just for reading or for both reading and writing:

Random AccessFile

new

```
RandomAccessFile fileVariable = new RandomAccessFile
   (file_name, access_string)
```

The access string is either "r" for read-only or "rw" for a file that can be both read from and written to. For example, the data file used by the telephone directory program is opened with:

```
RandomAccessFile finOut;
finOut = new RandomAccessFile ("Employees","rw");
```

Listing 12.12   FindDialog.java

```java
import java.lang.*;
import java.awt.*;
import java.awt.event.*;

public class FindDialog extends Dialog
{
    private FindDialog thisDialog;
    private TextField first, last;
    private Button theButton;
    private Font systemFont = new Font ("System",Font.BOLD,12);

    public FindDialog (DirectoryApp parent)
    {
        super (parent, "Search",true);
        thisDialog = this;
        addWindowListener (new WindowAdapter ()
        {
            public void windowClosing (WindowEvent theEvent)
                { thisDialog.dispose(); }
        } );

        setBackground (Color.white);
        Panel thePanel = new Panel();
        thePanel.setLayout (new GridLayout (2,2));
        thePanel.add (new Label ("      First Name:"));
        thePanel.add (first = new TextField ("",15));
        thePanel.add (new Label ("      Last Name:"));
        thePanel.add (last = new TextField ("",15));
        add ("Center",thePanel);

        thePanel = new Panel();
        thePanel.setFont (systemFont);

        theButton = new Button ("OK");
        theButton.addActionListener (new ActionListener ()
        {
            public void actionPerformed (ActionEvent theEvent)
            {
                ((DialogProcessor) getParent()).processDialog (thisDialog,
                    new KeyHolder (first.getText(),last.getText()));
                thisDialog.dispose();
            }
        } );
        thePanel.add (theButton);
```

Continued next page

Listing 12.12(Continued)   FindDialog.java

```
        theButton = new Button ("Cancel");
        theButton.addActionListener (new ActionListener ()
        {
            public void actionPerformed (ActionEvent theEvent)
                { thisDialog.dispose(); }
        } );
        thePanel.add (theButton);
        add ("South", thePanel);
        setSize (375, 100);
    }
}

class KeyHolder
{
    private String first, last;

    public KeyHolder (String iFirst, String iLast)
    {
        first = iFirst;
        last = iLast;
    }

    public String getKey()
        { return (first + " " + last); }
}
```

Reading from a Random Access File

Reading from a random access file is a two-step process. First, a program must move the file pointer to the position where reading is to begin. Then it can actually read the data.

To move the file pointer, you use the **seek** method:

Random
AccessFile

seek

```
fileVariable.seek (offset);
```

The offset is the number of bytes from the beginning of the file, expressed as a long integer.

As an example, let's look at how the **Employee** class positions the file pointer for reading specific fields within a specific record. Notice first that there are a group of constants at the top of Listing 12.9 that provide field lengths and offsets. The field lengths are expressed as the number of characters; the offsets are in bytes. (Remember that each character in a string takes up two bytes.) Placing these constants at the beginning of the class makes it easy to locate

Listing 12.13   OutputCanvas.java

```java
import java.lang.*;
import java.awt.*;
import java.util.Hashtable;
import java.util.Enumeration;
import java.io.*;

class OutputCanvas extends Canvas
{
    private int dx, dy;
    private Font theFont = new Font ("Courier",Font.PLAIN,10);
    private String first, last, office;
    private int ext;
    private boolean all;
    private Hashtable theTable;
    private RandomAccessFile fin;

    public OutputCanvas(String iFirst, String iLast, String iOffice, int iExt)
    {
        setBackground (Color.white);
        first = iFirst;
        last = iLast;
        office = iOffice;
        ext = iExt;
        all = false;
    }

    public OutputCanvas (Hashtable inTable, RandomAccessFile theFile)
    {
        setBackground (Color.white);
        theTable = inTable;
        fin = theFile;
        all = true;
    }

    public void translate (int x, int y)
    {
        dx = x;
        dy = y;
        repaint();
    }

    public void paint (Graphics graphObject)
    {
        graphObject.translate (-dx, -dy);
        graphObject.setFont (theFont);

        int base = 12;
```

Continued next page

Listing 12.13(Continued)   OutputCanvas.java

```java
    if (all)
    {
        try
        {
            Employee theEmployee = new Employee();
            Index indexObject;
            String ID;
            Enumeration theEnumerator = theTable.elements();
            while (theEnumerator.hasMoreElements())
            {
                indexObject = (Index) theEnumerator.nextElement();
                ID = indexObject.getID();
                graphObject.drawString (theEmployee.readFirstName
                    (fin,ID) + " " +
                    theEmployee.readLastName (fin,ID), 10, base);
                base += 12;
                graphObject.drawString ("  Office: " +
                    theEmployee.readOfficeNumb (fin,ID) +
                    " Extension: " +
                    theEmployee.readExtension (fin,ID),10, base);
                base += 24;
            }
        }
        catch (IOException theException)
        {
            System.out.println
                ("Problem reading data file while listing all.");
        }
    }
    else
    {
        graphObject.drawString (first + " " + last,10,base);
        base += 12;
        graphObject.drawString ("  Office: " + office + " Extension: " +
            ext,10, base);
    }
    }
}
```

Listing 12.14   DirectoryApp.Java

```java
import java.lang.*;
import java.io.*;
import java.awt.*;
import java.awt.event.*;
import java.util.Hashtable;
```

Continued next page

Listing 12.14(Continued)   DirectoryApp.Java

```java
import java.util.Enumeration;

// for getting data from dialog boxes
interface DialogProcessor
{
    public void processDialog (Dialog theDialog, Object theObject);
}

public class DirectoryApp extends Frame implements DialogProcessor
{
    private DirectoryApp thisWindow;
    private int lastID = 0;
    private Hashtable theIndex;
    private RandomAccessFile finOut;
    private Employee theEmployee = new Employee();
    private InputDialog inputWindow;
    private FindDialog findWindow;
    private Scrollbar vertical;
    private OutputCanvas theCanvas;

    public DirectoryApp()
    {
        thisWindow = this;
        setTitle ("Telephone Directory");
        setUpWindow();
        boolean keep_going = initialize();
        if (!keep_going)
            System.exit(0);
    }

    public void setUpWindow()
    {
        addWindowListener (new WindowAdapter ()
        {
            public void windowClosing (WindowEvent theEvent)
            {
                try // write index to sequential file
                {
                    PrintStream fout = new PrintStream
                        (new FileOutputStream ("Index"));
                    fout.print (lastID);
                    fout.print ("\n");
                    Enumeration theEnumerator = theIndex.elements();
```

Continued next page

Listing 12.14(Continued)   DirectoryApp.Java

```java
                while (theEnumerator.hasMoreElements())
                {
                    Index indexObject =
                        (Index) theEnumerator.nextElement();
                    indexObject.write (fout);
                }
            }
            catch (IOException theException)
            {
                System.out.println ("Couldn't write index file.");
            }

            System.exit(0);
        }
    } );

    // Menus
    MenuBar mbar = new MenuBar();
    Menu theMenu = new Menu ("Directory");
    MenuItem newEntry = new MenuItem ("Add New Entry");

    // Handle adding a new person to directory
    newEntry.addActionListener (new ActionListener ()
    {
        public void actionPerformed (ActionEvent theEvent)
        {
            inputWindow = new InputDialog (thisWindow);
            inputWindow.show();
        }
    } );
    theMenu.add (newEntry);

    // Handle finding one person's phone #
    MenuItem find = new MenuItem ("Find a Telephone Number");
    find.addActionListener (new ActionListener ()
    {
        public void actionPerformed (ActionEvent theEvent)
        {
            findWindow = new FindDialog (thisWindow);
            findWindow.show();
        }
    } );
    theMenu.add (find);
```

Continued next page

Listing 12.14(Continued)　DirectoryApp.Java

```java
    // Handle displaying a list of the entire directory
    MenuItem list = new MenuItem ("List Complete Telephone Directory");
    list.addActionListener (new ActionListener ()
    {
        public void actionPerformed (ActionEvent theEvent)
        {
            theCanvas = new OutputCanvas(theIndex, finOut);
            thisWindow.add ("Center",theCanvas);
            Dimension theSize = theCanvas.getSize();
            vertical.setValues (0, theSize.height,0,1000);
            thisWindow.show();
        }
    } );
    theMenu.add (list);

    mbar.add (theMenu);
    setMenuBar (mbar);

    add ("East",vertical = new Scrollbar (Scrollbar.VERTICAL));
    vertical.setBlockIncrement (300);
    vertical.addAdjustmentListener (new AdjustmentListener ()
    {
        public void adjustmentValueChanged (AdjustmentEvent theEvent)
        {
            theCanvas.translate (0,vertical.getValue());
            repaint();
        }
    } );
}

// read index file and make hash table; open data file
private boolean initialize()
{
    theIndex = new Hashtable ();
    try
    {
        DataInputStream fin = new DataInputStream
            (new FileInputStream ("Index"));
        String inputLine = fin.readLine();
        lastID = Integer.parseInt (inputLine);
        Index indexObject;
        for (int i = 1; i <= lastID; i++)
        {
            indexObject = new Index (fin);
            theIndex.put (indexObject.getKey(), indexObject);
        }
    }
```

Continued next page

Listing 12.14(Continued)   DirectoryApp.Java

```java
        catch (IOException theException)
        {
           System.out.println
           ("Couldn't open index file. Starting new files.");
        }

        try
        {
           finOut = new RandomAccessFile ("Employees","rw");
        }
        catch (IOException theException)
        {
           System.out.println ("Couldn't open data file. Can't continue.");
           return false;
        }
        return true;
    }

    public void processDialog (Dialog theDialog, Object theData)
    {
        if (theDialog == inputWindow)
        {
           Employee theEmployee = (Employee) theData;
           if (theEmployee.getFirstName() == "" ||
               theEmployee.getLastName() == "")
           {
               System.out.println ("You must enter a full employee name.");
               return;
           }
           lastID++;
           String newID = Integer.toString (lastID);
           theEmployee.setID (newID);
           Index indexObject = new Index (newID, theEmployee.getFirstName(),
               theEmployee.getLastName());
           theIndex.put (indexObject.getKey(), indexObject);
           try
               { theEmployee.write (finOut); }
           catch (IOException theException)
               { System.out.println ("Couldn't write new employee"); }
        }
        else // must be Find dialog
        {
           KeyHolder theKey = (KeyHolder) theData;
           String key = theKey.getKey();
```

Continued next page

Listing 12.14(Continued)   DirectoryApp.Java

```
            if (key == "")
            {
                System.out.println ("You must enter a person's name.");
                return;
            }
            Index indexObject = (Index) theIndex.get (key);
            if (indexObject == null)
            {
                System.out.println ("That person isn't in the directory.");
                return;
            }
            String theID = indexObject.getID();
            try
            {
                String first = theEmployee.readFirstName (finOut, theID);
                String last = theEmployee.readLastName (finOut, theID);
                String office = theEmployee.readOfficeNumb (finOut, theID);
                int ext = theEmployee.readExtension (finOut, theID);

                theCanvas = new OutputCanvas(first,last,office,ext);
                thisWindow.add ("Center",theCanvas);
                Dimension theSize = theCanvas.getSize();
                vertical.setValues (0, theSize.height,0,1000);
                thisWindow.show();
            }
            catch (IOException theException)
                { System.out.println ("Couldn't read data file."); }
        }
    }

    public final static void main (String args[])
    {
        DirectoryApp theApp = new DirectoryApp ();
        theApp.setSize (300,300);
        theApp.show();
    }
}
```

them when making changes to the file layout. In fact, if a programmer wants to change the size of a field, the only changes that have to be made to the class are to those constants. (An existing data file will also have to be rewritten, which is another issue entirely.)

Using those constants, the class subtracts 1 from the record ID and multiplies that by the record length. Then it adds any offset that is needed from the start of the record. This value is passed as an input argument to the seek method. For example, to position the record pointer for reading the last name, the class does the following:

```
fin.seek ((((Long.parseLong(inID) - 1) * RECORD_LENGTH) +
    LAST_OFFSET);
```

Note that the string value of the record ID is converted to a long integer before arithmetic is performed.

Note

Like other file I/O operations, a call to the seek method throws an IOException that must be caught.

Note

There was no compelling reason why the record ID was stored as a string other than to give you another example of how string to numeric conversions can be performed on the fly. If you're never going to show the user a record number, then in most cases you might as well make it a long integer and avoid the conversion.

There is a collection of methods that read data of varying sizes from a random access file, including the following:

Random
AccessFile

readX

- readBoolean ()
- readByte ()
- readUnsignedByte ()
- readShort ()
- readChar ()
- readInt ()
- readLong ()
- readFloat ()
- readDouble ()
- readLine ()

With the exception of readLine, each returns a single piece of data of the type indicated by its name. The readLine method returns a line terminated by a newline character (\n).

Notice that there is no method for reading a string. Strings must be read one character at a time. The telephone directory program therefore includes its own readString method:

```
private String readString (RandomAccessFile fin, int howLong)
    throws IOException
    {
        String theString = "";
        for (int i = 1; i <= howLong; i++)
            theString += fin.readChar();
        return theString.trim();
    }
```

The method requires a reference to the random access file and the number of characters to be read as input parameters. Repeated calls to readChar then copy the entire field from the data file. The method finishes by trimming any trailing blanks from the field and returning the completed string to the calling method.

Writing to a Random Access File

Writing to a random access file is just the converse of writing to it: You move the file pointer to the location where writing should begin and then call a write method to write the data. As with reading, there are a group of methods that write data of various types:

Random
AccessFile

writeX

- writeBoolean (boolean)
- writeByte (int)
- writeShort (int)
- writeChar (char)
- writeInt (int)
- writeLong (long)
- writeFloat (float)
- writeDouble (double)
- writeBytes (String)
- writeChars (String)

Each method takes an input parameter of the type of data it will be writing. Both the `writeBytes` and `writeChars` methods write strings. However, the `writeBytes` method packs each character into a single byte; the `write-Chars` method preserves the two-byte Unicode.

The telephone directory's `Employee` class writes a new employee's data with:

```
fout.seek (((Long.parseLong(ID) - 1) * RECORD_LEN));
fout.writeChars (padString (ID_SIZE,ID));
fout.writeChars (padString (NAME_SIZE,firstName));
fout.writeChars (padString (NAME_SIZE,lastName));
fout.writeChars (padString (OFFICE_SIZE,officeNumb));
fout.writeInt (extension);
```

Notice that the first step is to position the file pointer at the end of the file. This ensures that the new record will be appended to the file, without overwriting any data currently stored.

Creating Your Own Exceptions

Java's exception mechanism provides a framework from which you can define your own exceptions to trap and handle errors that are specific to your program. As an example, we'll be working with a modified version of the customer list program that you first saw in Chapter 9.

One of the biggest problems with that program is that it provides no data validation. In particular, it is possible for the user to store a customer with no ID number or to attempt to search for a customer without entering a search key. We can use a custom exception to trap that error and display an appropriate error message.

Defining a Custom Exception Class

To use a custom exception, you must first derive a class for that exception from `Exception` (or if appropriate, a subclass of `Exception`). The new exception class, such as the `NoIDException` in Listing 12.15, needs to provide only two methods: a constructor with no input parameters and a constructor that takes a string containing a detailed error message as a parameter.

Listing 12.15   NoIDException.java

```
import java.lang.*;

class NoIDException extends Exception
{
    public NoIDException ()
        { }

    public NoIDException (String message)
    {
        super (message);
    }
}
```

Throwing the Exception

When you are working with file I/O, Java throws an exception for you whenever a throwable condition (for example, an unexpected end-of-file) occurs. However, a program must explicitly test for an error condition and throw a custom exception. To see how this works, take a look at the modified `action-Performed` method for the customer list's Find button (Listing 12.16).

Listing 12.16   Throwing and catching a custom exception

```
public void actionPerformed (ActionEvent theEvent)
{
    try
    {
        String theID = IDField.getText(); // grab ID
        if (theID.length() < 1)
            throw new NoIDException ();
        Customer theCustomer = (Customer) theTable.get (theID);
        System.out.println ("\nCustomer #" + theID + ": " +
            theCustomer.getFirstName() + " " +
            theCustomer.getLastName() + "\n                    " +
            theCustomer.getPhone() + " Extension " +
            theCustomer.getExtension ());
        IDField.setText ("");  // clean out field
    }
    catch (NoIDException theException)
    {
        System.out.println ("\nPlease enter an ID number.");
    }
}
```

The method works in the following way:

- Retrieve the contents of the text field that should contain an ID number (`IDField`) into a string variable (`theID`).
- Check the length of the string.
- If the length of the string is less than 1, throw the exception. To throw an exception, you use the keyword `throw` followed by code needed to create an exception object:

```
throw new ExceptionClass();
```

In this particular example, the exception class is `NoIDException`:

```
throw new NoIDException();
```

- If the exception has been thrown, jump immediately to the `catch` block. Otherwise, continue with the contents of the `try` block.

In our particular example, the `catch` block displays an error message in the console window. You might, however, choose to provide a dialog box presenting an error message at that point.

Summary

Java views I/O as streams of bytes traveling in a series. To perform file I/O, you create objects from the appropriate stream classes. The file input and output stream classes set up connections between a program and files. Input to and output from those streams pass through data and print streams that make it possible to work with Java data types rather than individual bytes.

File I/O requires exception handling. Opening, reading from, and writing to files can cause runtime errors from which a program cannot automatically recover. A program must therefore place file I/O statements within a `try` block that is associated with a `catch` block. The `catch` block contains error handling code. Methods that perform file I/O but don't catch errors must indicate the possibility of throwing one or more types of errors.

Java's AWT provides a file dialog class that displays the File Open and File Save dialog boxes. A program can use those dialog boxes to let a user choose a file name.

To write to a sequential text file, a program prints individual values to a print stream, which is connected to a file output stream. To read from a file, a program reads an entire line of text using a file input stream and a data input stream. The text must then be parsed into the individual fields that make up the text, usually using a string tokenizer object. Then, the fields can be converted to the appropriate data type.

Random access files provide a file pointer that a program can move. Reading and writing take place beginning at the file's current position. To simplify access, most random access data files use fixed field lengths.

Java programs can create their own exception classes. In that case, a program must explicitly throw an exception for it to be caught by a `catch` block and handled.

Exercises

1. Write and test a program for a college admissions office. The data handling object used by this program represents an academic year. Include the following pieces of data:

    *   Academic year
    *   Number of people who asked for information about admission to the college
    *   Number of people who applied for admission
    *   Number of people who were accepted
    *   Number of those accepted who actually attended

    The program should be able to handle data for up to 10 years. It should include the following capabilities:

    *   Read current data values from a file when the program begins.
    *   Write data values to a file when the program ends.
    *   Give the user the opportunity to create new objects and enter data for them.
    *   Prepare a nicely formatted report that shows all of the current data.

2. Write and test a program that manages data about the distance driven by cars in a corporation's fleet. For each car, the program should store its vehicle identification number (VIN) and the number of miles driven each day in a seven-day period. The data should be stored in a text file when the

program ends and loaded into main memory each time the program begins. Give the user the opportunity to create new car objects and view a report that shows the average miles driven by each car each week.

3. Write a program that plays the game of Hangman (the word guessing game). The data handling object, which represents a game, should store the solution word (the word the player is trying to guess), the correct guesses so far, the number of guesses made, and the maximum guesses allowed. (Maximum guesses are equal to the length of the solution word plus seven.)

    Create a text file for the program that contains a list of words to be used as solutions. You can use any text editor to do this by placing one word on a line; press the carriage return at the end of each word. When the program begins, read those words into an array of strings. At the beginning of each game, randomly select a word from the solutions array and store it in the game object.

    Methods of the game class should include evaluating a guess against the solution, storing a correct guess in its proper position in the word, and storing the number of guesses made. (*Hint:* Because you can't modify characters in a string, you'll need to use an array of characters to store the correct guesses.) After each guess, the game object should determine the game status (won, in progress, or maximum number of guesses exceeded). After each guess that doesn't result in a win or a loss, print out the letters guessed correctly in their correct position in the word, using underscores (_) as placeholders for letters not yet guessed. Be sure to allow the player to play many games before exiting the program

4. Write a program to manage the live animal inventory for a pet shop that handles cats, dogs, aquarium fish, reptiles, and small mammals (for example, rabbits, gerbils, and hamsters). Include data such as the type of animal, its living conditions, its feeding and care requirements, and the number of individuals currently in stock. Allow the user to do the following:

    *   Load the inventory data from a text file
    *   Perform interactive input for any type of animal
    *   Remove individuals from inventory when they are sold. (*Hint:* All you need to do is find the correct type of animal in the array, vector,

or hash table of animal objects and then decrement the number in stock.)

- Display the entire inventory.
- Save the inventory data to a text file

5. Modify the program you wrote for Exercise 4 so that it uses custom exceptions to provide data validation. You should check for animal identifiers whenever you are storing or retrieving data interactively.

6. Write a program to manage the "cars wanted" list of an exotic car dealership. The data handling classes should be part of an inheritance hierarchy and include data about the customers along with descriptions of the vehicles for which customers are searching. Include methods to do the following:

- Load data from a text file when the program is launched
- Perform interactive entry of customers and their requests
- Display the requests of a specific customer
- Find out whether a specific car that has just come onto the dealership lot matches any request stored by the program
- Save the data to a file

7. Write a program that manages an investment portfolio, including stocks, bonds, CDs, and mutual funds. Include data about the name of the investment, the amount held, and the current unit value. Include methods to load data from a text file, enter new investments, modify the current value of all investments held, compute the total value of the portfolio, and write the data to a text file.

8. Modify the program you wrote for Exercise 7 so that it handles multiple investment portfolios. One way to approach this is to add a class that represents the investors. Each investor object can own multiple portfolio objects, each of which is made up of multiple holdings.

9. Modify the program you wrote for Exercise 8 so that it performs data input validation using custom exception classes. Before you begin, spend time looking at the data the program is manipulating so that you can identify where data validation is required.

10. The telephone directory program uses simple `if` statements for validating input and indicating that a search for an employee has failed. Replace those statements with custom exceptions. Create an error message dialog box class that displays a meaningful error message whenever an error occurs.

11. The telephone directory program lets you enter new employees, but doesn't provide any code for maintaining them. Modify the program so that you can change an employee's office location and extension. Then add code that lets you delete an employee.

12. Write a program that maintains a simple accounts receivable system for a small business. Each account contains a customer's name, address, telephone number, and amount owed along with an ID number that is the same as the record number of the account in a random access file. When a payment comes in, allow the user to enter the customer's ID number. Then retrieve the amount owed, decrement it by the amount paid, and write the new value back to the file. Also prepare a report that shows how much each customer in the file owes.

13. Write a program that manages a retail company's purchase orders. Each order has a number that corresponds to its record number in a random access file. An order has the following data:

    - Vendor name
    - Vendor telephone
    - Date of order
    - Total amount of order
    - Record numbers of the order's line items (allow space for 20)

    The items on the order are stored in a separate random access file. Each order line item has the following data:

    - Order number
    - Line number
    - Item number
    - Quantity
    - Price for each item

Allow the user to enter new orders with up to 20 line items. Store only as many records as there are line items. (No fair leaving space for unused line items!) Also let the user view all the data about a specific order (including line items) by entering just the order number. (*Note:* This program presents a tough problem because the number of line items per order isn't fixed. To make this work, you'll need to keep track of the last record number used in the line items file.)

13

Images, Animation, and Threads

OBJECTIVES:

In this chapter you will learn to:

- Import import images into Java applications and applets.
- Understand the problems that arise when loading images over a network.
- Use buffering to improve image loading.
- Use multiple threads to support animation and periodic activities.

Part of the hype surrounding Java is the language's ability to support animation. If you were to believe what you read, then you would think that anyone with a little bit of programming expertise could write a Java program that makes images dance across the screen. Unfortunately, although a Java program certainly can do animation, it's nowhere as easy as you might think.

In this chapter we're going to approach animation somewhat slowly. First, we'll look at loading static images into a Java program, and spend some time looking at what you have to do to make images appear smoothly when their source is a network rather than the local machine. Then, we'll turn to the issue of threads, which is fundamental to controlling animation.

Note

If all you want to do is to put animated images on a web page, then there is a much easier way to do it than writing a Java applet: Use something like the shareware program GIFBulder, which combines and animates a set of GIF images without any programming.

Loading Static Images

InFigure 13.1 you can see a Java application that loads a GIF image. (The image is a colorful picture of an indoor garden in Montreal that is part of a Wizard of Oz display.) All this application does is create a window and display the image.

Figure 13.1   A Java application that loads an image

The program for this application appears in Listing 13.1. As you would expect, the program has a **main** method, a constructor that sets the window's title and background color, and a window listener that traps an event in the window's close box. The last line in the constructor and the **paint** method are responsible for the image.

Listing 13.1 bigImage.java

```
iimport java.awt.*;
import java.awt.event.*;

public class bigImage extends Frame
{
    private Image theImage;

    public bigImage()
    {
        addWindowListener (new WindowAdapter()
        {
            public void windowClosing (WindowEvent theEvent)
                { dispose(); }
        } );

        setTitle ("Large Colorful Image Display");
        setBackground (Color.white);

        theImage = Toolkit.getDefaultToolkit ().getImage ("flowers.GIF");
    }

    public void paint (Graphics graphObject)
        { graphObject.drawImage (theImage, 10,10, this); }

    public static void main (String args[])
    {
        bigImage theApp = new bigImage();
        theApp.resize (400,300);
        theApp.show();
    }
}
```

Displaying an image requires two steps: loading the image and drawing the image. The processing for drawing the image is the same, regardless of the image's source. The way in which you load an image depends on the location of the image, and to some extent whether the program is an application or an applet.

Loading an Image from the Local Machine

To load an image that is stored in a file on the same machine running a Java application, you work with an object of the `Toolkit` class. A `Toolkit` object connects the AWT methods you use in your program with the underlying graphics toolkit of the specific platform on which a program is running.

ToolKit

getDefault
ToolKit

To obtain a reference to the toolkit object being used by your program, you use the static method `getDefaultToolkit`:

```
ToolKit theKit = ToolKit.getDefaultToolkit();
```

You then ask the toolkit object to load the image into an object of class `Image`:

ToolKit

getImage

```
Image theImage = theKit.getImage ("flowers.GIF");
```

Notice in Listing 13.1 that these two steps have been combined into a single statement:

```
theImage =
    Toolkit.getDefaultToolkit ().getImage ("flowers.GIF");
```

In this case, the `getImage` method takes a single input parameter: a string containing the path name of graphics file.

Note

Don't forget that applets can't access files on the client's machine. Therefore, the technique just described will only work with applications.

Loading Images Over a Network

When the image you want to load is located on a network, rather than on the machine on which a Java program is running, you don't need to worry about the toolkit the program is using. All you need to do is specify a URL for the image. You can supply a complete URL or, if the image is stored relative to the location of the HTML document running the applet displaying the image, you can ask Java for the URL of the document and then specify the image path from that location. These techniques are used primarily with applets.

URL

new

Supplying a Complete URL

To supply a complete URL as the location of an image, you create an object of the URL class. (The URL class can be found in `java.net`, which you must import into your source code.) Because creating a URL can throw a malformed URL exception, the `new` statement must be surrounded by a `try/catch` block, as in Listing 13.2.

Listing 13.2   Creating a URL object

```
try
{
    URL theURL = new URL ("http://www.someSite.com/images/flowers.GIF"
}
catch (MalformedURLException theException)
{
    // error message to user goes here
}
```

Applet

getImage

Once you have the URL object, you can use it as an input parameter to the `Applet` class's `getImage` method:

```
theImage = getImage (theURL);
```

Supplying a Relative URL

Applet

get-
Document-
Base

When an image is stored relative to the URL of the HTML document running an applet, the applet can retrieve that URL while it is running:

```
URL theURL = getDocumentBase();
```

Then, you can combine that URL with the path of the image relative to the URL to load the image:

```
theImage = getImage (theURL,"flowers.GIF");
```

If you look at the applet version of the simple image-loading program in Listing 13.3, you'll see that obtaining the document URL and loading the image have been combined into a single statement.

Listing 13.3   Loading an image into an applet over a network

```
import java.awt.*;
import java.applet.*;

public class bigImage extends Applet
{
    Image theImage;

    public void init()
    {
        theImage = getImage (getDocumentBase(),"flowers.GIF");
    }

    public void paint (Graphics graphObject)
    {
        graphObject.drawImage (theImage, 10,10, this);
    }
}
```

Drawing Images

Getting an image doesn't draw the image; it simply loads the image into main memory. A program must then draw the image directly onto a window or canvas. (In the examples you are seeing, drawing takes place directly in the window to keep the programs short. However, you can just as easily draw onto a canvas and then add the canvas to a container.)

Graphics

drawImage

To perform the drawing, you ask an object of the `Graphics` class to do the work in a `paint` method, just as you do when drawing directly with AWT methods:

```
graphObject.drawImage (theImage, 10,10, this);
```

The first input parameter is an image object containing the previously loaded image. The second two parameters are the X- and Y- coordinates of where the top left corner of the image should be placed. Both measurements are relative to the surface on which you are drawing, whether it is a window or a panel.

The third input parameter is an *image observer*, the object that should be notified when drawing of the image is complete. This version of the program doesn't make any use of the image observer, but as you will see in the next section, an image observer is an essential part of making an image appear smoothly when it is loaded across a network.

Using Buffering to Smooth Network Image Loading

If you run the applet in Listing 13.3, you will discover that the image will indeed load and display in a web browser. However, loading will be very, very slow and the image will flicker constantly until drawing is complete.

Note   There's no way to demonstrate the slow, flickering load with a screen shot, so you should try the program yourself to see what happens. You will probably find it easier to work with a web browser than an applet viewer because some applet viewers aren't smart enough to realize that although you're using a URL to specify the location of the image file, the image is still on the local machine and you don't need a live Internet connection to retrieve the image.

The slow, flickering load occurs because the Java virtual machine isn't calling `paint` whenever it notices that the screen needs to be redrawn. Instead, it's calling a method named `update`, which erases and then repaints the entire area. Given that the image is loading slowly over the network, `update` is called repeatedly while the image transfer is occurring.

There are two parts to the solution:

- Override the `update` method with code that simply repaints the area, rather than erasing it completely each time.
- Delay drawing anything until the entire image is loaded. This technique, known as *buffering*, means that you draw the image in main memory until the entire image is present. Then, you draw it all at once on the screen.

In Listing 13.4 you can find yet another version of the applet that loads the indoor garden image. This particular version uses buffering. When you run it, you will notice a *very* slight delay as the image loads. Then, the entire image appears on the screen, without any flickering.

Image Observers and Detecting Image Completion

To implement buffering, an applet must be able to be notified when an image has been completely rendered in main memory. This means you must give it the characteristics of an image observer by implementing the `ImageObserver`

Listing 13.4   Using buffering to smooth image loading

```
import java.awt.*;
import java.applet.*;
import java.awt.image.ImageObserver;

public class bigImage extends Applet implements ImageObserver
{
    private Image theImage;
    private Image buffer;
    private boolean loaded = false;

    public void init()
        { theImage = getImage (getDocumentBase(),"flowers.GIF");}

    public void update (Graphics graphObject)
        { paint (graphObject); }

    public void paint (Graphics graphObject)
    {
        if (!loaded)
        {
            buffer = createImage (1,1);
            Graphics bufferGraph = buffer.getGraphics();
            bufferGraph.drawImage (theImage,10,10,this);
            bufferGraph.dispose();
            return;
        }

        buffer = createImage (theImage.getWidth(this),
            theImage.getHeight(this)); // size of illustration
        Graphics bufferGraph = buffer.getGraphics();
        bufferGraph.drawImage (theImage, 10,10, null);
        bufferGraph.dispose();

        graphObject.drawImage (buffer, 10,10, this);
    }

    public boolean imageUpdate (Image theImage, int infoflags, int x, int y,
        int width, int height)
    {
        if ((infoflags & ImageObserver.ALLBITS) != 0)
        {
            loaded = true;
            repaint();
            return false; // no more needs to be loaded
        }
        return true; // yes, more needs to be loaded
    }
}
```

interface and writing code for an `imageUpdate` method. The `ImageObserver` interface is actually implemented by the `Component` class. `Applet` therefore inherits it because of the following inheritance hierarchy:

```
Component <- Container <- Panel <- Applet
```

The Java virtual machine calls `imageUpdate` whenever a program calls a method that requests information about an image (such as its width or height) or asks that the image be drawn.

Note

If you use the `drawImage` method with `null` for the last parameter (the image observer), then `imageUpdate` isn't called.

The `imageUpdate` method returns TRUE if the image *isn't* complete, indicating that further updates will be needed, and FALSE if the image is complete and further updates aren't needed. (Yes, this is a bit counterintuitive.) However, because the `imageUpdate` method comes from an interface, rather than from a base class, there is no implementation of the method to inherit. The code you write for that method must determine whether loading of the image is complete.

Image-
Observer

image-
Update

When the Java virtual machine calls `imageUpdate`, it provides you with several pieces of information about the image as input parameters:

- A reference to the image.
- A set of flags that indicate the status of the image. We will discuss these flags more in a moment.
- The X- and Y-coordinates of the image's location. (May not be valid, depending on the status of the image.)
- The height and width of the image. (May not be valid, depending on the status of the image.)

The flags that indicate the status of the image (stored in the variable `infoflags` in Listing 13.4) are contained in a single integer. Some of the bits in that integer have a special meaning. For example, if bit 0 has a 1 in it, then the width of the image is valid and can be used; if bit 1 has a 1 in it, then the height of the image is valid. If bit 6 has a value of 1, then the image is complete.

Each of the bits is assigned a constant in the `ImageObserver` class. For our purposes, we'll use the constant `ALLBITS`, which holds a 32 (the value of an integer if only bit 6 is set).

Java has no method for testing an individual bit, but you can get the same effect by using the bit-wise AND operator (&). Keep in mind that when you AND two bits together, the result will be 1 only if both bits are one. Therefore, if we take the `infoflags` integer and perform a bit-wise AND between that value and the constant `ALLBITS`, the result will be TRUE (in other words, non-zero), only if bit 6 is set in `infoflags`. The state of the rest of the bits in `infoflags` has no effect on the result because with the exception of bit 6, all bits in `ALLBITS` are 0. A program therefore tests that an image is completely loaded with:

```
if ((infoflags & ImageObserver.ALLBITS) != 0)
```

In our particular example, when the `imageUpdate` method detects that the image is complete, it changes the value in the boolean `loaded` and then calls `repaint`. As you will see in the next section, what happens in `paint` depends on the value of `loaded`.

Buffering the Image

The idea behind buffering is that you set aside a special area in main memory (a *buffer*) into which you can draw an image as it arrives slowly over the network. Then, when the image is complete, you draw to the screen from the buffer.

The trick with buffering is to trigger the loading of the image, even though you may only have only a small part of it. We do this by creating a tiny image (1 pixel wide by 1 pixel high) for the buffer. If the image isn't loaded (the `loaded` boolean in Listing 13.4 is FALSE), then the program draws whatever it has in the buffer and doesn't draw anything on the screen. However, if the image is complete, then the program draws the entire image in the buffer and then copies it to the screen. The result is an image that appears quickly and smoothly. (Well, it appears as fast as it can, depending on the speed of the network connection ...)

Component

The buffer itself is an object of the `Image` class that is created with the `createImage` method:

create-
Image

```
Image buffer = createImage (width, height);
```

If the image isn't completely loaded, then we make the width and height equal to 1:

```
Image buffer = createImage (1,1);
```

Conceptually, the next step is to draw into the buffer. However, drawing is performed by graphics objects, and although the paint method has a graphics object for the applet, it doesn't have one for the buffer. Therefore, before a program can draw into a buffer, it must obtain a reference to the graphics object associated with the buffer:

Image

get-
Graphics

```
Graphics bufferGraph = buffer.getGraphics();
```

Then the program can use that graphics object to do the drawing:

```
bufferGraph.drawImage (theImage,10,10,this);
```

Immediately after finishing drawing, a program should release the memory used by the graphics object:

Graphics

dispose

```
bufferGraph.dispose();
```

In Java programs, objects are "orphaned" in main memory all the time. When you exit a method in which an object was created, the variable that holds a reference to the object is destroyed. If you assign a second object reference to a variable that previously referenced an object, the first reference is lost. Under most circumstances, Java periodically cleans up these inaccessible objects and makes the memory they occupied available to the program with a process known as *garbage collection*. Java does not, however, clean up inaccessible graphics objects. You must therefore be certain to include the call to dispose.

Image

getWidth

Image

getHeight

If image loading is completed, then a program should create a buffer that is the exact size of the image. You can retrieve the width of the image with the getWidth method and the height with getHeight, both of which take a reference to the image observer object as an input parameter. In that case, the call to createImage looks like:

```
buffer = createImage
    (theImage.getWidth(this),theImage.getHeight(this));
```

Then the program obtains the image's graphics object, draws the image in the buffer, and then disposes of the graphics object. The final step is to render the image of the screen by drawing it in the applet's graphics object, taking the source of the image from the buffer:

```
graphObject.drawImage (buffer, 10,10, this);
```

MultiThreading Concepts

Strictly speaking, a thread is an independent execution unit that can compete for system resources, such as CPU time and disk files. When a program has more than one thread—in other words, it is *multithreaded*—it means that the program's work is broken up into multiple, independent strands that run in parallel. A multitasking operating system allocates CPU time to each thread, making it possible for the same program to be doing more than one thing at once.

There are many reasons to write a multithreaded program, but two common ones are to support animation and programs that perform periodic, or timed, actions. In the remainder of this chapter, you will see examples of both types of programs. The animation program cycles a stoplight through green, yellow, and red. The periodic program displays a year 2000 countdown clock that counts down the years, months, days, hours, minutes, and seconds until the beginning of 2000.

Why does animation require multiple threads? Because once the animation is started, there needs to be some way to stop it. Unless there is a separate thread that checks for a user's actions, the animation will continue uninterrupted. Why do periodic events need multiple threads? Because something must trigger the periodic actions at specific intervals. In the example you are going to see, the periodic activity is updating the clock's display.

Warning If you attempt to use a buffering technique without checking for image completion, you may find that your program doesn't draw anything. This is because once Java starts drawing the image, it creates a separate thread for loading the image, finishes executing the method that loads the thread, and then continues to execute other methods in the applet using additional threads. The applet therefore won't wait for the image to complete loading before it draws the screen.

Thread Objects

A Java thread is an object that is either derived from the Thread class or implements the interface Runnable. Applets, for example, must inherit from the Applet class and therefore have no choice but to use the interface. Both the Thread class and the Runnable interface provide three methods that are usually overridden in a multithreaded program:

- run: Code that should be executed whenever a thread gets a chance to run is placed in the run method. A program never calls this method directly, however.
- start: The start method initializes a new thread and calls the thread's run method. Java generates an exception if a program calls start more than once.
- stop: The stop method kills a thread and runs its contents before the resources (in particular, main memory) used by the thread are released.

Thread States

When the Java virtual machine or a Java program creates a thread, it can be in one of four states:

- New: A new thread has just been created and is not yet ready to run.
- Runnable: A runnable thread is capable of being run. This means that it has been initialized and that it is not waiting for an I/O operation to complete. When the CPU becomes available, this thread can be run. At any given time, one runnable thread will be running. In other words, it will have control of the CPU. However, there is no way to tell the difference between a runnable thread that is waiting for a turn to execute and the single thread that is actually executing.
- Blocked: A blocked thread is a thread that could not run even if the CPU were available. One reason for a thread to become blocked is that it must wait for I/O to complete. A thread may also become blocked if the program calls sleep (the thread waits for a specified number of milliseconds), suspend (the thread waits until another object calls its resume method), or wait (the thread waits until it is notified with a call to notify that it can proceed). You will read more about these methods in the rest of this chapter.

- Dead: A dead thread is a thread that is no longer active. Threads die when the `run` method in which they are contained completes or if another object calls the thread's `stop` method.

During its life, a thread may make several *state transitions*, switching between the preceding states depending on how it is handled by its program. You can find the major thread state transitions and the `Thread` class methods that are used to make those transitions in Figure 13.2.

Figure 13.2   Thread state transitions

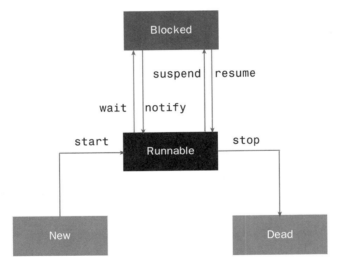

For example, the first transition a thread makes is the one from New to Runnable.

```
New -> Runnable
```

A Runnable thread may go from Runnable to Blocked and Blocked to Runnable several times during its life:

```
Runnable -> Blocked
Blocked -> Runnable
```

As you might expect, a thread only goes from Runnable to Dead once:

```
Runnable -> Dead
```

Note that a thread cannot go directly from Blocked to Dead. It must be made Runnable before it can be killed.

When a program needs to know the current state of a thread, it asks the thread by calling the thread's `isAlive` method. The method call returns TRUE if the thread is Runnable or Blocked, and FALSE if it is New or Dead. Note that this only identifies currently active threads. It won't tell you, for example, whether a thread is new and hasn't started running or if a thread is dead. It also can't differentiate between a Runnable and Blocked thread.

Thread Behavior

The threads in a program can be either *cooperative* or *selfish*. A cooperative thread uses the `sleep` method to put itself to sleep for a short period of time so other threads can have a chance to run. Alternatively, a thread can call `yield` to indicate that it's all right to interrupt the thread's processing.

A selfish thread doesn't indicate its willingness to give up control of the program. If a program contains selfish threads, then it may be difficult to get the program to respond to user actions. For example, suppose a program has two threads, one to display animated images and another to detect user actions. If the animation thread is selfish, then—*depending on the operating system*—the user may not be able to stop the animation easily because the program won't be checking for user input very often.

One of the benefits of programming in Java is that, assuming you write Java code that doesn't include any platform-specific features, then the same program will run unmodified on any platform that has a Java virtual machine. This means that you can't count on having an operating system that interrupts threads on its own. It is therefore up to you as a programmer to write a multi-threaded program in such a way that all your threads are well behaved.

Thread Synchronization

If you have taken a database management course, then you are familiar with the problems that can occur if a DBMS doesn't control concurrent access to the same data objects. Like database systems, multithreaded programs can run into problems when two threads of the same program are modifying the same object at the same time.

To help you understand the type of problem that arises, assume that someone has written a retail store inventory program with multiple threads to support multiple users. In Figure 13.3 you can see what happens when two different users try to find out if there are enough widgets in stock to fill someone's order. The first thread retrieves 100 widgets; so does the second. When the first thread sells those 100 widgets, the inventory drops to 0. Unfortunately, the second thread doesn't know that the widgets have been sold, and it therefore proceeds to sell 100 nonexistent items.

Figure 13.3   The effective of conflicting multithreaded actions

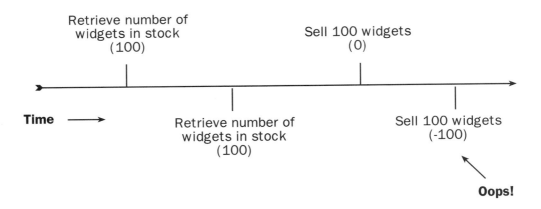

To avoid problems of this type, you need to prevent the second thread from executing the methods that retrieve inventory levels and record sales until the first thread has finished. You therefore make the retrieval and sales methods *synchronized methods*. Once the first thread begins executing any synchronized method in the widget object, no other thread can execute any synchronized method belonging to that object until the first thread completes its work. If a thread cannot execute a method that it needs, Java makes it wait until the object is available.

Objects that can block threads and then notify them when they execute a method for which they are waiting are called *monitors*. A monitor is therefore any object that has one or more synchronized methods.

A synchronized method includes the keyword `synchronized` in its first line:

```
public class synchronized returnDataType className
```

Writing a Program with Animation

For your first multithreaded program, we'll extend the image concepts you've been reading about in the beginning of this chapter to provide an animated applet that cycles through green, yellow, and red stoplights (Figure 13.4).

Figure 13.4 The animated stoplight applet

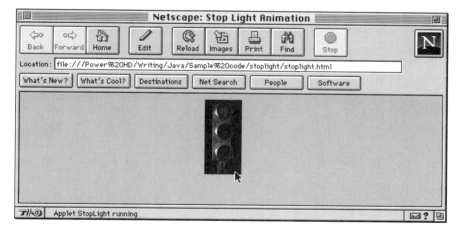

Before writing code for an animation, you must first have the individual images through which the animation will cycle. They can be stored in separate files, but it is much easier to write the animation program if the images are together in one, as in Figure 13.5. Place the images one on top of the other, with no space in between, as if they were part of an old-fashioned filmstrip.

Figure 13.5   The stoplight images (lights.GIF)

You can display animation directly in a window or on a canvas. The animated stoplight program, however, draws directly on the applet to keep the program a bit shorter. The stoplight program (Listing 13.5) therefore has one class that is derived from `Applet`. To give it the characteristics of a thread, it also implements the `Runnable` interface.

Some of the code in the stoplight applet is the same as what you saw when displaying a static image. In particular, the program overrides the `update` method to prevent complete erases each time the window is redrawn and uses buffering in the `paint` method to prevent drawing an image until the entire contents of the image file have been loaded over the network. The major difference you should notice is in the call to `drawImage` in the `paint` method. Although the program does draw the entire contents of the image file, the origin of the applet window is offset so that only one of the images appears. This is the same technique that you saw when scrolling the contents of a window, where the Y-coordinate of the top left corner is offset by a negative value to make the viewable area other than the top left corner of what is being drawn. By changing the number of the current image (numbered beginning with 0 and stored in `currentFrame`), the program changes the location of the origin and therefore determines which image can be seen.

Listing 13.5   StopLight.java

```java
import java.awt.*;
import java.awt.image.ImageObserver;
import java.applet.*;
import java.lang.*;
import java.util.*;
import java.awt.event.*;

public class StopLight extends Applet implements Runnable
{
    private Image theImage;
    private int numbImages = 3;
    private int imageWidth = 0;
    private int imageHeight = 0;
    private Thread runner = null;
    private int currentFrame = 0;
    private boolean loaded = false;
    private boolean stopped = false;

    public void init ()
    {
        addMouseListener (new MouseAdapter ()
        {
            public void mousePressed (MouseEvent theEvent)
            {
                StopLight theApplet = (StopLight) theEvent.getSource ();
                if (loaded)
                {
                    if (runner != null && runner.isAlive ())
                    {
                        if (stopped)
                        {
                            showStatus ("Click once to stop animation.");
                            runner.resume ();
                        }
                        else
                        {
                            showStatus ("Click once to start animation.");
                            runner.suspend ();
                        }
                        stopped = !stopped;
                    }
                    else
                    {
                        stopped = false;
                        currentFrame = 0;
                        runner = new Thread (theApplet);
                        runner.start ();
```

Continued next page

Listing 13.5(Continued)   StopLight.java

```
                }
            }
        }
    } );
}

public void start()
{
    if (runner == null)
    {
        runner = new Thread (this);
        runner.start();
    }
}

public void stop()
{
    if (runner != null && runner.isAlive())
    {
        runner.stop();
        runner = null;
    }
}

public synchronized void loadImage()
{
    if (loaded)
        return;
    theImage = getImage (getDocumentBase(),"lights.GIF");

    while (!loaded)
        try
        {
            wait();
        }
        catch (InterruptedException theException)
        { }
    resize (imageWidth, imageHeight / numbImages);
}

public void run()
{
    if (!loaded)
        loadImage();
```

Continued next page

Listing 13.5(Continued)   StopLight.java

```java
        while (runner != null)
        {
            repaint();
            try
            {
                Thread.sleep (200);
            }
            catch (InterruptedException theException)
            { }
            currentFrame = (currentFrame + 1) % numbImages;
        }
    }

    public void paint (Graphics graphObject)
    {
        if (!loaded)
        {
            Image buffer = createImage (1,1);
            Graphics bufferGraph = buffer.getGraphics();
            bufferGraph.drawImage (theImage,0,0,this);
            bufferGraph.dispose();
            return;
        }
        graphObject.drawImage (theImage, 0, -(imageHeight / numbImages) *
    currentFrame,null);
    }

    public void update (Graphics graphObject)
    {
        paint (graphObject);
    }

    public synchronized boolean imageUpdate (Image theImage, int infoflags, int
    x,
        int y, int width, int height)
    {
        if ((infoflags & ImageObserver.ALLBITS) != 0)
        {
            imageWidth = theImage.getWidth (null);
            imageHeight = theImage.getHeight (null);
            showStatus ("Click once to stop animation.");
            loaded = true;
            notify();
            return false;
        }
        return true;
    }
}
```

Creating the Animation Thread

To create a thread, a program creates an object of class `Thread`. In the stoplight program, this occurs in the applet's `start` method. Because a thread runs a portion of the program, the variable that represents the thread is usually named `runner`:

Thread

```
runner = new Thread (this);
```

new

The parameter passed to the thread object's constructor is a reference to the object whose `run` function is to be called by the thread. In this case, that object is the applet itself.

To begin image loading and the animation, the applet calls the thread's `start` method:

```
runner.start();
```

Note

Both the `Applet` class and the `Thread` class have `start` methods. An applet's `start` method runs whenever the user opens or returns to a web page; a program never needs to call the method directly. However, a thread won't become runnable until a program calls its `start` method directly.

Dealing with a Partially Loaded Image File

A thread's `start` method calls the `run` method of the object specified when the thread was created. If the image is loaded, then the thread goes to sleep for 200 milliseconds by calling the `Thread` class method `sleep`, ensuring that each image within the image file stays on the screen for that period of time:

Thread

```
runner.sleep (200);
```

sleep

When it wakes up, it repaints the screen and changes the value of the current frame, which in turn changes the origin of the visible portion of the image, providing the visual illusion that the image the viewer is seeing is actually moving.

If the image isn't loaded, then the thread needs to load the image, calling the applet's `loadImage` method. Notice first that the `loadImage` method is a synchronized method. This prevents more than one thread from attempting to load the same image at the same time.

Object

wait

What should the thread do while the image file is being transferred over the network? In this case, the thread must wait for the image; we don't want it to start animating from an incomplete image file. Therefore, the `loadImage` method calls the `Object` class method `wait`, which causes the thread to wait indefinitely until some other object notifies it that it can proceed. Notice in Listing 13.5 that `wait` can throw an `InterruptedException` and that the call must therefore be placed in a `try/catch` block. Although there's nothing you can do if an exception occurs, the `try/catch` structure must be included.

Starting the Animation

The stoplight program has an `imageUpdate` method to implement its behavior as an image observer. (Keep in mind that the `Applet` class inherits from `Panel`, which in turn inherits from `Container`, which inherits from `Component`, which implements the `ImageObserver` interface.) This method, which is called periodically during the image loading process, begins with the test you saw earlier in this chapter for determining when an image load is complete. Assuming the entire image file is complete in main memory, the method does the following:

Applet

show-
Status

Object

notify

- Obtains the width of the image.
- Obtains the overall height of the image. (All you need to know to calculate the coordinates of a single image is the total number of images in the image file (`numbImages`) and the number of the current image (`currentFrame`).)
- Changes the status line at the bottom of the web browser using the `Applet` class's `showStatus` method, which takes the status line message as an input parameter.
- Changes the `loaded` boolean to indicate that loading is complete.
- Calls the `Object` class's `notify` method to tell the waiting thread that it can proceed.

Warning

If you suspend a thread by calling `wait`, don't forget to `notify` it to resume execution. Otherwise, it will wait forever.

Controlling the Animation with Mouse Clicks

A user viewing the stoplight applet can start and stop the animation by clicking on the applet. The applet implements this behavior by registering a mouse event listener (a class that extends `MouseAdapter`). The code then implements either the `mouseClicked` or `mousePressed` method to trap the click of a mouse in the applet window.

The stoplight applet uses the `mousePressed` method, which first checks to see if a thread exists and if it is alive:

```
if (runner != null && runner.isAlive())
```

Assuming an existing thread is alive, it then must take different actions based on whether the animation is currently running or stopped. The stoplight applet keeps track of this with its `stopped` boolean.

If the animation is running, the `mousePressed` method changes the status line and suspends the thread:

Thread

suspend

```
showStatus ("Click once to start animation.");
runner.suspend();
```

The `suspend` method causes a thread to stop executing, freezing it at the point at which `suspend` is called.

If the animation has been stopped, the `mousePressed` method changes the browser's status line and starts the animation running again:

Thread

resume

```
showStatus ("Click once to stop animation.");
runner.resume();
```

The `resume` method causes a suspended thread to pick up execution where it left off. The method call is only valid after a thread has been suspended with the `suspend` method.

When a mouse down event occurs but no animation thread is available, the `mousePressed` method creates a new thread and jump starts its execution by calling `start`.

Stopping the Animation

The mousePressed method in the mouse event listener takes care of managing the animation while the user is continuing to view the same web page. In addition, the applet must take care of stopping the animation when the user leaves the web page by either viewing another page or quitting the browser. This is where the applet's stop method comes into play.

The stop method checks to see if there is a live thread. In this case, however, if a live thread exists, then we want to kill it, not just suspend it:

Thread

stop

```
runner.stop();
```

Writing a Program with a Periodic Thread

Threads that require attention at regular intervals are known as *periodicals* or *timers*. Once of the most common uses of a periodical is to update a display that changes regularly. For example, you may have seen a billboard that counts up the size of the U.S. national debt each second. Our example of a periodical is only a bit less sinister: It is a clock that shows you the years, months, days, hours, minutes, and seconds until the beginning of the year 2000 (Figure 13.6). It updates itself approximately once a second.

Figure 13.6   The year 2000 countdown clock

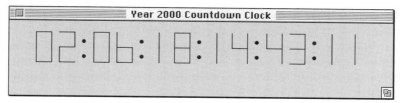

The numbers in the display are created by drawing lines with the draw-Line method. The dots separating pairs of digits are drawn with fillOval. The entire display is placed on a canvas, which is then installed in the program's main window. (This is an application, not an applet, although there is certainly no reason you couldn't turn it into an applet.)

The application class (Listing 13.6) is very simple. Its main method creates an object of the class, registers a window listener, resizes the window, and shows it. The constructor creates a canvas for the clock display and adds it to the application object's window. All of the work dealing with the display itself and the thread that handles the timing is taken care of by the canvas class (Listing 13.7) and by a timer class derived from Thread (Listing 13.8).

Listing 13.6   countdownClock.java

```java
import java.awt.*;
import java.lang.*;
import java.util.*;
import java.awt.event.*;

public class countdownClock extends Frame
{
    private clockDisplay theCanvas;

    public countdownClock()
    {
        setTitle ("Year 2000 Countdown Clock");
        setLayout (new FlowLayout());
        theCanvas = new clockDisplay();
        add (theCanvas); // add the canvas showing intial clock
    }

    public static void main (String args[])
    {
        class windowListener extends WindowAdapter
        {
            public void windowClosing (WindowEvent theEvent)
            {
                Window theWindow = (Window) theEvent.getSource();
                theWindow.dispose();
                //System.exit(0);
            }
        }

        Frame theClock = new countdownClock();
        theClock.addWindowListener (new windowListener());
        theClock.resize (500,100);
        theClock.show();
    }
}
```

Actions of a Timer Class

The clockTimer class is an example of a relatively generic timer class. It has only two methods, a constructor and run. The constructor initializes the thread object with a reference to the object being timed and the interval at

Listing 13.7   clockDisplay.java

```java
import java.awt.*;
import java.lang.*;
import java.util.*;

interface Timed
{
    public void performUpdate (clockTimer timedObject);
}

class clockDisplay extends Canvas implements Timed
{
    int years, months, days, hours, minutes, seconds;

    public clockDisplay()
    {
        resize (450,75);
        clockTimer theTimer = new clockTimer (this, 1000);
        theTimer.start();
    }

    public void performUpdate(clockTimer timedObject)
    {
        repaint();
    }

    public void paint (Graphics graphObject)
    {
        findDifference();
        draw(graphObject);
    }

    private void findDifference()
    {
        Date now = new Date();
        years = 100 - now.getYear() - 1;
        if (now.getMonth() == 0 || now.getDate() == 1) // adjust for January 1
            years += 1;
        int thisMonth = now.getMonth();
        months = 11 - thisMonth;
        days = 0;
        switch (thisMonth)
        {
            case 0: // January
            case 2: // March
            case 4: // May
            case 6: // July
```

Continued next page

Listing 13.7(Continued)   clockDisplay.java

```
            case 7: // August
            case 9: // October
            case 11: // December
                days = 31 - now.getDate();
                break;
            case 3: // April
            case 5: // June
            case 8: // September
            case 10: // November
                days = 30 - now.getDate();
                break;
            // No leap years before 2000!
            case 1: days = 28 - now.getDate(); break;
        }

        hours = 23 - now.getHours();
        minutes = 59 - now.getMinutes();
        seconds = 59 - now.getSeconds();
    }

    private void draw(Graphics graphObject)
    {
        int digit;
        digit = years / 10;
        decideDraw (10,10,graphObject,digit);
        digit = years % 10;
        decideDraw (40,10,graphObject,digit);
        graphObject.fillOval (70,20,5,5);
        graphObject.fillOval (70,40,5,5);

        digit = months / 10;
        decideDraw (85,10,graphObject,digit);
        digit = months % 10;
        decideDraw (115,10,graphObject,digit);
        graphObject.fillOval (145,20,5,5);
        graphObject.fillOval (145,40,5,5);

        digit = days / 10;
        decideDraw (160,10,graphObject,digit);
        digit = days % 10;
        decideDraw (190,10,graphObject,digit);
        graphObject.fillOval (220,20,5,5);
        graphObject.fillOval (220,40,5,5);

        digit = hours / 10;
        decideDraw (235,10,graphObject, digit);
```

Continued next page

Listing 13.7(Continued)   clockDisplay.java

```java
        digit = hours % 10;
        decideDraw (265,10,graphObject,digit);
        graphObject.fillOval (295,20,5,5);
        graphObject.fillOval (295,40,5,5);

        digit = minutes / 10;
        decideDraw (310,10,graphObject, digit);
        digit = minutes % 10;
        decideDraw (340,10,graphObject,digit);
        graphObject.fillOval (370,20,5,5);
        graphObject.fillOval (370,40,5,5);

        digit = seconds / 10;
        decideDraw (385,10,graphObject,digit);
        digit = seconds % 10;
        decideDraw (415,10,graphObject,digit);
    }

    private void decideDraw (int x, int y, Graphics graphObject, int digit)
    {
        switch (digit)
        {
            case 0: drawZero (x, y, graphObject); break;
            case 1: drawOne (x, y, graphObject); break;
            case 2: drawTwo (x, y, graphObject); break;
            case 3: drawThree (x, y, graphObject); break;
            case 4: drawFour (x, y, graphObject); break;
            case 5: drawFive (x, y, graphObject); break;
            case 6: drawSix (x, y, graphObject); break;
            case 7: drawSeven (x, y, graphObject); break;
            case 8: drawEight (x, y, graphObject); break;
            case 9: drawNine (x, y, graphObject); break;
        }
    }

    private void drawZero (int x, int y, Graphics graphObject)
    {
        graphObject.drawLine (x, y, x+20,y); // top
        graphObject.drawLine (x, y, x, y+40); // left side
        graphObject.drawLine (x+20, y, x+20, y+40); // right side
        graphObject.drawLine (x, y+40, x+20, y+40); // bottom
    }

    private void drawOne (int x, int y, Graphics graphObject)
    {
        graphObject.drawLine (x + 10, y, x+10, y+40);
    }
```

Continued next page

Listing 13.7(Continued)   clockDisplay.java

```
private void drawTwo (int x, int y, Graphics graphObject)
{
    graphObject.drawLine (x, y, x+20, y); // top
    graphObject.drawLine (x+20, y, x+20, y+20); // top half left
    graphObject.drawLine (x, y+20, x+20, y+20); // middle
    graphObject.drawLine (x, y+20, x, y+40); // bottom half right
    graphObject.drawLine (x, y+40, x+20, y+40); // bottom
}

private void drawThree (int x, int y, Graphics graphObject)
{
    graphObject.drawLine (x, y, x+20,y); // top
    graphObject.drawLine (x+20, y, x+20, y+40); // right side
    graphObject.drawLine (x, y+20, x+20, y+20); // middle
    graphObject.drawLine (x, y+40, x+20, y+40); // bottom
}

private void drawFour (int x, int y, Graphics graphObject)
{
    graphObject.drawLine (x, y, x, y+20); // top half right
    graphObject.drawLine (x, y+20, x+20, y+20); // middle
    graphObject.drawLine (x+20, y, x+20, y+40); // right side
}

private void drawFive (int x, int y, Graphics graphObject)
{
    graphObject.drawLine (x, y, x+20,y); // top
    graphObject.drawLine (x, y, x, y+20); // top half right
    graphObject.drawLine (x, y+20, x+20, y+20); // middle
    graphObject.drawLine (x+20, y+20, x+20, y+40); // bottom half left
    graphObject.drawLine (x, y+40, x+20, y+40); // bottom
}

private void drawSix (int x, int y, Graphics graphObject)
{
    graphObject.drawLine (x, y, x, y+40); // left side
    graphObject.drawLine (x, y+20, x+20, y+20); // middle
    graphObject.drawLine (x+20, y+20, x+20, y+40); // bottom half left
    graphObject.drawLine (x, y+40, x+20, y+40); // bottom
}

private void drawSeven (int x, int y, Graphics graphObject)
{
    graphObject.drawLine (x, y, x+20,y); // top
    graphObject.drawLine (x+20, y, x+20, y+40); // right side
}
```

Continued next page

Listing 13.7(Continued)   clockDisplay.java

```
private void drawEight (int x, int y, Graphics graphObject)
{
    graphObject.drawLine (x, y, x+20,y); // top
    graphObject.drawLine (x, y, x, y+40); // left side
    graphObject.drawLine (x+20, y, x+20, y+40); // right side
    graphObject.drawLine (x, y+40, x+20, y+40); // bottom
    graphObject.drawLine (x, y+20, x+20, y+20); // middle
}

private void drawNine (int x, int y, Graphics graphObject)
{
    graphObject.drawLine (x, y, x+20,y); // top
    graphObject.drawLine (x+20, y, x+20, y+40); // right side
    graphObject.drawLine (x, y, x, y+20); // top half right
    graphObject.drawLine (x, y+20, x+20, y+20); // middle
}
}
```

which the timed object should be updated (stored in howLong). The timed object is of class Timed, an interface that you can see at the top of Listing 13.7. Any class that needs the services of a timer thread will need to implement this interface.

The constructor also makes the thread a *daemon thread*. A daemon thread exists only to take care of other threads in the program. Most important, its existence (or non-existence) doesn't affect the end of the program. When all the non-daemon threads in a program end, the daemon thread ends automatically. By making the timer thread a daemon thread, it is killed automatically when the user quits the countdown clock application. We therefore don't need to write code to kill the thread.

To make a thread a daemon thread, call setDaemon with an input parameter of TRUE:

Thread

```
setDaemon(true);
```

setDaemon

The run method includes an infinite loop that continues as long as the thread is alive. (This is a safe thing to do only because the thread is a daemon thread that will die automatically at the program's end.) The loop causes the thread to sleep for the specified interval (in this case, it will be 1000 milliseconds) and then runs the timed object's performUpdate method, the method inherited from the Timed interface.

Listing 13.8   clockTimer.java

```java
import java.awt.*;
import java.lang.*;
import java.util.*;

class clockTimer extends Thread
{
    private Timed timedObject;
    private int howLong;

    public clockTimer (Timed itimedObject, int ihowLong)
    {
        timedObject = itimedObject;
        howLong = ihowLong;
        setDaemon (true);
    }

    public void run()
    {
        while (true)
        {
            try
                { sleep (howLong); }
            catch (InterruptedException theException)
            { }
            timedObject.performUpdate(this);
        }
    }
}
```

Actions of the Timed Object

The timed object in the countdown clock program is the canvas that displays the clock. The canvas class implements the `Timed` interface and therefore has a `performUpdate` method that triggers the actions that need to be performed each time the thread wakes up. However, before the thread can call `performUpdate`, something has to create and start the thread.

Thread creation takes place in the canvas's constructor. It first creates a new `clockTimer` object:

```java
clockTimer theTimer = new clockTimer (this, 1000);
```

Then it starts the thread:

```java
theTimer.start ();
```

The `performUpdate` method itself is deceptively simple. It contains nothing more than a call to `repaint`. However, if you look at the `paint` method (which is called by `repaint`), you'll see that `paint` triggers a lot of work going on to determine the interval between midnight on January 1, 2000 and the current date, all of which is collected in the `findDifference` method.

An Aside: Working with Java Dates

Given the calendar we use, dates are always problematic. Java does provide a date class that handles both dates and times, although it is not quite complete. In particular, it doesn't perform date arithmetic, making it easy to find out the difference between two dates or to add a fixed interval to a date. The countdown clock program must therefore engage in all sorts of strange computations to determine how many years, months, days, hours, minutes, and seconds to display.

Date

new

The first task is to read the current system date and time. To do this, all you have to do is create an object of class **Date**:

```
Date now = new Date();
```

Then you can extract parts of the date and time to work with them individually:

Date

get...

- `getYear`: Extracts the year from a date object as the number of years from 1900. The year 2000, for example, returns 100.
- `getMonth`: Extracts the month from a date object as a month number. Months are numbered beginning with 0 (January).
- `getDate`: Extracts the day of the month. (The `getDay` method gets the day of the week, with Sunday numbered as 0.)
- `getHours`: Extracts the hours.
- `getMinutes`: Extracts the minutes.
- `getSeconds`: Extracts the seconds.

Once the canvas has the parts of the current date, it can subtract them from parts of January 1, 2000 and come up with the values of the digits to be drawn. At this point, the `draw` method takes over and performs the actual drawing of the display.

Warning

The Java date class doesn't validate dates. It is therefore possible to create a date such as February 30. Depending on the way in which a program uses dates, you may need to add your own validation code.

Summary

To display an image in a Java program, you first load the image from a file (either from a local disk or over a network). Then you draw the image in a window or on a canvas.

Because images appear slowly over a network, they can flicker as they are updated as they are partially drawn. To smooth and speed up the drawing of slowly loading images, programs use buffering, where an image is drawn into a main memory buffer until it is completely loaded. When the image is loaded, it is transferred from the buffer to the screen. Buffering code must also include code that notifies the object drawing the image when image loading is complete. Otherwise, the program may not draw anything at all.

A thread is a sequence of executable code that can compete independently for system resources. Java programs can be multithreaded, having more than one thread active at a time. Cycling through a sequence of images to perform animation requires a separate program thread. Programs that require periodic updates also use a separate thread to perform the updates at regular intervals.

Threads can be in one of four states. A new thread is a thread whose object has been created but that isn't yet running. A runnable thread is a thread that can run whenever the CPU becomes available. A blocked thread is a thread that cannot run because it is waiting for I/O or because something in the program has caused it to wait. A dead thread is a thread that is no longer available.

Some methods used by multithreaded programs must be synchronized to prevent more than one thread from calling the method at one time. This prevents problems that may occur if more than one thread were to attempt to update the same object at the same time.

Exercises

1. Write a program or applet that displays a working stopwatch. (It can be analog or digital, although the digital display is by far easier.) Include a Reset button that sets the watch to 00:00. Include a Start button that starts

timing in one-second intervals and a Stop button that stops the watch. Stopping the watch should leave the time at which the watch was stopped on the screen until the user either exits the program (or leaves the web page) or resets the watch.

2. Write a program or applet the makes a ball (a 10 by 10 pixel oval) bounce around a window. The ball should start at either the left or right edge of the window and travel toward the top or bottom at a randomly selected angle. When the ball hits a side of the window, it should bounce off at another randomly selected angle. Write the multithreading in this program so that the program generates a new thread object (and thus another ball) each time the user clicks the mouse button anywhere in the window. (*Hint:* Trap a MOUSE_DOWN event to detect the mouse button click.)

3. Write a program that makes a corporate logo move from left to right across the screen. This will work best as an applet, given that it is the type of animation that is often seen on web sites. For the logo, you can create a GIF image using a graphics program or download something from the web. Then, use a graphics program to create the logo in various positions across the screen. (All you have to do is move the logo to the right a bit and then add the image to your image file.)

4. Write a Java program that performs a "reminder" service. The program should allow the user to enter the tasks about which he or she wants to be reminded and the times at which the reminding should occur. When a reminder should occur, the program should "wake up" and display something appropriate on the screen. (*Hint:* The timer in this program should check regularly to see if there are any tasks about which the user should be reminded at the time a given check is being performed.)

5. As you read in this chapter, the Java Date class doesn't perform any validation. This means that many programs that use dates will need to include their own validation code. One way to avoid writing the same validation code over and over again is to derive a new class from Date that adds the necessary checks for a valid date. The new class could also include the date arithmetic capabilities missing from the Java class. For this exercise, create such a derived date class. The class should do the following:

- Verify that all values for a date are within acceptable ranges. Decide how you will notify a programmer and/or a user that a date can't be constructed because some of the values are out of range.
- Perform date addition, allowing a program to add a number of days (an integer) to a date to produce another date.
- Perform date subtraction, allowing a program to subtract a number of days (an integer) from a date to produce another date.
- Find the difference between two dates, expressed as a number of days.

Write a program that demonstrates that the features you have added to your date class work properly.

Glossary

Abstract class: A class containing at least one abstract method and from which no objects can be created.

Abstract method: A method in a base class that has no implementation and therefore must be overridden in derived classes.

Accessor method: A method that returns the value in a single variable to a calling method.

Actor: In object-oriented analysis, someone who acts to use some part of an information system.

Applet: A Java program that runs inside a World Wide Web browser.

Application object: An object that represents a computer program.

Argument: A value passed into a method when the method is called.

Attribute: A piece of data that describes an object.

Bind: Connect an object to the code of its class's methods.

Bubble sort: A sorting algorithm that examines successive pairs of values and swaps them if they are in the wrong order. The sort makes repeated passes through the values until no swapping occurs, indicating that the values are in the correct order.

Buffer: A temporary holding area in main memory for data during an I/O process.

Buffering: Using a main memory location as temporary storage while a slow operation, such as loading an image over a network, is in progress.

Bytecode: A generic form of a Java program that can be understood by a Java interpreter and translated to machine language at runtime.

Container: A component, such as a window, that can contain other components.

Class: The template from which objects of the same type are created.

Class variable: A variable that describes all objects declared from a class.

Collision: Objects whose key transformations produce the same location in a hash table.

Component: A single graphic element in a Java program.

Concatenation operator: A plus sign, used to add strings together by pasting one string onto the right end of another.

Constructor: A method that is executed automatically when an object is created from a class.

Container class: A class whose sole purpose is to contain and manage objects of another class.

Cooperative thread: A thread that willingly gives up control to other threads in the program.

Copy constructor: A constructor that initializes an object with data copied from an object of the same class.

Daemon thread: A thread whose sole purpose is to serve other program threads.

Delimiter: A character used to separate fields or records in a text file.

Delimited text files: Text files that use a special character between fields and a different character between records.

Dot notation: The syntax for calling a method using a pointer to an object, a period, and the name of the method.

Enumerator: An object that retrieves the items in a hash table in key order.

Event-driven program: A program that waits for something to happen, identifies what occurred, and then takes action based on the action.

Exception: An error that occurs while a program is running that causes the program to stop if the error isn't trapped and handled.

Field: A single piece of data in a text file.

Garbage collection: Periodically collecting all unrefined memory, freeing it for use again.

Hash code: The value generated by a hash table from an object's key, used to place the object in a specific location in the table.

Hashing algorithm: A formula used to transform a key into a location in a hash table.

Image observer: The object that is to be notified when rendering of an imported image is complete.

Immutable: A property of the Java strings such that the individual characters in a string cannot be modified.

Instance (of a class): An object created from a class.

Instantiate (an object): Create an object from a class.

Interface: A specification of methods that a class will implement.

Interpreter: A program that takes Java bytecodes and translates them into machine language instructions as a program is running.

Layout manager: An object that governs the placement of components in a container.

Local variable: A variable used by a method as temporary storage while the method is running.

Member function: The actions an object knows how to perform.

Memory leak: Memory space that is allocated and then lost and never recovered.

Message: Instructions sent to an object telling it to perform one of the actions it knows how to do.

Modal dialog box: A dialog box that the user must close before performing any more actions with the program.

Modeless dialog box: A dialog box that acts like any other window, permitting a full range of actions with the program while the dialog box is on the screen.

Monitor: An object that can block more than one thread from executing a method at any given time.

Multiple inheritance: Deriving a class from more than one base class.

Multithreaded: Able to support more than one thread at a time.

Mutator method: A method that changes the value in a single variable.

Object: An entity in a data processing environment that has data that describe it and actions that it can perform.

Object-oriented programming: A paradigm for designing and developing application programs that encapsulate data and the actions data can perform into objects.

Overloading: Having more than one method with the same name but different signatures in the same class.

Overriding: In a derived class, reimplanting a method from a base class.

Package: A group of related Java classes, stored together under a single name.

Paradigm: A theoretical model that can be used as a pattern for some activity.

Parameter list: A list of input arguments used by a method.

Pass by reference: Passing the address of a parameter into a method rather than the value of the parameter itself.

Pass by value: Passing a copy of a parameter into a method.

Periodical: A thread that requires attention at regular intervals.

Plug-in: A stand-alone piece of code that adds functionality to a program.

Pointer: The main memory address of the beginning of a block of storage.

Precision: In a floating point number, the number of digits to the right of the decimal point.

Project: A way of organizing the files in a program so that the compiler knows which source code files and libraries are used by a program.

Queue: A waiting list accessed in first in, first out order.

Record: In a text file, the collection of all the data that describe a single object.

Reference variable: A variable that holds the main memory location (a pointer to) an object.

Scope (of a variable): Accessibility and visibility of a variable.

Selfish thread: A thread that does not give up control to other threads, often making the program unresponsive to user actions.

Services: The actions an object knows how to perform.

Signature: The combination of a method's name and argument list, which constitutes an identifier for that method.

State transition: The movement of a thread from one state to another.

Static method: A method that doesn't operate on an object of its class.

Strongly typed: A description of a programming language in which all variables must be given a data type.

Structured programming: A programming paradigm in which programs are built from only three structures (simple sequence, iteration, and selection).

Substring: A portion of a string.

Synchronized method: A method that permits only one thread to execute it, and any other synchronized methods belonging to its object, at a time.

Timer: A thread that requires attention at regular intervals.

Token: A piece of data in a text string separated from other tokens by some known delimiter.

Use case scenario: In object-oriented analysis, a description of the way in which a user can interact with an information system.

Variable: A piece of data that describes an object; a label on a main memory storage location.

Virtual machine: The software that interprets a Java program at runtime.

Index